The Brothers Karamazov

The Brothers Karamazov

by

Fyodor Dostoyevsky
(Translated by Constance Garnett)

Adapted by Joseph Cowley
Classics Condensed by Cowley

Strategic Book Publishing and Rights Co.

Strategic Book Publishing and Rights Co.
12620 FM 1960, Suite A4-507
Houston TX 77065
www.sbpra.com

For information about special discounts for bulk purchases, please contact Strategic Book Publishing and Rights Co. Special Sales, at bookorder@sbpra.net.

ISBN: 978-1-63135-610-0

This work meets the specifications for ESL students reading at level 4 of the Ladder series.

To my brother William Cowley, whose generosity has made the publication of many of these volumes possible. JGC

Table of Contents

Volume One

Cast of Main Characters

Agrafena Alexandrovna (Grushenka) – woman desired by Fyodor and Dmitri Karamazov

Grigory – man servant of Fyodor Karamazov

Grushenka – Agrafena Alexandrovna

Herzenstube – doctor in the district

Hohlakov, Madame – wealthy lady in district

Karamazov, Alexey (Alyosha) – third son of Fyodor Karamazov

Karamazov, Dmitri (Mitya) – eldest son of Fyodor Karamazov

Karamazov, Fyodor Pavlovitch – the father, a wealthy landowner

Karamazov, Ivan – second son of Fyodor Karamazov

Katerina Ivanovna – woman to whom Dmitri Karamazov is engaged

Lise – daughter of Madame Hohlakov, in love with Aloysha

Marfa – wife of Grigory

Misha – nickname for Rakitin, a friend of Aloysha's

Rakitin, Pyotr Fomitch – divinity student

Samsonov – old merchant, Gruishenka's benefactor

Smerdyakov – valet of Fyodor Pavlovitch

Zossima, Father – elder in local monastery

PART I

✺

Book I • The History of a Family

Chapter I

Fyodor Pavlovitch Karamazov

Fyodor Pavlovitch Karamazov was married twice and had three sons, the eldest, Dmitri, by his first wife, and Ivan and Alexey, by his second. His first wife, an intelligent, beautiful young woman, came from a wealthy family. No one knows why she married the old fool, except that she was strong-minded, and perhaps the idea of running away to marry seemed exciting. \

Immediately after they were married, she realized she made a mistake and had nothing but hate for her husband. They began to live a terrible life, with ever-lasting fights. When their only son, Dmitri, was three years old, she ran away, leaving the child in her husband's hands. When Fyodor Karamazov at last got word that she was in Petersburg, he was getting ready to go for her when he received news of her death from a disease.

Chapter II

He Gets Rid of His Eldest Son

Fyodor Pavlovitch took no care with the child of his marriage, but left him in the care of a servant, old Grigory. The child was almost a year in his charge, until a cousin of Mitya's mother, visiting from Paris, heard about the child and told Fyodor Pavlovitch he wished to provide for the child's education. He was appointed joint guardian of the child, and took the boy to Paris with him, where he put him in charge of a lady in Moscow. Dmitri Fyodorovitch, Mitya, was the only one of Fyodor Pavlovitch's three sons who grew up thinking he had property, a house left him by his mother, and would receive a sum of money on coming of age.

He saw his father for the first time when he visited the town to settle with him about his property. He did not stay long, but hurried to get away after obtaining a sum of money and an agreement for future payments. His father was well satisfied with this arrangement, for he gathered that the young man was of strong passions, not patient, and was free living, and that if he only got enough ready money he would be satisfied.

His father then him small amounts of money from time to time. And when, four years later, Mitya came a second time to settle with his father, he was shocked to find he had nothing left, that he had received the whole value of his property. The young man suspected he had been cheated.

Chapter III

The Second Marriage

Shortly after getting four-year-old Mitya off his hands, Fyodor Pavlovitch married a second time. This marriage lasted eight years. His second wife was a young girl whose parents had died, and who grew up in the house of a widow, a wealthy old lady who made her life a living hell. Fyodor Pavlovitch made her an offer; inquiries were made, and he was refused.

As in the case of his first wife, he proposed running away to get married. There is little doubt the young woman would not have married him had she known more about him. But what could a girl of sixteen know, except that she would be better at the bottom of the river than remaining with the widow.

Because Fyodor Pavlovitch received no money for marrying her, he did not treat her with respect. Instead, he took advantage of her gentleness, and trampled on the basic decencies of marriage by gathering loose women in his house for wild parties. In the end this unhappy young woman had a breakdown. At times, after terrible fits, she even lost her reason. Yet she bore Fyodor Pavlovitch two sons. When she died, the first son, Ivan, was eight and Alexey was four.

The same thing happened to the two boys as to their brother Mitya. They were left by their father to be looked after by the same Grigory. When the old lady who had brought up their mother heard of the girl's illness and death, she came to town one evening to see the boys.

Fyodor Pavlovitch came in to her drunk. Without a word, she slapped him twice on the face, seized him by the hair, and shook him. Then she went to the cottage to see the two boys. Seeing them with dirty faces and soiled clothes, she also gave Grigory a box on the ear, and drove off with the children. Fyodor Pavlovitch decided it was a good thing, and gave her his consent to do anything regarding their education.

The old lady died soon after this, leaving the boys in her wills a thousand rubles each "for their instruction." The money was left in the hands of Yefim Polenov, who was an honest man.

He wrote to Fyodor Pavlovitch but, finding he could get nothing from him for his children's education, took a personal interest in them. He put the two thousand rubles left them by the widow in a bank, so that by the time they came of age their money had doubled, and educated them at his own expense.

Ivan was quiet and seldom spoke, but began to show a talent for learning. As a result, he left Yefim Polenov when he was thirteen to enter a Moscow high school, boarding with a well-known teacher, a friend of Yefim's. Neither of these men was living when Ivan entered the university four years later.

The inheritance left by the widow was delayed by formalities, but he succeeded in getting work, at first giving lessons, then getting paragraphs on minor news events into the newspapers. Having once got into touch with the editors, he always kept in touch with them, and in his later years at the university published reviews of books on various subjects, so that he became well known.

When he left the university and was preparing to go abroad, Ivan published in one of the more important journals an article that drew a lot of attention. The article dealt with a subject being debated everywhere at the time—the position of the church courts. What was striking about the article was its tone, and unexpected conclusion. Many of the Church regarded him as on their side. Yet even atheists joined them in their applause.

This article reached the monastery in the town where his father lived. Learning the author's name, the monks were interested in his being a son of "that Fyodor Pavlovitch." Just then the author appeared in town, staying with his father. It seemed strange that a young man so learned should live with a father who had paid no attention to him all his life. It was learned only later that Ivan had come at the request of his brother, Dmitri, whom he saw for the first time on this visit, though they had exchanged letters. The family was now together for the first time, for the younger brother, Alexey, had been for the last year in the monastery, and seemed willing to live there for life.

Chapter IV

The Third Son, Alyosha

Alexey, Alyosha as he was called, was only twenty, his brother Ivan twenty-four, and Dmitri twenty-seven at the time. Alyosha took on the monastic life because it struck him as the ideal way for his struggle from the world of evil to the light of love. Life struck him this way because he found at that time the famous elder, Zossima, to whom he became attached.

But Alyosha had been strange from his cradle. In his childhood and youth he talked little, not because he was not social, but from inner concerns that had nothing to do with other people. He was fond of people, and put his trust in them: yet no one ever looked on him as simple-minded or without experience. There was something about him, also, which made one feel at once that he did not care to be a judge of others.

Coming at twenty to his father's house, which was filled with sin, he withdrew in silence when to look on was unbearable, but without the slightest sign of judging. His father, who was sensitive and ready to take offense, didn't trust him at first, and was not happy to have him there. But within two weeks he took to embracing and kissing him, often with drunken tears, feeling a deep affection such as he had never felt before.

At the time of Yefim Polenov's death, Alyosha had two more years to complete high school, but left to see his father about a plan he had. When he got to the town he made no answer to his father's inquiry about why he had come before completing his studies. It became clear he was looking for his mother's grave. But it can hardly have been the only reason.

Fyodor Pavlovitch could not show him where his second wife was buried, for he had never visited her grave. Three or four years after her death, he went to the south of Russia, where he developed his ability for making and piling up money. He returned to the town only three years before Alyosha, looking aged, and acting not with more dignity, but with more nerve.

He liked making fools of others, and his parties with women were more shocking than ever. Of late, too, his face looked swollen, and he was more frequently drunk. If it had not been for Grigory, who looked after him, Fyodor Pavlovitch might have got into terrible scrapes. Alyosha's arrival affected his moral side, as though something had awakened in him.

"Do you know," he said, looking at Alyosha, "you are like her, 'the crazy woman'"—he meant Alyosha's mother.

Grigory pointed out the "crazy woman's" grave to Alyosha, showing him the stone on which were inscribed the name and age of the dead woman and the date of her death. Grigory had put it up at his own expense after Fyodor Pavlovitch went south.

Alyosha showed no emotion listening to Grigory's account of putting it up with bowed head, and walked away without saying a word. Not long after this he told his father he wanted to enter the monastery. He explained that this was his strong desire, and that he was asking his consent.

The old man knew that the elder Zossima, who was living there, had made a special impression upon Alyosha, and said, after listening in silence, "That is the most honest monk among them," he observed, after listening in silence. "So that's where you want to be?"

He was half drunk, and grinned at him.

"I had a sense you would end in something like this," he said. "You were making straight for it. Well, you have your own two thousand. And I'll never desert you, my angel. I'll pay what's wanted for you, if they ask for it. But, of course, if they don't ask, why should we worry them? So you want to be a monk? I'm sorry to lose you, Alyosha; I've grown fond of you. Well, you'll pray for us sinners. I've always wanted someone to pray for me. Besides, it will be better for you with the monks than here with me—a drunken old man and loose women. That's why I let you go. You will be healed and come back again. You're the only person in the world who has not condemned me."

Chapter V

Elders

Alyosha was at this time a clear-eyed lad of nineteen. He was very handsome, graceful, moderately tall, with dark brown hair, a regular, oval-shaped face, and wide-set dark gray eyes; he was very thoughtful, and apparently very serene. Some people were of the opinion that he was stupid and undeveloped because he had not finished his studies.

That he did not finish his studies is true, but to say he was stupid would be a great mistake. He entered upon this religious path only because it struck his imagination as an ideal means of escape from darkness to light. He was convinced of the existence of God and life after death, and said: "I want to live forever, and will accept nothing less than a life that leads to that."

In the monastery he met this elder, one who took your soul, your will, into his soul and his will. When you choose an elder, you renounce your own will and yield to him in complete submission. This is undertaken in the hope of self-mastery, in order, after a life of obedience, to attain perfect freedom from self; to escape the lot of those who live their whole life without finding their true selves.

The elder Zossima was sixty-five. He had, no doubt, impressed Alyosha by some odd quality of his self. Alyosha lived in the cell of the elder, who was very fond of him and let him wait upon him. It must be noted that Alyosha was bound by no obligation and could go where he pleased, when he pleased. Though he wore monastic dress, it was by choice.

It was said that so many people had for years past come to confess their sins to Father Zossima and beg him for words of advice and healing, that he had acquired the keenest intuition and could tell from an unknown face what a new-comer wanted, and what was the suffering his conscience. He sometimes astounded and alarmed his visitors by his knowledge of their secrets.

Alyosha noticed that almost all who went in to the elder for the first time, with fear and uneasiness, came out with bright and happy faces. He was particularly struck by the fact that Father Zossima was not at all stern. On the contrary, he was almost always gay. Some say he was more drawn to those who were more sinful, and loved them the more.

Alyosha had complete faith in the miraculous power of the elder. He saw many who came with sick children or relatives, who returned shortly after and, falling in tears at the elder's feet, thank him for healing them. Whether they had really been healed or were simply better in the natural course of the disease was a question which did not exist for Alyosha, for he fully believed in the spiritual power of his teacher.

His heart throbbed when the elder came out to the gates to the waiting crowd of people who came from all over for his blessing. They fell down before him, wept, kissed his feet, kissed the earth on which he stood, and cried, while the women held up their children and brought the sick "possessed with evils."

The elder spoke to them, prayed over them, blessed them, and dismissed them. Of late he had become so weak through illness that he was sometimes unable to leave his cell, and the people waited for days. Alyosha did not wonder why they loved him. He knew that for the humble soul of the peasant, it was the greatest need and comfort to find someone or thing holy to fall down and worship. He understood that this was how the people felt, and that the elder was this saint and custodian of God's truth.

"He is holy. He carries in his heart the secret of renewal for all: that power which will, at last, establish truth on the earth, and all men will be holy and love one another. There will be no more rich or poor, no mighty or humbled; all will be as the children of God, and the Kingdom of Christ will come."

That was the dream in his heart.

The arrival of his two brothers, whom he had not known till then, made a great impression on Alyosha. He more quickly made friends with his half-brother Dmitri than with Ivan. He was interested in Ivan, but when the latter had been two months in town, though they met fairly often, they were still not intimate. Alyosha was naturally silent, while his brother Ivan looked curiously at him, but seemed not be thinking of him. Alyosha put down his brother's indifference at first to the difference in their age and education. But he also wondered if the absence of curiosity and sympathy in Ivan might be due to something else.

He fancied Ivan was absorbed in something—that he was striving towards some goal, hard to attain, and that was why he had no thought for him. Alyosha wondered, too, whether there was not some contempt on the part of the learned atheist for him—a foolish novice. He could not take offense at this, if it existed; yet, with an uneasy shame which he did not understand, he waited for his brother to come nearer to him.

Dmitri spoke of Ivan with deep respect. From him Alyosha learnt the details of the important affair which had of late formed such a close bond between the two. Dmitri's references to Ivan were the more striking since Dmitri was, compared with Ivan, almost without education, and the two brothers were so different in personality and character.

It was at this time the members of the family gathered in the cell of the elder who had such a powerful influence on Alyosha. The discord between Dmitri and his father was at its worst, and relations had become even more strained. Fyodor Pavlovitch suggested, apparently as a joke, that they should all meet in Father Zossima's cell so that, without appealing directly to him, they might come to an understanding. Dmitri, who had never seen the elder, accepted the challenge.

Alyosha was much troubled when he heard of the proposed visit. Of all of them, Dmitri was the only one who could regard the interview seriously. Alyosha was well aware that Ivan would come from curiosity, while his father might have in mind some trick, and waited for the day with heavy heart. His chief anxiety was for the elder. He trembled for him, and dreaded any slight to him, especially the biting wit of highly educated Ivan.

He wanted to warn the elder, but said nothing. He only sent word the day before, to his brother Dmitri, that he loved him and expected him to keep his promise. Dmitri could not remember what he had promised, but he answered by letter that he would do his best not to let himself be angered. But though he had a deep respect for the elder and for his brother Ivan, he was convinced the meeting was either a trap for him or a joke.

"Nevertheless I would rather bite out my tongue than be lacking in respect to the sainted man of whom you think so highly," Dmitri wrote.

Book II • An Unfortunate Gathering

Chapter I

They Arrive at the Monastery

It was a warm, bright day at the end of August. The visitors arrived just as the last mass was over. In an ancient, but roomy, hired carriage came Fyodor Pavlovitch, with his son Ivan (Dmitri was late). They left the carriage at the hotel, and went to the monastery on foot. Just then a little, old bald-headed man wearing a summer coat came up.

Lifting his hat, he introduced himself as Maximov and said, "Father Zossima lives in a cell the other side of the trees."

"I know it's the other side of the trees," said Fyodor Pavlovitch, "but we don't remember the way. It is a long time since we've been here."

"This way, by the gate. Come with me, I'll show you."

They came out of the gate and turned towards the trees. Maximov, a man of sixty, ran rather than walked, turning sideways to stare at them with curiosity.

"I've been there," said Maximov.

But his talk was cut short by a pale-looking monk who, with a deep bow, announced: "The Father Superior invites all of you to dine with him after your visit. At one o'clock. And you also," he added, addressing Maximov.

"That I certainly will," said Fyodor Pavlovitch. "We've all given our word to behave properly.... Dmitri Fyodorovitch is not here yet. It would be a capital thing if he didn't turn up. So we will come to dinner. Thank the Father Superior."

"It is my duty now to conduct you to the elder," answered the monk.

"If so, I'll go straight to the Father Superior," said Maximov.

"The Father Superior is engaged just now," said the monk.

"Here's the elder's cell," cried Fyodor Pavlovitch.

He made the sign of the cross to the saints on the gates.

"When you go to Rome you must do as the Romans do. Here there are twenty-five saints being saved. They eat cabbage. And not one woman goes in at this gate. That's what's remarkable. But I did hear the elder receives ladies."

"Women of the people are here now," said the monk, "waiting at the gate. For ladies of higher rank two rooms have been built next to the gate, outside the grounds. The elder goes to them by an inner passage when he is well enough."

"So there are ways, after all, to creep out to the ladies. Don't suppose, holy father, I mean any harm. But do you know that at Athos not only the visits of women are not allowed, but no creature of the female sex—no hens, nor cows."

There were rare and beautiful autumn flowers growing round the church and between the graves; and the wooden house where the elder lived was also surrounded with flowers.

"Was it like this in the time of elder Varsonofy? They say he used to beat even ladies," said Fyodor Pavlovitch.

"The elder Varsonofy did at times seem strange, but a great deal that's told is foolish. He never beat anyone," answered the monk. "Now, gentlemen, if you wait a bit, I'll announce you."

Chapter II

The Old Fool

They entered the room at the moment the elder came in from his bedroom. There were already there two monks, both in delicate health, though not old, and a tall young man, a divinity student named Rakitin.

Father Zossima was accompanied by a novice and Alyosha. The two monks rose and greeted him with a deep bow, touching the ground with their fingers. Blessing them, the elder replied with as deep a bow to them and asked their blessing. Fyodor Pavlovitch did the same. Ivan bowed, but kept his hands at his sides. The elder was a short, bent man with weak legs; though only sixty-five, he looked ten years older.

A clock on the wall struck twelve, and the discussion began.

"Right on time," cried Fyodor Pavlovitch, "but no sign of my son Dmitri. I ask that he be forgiven, sacred elder! To be on time is the courtesy of kings...."

Father Zossima looked at him in silence.

"I am a fool," Fyodor Pavlovitch went on, thrown off balance by the elder's silence. "But I believe in God, though I have had doubts. I'll just listen."

Such oddness puzzled the visitors. Alyosha stood with hanging head, on the verge of tears. What seemed strangest of all was that his brother Ivan, on whom he had rested his hopes, and who alone had influence on his father, sat unmoved, seeming to be waiting to see how it would end. Alyosha did not dare to look at Rakitin, the student.

"Great elder, speak! Does my liveliness spoil things for you?" Fyodor Pavlovitch cried, holding the arms of his chair as though ready to leap up if the answer were yes.

"I beg you not to be uneasy," the elder said. "Make yourself at home. And, above all, don't be so shamed for yourself; for that is at the root of it all."

"Make myself at home? Be my natural self? Oh, that is too much, but I accept it with joy. Do you know, blessed Father, you'd better not invite me to be my natural self. Don't risk it.... Holy Being, I am running over with happiness just to be here."

He threw up his hands, and cried, "Blessed be the womb that bare you. When you said just now, 'Don't be so shamed for yourself, for that is at the root of it all,' you read me to the core. I always feel when I meet people that I am lower than everyone, and that they all take me for a fool. So I say, 'Let me play the fool. I am not afraid of what you think, for every one of you is worse than I am.' That is why I am a fool. It is from shame, great elder. If I were sure everyone would accept me as the wisest of men, what a good man I should be!"

Falling to his knees, he cried, "What must I do to gain heaven?"

It was difficult even now to decide if he was joking or not.

Father Zossima said with a smile, "You have known for a long time what you must do: don't give way to drunkenness and wild speech; don't give way to lust; and, above all, to the love of money. Close your taverns, at least two. And—don't lie."

"You mean to anyone?"

"Above all, to yourself. The man who lies to himself cannot know the truth within or around him, and so loses all respect

18

for himself and others. And having no respect he ceases to love, and to avoid thinking about it he gives way to passions and pleasures, and sinks to the level of an animal. He who lies to himself is more easily offended. But get up, I beg you. All this is play acting...."

"Blessed man! Give me your hand to kiss."

Fyodor Pavlovitch got up and kissed the elder's thin hand.

"You said that so well. Yes, I have been all my life taking offense, for it is not pleasant to be insulted! I have been lying my whole life. Great elder, by the way, I was forgetting, though I had been meaning for the last two years to come here to ask you something. Is it true, great Father, the story told in the *Lives of the Saints* of a holy saint martyred for his faith who, when his head was cut off, picked it and walked away?"

"No, it is not true," said the elder, rising from his seat.

"Excuse me, gentlemen, for leaving you a few minutes," he said. "I have visitors waiting to see me who arrived before you. But don't tell lies all the same," he added, turning to Fyodor Pavlovitch with a good-humored face.

He started out. Alyosha and the novice flew to escort him down the steps. Alyosha was glad to get away; he was glad, too, that the elder was good-humored and not offended. Father Zossima was going to the gate to bless the people waiting for him there. But Fyodor Pavlovitch stopped him at the door.

"Blessed man!" he cried. "Allow me to kiss your hand again. With you I could still talk, still get on. Do you think I always lie and play the fool like this? I have been acting like this to try you. I have been testing you to see whether I could get on with you. Is there room for my humility beside your pride? But now, I'll sit and be quiet."

Chapter III

So Be It! So Be It!

It was half-past twelve when the elder returned, but Dmitri, on whose account they had all met, had still not appeared. He seemed almost to have been forgotten, and when the elder entered the cell he found his guests in eager conversation. The discussion died for a moment when he entered, but, seating himself, he looked at them as though inviting them to go on. Alyosha saw he was exhausted and making a great effort. But he evidently did not want to break up the party.

"We are discussing this gentleman's most interesting article," said Father Iosif, the librarian, addressing the elder, and indicating Ivan. "He brings forward much that is new, but I think the argument cuts both ways. It is an article written in answer to a book by an ecclesiastical authority on the ecclesiastical court, and the scope of its authority."

"I'm sorry I've not read it, but I've heard of it," said the elder to Ivan.

"He takes an interesting position," said the Father Librarian. "As far as Church authority is concerned he seems to be opposed to the separation of Church and State."

"That's interesting. But in what sense?" Father Zossima asked Ivan.

The latter answered him with modesty.

"I start from the position that the mix-up between the principles of Church and State will go on forever, for there is no middle ground between them in such questions as law, for example. It is, in fact, impossible in any real sense to define their responsibilities My clerical opponent maintains that the Church holds a precise and defined position in the State. I, on the other hand, believe that the Church ought to include the State, and not simply occupy a corner in it!"

"Perfectly true," Father Païssy, the silent, learned monk, said.

"Observe the answer he makes to these ideas of his opponent," said Father Iosif. "His opponent says, first, that 'no social organization ought to take to itself power to take over the civic rights of its members.' Second, that 'criminal and civil over-sight ought not belong to the Church, for it does not fit in with its divine nature,' and, third, 'the Church is a kingdom not of this world.'"

"An unworthy play upon words!" Father Païssy broke in. "I have read the book you answered," he said, turning to Ivan, "and was shocked by the words 'the Church is a kingdom not of this world.' If it is not of this world, then it cannot exist on earth. In the Gospel, 'not of this world' is not used in that sense. Our Lord Jesus Christ came to set up the Church on earth. The Kingdom of Heaven is not of this world, but it is only entered through the Church, established upon earth. And so it is a play upon words. The Church is a kingdom ordained to rule, and so must rule over all the earth."

He ceased speaking as though checking himself.

After listening with respect, Ivan went on, addressing the elder: "The whole point of my article lies in the fact that for the first centuries Christianity only existed in the Church. When the Roman Empire became Christian, it included the Church but stayed pagan. The Christian Church entering into the State could surrender no part of its principles, and only pursue those aims revealed by God. In that way it is not the Church that should seek a position in the State, but that every State should be, in the end, completely transformed into the Church. This is why the author, when he declares the states are permanent, is going against the Church and its sacred, eternal calling."

"In brief," Father Païssy broke in again, "according to these theories, the Church ought to be included in the State, as though this would be an advance from a lower to a higher form. If the Church resists, some corner will be set apart for her in the State. But we should demand not that the Church pass from a lower into a higher type, but that the State should end by being worthy to become the Church!"

"In reality it is so now," said the elder. "If anything preserves society and changes the criminal, it is the law of Christ speaking in his deeper self. It is only by recognizing his wrong-doing as a son of a Christian society that he recognizes his sin against society—that is, against the Church. So it is only against the Church, and not against the State, that the criminal can recognize he has sinned. But the Church, like a loving mother, holds apart from actively punishing him, as the sinner is severely punished already by the civil law, and there must be at least someone to have pity on him.

"If the Church were introduced in full force, if the whole of the society were changed into the Church, not only the judgment of the Church would have influence on reforming the criminal, but possibly the crimes themselves would be much reduced. There is no doubt the Church would look upon the criminal and crime quite differently, and would succeed in restoring the excluded, restraining those who plan evil, and regenerate the fallen.

"It is true," the elder added with a smile, "the Christian society now is not ready, but it continues unshaken in its expectation of a complete change from a society almost without God into a single universal and all-powerful Church. So be it! Even if it be at the end of time, it is fated! And there is no need to be troubled about times and seasons, for these are in the wisdom of God, in His foresight and love. And what in human reckoning seems far off, may be close at hand. So be it!"

"So be it!" Father Païssy repeated.

Alyosha watched it all with beating heart. The conversation stirred him deeply. He glanced at Rakitin and, from the color in his cheeks guessed that he, too, was no less excited. But just then, the door opened, and the guest long expected, Dmitri Fyodorovitch, came in. His appearance caused some surprise.

Chapter IV

Why Is Such A Man Alive?

Dmitri Fyodorovitch, a young man of twenty-eight, looked older than his years. He was physically strong, yet his face was thin, his cheeks hollow and pale. His dark eyes had a determined look, yet there was something not clear in them. He was stylishly dressed, with black gloves and a top-hat. From the door he, glanced at everyone, then went to the elder and bowed to him.

Father Zossima, rising, blessed him.

Dmitri kissed his hand with respect, and with intense feeling, said: "Please be so generous as to forgive me for having kept you waiting, but Smerdyakov, the valet, told me, by way of my father, that the meeting was for one. Now I learn—"

"Be not disturbed," said the elder. "You're a little late. It is of no matter...."

"I'm extremely obliged to you, and expected no less from your goodness."

Saying this, Dmitri bowed again. Then, turning to his father, he made him, too, a low bow. Although his father was taken by surprise, he jumped up and made his son a bow as low in return. Without a word, Dmitri sat on the empty chair near Father Païssy, prepared to listen to the conversation.

"Our liberal thinkers," Ivan went on, "often mix the results of socialism with those of Christianity. But it's not only Liberals who do this...."

"Excuse me," Dmitri cried. "I couldn't help but overhear your conversation as I waited to enter. If I've heard right, crime must not only be permitted but even recognized as the inevitable outcome of his position for every infidel! Is that so?"

"Quite so," said Father Païssy.

"I'll remember it."

Having uttered these words, Dmitri ceased speaking.

"Is that really your belief as to what will happen if faith in immortality is no more?" the elder asked Ivan.

"Yes. That was what I meant. There is no virtue if there is no immortality."

"You are blessed in believing that, or else most unhappy."

"Why unhappy?" Ivan asked, smiling.

"Because you probably don't believe yourself in life after death, or in what you have written on Church authority."

"Perhaps you are right! But it wasn't a joke," Ivan said.

"That's true," said the elder. "But the question is still causing you uneasiness. The martyr likes to toy with despair. In the mean-time, you avoid thinking about it with magazine articles and discussions, though you don't believe your own words, and mock at them inwardly. That question you have not answered begs for an answer."

"But can it be answered by me? Can I say yes?" Ivan asked.

"If you can't say yes, you will never be able to say no. You know that that question is in your heart, and all its suffering is due to it. But thank the Creator who has given you a heart capable of such suffering; of thinking and seeking higher things. God grant that your heart will attain the answer on earth."

The elder raised his hand and would have made the sign of the cross over Ivan. But the latter rose to receive his blessing, and kissing his hand went back to his place in silence. This action and the conversation, which was so surprising from Ivan, impressed everyone, so that all were silent for a moment.

At the same moment Fyodor Pavlovitch jumped up.

"Holy elder," he cried, pointing to Ivan, "that is my son, flesh of my flesh, the dearest of my flesh! He is my most dutiful son, while this son, Dmitri, who has just come, against whom I am seeking justice, is the most undutiful! Judge and save us!"

"Speak without acting the fool, and don't begin by insulting your son," answered the elder in a faint, exhausted voice.

"This is what I knew would happen when I came here!" cried Dmitri. "Forgive it, reverend Father," he added. "I am not a religious man, and I don't even know how to address you properly, but you have been deceived and you have been too good-natured in letting us meet here. All my father wants is a scene. Why he wants it I believe I know."

"They all blame me!" cried Fyodor Pavlovitch. "They accuse me of hiding their money and cheating them, but isn't there a court of law? There they will reckon out for you, Dmitri Fyodorovitch, from your notes, your letters, and your agreements, how much money you had, how much you have spent, and how much you have left. He several times spent a thousand or two for the ruin of some respectable girl. Would you believe it, Holy Father, he has compromised the girl by promising to marry her, yet before her very eyes dances attendance on someone else. That's why he is without respect for me, trying to get money from me, though he has wasted thousands on this woman already. He's always borrowing money for the purpose. From whom do you think? Shall I say, Mitya?"

"Be silent!" cried Dmitri. "Don't dare in my presence to darken the good name of an honorable girl! That you should say a word about her is an outrage!"

"Mitya!" cried Fyodor Pavlovitch. "Is your father's blessing nothing?"

"Shameless hypocrite!" cried Dmitri in a fury.

"He says that to his father! What would he be with others?"

Dmitri was trembling with anger.

"Father, you reproach me for having a weakness for that lady when you yourself told her to charm me! She told me so. You wanted to put me in prison because you're jealous of me, because you'd begun to force your attentions on her. So here you have this father who blames his son who is like him! Gentlemen, forgive my anger, but I knew this crafty old man would only bring you together to create a scene. I came to forgive him if he held out his hand! But he has just insulted not only me, but a young lady for whom I feel such love that I dare not take her name in vain. I know his game...."

He could not go on. His eyes shone and he breathed deeply.

Everyone in the cell was stirred. All except Father Zossima stood up. He sat still and pale, not from the excitement but from weakness. He raised his hand as though to check the storm, but seemed to be waiting for something, watching them intently, as though trying to make out something which was not clear.

"Dmitri Fyodorovitch," yelled Fyodor Pavlovitch, "if you were not my son I would challenge you this instant to a duel ... with pistols, at three yards!"

Dmitri frowned painfully, and looked with hate at his father.

"I thought," he said in a soft, controlled voice, "that I was coming to my native place with the angel of my heart, my love, to hold dear his old age, and I find nothing but an evil old man, bent on destroying this creature that I love!"

"A duel!" yelled the old man again. "Let me tell you all there has never been a more honest woman than this 'creature,' as you have dared to call her! And you, Dmitri Fyodorovitch, have abandoned your loved one for that 'creature,' so you must have thought your loved one couldn't hold a candle to this woman called a 'creature'!"

"Shame!" broke from Father Iosif.

"Why is such a man alive?" Dmitri shouted with anger.

"Listen to the father-killer!" cried Fyodor Pavlovitch. "That's your answer to your 'shame!' That 'creature,' that 'woman of loose behavior,' is holier than you   are, who seek to save your souls! She fell in her youth, ruined by society. But she loved much, and Christ forgave the woman 'who loved much.'"

"It was not for such love Christ forgave her," broke from Father Iosif.

"Yes, it *was for that*, monks! You save your souls here, eating cabbage, and think you are holy. You eat fish, and think you bribe God with fish."

"This is not to be put up with!" was heard on all sides.

But the scene was cut short in a most unexpected way. Father Zossima rose from his seat and, with Alyosha supporting him by the arm, moved towards Dmitri. Reaching him, he sank on his knees before him. Alyosha thought he had fallen from weakness, but this was not so. The elder bowed down at Dmitri's feet till his forehead touched the floor. Surprised, Alyosha failed to help him get up.

There was a faint smile on the elder's lips.

"Good-by! Forgive me, all of you!" he said, bowing on all sides.

Dmitri stood for a few moments in shock. Bowing down to him—what did it mean? Suddenly he cried, "Oh, God!" and hid his face in his hands. He rushed out of the room. All the guests ran after him in their confusion, not saying good-by or bowing to their host. Only the monks went up to him for a blessing.

"What did it mean, falling at his feet like that?" asked Fyodor Pavlovitch.

The monk who had invited them to dine with the Superior met them as they came down the steps from the elder's cell.

"Forgive me," Fyodor Pavlovitch cried. "I was carried away. After such a scene, how can I eat up the monastery's sauces? Please excuse me!"

Chapter V

A Young Man Bent on a Career

Alyosha helped Father Zossima to his bedroom, a little room with a narrow bedstead and a strip of felt for a mattress. In the corner under the icons was a reading-desk, with a cross and the Gospel on it. The elder sank exhausted on the bed, and looked up at Alyosha.

"Go, my dear boy," he said. "You are needed there."

"Let me stay here," Alyosha begged.

"You are more needed there. You will be of service. If evil spirits rise, say a prayer. And remember, my son, this is not the place for you in the future. When it is God's will to call me, leave the monastery. Go away for good."

Alyosha started.

"This is not your place. I bless you for great service in the world. Yours will be a long journey. You'll have to take a wife. You'll have to bear *all* before you come back. There will be much to do. But I don't doubt of you, and so I send you forth. Christ is with you. Do not abandon Him and He will not abandon you. You will see great sorrow, but in that sorrow you will be happy. This is my last message to you: in sorrow seek happiness. Work unceasingly. Remember my words, for although I shall talk with you again, not only my days but my hours are numbered."

Alyosha's face showed strong emotion.

"What is it?" Father Zossima asked, smiling gently. "The worldly may follow the dead with tears, but here we rejoice. We rejoice and pray for him. Leave me, I must pray. Be near your brothers. Not one, but both."

Father Zossima raised his hand to bless him. Alyosha made no protest, though he longed to remain. He longed, also, to ask what his bowing to Dmitri meant. But he knew the elder would have explained it if he had thought fit. It impressed Alyosha; it was a mystery, but he believed it had great meaning.

As he hurried to the monastery, he heard again Father Zossima's words about his approaching end. What he said so exactly must come to pass. But what would Alyosha do without him? How could he live without seeing and hearing him? Where should he go? He had told him not to weep, but it was long since he had known such pain. He hurried through the wood to the monastery.

At the turn of the path he saw Rakitin.

"Are you waiting for me?" asked Alyosha.

"Yes," said Rakitin. "You are hurrying to the Father Superior to serve at the dinner. I shan't be there, but tell me one thing, Alexey, what does that vision mean?"

"What vision?"

"That bowing to your brother, Dmitri. And didn't he tap the ground with his head!"

"You speak of Father Zossima?"

"Yes, of Father Zossima."

"Tapped the ground with his head?"

"Yes. What does that vision mean?"

"I don't know what it means, Misha."

"I knew he wouldn't explain it! There's nothing wonderful about it, only the usual show. But there was an object in his doing it. All the pious people in the town will talk about it and spread the story, wondering what it meant. The old man really has a keen nose; he sniffed a crime. Your house stinks of it."

"What crime?"

"It'll be in your family, this crime. Between your brothers and your rich old father. Father Zossima threw himself down to be ready for what may turn up. If something happens, it'll be: 'The holy man saw it coming—to his glory: 'He saw the coming crime and marked the criminal!' That's the way with these people; they beat a just man and fall at the feet of a murderer."

"What crime? What murderer? What do you mean?"

Alyosha stopped. Rakitin, too.

"What murderer? As though you didn't know! I'll bet you've thought of it before. Alyosha, you always speak the truth. Have you thought of it or not?"

"I have," answered Alyosha in a low voice.

Even Rakitin was taken aback.

"What? Have you really?" he cried.

"I ... I've not exactly thought it," said Alyosha, "but directly you began speaking, I fancied I had thought of it myself."

"You see? Looking at your father and your brother Mitya today you thought of a crime. Then I'm not mistaken?"

"Wait a minute," Alyosha broke in. "What has led you to see all this? Why does it interest you? That's the first question."

"Two questions. I'll deal with them separately. First, I shouldn't have seen it if I hadn't suddenly understood your brother Dmitri. I caught the whole man from one trait. These honest but passionate people have a line which must not be crossed. If it is, he'll run at your father with a knife. But your father's a drunken old sinner who can never draw the line—if they both let themselves go, they'll come to grief."

"No, Misha. It won't come to that."

"But why are you trembling? Your Mitya may be honest, but he's—filled with sexual desire. That's the very essence of him. It's your father that has given him that desire. I wonder at you, Alyosha, how you can have kept your purity. You're a Karamazov, you know! In your family desire is a disease. But now these three Karamazovs are watching one another, with knives in their belts."

"You are wrong about that woman. Dmitri hates her."

"Grushenka? No, brother, he doesn't. Since he left the one he was to marry for her, he doesn't hate her. That's something you don't understand. A man will fall in love with a woman's body, or even a part of a woman's body, and he'll abandon everything for her, sell his father and mother, too. If he's honest, he'll steal; if he's humane, he'll murder; if he's faithful, he'll deceive. Even if he hates Grushenka, he can't tear himself away."

"I understand that," Alyosha said.

"Well, maybe you do, since you say it," said Rakitin. "So you've thought about it! You're a quiet one, Alyosha. The devil only knows what you've thought, and what you know already! You are pure, but I've been watching you. You're a Karamazov yourself, filled with desire from your father, and a crazy saint from your mother. Do you know, Grushenka has been begging me to bring you along. 'I'll pull off his cassock,' she says. I wondered why she took such an interest in you. Do you know, she's an unusual woman!"

"Thank her and say I'm not coming," said Alyosha. "Finish what you were saying."

"There's nothing to finish. It's all clear. It's the same old story, brother. You're all filled with sexual desire, and crazy! Your brother Ivan writes religious articles as a joke, though he doesn't believe in God, and admits it. He's trying to get the woman Mitya was to marry for himself, and I fancy he'll succeed. What's more, it's with Mitya's consent. Mitya will give her up to him to be rid of her, and escape to Grushenka.

"He recognizes his evil nature and goes on with it! Let me tell you, too, the old man, your father, is standing in Mitya's way. He has gone crazy over Grushenka. It's on her account he made that scene in the cell just now. He's worse than a tom-cat in love. At first she was only employed by him in connection with his taverns and in some other shady business, but now he realizes all she is and has gone wild about her.

"He keeps angering her with his offers, not honorable ones, of course. And they'll come to a terrible end over her! But Grushenka favors neither of them. She's playing with them, considering which one she can get the most out of. Though she might get a lot of money from the papa, he wouldn't marry her, and maybe he'll shut his purse in the end.

"That's where Mitya comes in; he has no money, but he's ready to marry her! To desert Katerina Ivanovna, who's rich, and marry Grushenka, who has been the lover of the old merchant. What craziness! Murder may well come to pass from all this, and that's what your brother Ivan is waiting for.

"He'll carry off Katerina Ivanovna, for whom he is pining, and pocket her dowry of sixty thousand. And he won't be wronging Mitya, but doing him the greatest service. For Mitya, only last week when he was with some gypsy girls, drunk, in a tavern, cried aloud that he was not worthy of the woman, Katya, to whom he was engaged, but that his brother Ivan was the man who deserved her. And Katerina Ivanovna will not in the end refuse such a fascinating man as Ivan. She's hesitating between the two of them. And how has Ivan won you all over? He is laughing at you, and enjoying himself at your expense."

"How do you know?" Alyosha asked.

"Why do you ask? Are you frightened? It shows you know I'm speaking the truth."

"You don't like Ivan. Ivan wouldn't be tempted by money."

"Really? And the beauty of Katerina Ivanovna? It's not only the money, though a fortune of sixty thousand is not something to turn your nose up at."

"Ivan is above that. He wouldn't make up to any one for thousands. It is not money, not comfort Ivan is seeking. Perhaps it's suffering he is seeking."

"What wild dream now?"

"He has a stormy spirit. He is in great doubt. He doesn't want millions, but an answer to his question."

"That's plagiarism, Alyosha. You're quoting your elder. Ah, Ivan has set you a problem!" cried Rakitin. "And the problem's a stupid one. It is no good guessing it. Rack your brains—you'll understand it. His article is ridiculous. And did you hear his stupid theory just now: if there's no immortality, there's no virtue, and everything is lawful. A good theory for evil people! He's showing off. His whole theory is a joke! Humanity will find the power to live for virtue without believing in immortality. It will find it in love for freedom, equality, and in each other."

Rakitin could hardly hold himself back, but he stopped.

"That's enough," he said. "Why are you laughing? You think I'm a fool?"

"I've never dreamed of you as a fool. You are clever but ... never mind, I was silly to smile. I understand you getting hot about it. I would guess from your warmth that you are not without interest in Katerina Ivanovna yourself; I've thought that for a long time. That's why you don't like Ivan. You're jealous!"

"And jealous of her money, too? Won't you add that?"

"I'll say nothing about money; I'm not going to insult you."

"I believe it, since you say so, but to hell with your brother Ivan. Don't you know one might dislike him, apart from Katerina Ivanovna? And why should I like him? He puts me down, you know. Why haven't I a right to put him down?"

"I never heard of his saying anything about you."

"The day before yesterday, at Katerina Ivanovna's, he was running me down for all he was worth. He was so good as to express the opinion that, if I don't go in for the career of a monk, I shall be sure to go to Petersburg and get on to some magazine as a reviewer, that I shall write for the next ten years, and in the end become the owner of the magazine, and bring it out on the liberal side, with a touch of socialism, but keeping a sharp look out all the time, that is, keeping in with both sides and taking in the fools. According to your brother, the tinge of socialism won't keep me from putting aside the proceeds, until, at the end of my career, I build a great house in Petersburg, move my publishing offices there, and let out the upper stories to lodgers."

"Ah, Misha, that's just what will happen," cried Alyosha.

"You are pleased to make fun of me, too, Alexey Fyodorovitch."

"I'm joking, forgive me. But who told you all this? You weren't at Katerina Ivanovna's when he was talking about you?"

"I heard him, for I was sitting in Grushenka's bedroom and I couldn't go away because Dmitri Fyodorovitch was there."

"Oh, yes, I'd forgotten she was a relation of yours."

"Grushenka a relation of mine!" cried Rakitin, turning red. "Are you mad? You're out of your mind!"

"Why, isn't she a relation of yours? I heard so."

"Where can you have heard it? You Karamazovs talk of being a noble family, but your father ran about playing the fool at other men's tables. I may be only a priest's son, and dirt in the eyes of nobles like you, but I have a sense of honor, too. I couldn't be a relation of Grushenka, a loose woman!"

Rakitin was very up-set.

"Forgive me, for goodness' sake; I had no idea ... besides ... how can you call her a loose woman? Is she ... that sort?" Alyosha turned red. "I tell you again, I heard she was a relation of yours. You often go to see her, and you told me yourself you're not her lover. I never dreamed that you of all people had such contempt for her! Does she deserve it?"

"I may have my reasons for visiting her. But as for a relationship, your brother, or even your father, is more likely to make her yours than mine. Well, here we are. You'd better go to the kitchen. They can't have finished dinner so soon! Here's your father, and your brother Ivan after him. They've left the Father Superior's. Look, Father Isidor's shouting something after them. And your father's shouting and waving his arms. I expect he's swearing. And there's old Maximov running!—there must have been a row."

There was reason for Rakitin's exclamations. There had been a scene.

Chapter VI

A Shocking Scene

They entered the Father Superior's rooms, in which everything shone with cleanliness. There were flowers in the windows, and a beautifully decorated table on which were three kinds of bread, two bottles of wine, and a jug of kvass.

Rakitin was not important enough to be invited. Only Father Iosif, Father Païssy, and one other monk were invited. They were waiting when Ivan arrived. The Father Superior, a tall, thin, but not vigorous old man with black hair streaked with gray, stepped into the room. He bowed to his guests in silence.

"Pray be seated, gentlemen," he said.

He stood before the holy image and began to say grace. All bent their heads. It was at this moment that Fyodor Pavlovitch, who had really meant to go home, remembered his words at the elder's: "I always feel when I meet people that I am inferior, and that's why I act the fool." He decided, "Well, since I have begun I might as well continue."

He told the coachman to wait, and with rapid steps returned to the Father Superior's. He had no clear idea what he would do, but he knew he could not control himself, and that a touch might drive him to being his worst. He appeared in the Father Superior's dining-room at the moment when the prayer was over, and all were moving to the table.

Standing in the doorway, he cried: "They thought I had gone, and here I am again!"

For one moment everyone stared at him without a word.

"Your reverence," cried Fyodor Pavlovitch. "Am I to come in or not? Will you receive me as your guest?"

"You are all welcome," said the Superior. "Gentlemen!" he added, "I beg you to lay aside your differences and be united in love and family harmony—with prayer to the Lord at our table."

"No, excuse me," Fyodor Pavlovitch said. "Allow me to finish. Father Superior, though I play the fool, I am the soul of honor, and I want to speak my mind. My son, Alexey, is here, being saved. I am his father; I care for his welfare. While I've been playing the fool, I have been listening, and, Holy Father, I am angry. Confession is a great sacrament, but in the cell they kneel and confess aloud. Can that be right? It was said by the Holy Fathers that we should confess in secret: then only will it be a mystery. I shall write to the Synod, and take my son home."

"What is happening? What's this?" cried the monks.

"Pardon me!" said the Father Superior. "It was said of old, 'Many have begun to speak against me and have uttered evil sayings. Hearing it, I have said to myself: it is the correction of the Lord. He has sent it to heal my soul.' And so we thank you, honored guest!" and he made Fyodor Pavlovitch a low bow.

"Old phrases and gestures. We know all about them. I don't like falsehood, Fathers, I want the truth. But the truth is not found in eating fish! Monks, why do you fast? Why do you expect reward in heaven for that? Why, for reward like that I will come and fast too! No, saintly monks, try being virtuous in the world, do good to society without shutting yourself up at other people's expense, and without expecting a reward for it—you'll find that a bit harder. What have they got here?"

He went up to the table.

"Old port wine, and mead. That is something beyond fish. Look at the bottles the fathers have brought out! And who has provided it all? The Russian peasant, the laborer, brings here the pennies earned by his hand, wringing it from his family and the tax-gatherer! You bleed the people, holy fathers."

"This is too disgraceful!" said Father Iosif.

"Well, Father, I will leave now! I am not coming again. You may beg me on your knees, I shan't come. I sent you a thousand rubles, so you have begun to keep your eye on me. I'll say no more. I am taking my revenge for all the humiliation I endured," he said, and thumped the table with his fist.

"This monastery has played a great part in my life! It has cost me many bitter tears. You used to set my wife, the crazy one, against me. You cursed me with bell and book, you spread stories about me. Enough, fathers! This is the age of Liberalism, the age of steamers and railways. Neither a thousand, nor a hundred rubles, will you get out of me!"

The monastery never had played any great part in his life, and he never shed a bitter tear owing to it. But he was so carried away by his fake emotion that, for a moment, he almost believed it. He was so touched he almost wept.

The Father Superior bowed his head, and again spoke impressively: It is written again, 'Bear gladly any dishonor that come to thee by no act of your own, be not confounded, and hate not him who has dishonored thee.'"

"Fathers, I will go. But I will take my son, Alexey, away from here forever. Ivan Fyodorovitch, my most dutiful son, permit me to order you to follow me. Come and see me now in the town. Instead of fish, I will give you roast pig. We'll have dinner with drinks and wine...."

He went out, shouting and waving his arms.

It was at that moment Rakitin saw him and pointed him out to Alyosha.

"Alexey!" his father shouted, catching sight of him. "You come home to me today, for good, and bring your pillow and mattress."

Alyosha stood rooted to the spot. Fyodor Pavlovitch got into the carriage, and Ivan was about to follow him in silence, without even saying good-by to Alyosha. But at this point Maximov ran up to the carriage, afraid of being late. He was in such a hurry that he put his foot on the step on which Ivan's left foot was resting, and kept trying to jump in.

"I am going with you!" he shouted, laughing. "Take me, too."

"There!" cried Fyodor Pavlovitch, delighted. "How did you tear yourself away? You must be a brazen-faced fellow! I am that myself, but I am surprised at you, brother! Jump in! Let him pass, Ivan. It will be fun. He can lie somewhere at our feet. Will you lie at our feet? Or perch on the box with the coachman. Skip on to the box!"

But Ivan, who had by now taken his seat, gave Maximov a shove and sent him flying, angrily shouting to the coachman, "Drive on!"

"What are you doing?" Fyodor Pavlovitch protested.

But the carriage had already driven away.

Ivan made no reply.

"Well, you are a fellow," Fyodor Pavlovitch said again.

After a pause, looking at his son, he said, "It was you who got up all this monastery business. You urged it, you approved of it. Why are you angry now?"

"You've talked rot enough. You might rest a bit now," Ivan said.

Fyodor Pavlovitch was silent again for two minutes.

"A drop of something to drink would be nice," he observed.

Ivan made no response.

Book III • Those with Physical Desires

Chapter I

The Help's Quarters

The Karamazovs' house was a pleasant-looking old house of two stories with a red roof. There were all sorts of unexpected little cupboards and closets and staircases. The house was built for a large family; but there was no one living in it but Fyodor Pavlovitch and Ivan. The lodge in the yard was a roomy, solid building in which the three servants lived: old Grigory, his wife Marfa, and a young man called Smerdyakov.

Grigory was honest, but obstinate if he believed he was right. His wife, Marfa Ignatyevna, had obeyed him all her life, yet she had pestered him terribly after the freeing of the serfs. She wanted them to leave Fyodor Pavlovitch and open a shop in Moscow with their small savings. But Grigory said that was "nonsense," and their "duty" was to stay with their old master.

"Do you understand what duty is?" he asked her.

"I understand what duty means, Grigory Vassilyevitch, but why it's our duty to stay here I never shall understand," Marfa answered.

"Well, don't understand then. But so it shall be. And you hold your tongue."

And so they did not go away, and Fyodor Pavlovitch paid them a small sum for wages regularly. Grigory knew, too, that he had an influence over his master. Fyodor Pavlovitch, strong "in some affairs of life," found himself, to his surprise, extremely feeble in other areas. He was afraid of his weaknesses. There are times when one has to keep a sharp look out. And that's not easy without a trustworthy man, like Grigory.

Many times Fyodor Pavlovitch only just escaped a beating through Grigory's stepping in, and on each occasion the old servant gave him a good lecture. But it wasn't only beatings that Fyodor Pavlovitch was afraid of. There were graver occasions, which Fyodor Pavlovitch could not explain, when the craving for someone faithful and devoted came upon him. Corrupt and cruel, Fyodor Pavlovitch was sometimes overcome by fear.

"My soul's simply quaking in my throat at those times," he used to say.

At such moments he liked to feel there was near at hand a strong, faithful man who had seen all his sinning and knew all his secrets, but was ready to overlook them and, in case of need, defend him. From whom? From somebody unknown, but terrible and dangerous. It happened sometimes that Fyodor Pavlovitch went at night to the lodge to wake Grigory and fetch him. When the old man came, Fyodor Pavlovitch would begin talking about the most trivial matters, and would soon let him go again. After he had gone, Fyodor Pavlovitch would go to bed and sleep the sleep of the just.

On the outside, Grigory acted with dignity and in silence. It was impossible to tell whether he loved his meek wife; but he really did, and she knew it. Marfa Ignatyevna was by no means foolish; she was probably cleverer than he, or, at least wiser in worldly affairs, and yet she gave in to him in everything without question, and respected him for his spiritual superiority. Grigory thought over his cares alone, so that Marfa Ignatyevna had long grown used to knowing that he did not need her advice. She felt that her husband respected her silence, and took it as a sign of her good sense.

God had not blessed them with children. One child was born, but died. Grigory was fond of children, and was not ashamed of showing it. When Adelaïda Ivanovna ran away, Grigory took Dmitri, then a child of three, combed his hair and washed him in a tub with his own hands, and looked after him for almost a year. Afterwards he looked after Ivan and Alyosha, for which the general's widow rewarded him with a slap in the face.

It happened that, on the very night after the burial of their own child, Marfa was wakened by the wail of a new-born baby. Frightened, she woke her husband. He listened and said he thought it was someone groaning, "It might be a woman." He got up and dressed. It was a rather warm night in May. As he went down the steps, he heard groans coming from the garden. But the gate from the yard into the garden was locked at night, and there was no other way of entering it, for there was a high fence.

Grigory lit a lantern, took the garden key, and taking no notice of the fears of his wife, went into the garden. There he heard the groans coming from the bath-house near the garden gate. Opening the door of the bath-house, he saw a sight which petrified him. An idiot girl, who wandered about the streets and was known by the nickname Lizaveta Smerdyastchaya (Stinking Lizaveta), had got into the bath-house and given birth to a child.

She lay dying, with the baby beside her.

She said nothing, for she had never been able to speak.

Chapter II

Lizaveta

Lizaveta was a little creature, not five foot. Her broad face had a look of blank idiocy, and the fixed stare in her eyes was unpleasant. She wandered about, summer and winter, bare-foot and wearing nothing but a dress. Her coarse, black hair curled like lamb's wool, forming a cap on her head. It was always crusted with mud and leaves, as she slept on the ground.

Her father, a homeless, sickly drunk called Ilya, had lived many years as a work-man. Her mother was long dead. Everyone was ready to look after her as, being an idiot; she was especially dear to God. Many tried to clothe her better, rigging her out with high boots and sheepskin coat for the winter. But though she allowed them to dress her up without resisting, she went away, usually to the cathedral porch, where, removing the clothes and leaving them in a pile there, she walked away.

When her father died it made her even more acceptable in the eyes of the religious persons as an orphan. In fact, everyone seemed to like her; even the boys did not tease her. She would walk into strange houses and no one drove her away. Everyone was kind to her and gave her something. If she was given a copper, she would take it and at once drop it in the alms-box of the church or prison. If she were given a roll or bun in the market, she would hand it to the first child she met. Sometimes she would stop one of the richest ladies in the town and give it to her, and the lady, pleased, would take it.

She herself never tasted anything but black bread and water. If she went into an expensive shop where costly goods or money were lying about, no one kept watch on her, for they knew that if she saw thousands of rubles overlooked by them, she would not touch a penny. She slept either in the church porch or climbed over a hurdle into a kitchen garden. Once a week she turned up "at home," the house of her father's former employers, and in the winter went there every night to sleep in the passage or cow house. People were amazed she could stand such a life, but she was used to it, and, though tiny, was healthy.

It happened one clear, warm, moonlit night in September many years ago, five or six drunken men were returning from the club at a very late hour. They passed the "back-way" between the gardens of the houses, with fences on either side. Lying in the tall grass at the side of the road, they saw Lizaveta asleep. They stopped to look at her, laughing and joking about taking advantage of her. It occurred to one young gentleman to ask whether anyone could possibly look upon such an animal as a woman.... They all declared it was impossible.

But Fyodor Pavlovitch, who was among them, declared that it was by no means impossible. It is true that at that time he was overdoing his part as a fool. It was just at the time when he had received the news of his first wife's death in Petersburg, and was drinking and behaving so shamelessly that even the most reckless among them were shocked. They laughed; and one of them challenged him to act on it. The others repelled the idea, although still with hilarity, and at last went their way.

Later on, Fyodor Pavlovitch swore that he had gone with them, and perhaps it was so, for no one knows for certain. But five or six months later, all the town was talking of Lizaveta's condition, and trying to find out who had wronged her. A rumor was that this person was no other than Fyodor Pavlovitch. At the time, Grigory stood up for him, provoking quarrels, and succeeded in bringing some people round to his side.

"It's the wench's own fault," he said, and the man responsible was Karp, a convict who had escaped from prison. This sounded like the truth, for it was remembered that Karp had been in the area at that time and had robbed three people. But the affair and the talk did not turn away popular sympathy from Lizaveta. She was better looked after than ever. A widow named Kondratyev took her in, meaning not to let her go until after the birth.

They kept a constant watch over her, but in spite of that she escaped on the last day. She made her way into Fyodor Pavlovitch's garden. Grigory rushed to Marfa and sent her to Lizaveta, while he ran to fetch a midwife. They saved the baby, but Lizaveta died. Grigory brought the baby home and, making his wife sit down, put it on her lap.

"A child of God—an orphan is akin to all," he said, "and to us above others. Our little lost one has sent us this, who has come from a holy innocent."

So Marfa brought up the child. He was christened Pavel, to which people were not slow in adding Fyodorovitch (son of Fyodor). Fyodor Pavlovitch did not object to this, and thought it amusing. The townspeople were pleased at his adopting the foundling. Later Fyodor Pavlovitch invented a surname for the child, calling him Smerdyakov, after his mother's nickname. So this Smerdyakov became Fyodor Pavlovitch's second servant, and was living in the lodge with Grigory and Marfa at the time our story begins.

Chapter III

The Confession of a Man of Passion – 1

Alyosha remained for some time uncertain after hearing the command his father shouted to him from the carriage. But his father's shouts did not frighten him. He understood perfectly that they were merely "a flourish." He knew his father would let him go back to the monastery the next day, maybe even that evening.

An anxiety of a different sort disturbed him just now. It was the fear of a woman, Katerina Ivanovna, who had begged him in the note handed to him by Madame Hohlakov to come and see her. The request aroused an uneasy feeling, not because he didn't know what she would say, and not because he was afraid of her as a woman. Though he knew little of women, he had spent his life, from early childhood, entirely with women.

He was afraid of that particular woman, and had been from the first time he saw her. He thought of her as a beautiful, proud, imperious girl. But it was not her beauty that troubled him; it was something else. And not knowing what caused his fear only increased it. The girl's aims were of the noblest, he knew. She was trying to save his brother Dmitri, though he had behaved badly to her. Alyosha recognized this, but a shiver ran down his back as he neared her house.

He reflected that he would not find Ivan with her, for Ivan was certainly with his father. Dmitri he was even more certain not to find there. So his conversation would be with her alone. He had a great longing to see his brother Dmitri before that interview. Without showing him the letter, he could talk to him about it. But Dmitri lived a long way off.

Crossing himself, he turned in the direction of his terrible lady.

Meanwhile his father was expecting him, and he had not forgotten his command. He might not be reasonable, so he had to hurry to get there and back. He decided to take a short cut by the back-way, which meant climbing over fences and crossing back-yards. On reaching the garden next door to his father's, he raised his head and came upon something quite unexpected.

Over the fence, in the garden, Dmitri, mounted on something, was leaning forward, trying to get his attention, obviously afraid to utter a word for fear of being overheard.

Alyosha ran up to the fence.

"It's a good thing you looked up.," Mitya said in a whisper. "Climb in here quickly! How splendid you've come! I was just thinking of you!"

Alyosha was delighted too, but he did not know how to get over the fence. Mitya put his hand under his elbow to help him, and, tucking up his monk's dress, Alyosha leapt over the fence.

"Well done! Now come along," said Mitya in a whisper.

"Where?" asked Alyosha. "There's no one here. Why do you whisper?"

"Why do I whisper? Jesus!" cried Dmitri loudly. "You see what silly tricks nature plays. I'm here in secret and on the watch. I'll explain later, but, knowing it's a secret, I began whispering like a fool, when there's no need. Let us go."

Dmitri led his brother to a secluded corner where, in a thicket of old bushes, there stood a broken-down green summer-house blackened with age. Its walls were of lattice-work, but there was still a roof for shelter, though the floor was rotting. In it was a wooden table, and round it some benches. Alyosha saw his brother's excited condition, and on entering the arbor saw half a bottle of brandy and a glass on the table.

"That's brandy," Mitya laughed. "I see your look: 'He's drinking again!' But I'm not drinking, I'm only 'relaxing,' as that pig, Rakitin, says. Sit down. I could take you in my arms, Alyosha, and crush you, for in the whole world I love no one but you!"

He uttered the last words in a sort of joy.

"No one but you and one 'jewel' I have fallen in love with, to my ruin. But being in love doesn't mean loving. You may be in love with a woman and yet hate her. Sit down here by the table and I'll sit beside you and look at you. I'd better speak quietly, for you can never tell what ears are listening. Why have I been thirsting for you all these days? Because it's only to you I can tell everything; because I must, because tomorrow life is ending and beginning. Have you ever dreamt of falling into a pit? That's just how I'm falling, but not in a dream. I'm not afraid, so don't you be afraid. Where were you going?"

"I was going to father's, but I meant to go to Katerina Ivanovna's first."

"To her, and to father! What a coincidence! Why was I waiting for you? Why, to send you to father and to Katerina Ivanovna, to have done with her and with father. And here you are on your way to see both."

"Did you really mean to send me?" cried Alyosha, unhappy.

"You knew it! And I see you understand it all at once. But be quiet for a time." Dmitri thought a moment.

"She's asked you, written you a letter or something, that's why you're going? You wouldn't be going except for that?"

"Here is her note." Alyosha took it from his pocket.

Mitya looked through it.

"And you were going the back-way! Oh, gods, I thank you for sending him by the back-way, and he came to me! Listen, Alyosha! I mean to tell you everything. You will hear and judge and forgive. And that's what I need. Listen! If two people break away from everything and fly off into the unknown, and before flying off to ruin he comes to someone else and says, 'Do this for me'—some favor that could only be asked on one's deathbed—would that other refuse, if he were a brother?"

"I will do it, but tell me what it is, and hurry," said Alyosha.

"Don't be in a hurry, Alyosha There's no need to hurry. The world has taken a new turn. Ah, Alyosha, what a pity you can't understand joy."

Alyosha made up his mind to wait. Mitya sank into thought.

"Alyosha," he said, "you're the only one who won't laugh. I should like to begin my confession. Don't think I'm talking nonsense because I'm drunk. I'm not a bit drunk. But I've made a decision. Don't be uneasy. I'm talking sense, and I'll come to the point in a minute. I won't keep you in suspense. Stay…."

He raised his head, then broke into sobs and seized Alyosha's hand.

"My dear, there's a terrible amount of suffering for man on earth. Don't think I'm only a brute wallowing in drink. I hardly think of anything but of the degraded man I am. The difficulty is how am I to go on? Can I reform? Never! For I'm a Karamazov. When I leap into the pit, I go headlong. Let me be vile and base, only let me kiss the hem of the veil in which God is shrouded. I may follow the devil, but I am Thy son, O Lord.

"I am in tears. It may be foolishness that everyone would laugh at, but you won't, Alyosha. I want to tell you now about the insects to whom God gave lust. I am that insect, brother. All we Karamazovs are, and, angel as you are, that insect lives in you, too, and will stir up a tempest in you. Beauty is a terrible thing, because it has not been fathomed.

"I am not a cultivated man, brother, but I've thought a lot about this. It's terrible what mysteries there are that we must solve. I can't endure the thought that a man of lofty mind and heart begins with the ideal of the Madonna and ends with Sodom. What to the mind is shameful is beauty to the heart. Believe me, beauty is found in Sodom. The awful thing is that beauty is a mystery. God and the devil are fighting there and the battlefield is the heart of man."

Chapter IV

The Confession of a Man of Passion – 2

"I was leading a wild life then," said Dmitri. "I spent thousands seducing young girls. That's a lie; I didn't need money for *that*. I threw away money on music and drinking. Sometimes I gave money to the ladies. But I liked dark back-alleys—there one finds adventures and surprises. I loved vice, the shame of it. Once, riding in a sledge on a dark, winter night, I began squeezing a girl's hand and forced her to kiss me. She was a sweet, gentle, submissive creature, and allowed me much in the dark.... You're blushing!"

"I wasn't blushing at what you were saying," Alyosha said. "I blushed because I am the same as you are."

"You? Come, that's going a little too far!"

"No, it's not," said Alyosha. "The ladder's the same. I'm at the bottom, you're above. It's all the same. Any one on the bottom is bound to go to the top."

"Then one ought not to step on it at all."

"Anyone who can help it had better not."

"But can you?"

"I think not."

"Hush, Alyosha! I could kiss your hand, you touch me so. That rogue Grushenka has an eye for men. She told me once that she'd devour you one day. But let's pass to my vileness. The old man told lies about my ruining the innocent, but there really *was* something of the sort, though it did not come off. The old man has blamed me with what never happened; I never told anyone about it. You're the first, except Ivan. Ivan knows everything. But he's a tomb."

"A tomb?"

"Yes."

Alyosha listened with great attention.

"I was lieutenant in a regiment, well received in the little town. I spent money right and left. They thought I was rich, but I must have pleased them in other ways as well. My colonel, who was an old man, took a sudden dislike to me. But I had powerful friends in the town, so he couldn't do me much harm.

"He was really a very good sort. He had a daughter of four and twenty living with him and an aunt. The aunt was simple and illiterate; the niece simple but lively. Her name was Agafya Ivanovna, and I never knew a woman of more charm! She was tall and stout, with a full figure and beautiful eyes.

"She had not married, although she had had two suitors she refused. I was intimate with her, not in 'that' way, it was pure friendship. I have often been friendly with women quite innocently. I used to talk to her with shocking openness, and she only laughed. Many women are like that. She and her aunt lived in her father's house with a sort of humility, not feeling on an equal with other people. But the colonel was a very different matter. He was one of the chief people in the district. He kept open house, gave suppers and dances.

"At the time I arrived, all the town was talking of the expected return of the colonel's second daughter, a great beauty who had just left a fashionable school in the capital. This daughter, Katerina Ivanovna, was the child of his second wife. When the young lady came from boarding-school on a visit, the whole

town revived. Our most distinguished ladies gave balls in her
honor. I took no notice. I saw her eyes taking my measure one
evening, but I didn't go up to her, as though to avoid meeting
her. When I did speak to her at an evening party not long after,
she hardly looked at me. 'Wait, I'll have my revenge,' thought I.

"What made it worse was that 'Katenka' was not an innocent
boarding-school miss, but a person of character, proud and high-
principled; she had education and intellect, and I had neither.
Meanwhile, I spent my time in drink and riot, till the lieutenant-
colonel put me under arrest for three days. Just at that time
father sent me six thousand rubles in return for my sending him
a deed giving up all claims upon him. I also got a letter from
a friend telling me something of great interest: the authorities
were not satisfied with our lieutenant-colonel. He was suspected
of irregularities. When the commander of the division arrived,
he kicked up the devil. Soon afterwards the lieutenant-colonel
was ordered to retire. Suddenly there was a marked coolness
in the town towards him and his family. Then I took my first
step. I met Agafya Ivanovna, with whom I'd always kept up a
friendship, and said, 'Do you know there's a deficit of 4,500
rubles of government money in your father's accounts?'

"'Why do you say so? When the general was here everything
was fine.'

"'Then it was, but now it isn't.'

"She was terribly scared.

"'Don't frighten me!' she said. 'Who told you so?'

"'Don't be uneasy,' I said, 'I won't tell anyone. But when they
ask for that 4,500 rubles from your father and he can't produce
it, he'll be tried and made to serve as a soldier in his old age,
unless you'd like to send me your young lady secretly. I've just had
money paid me. I'll give her four thousand, if you like, and keep
the secret religiously.'

"'You beast!' she said. 'You wicked beast! How dare you!'

"She went away furious, while I shouted after her that the secret should be kept safe. Agafya and her aunt, I may say, behaved like perfect angels all through this business. They genuinely adored their 'Katya,' thought her far above them, and waited on her hand and foot. Agafya told her of our conversation, and of course that's all I wanted.

"When the new major arrived to take command, the lieutenant-colonel was taken ill, couldn't leave his room for two days, and didn't hand over the money. Dr. Kravchenko declared that he really was ill. But I knew for a fact that for the last four years the money had never been in his hands except when the Commander made his visits of inspection.

"He used to lend it to a trusted person called Trifonov, an old widower, who used to go to the fair, do a profitable business with the money, and return the sum to the colonel, bringing with it a present from the fair, as well as interest on the loan. But this time Trifonov brought nothing back. The lieutenant-colonel flew to him, but Trifonov said to him: "'I've never received any money from you, and couldn't possibly have received any.'

"That was all the answer he got. So now our lieutenant-colonel is confined to the house with a towel round his head. All at once an orderly arrives with the book and the order to 'hand over the battalion money.' He signed the book, stood up, saying he would put on his uniform, ran to his bedroom, loaded his double-barreled gun with a service bullet, took the boot off his right foot, fixed the gun against his chest, and began feeling for the trigger with his foot.

"But Agafya, remembering what I had told her, had her suspicions. She peeped into the room just in time. She rushed in, flung herself upon him, and the gun went off, but hurt no one. The others ran in, took away the gun, and held him. I heard all about this afterwards. I was at home, preparing to go out, when the door opened, and facing me stood Katerina Ivanovna.

"No one had seen her in the street, so no one knew of it in the town. I lodged with two decrepit old ladies who looked after me. They were ready to do anything for me, and at my request were silent. Of course I grasped the position at once. She walked in, her dark eyes flashing, but on her lips I saw fear.

"'My sister told me,' she began, 'that you would give me 4,500 rubles if I came to you for it—myself. I have come....'

"She couldn't keep it up. She was frightened, her voice failed her, and the corners of her mouth quivered. Alyosha, are you listening?"

"Mitya, I know you will tell the whole truth," said Alyosha.

"I am telling it. I shan't spare myself. My first idea was a Karamazov one. I looked her up and down. You've seen her? She's a beauty. But she was beautiful in another way then. At that moment she was beautiful because she was noble and proud, and I was not. She was at my mercy. I could scarcely breathe. But at that second a voice whispered in my ear, 'But when you come tomorrow to make your proposal, she won't see you; she'll order her coachman to kick you out. 'Publish it through the town,' she would say, 'I'm not afraid of you.'

"That is how it would be, no doubt of it.

"I longed to play her the nastiest trick. 'Four thousand! I was joking,' I said. You've been counting your chickens too easily, madam. Two hundred, if you like, but four thousand is not a sum to throw away.' She'd have run away. But it would have been worth it. It has never happened to me with any other woman, to look at her at such a moment with such hate—which is only a hair's-breadth from love.

"I did not keep her long. I went to the table and took out a bank-note for five thousand rubles. I showed it to her in silence,

folded it, handed it to her, opened the door, and made her a deep
bow! She gazed at me for a second, then softly, gently, bowed
down to my feet, her head to the floor. Then she ran away. I was
wearing my sword. I nearly stabbed myself with it. But I didn't.
Well, that's my 'adventure' with Katerina Ivanovna. So now Ivan
and you know.

Chapter V

The Confession of a Man of Passion – 3

"Now," said Alyosha, "I understand the first half."

"You understand the first half. That is a drama. The second is a tragedy."

"I understand nothing of that second half," said Alyosha.

"Do you suppose I do?"

"Dmitri. There's one important question. You were engaged, are you still?"

"We weren't engaged for three months. The next day I told myself the matter was closed. It seemed quite wrong to make her an offer. The day after her visit the maid slipped round with an envelope addressed to me. It contained the change out of the banknote. Not a note of explanation—nothing!

The lieutenant-colonel produced the money, to everyone's surprise. But he no sooner paid it than he fell ill, and died five days later. Ten days after his funeral, Katerina Ivanovna, with her aunt and sister, went to Moscow. I received a note: 'I will write you. Wait. K.' And that was all.

"In Moscow their fortunes changed. The general's widow lost her two nieces—both died of small-pox. The old lady, prostrate with grief, welcomed Katya as a daughter, and changed her will in Katya's favor. She also gave her eighty thousand rubles as a marriage portion.

"I received by post four thousand five hundred rubles. I was speechless. Three days later came the promised letter. She offers to be my wife. 'I love you madly,' she says. 'Even if you don't love me, be my husband. I won't tie you down or be in your way. I'll be your slave. I want to love you forever. I want to save you from yourself.'

"Alyosha, I am not worthy to repeat those words. That letter stabs me even now. I wrote her an answer at once, with tears. One thing I shall feel shame about forever. I referred to her being rich and having a dowry while I was only a beggar! I mentioned money! I ought to have borne it in silence, but it slipped from my pen. Then I wrote at once to Ivan, and told him all I could about it in a letter of six pages, and sent him to her.

"Why do you look like that? Yes, Ivan fell in love with her. I know I did a stupid thing, but perhaps that stupid thing may be the saving of us all. Don't you see what a lot she thinks of Ivan? When she compares us, do you suppose she can love a man like me, especially after all that has happened? But she *does* love a man like him, and not a man like me. She loves her own *virtue*, not me."

Those words slipped from Dmitri.

"I swear, Alyosha," he cried, angry at himself; "you may not believe me, but I swear that though I smiled at her feelings just now, I know I am a million times baser in soul than she, and that her feelings are sincere. That's the tragedy of it. As for Ivan, I can understand how he must be cursing nature now—with his intellect! To see the preference given to a man who, though engaged, can't restrain his nature! And he is rejected. Why? Because she wants to sacrifice her life out of gratitude. I've never said a word of this to Ivan, and Ivan of course has never dropped a hint to me. But destiny will be done. The best man will hold his ground while the baser one will vanish into his back-alley—where he's at home and where he will sink in filth. I've been talking foolishly. But it will be so. She will marry Ivan."

"Stop, Dmitri," Alyosha said. "There's one thing you haven't made clear: you're still engaged, aren't you? How can you break off the engagement if she doesn't want to?"

"Yes, formally engaged. It was all done on my arrival in Moscow. The general's wife blessed us and—would you believe it?—congratulated Katya. 'You've made a good choice,' she said, 'I see right through him.' And—would you believe it?—she didn't like Ivan, and hardly greeted him. I talked with Katya. I told her about myself. She listened, but made me promise to change. I gave my promise, and here—"

"What?"

"I called to you today—to send you to Katerina Ivanovna and—"

"What?"

"Tell her I shan't see her again. Say, 'He sends you his compliments.'"

"Is that possible?"

"That's why I'm sending you. How could I tell her myself?"

"And where are you going?"

"To the back-alley."

"To Grushenka, then!" Alyosha said. "Can Rakitin really have told the truth? I thought you had just visited her, and that was all."

"Can an engaged man pay such visits? As soon as I began visiting Grushenka I ceased to be engaged. Why do you look at me? I went in the first place to beat her. I had heard that that father's agent had given her an I.O.U. of mine so she could sue me for it, to put an end to me. They wanted to scare me. I knew about her old merchant, who's ill now; but he's leaving her a decent little sum. I knew, too, that she was fond of money, that she's a merciless cheat and swindler. I went to beat her, and I stayed.

"I know that everything is over, that there will never be anything more for me. And though I'm a beggar, I had three thousand just then in my pockct. I drove with Grushenka to Mokroe, got wine, and made all the workers and girls drunk. I sent the thousands flying. In three days' time I was stripped bare, but a hero. Do you suppose the hero had gained his end? Not a sign of it. 'I'll marry you if you like,' she said, 'you're a beggar, you know. Say you won't beat me, and will let me do anything I choose, and I will marry you.' She laughed!"

"And do you really mean to marry her?"

"At once, if she will. And if she won't, I shall stay all the same. I'll be the slave at her feet. Alyosha!" he cried, "Do you know this is all a senseless dream, for there's a tragedy here. I may not be a good man, but a thief I never can be. Well, I am a thief. That very morning, before I went to beat Grushenka, Katerina Ivanovna sent for me and, in secrecy, asked me to go to another town and post three thousand rubles to Agafya Ivanovna in Moscow, so nothing should be known of it in town.

"I had that three thousand rubles in my pocket when I went to see Grushenka, and it was that money we spent at Mokroe. Afterwards I pretended I had been to the town, but did not show her the post office receipt. I said I had sent the money and would bring the receipt, and so far I haven't. Now what are you going to her today to say? 'He sends his wishes,' and she'll ask you, 'What about the money?' You might say to her, 'He's a beast with passions he can't control. He didn't send your money, but wasted it, because he couldn't control himself.' He told me to say 'he sends his best wishes.'"

"Mitya, you are unhappy! But not as unhappy as you think."

"Do you suppose I'd shoot myself because I can't get three thousand to pay her back? That's just it. I shan't shoot myself. I haven't the strength. Now I'm going to Grushenka. I don't care what happens."

"And what then?"

"I'll be her husband if she will have me, and when her lovers come, I'll go into the next room. I'll clean her friends' boots, make their tea, run their errands, do whatever she asks."

"Katerina Ivanovna will understand," Alyosha said. "She'll understand and forgive you. She'll see that no one could be more unhappy than you are."

"She won't forgive everything," said Dmitri. "This is something in it that no woman can forgive. Do you know what the best thing to do is?"

"What?"

"Pay back the three thousand."

"Where can we get it? I have two thousand. Ivan will give you another thousand—that makes three. Take it and pay it back."

"And when would you get your three thousand? You're not of age yet. Besides, you must take my farewell to Katerina Ivanovna today. Tomorrow will be too late. I shall send you to father."

"To father?"

"Yes, to father first. Ask him for three thousand."

"But, Mitya, he won't give it."

"I know he won't. Do you know the meaning of despair?"

"Yes."

"Legally he owes me nothing. I know that. But, still, he owes me something. He started with twenty-eight thousand of my mother's money and made a hundred thousand with it. Let him give me back only three out of the twenty-eight, and he'll draw me out of hell; it will make up for many of his sins. For that three thousand I'll make an end of everything, and he shall hear nothing more of me from now on. Forever. For the last time I give him the chance to be a father. Tell him God Himself sends him this chance."

"Mitya, he won't give it for anything."

"I know he won't. Only a few days ago he found out that Grushenka is perhaps not joking, and really means to marry me. Do you suppose he's going to give me money to help to bring that about when he's crazy about her himself? Also, I know that for the last five days he has had three thousand changed into notes of a hundred rubles, packed into an envelope and tied with red tape. I know all about it! On the envelope is written: 'To my angel, Grushenka, when she comes to me.'

"He scrawled it himself in secret, and no one knows it's there except Smerdyakov, whom he trusts like himself. He has been expecting Grushenka for the last four days; he hopes she'll come for the money. He has sent her word of it, and she has said that perhaps she'll come. And if she does go, can I marry her after that? You understand now why I'm here and on the watch."

"For her?"

"Yes. No one knows I am on watch here."

"No one but Smerdyakov knows, then?"

"No one. He will let me know if she goes to the old man."

"It was he told you about the money, then?"

"Yes. It's a secret. Even Ivan doesn't know. The old man is sending Ivan on a two or three days' journey. A buyer has turned up for the woods: he'll give eight thousand for the timber. So the old man keeps asking Ivan to go to arrange it. It will take him two or three days. That's what the old man wants, so that Grushenka can come while he's away."

"Then he's expecting Grushenka today?"

"No, she won't come today; there are signs. She's certain not to come," cried Mitya. "Smerdyakov thinks so, too. Father's drinking now. He's sitting at table with Ivan. Go to him, Alyosha, and ask for the three thousand."

"Mitya, dear, what's the matter with you?" cried Alyosha.

For one moment the thought struck him that Dmitri was mad.

"What is it? I'm not insane," said Dmitri. "No fear. I am sending you to father, and I know what I'm saying. I believe in miracles."

"In miracles?"

"In a miracle of Divine Providence. God knows my heart. He sees my despair. He sees the whole picture. Surely He won't let something awful happen. Alyosha, go!"

"I'm going. Tell me, will you wait for me here?"

"Yes. I know it will take time. He's drunk now. I'll wait three hours—four, five, six. Only remember you must go to Katerina Ivanovna today, if it has to be at midnight, *with the money or without*, and say, 'He sends his best wishes.'"

"Mitya! What if Grushenka comes today—or tomorrow, or the next day?"

"Grushenka? I shall see her. I shall rush out and prevent it."

"And if—"

"If there's an if, it will be murder. I couldn't endure it."

"Who will be murdered?"

"The old man. I shan't kill her."

"Brother, what are you saying?"

"Oh, I don't know. Perhaps I shan't kill him. But I'm afraid I will hate him so at that moment. I hate his ugly throat, his nose, his eyes. I'm afraid that may be too much for me."

"I'll go, Mitya. I believe God will order things so nothing awful happens."

"I'll sit and wait for the miracle. And if it doesn't come to pass—"

Alyosha went thoughtfully towards his father's house.

Chapter VI

Smerdyakov

Alyosha found his father at table. The dinner was over, but coffee and preserves had been served. Fyodor Pavlovitch liked sweet things with his drinks after dinner. Ivan was at the table sipping coffee, the servants, Grigory and Smerdyakov, standing by. Everyone seemed in good spirits.

Before he entered the room, Alyosha heard the shrill laugh he knew so well, and could tell that his father had only reached the good-humored stage.

"Here he is! Here he is!" yelled Fyodor Pavlovitch at seeing him. "Sit down. The coffee is hot and good. I don't offer you a drink, you're fasting. But would you like some? No; I'd better give you our famous wine. Smerdyakov, go to the cupboard, the second shelf on the right. Here are the keys. Look sharp!"

Alyosha refused the liqueur.

"If you won't have it, we will," said Fyodor Karamazov. "Have you dined?"

"Yes," answered Alyosha, who had only had a piece of bread and a glass of kvass in the Father Superior's kitchen. "Though I should like some coffee."

"Bravo, my darling! He'll have some coffee. Does it want warming? No, it's boiling. My Smerdyakov's an artist at coffee and at fish soup, too. You must come one day and have some.

But, stay; didn't I tell you this morning to come home with your mattress and pillow? Have you brought your mattress?"

"No, I haven't," said Alyosha, smiling.

"Ah, but you were frightened this morning, weren't you? There, my darling, I couldn't do anything to trouble you. Do you know, Ivan, I can't resist the way he looks one straight in the face and laughs? Alyosha, let me give you a father's blessing."

Alyosha rose, but Fyodor Pavlovitch had already changed his mind.

"No," he said. "I'll just make the sign of the cross over you. We've a treat for you. Balaam's ass has begun talking to us here—and how he talks!"

Balaam's ass, it appeared, was the valet, Smerdyakov. He was a young man of about four and twenty, remarkably unsociable. Not that he was shy. In fact, he was conceited and seemed to look down on everybody. He was brought up by Grigory and Marfa, but grew up "with no sense of gratitude," as Grigory expressed it. In his childhood he was fond of hanging cats and burying them with ceremony. All this he did on the sly, with the greatest secrecy. Grigory caught him once and gave him a sound beating.

"He doesn't care for you or me," Grigory used to say to Marfa, "and he doesn't care for anyone. Are you a human being?" he said, addressing the boy directly. "You're not a human being. You grew from the mildew in the bath-house. That's what you are."

Smerdyakov, it appeared, never forgave him those words. Grigory taught him to read and write, and when he was twelve years old began teaching him the Scriptures. But this teaching came to nothing.

At the second or third lesson the boy suddenly grinned.

"What's that for?" asked Grigory.

"Oh, nothing. God created light on the first day, and the sun, moon, and stars on the fourth day. Where did the light come from on the first day?"

Grigory was thunder-struck. "I'll show you where!" he cried, and gave the boy a slap on the cheek. The boy took the slap without a word, but withdrew into his corner again for some days.

A week later Smerdykov had his first attack of the disease to which he was subject all the rest of his life—epilepsy. When Fyodor Pavlovitch heard of it, his attitude to the boy changed. Till then he had taken no notice of him, though he never scolded him, and always gave him a penny when he met him. Sometimes, when he was in good humor, he would send the boy a sweet from his table.

As soon as he heard of his illness, he showed an interest in him, and sent for a doctor. But the disease was not to be cured. The fits occurred, on average, once a month, but at various intervals. The fits varied too, in strength: some light, some severe. Fyodor Pavlovitch told Grigory never to hit the boy, and began allowing him to come upstairs to him. He would not let him be taught anything for a time. But one day when the boy was fifteen, Fyodor Pavlovitch saw him at the bookcase reading the titles through the glass. Fyodor Pavlovitch had a fair number of books—over a hundred—but no one ever saw him reading. He gave Smerdyakov the key of the bookcase.

"Come, read. You'll be better reading than hanging about the courtyard. Come, read this," and Fyodor Pavlovitch gave him a book.

He read a little but didn't like it.

"Why? Isn't it funny?" asked Fyodor Pavlovitch.

Smerdyakov did not speak.

"Answer!"

"It's all untrue," mumbled the boy with a grin.

"Then go to the devil! Stay, here's a history. That's all true. Read that."

But Smerdyakov did not get through ten pages. He thought it dull.

So the bookcase was closed again.

Shortly afterwards Grigory reported to Fyodor Pavlovitch that Smerdyakov was beginning to show a great care about everything. He would sit before his soup, take up his spoon and look into the soup, bend over it, examine it, take a spoonful and hold it to the light.

"What is it? A bug?" Grigory would ask.

"A fly, perhaps," observed Marfa.

The youth never answered, but he did the same with everything. He would hold a piece on his fork to the light, study it, and only then decide to eat it.

"What fine gentlemen's airs!" Grigory said.

When Fyodor Pavlovitch heard of this, he decided to make Smerdyakov his cook, and sent him to Moscow to be trained. He spent some years there and came back very changed. He looked old for his age. His face had grown wrinkled, yellow, and strangely unmanly. But in character he seemed almost exactly the same as before. He was just as unsociable, and showed not the slightest desire for any companions.

Fyodor Pavlovitch paid him a salary, almost the whole of which Smerdyakov spent on clothes, perfumes, and such. But he seemed to have as much contempt for the female sex as for men. Fyodor Pavlovitch began to regard him rather differently. His fits became more frequent, and on the days he was ill Marfa cooked.

"Why are your fits getting worse?" Fyodor Pavlovitch asked him. "Would you like to get married? Shall I find you a wife?"

Smerdyakov turned pale with anger, and made no reply. Fyodor Pavlovitch left him with an impatient gesture. The great thing was that he had absolute confidence in his honesty. It happened once, when Fyodor Pavlovitch was drunk, that he dropped in the yard three hundred-ruble notes he had just received. He only missed them the next day, and was searching his pockets when he saw them lying on the table. Where had they come from? Smerdyakov had picked them up and brought them in.

"Well, my lad, I've never met anyone like you," Fyodor Pavlovitch said, and gave him ten rubles. After that he not only believed in his honesty, but had, for some reason, a liking for him, although the young man looked at him as at every one and was always silent. He used sometimes to stop suddenly in the house, or yard or street, and stand lost in thought. If one touched him he would start and look as though woken and bewildered. And if he were asked what he had been thinking, he would not remember.

Chapter VII

The Discussion

Grigory, at the store, heard from the shopkeeper the story of a Russian soldier that had appeared in the newspaper. This soldier had been taken prisoner in a remote part of Asia, and threatened with an immediate, painful death if he did not turn his back on Christianity and follow Islam.

He refused, was tortured, flayed alive, and died praising Christ.

Grigory told the story at table.

Fyodor Pavlovitch liked, over dessert, to laugh and talk, if only with Grigory. This afternoon he was in a good-humor. Sipping his drink and listening to the story, he said they ought to make a saint of the soldier and take his skin to a monastery. "That would make the people flock, and bring the money in."

Grigory saw that Fyodor Pavlovitch was going to make fun of the story. Smerdyakov, standing by the door, smiled.

"What are you grinning at?" asked Fyodor Pavlovitch.

"My opinion is," Smerdyakov began loudly, "that if that soldier's exploit was so great there would have been, to my thinking, no sin in it if he had on such an emergency renounced the name of Christ and his own christening to save his life, for the good deeds which, in the course of years, he would do would make up for his cowardice."

"How could it not be a sin? You're talking nonsense. For that you'll go straight to hell and be roasted there like lamb," put in Fyodor Pavlovitch.

It was at this point that Alyosha came in, and Fyodor Pavlovitch was highly delighted at his appearance.

"We're on your subject," he said, making Alyosha sit down.

"As for lamb, there'll be nothing there for that either, if it's according to justice," Smerdyakov said.

"How do you mean 'according to justice'?" Fyodor Pavlovitch cried.

"He's a non-believer, that's what he is!" burst from Grigory.

"As for being a non-believer, Grigory Vassilyevitch," said Smerdyakov, "you'd better consider yourself that, once I am taken prisoner by the enemies of the Christians, and they demand I curse the name of God and give up my belief, I am fully entitled to act by my own reason, for there would be no sin in it."

"But you've said that before. Prove it," cried Fyodor.

"Soup-maker!" said Grigory.

"As for being a soup-maker, consider this, Grigory Vassilyevitch, without getting mean. As soon as I say to my enemies, 'No, I'm not a Christian, and curse God,' then at once, by God's high judgment, I become immediately and specially cursed, cut off from the Holy Church. So that at that very instant, not only when I say it aloud, but when I think it, I am cut off. Is that so or not?"

He addressed Grigory, though he was really answering Fyodor Pavlovitch.

"You're cursed," Grigory cried. "How dare you argue, you sinner, after—"

"Don't scold him, Grigory," Fyodor Pavlovitch said.

"You should listen, Grigory Vassilyevitch, for I haven't finished. At the moment I become cursed, I become one who does not believe, and my faith becomes of no use. Isn't that so?"

73

"Hurry and finish, my boy," Fyodor Pavlovitch said.

"And if I've ceased to believe, then I told no lie when the enemy asked whether I was a Christian, seeing I had already had my belief taken away by God Himself by reason of the thought alone. And if I have already lost my belief, in what manner and with what sort of justice can I be held responsible as a believer for having denied Christ, when, through the very thought alone, I had had my belief taken away? If I'm no longer a believer, then I can't give up Christ, for I've no belief to give up. That would mean that the Almighty would tell an untruth. And can the Lord of Heaven tell a lie, even in one word?"

Grigory was thunder-struck, looking at Smerdyakov with his eyes starting out of his head. Though he did not fully understand what was said, he caught something in this talk, and looked like a man who has hit his head against a wall.

Fyodor Pavlovitch emptied his glass and went off into his shrill laugh.

"Alyosha! What do you say to that! He must have been with the Jesuits. Oh, you stinking Jesuit, who taught you? Don't cry, Grigory, we'll reduce him to smoke and ashes in a moment. Tell me this, O fool; you may be right, but you have renounced your faith in your heart, and you say yourself that in that very hour you became cursed. And if you're cursed, they won't pat you on the head for it in hell. What do you say to that, my fine Jesuit?"

"There is no doubt I renounced it, but there was no special sin in that. Or if there was sin, it was the most ordinary."

"How's that the most ordinary?"

"Consider," Smerdyakov went on. "It is said in Scripture that if you have faith, even as a mustard seed, and bid a mountain move, it will move. Grigory Vassilyevitch, if I'm without faith and you have so great a faith, try telling a mountain to move. You'll see for yourself it won't move. That shows, Grigory

Vassilyevitch, that you haven't proper faith, and only accuse others of the same lack of faith. And since no one in our day, not only you, but no one, can move mountains—will God curse the whole population? And in His mercy will He not forgive even one? I believe, though I doubted, I shall be forgiven if I repent."

"It's characteristic of the people's faith," Ivan said. "It's true, isn't it, Alyosha? That's the Russian faith all over?"

"No, Smerdyakov has not the Russian faith at all," said Alyosha.

"Your words are worth a gold piece, O fool," cried Grigory Vassilyevitch, "and I'll give it to you today. Let me tell you, we here are all of little faith only from carelessness, and, in the second place, the Lord God has given us so little time that one hasn't even time to sleep enough, much less repent of one's sins. You have denied your faith when you'd nothing to think about! So, brother, that's a sin."

"A sin it may be, but Grigory Vassilyevitch, if I believed as I ought, then it really would have been a sin if I had not faced tortures for my faith. But it wouldn't have come to that, because I should only have had to say to the mountain, 'Move and crush the enemy,' and it would have moved and crushed him, and I should have walked away as though nothing had happened.

"But, suppose I cried to the mountain, 'Crush these enemies,' and it didn't crush them, how could I have helped doubting? I should know already that I could not attain to the Kingdom of Heaven. So why should I let them flay the skin from me to no good purpose? And, therefore, how could I be blamed if, not seeing my advantage or reward there or here, I should at least save my skin. So, trusting in the grace of the Lord, I hope I might be forgiven."

Chapter VIII

Over Drinks

The argument was over. But Fyodor Pavlovitch, who had been so gay, began gulping his drinks. "Get along with you, Jesuits!" he cried. "Go away, Smerdyakov. I'll send you the gold piece I promised you, but be off! Don't cry, Grigory. Go to Marfa. She'll comfort you. They won't let us sit in peace after dinner," he said as the servants left. "Smerdyakov always sticks his nose in after dinner. It's you he's interested in, Ivan. What have you done to fascinate him?"

"Nothing whatever," answered Ivan. "He's pleased to have a high opinion of me; he's a lackey and a mean soul. Raw material for revolution, however."

"For revolution?"

"There will be others and better ones. But there will be some like him as well. His kind will come first, and better ones after."

"And when will the time come?"

"The rocket will go off and fizzle out, perhaps. The peasants are not very fond of listening to these soup-makers, so far."

"Ah, but a fool like that thinks, and the devil knows where he gets to."

"He's storing up ideas," said Ivan.

"I know he can't bear me, or anyone else, even you, though you fancy he has a high opinion of you. And he despises Alyosha.

But he doesn't steal, that's one thing, and he's not a gossip, and doesn't wash our dirty linen in public. He makes capital fish pasties, too. But is he worth talking about so much?"

"Of course he isn't."

"As for the ideas he may be hatching, the Russian peasant needs beating. That I've always maintained. Our peasants steal, and don't deserve to be pitied. We've left off beating the peasants, but they go on beating themselves. And a good thing too. 'For with what measure ye mete it shall be measured to you again,' or how does it go? Anyhow, it will be measured. But Russia's all evil. My dear, if you only knew how I hate Russia.... That is, not Russia, but all this sin! Do you know what I like? I like wit."

"You've had another glass. That's enough."

"I'll have one more, then I'll stop. No, stay, you interrupted me. At Mokroe I was talking to an old man, and he said: 'There's nothing we like so much as sentencing girls to be beaten, and we always give the lads the job of doing it. The girl he beats today, the young man will ask to marry him tomorrow. So it quite suits the girls, too,' he said. Shall we go over and have a look at it? Alyosha, are we up-setting you?

"Don't be, child. I'm sorry if I was rude to your Superior this morning. I lost my temper. If there is a God, of course, I'm to blame, and I shall have to answer for it. But if there isn't a God at all, what shall we do with your Fathers? It's not enough to cut their heads off, for they keep back progress. Would you believe, Ivan, that idea pains me? No, you don't believe it; I see from your eyes. You believe what people say, that I'm only a fool. Alyosha, do you believe it?"

"No, I don't believe it."

"I believe you don't, and that you speak the truth. You are sincere and speak sincerely. But not Ivan. I'd make an end of your monks, though. I'd do away with all that mystic stuff, to bring all the fools to reason!"

"But why do away with it?" asked Ivan.

"That Truth may prevail."

"Well, if Truth were to prevail, you'd be the first to be done away with."

"I dare say you're right. I'm a fool!" burst out Fyodor Pavlovitch, striking himself on the forehead. "Well, your monastery may stand then, Alyosha, if that's how it is. And we clever people will sit snug and enjoy our drinks. You know, Ivan, it must have been so ordered by the Almighty. Ivan, is there a God or not? Speak seriously. Are you laughing again?"

"I'm laughing that you made a clever remark about Smerdyakov's belief in the existence of two saints who could move mountains."

"Why, am I like him, then?"

"Very much."

"Well, that shows I'm Russian, too. You may be caught the same way, though you are a thinker. Speak all the same, is there a God, or not?"

"No, there is no God."

"Alyosha, is there a God?"

"There is."

"Ivan, and is there life after death of some sort?"

"There is no life after death either."

"None? There's absolute nothingness then."

"Alyosha, is there life after death?"

"There is."

"God and life after death?"

"God and life after death. In God *is* life after death."

"It's more likely Ivan's right. To think what faith, what force, man has lavished for nothing on that dream, and for how many thousand years. Who is it laughing at man? Ivan! For the last time, is there a God or not?"

"And for the last time there is not."

"Who is laughing at mankind, Ivan?"

"It must be the devil," said Ivan, smiling.

"And the devil? Does he exist?"

"No, there's no devil, either."

"It's a pity. Damn it all, what wouldn't I do to the man who first invented God! Hanging would be too good for him."

"There would have been no civilization if they hadn't invented God."

"Wouldn't there have been? Without God?"

"No. And there would have been no drinks, either. But I must take your drinks away from you, anyway."

"Stop, dear boy, one more little glass. I've hurt Alyosha's feelings. You're not angry with me, my dear little Alyosha?"

"I'm not angry. I know your thoughts. Your heart is better than your head."

"My heart better than my head? Ivan, do you love Alyosha?"

"Yes."

"You must love him. Alyosha, I was rude to your elder this morning. I was excited. But there's wit in that elder, don't you think, Ivan?"

"Very likely."

"There is. He's a Jesuit. As he's a person of honor; there's a hidden anger boiling within him at having to pretend and affect holiness."

"But, of course, he believes in God."

"Not a bit. He tells everyone himself. Not everyone, but the clever people. He said to Governor Schultz not long ago: *Believe, but I don't know in what.*"

"Really?"

"He really did. But I respect him. He has such passion, though, that I should be afraid for my daughter or my wife if she went to him. You know, the year before last he invited us to tea, with drinks, and he began telling us about old times. We nearly split our sides. He told how he cured a paralyzed woman, then said to her, 'If my legs were not so bad I could dance with you.' What do you say to that? 'I've plenty of tricks in my time,' said he. He did Dernidov out of sixty thousand."

"He stole it?"

"Dernidov brought him the money as a man he could trust, saying, 'Take care of it for me, friend, there'll be a police search at my place tomorrow.' And he kept it. 'You have given it to the Church,' he declared. I said to him: 'You stole the money.' 'No,' said he, 'I didn't steal it, but I'm broad-minded.' But that was someone else. I've mixed him with someone else.... Come, another glass and that's all. Take the bottle, Ivan. I've been telling lies. Why didn't you stop me?"

"I knew you'd stop of yourself."

"That's a lie. You did it on purpose. You despise me in my own house."

"Well, I'm going away. You've had too much to drink."

"I begged you to go to Tchermashnya for a day or two, and you don't go."

"I'll go tomorrow if you're so set on it."

"You won't go. You want to keep an eye on me. That's what you want."

The old man had reached that state of drunkenness when he tries to pick a quarrel.

"Why are you looking at me? Your eyes say, 'You ugly drunk!' You're looking down on me. You've come here with some design. Alyosha, here, looks at me and his eyes shine. Alyosha doesn't put me down. Alexey, you mustn't love Ivan."

"Don't be ill-tempered with my brother," Alyosha said.

"All right. My head aches. Take away the brandy. It's the third time I've told you."

A slow, cunning grin spread over his face.

"Don't be angry with a feeble old man, Ivan. I know you don't love me, but don't be angry. You've nothing to love me for. Go to Tchermashnya. I'll come myself and bring you a present. I'll show you a girl there. I've had my eye on her a long time. She's still running about bare-foot. Don't be afraid of bare-footed girls—they're pearls!"

And he kissed his hand with a loud sound.

"To my thinking," he said, seeming to grow sober the instant he touched on his favorite topic. "Ah, you boys! Children, to my thinking ... I never thought a woman ugly in my life—that's been my rule! Can you understand that? How could you understand it? You've milk in your veins, not blood. You're not out of your shells yet. My rule has been that you can always find something interesting in every woman that you wouldn't find in any other. Only one must know how to find it, that's the point!

"To my mind there are no ugly women. The fact she is a woman is half the battle. Even in young girls you may discover something that makes you simply wonder that men have been such fools as to let them grow old without noticing them. Bare-footed girls or ugly ones, you must take by surprise. You must go after them till they're fascinated, up-set, shamed that such a gentleman should fall in love with such a nothing. Alyosha, I always used to surprise your mother, but in a different way. I paid no attention to her at all, but all at once, when the minute came, I'd be all devotion to her, crawl on my knees, kiss her feet, and I always reduced her to that tinkling, quiet, nervous, queer little laugh.

"I knew her attacks always began like that. The next day she would begin shrieking, and this little laugh was not a sign of delight, though it made a very good counterfeit. I took her to the monastery to bring her to her senses. The holy Fathers prayed her back to reason. But I swear, Alyosha, I never insulted the poor crazy girl! Only once, perhaps, in the first year, when she was fond of praying. She used to keep the feasts of Our Lady and turn me out of her room then. I'll knock that mysticism out of her, thought I!

"'Here,' said I, 'you see your holy image. You believe it's miraculous, but I'll spit on it and nothing will happen to me!' When she saw it, good Lord! I thought she would kill me. But she only jumped up, wrung her hands, then hid her face in them, trembling, and fell on the floor. Alyosha, what's the matter?"

The old man jumped up in alarm. From the time he began speaking about Alyosha's mother, a change had come over Alyosha's face. He flushed, his eyes glowed, his lips quivered. The old sot had gone on, noticing nothing, till the moment when something strange happened to Alyosha. Precisely what he was describing in the crazy woman was repeated with Alyosha. He jumped up from his seat as his mother was said to have done, wrung his hands, hid his face in them, and fell back in his chair, shaking and weeping.

"Ivan! Water, quickly! It's like her, exactly as his mother used to be. Spit some water on him, that's what I used to do to her. He's upset about his mother," he said.

"But she was my mother, too, I believe. Was she not?" said Ivan, with anger. The old man shrank before his flashing eyes. For a second; it seemed really to have escaped the old man's mind that Alyosha's mother actually was the mother of Ivan, too.

"Your mother?" he said, not understanding. "What do you mean? What mother are you talking about? Was she? Why, damn it! Of course she was yours too! My mind has never been so darkened before. Excuse me, why, I was thinking, Ivan...!"

He stopped, a drunken, half-senseless grin on his face. At that moment a loud noise was heard in the hall, the door was flung open, and Dmitri burst into the room. The old man rushed to Ivan in terror.

"He'll kill me! Don't let him get me!" he cried, hanging on to Ivan's coat.

Chapter IX

Lovers of the Flesh

Grigory and Smerdyakov ran into the room after Dmitri. They had struggled with him in the passage, refusing to admit him, on instructions given by Fyodor Pavlovitch. Taking advantage of the fact that Dmitri stopped on entering the room to look about him, Grigory ran round the table, closed the double doors on the opposite side of the room leading to the inner apartments, and stood before them, stretching wide his arms.

Seeing this, Dmitri uttered a scream and rushed at Grigory.

"Then she's there! She's hidden there! Out of the way, old man!"

He tried to pull Grigory away, but the old servant pushed him back. Beside himself with fury, Dmitri hit Grigory with all his might. The old man fell like a log, and Dmitri, leaping over him, broke in the door. "She's here!" he shouted. "I saw her turn towards the house just now, but I couldn't catch her. Where is she?"

"When Fyodor Pavlovitch heard him shout, "She's here!" his terror left him.

"Hold him!" he cried, dashing after Dmitri. Meanwhile Grigory got up from the floor, stunned. Ivan and Alyosha ran after their father. In the third room something was heard to fall on the floor: it was a large glass vase Dmitri upset.

"At him!" shouted the old man. "Help!"

Ivan and Alyosha caught the old man and brought him back.

"Why do you run after him? He'll murder you," Ivan cried.

"Ivan! Alyosha! She must be here. Grushenka's here. He said he saw her."

He was choking. Not expecting Grushenka, he was trembling all over.

"But you've seen for yourself she hasn't come," cried Ivan.

"But she may have come by the other entrance."

"You know that entrance is locked, and you have the key."

Dmitri reappeared in the drawing-room. He had, of course, found the other entrance locked. The windows of all the rooms were also closed, so Grushenka could not have come in anywhere nor have run out anywhere.

"Hold him!" cried Fyodor Pavlovitch. "He stole money in my bedroom."

Tearing himself from Ivan he rushed at Dmitri. But Dmitri clutched the old man by the tufts of hair and flung him on the floor. He kicked him two or three times in the face. The old man moaned. Ivan, though not so strong as Dmitri, threw his arms round him and pulled him away. Alyosha helped him with his slender strength, holding Dmitri in front.

"Mad man! You've killed him!" cried Ivan.

"Serve him right!" shouted Dmitri. "If I haven't killed him, I'll come again and kill him. You can't protect him!"

"Dmitri! Go away at once!" cried Alyosha.

"Alexey! You tell me. It's only you I can believe; was she here just now? I saw her creeping this way by the fence from the lane."

"I swear she's not been here, and no one expected her."

"But I saw her.... She must...

"I'll find out where she is.... Good-by, Alexey! Not a word about the money. Go to Katerina Ivanovna and be sure to say, 'He sends his best wishes to you!' Just 'best wishes' and farewell!"

Meanwhile Ivan and Grigory raised the old man and seated him. His face was covered with blood, but he was conscious and heard Dmitri's cries. He still fancied Grushenka was in the house.

Dmitri looked at him with hatred as he went out.

"I'm sorry I bloodied you! Beware, old man. I curse you," he cried, and ran out of the room.

"She's here. She must be here. Smerdyakov!" the old man called.

"No, she's not here, you crazy old man!" Ivan shouted. "Here, he's fainting! Water! A towel! Hurry, Smerdyakov!"

Smerdyakov ran for water.

At last they got the old man undressed and in bed. They wrapped a wet towel round his head. Exhausted by the drinks, his emotion, and the blows, he shut his eyes and fell asleep immediately.

Ivan and Alyosha returned to the drawing-room. Smerdyakov removed the fragments of the vase Dmitri had broken, while Grigory stood by the table, sadly, looking at the floor.

"Shouldn't you put a wet bandage on your head and go to bed, too?" Alyosha said to him. "We'll look after him. My brother gave you a terrible blow—on the head."

"He's hurt me!" Grigory said.

"He's 'hurt' his father, not only you," said Ivan.

"I used to wash him in his tub. He's hurt my feelings," repeated Grigory.

"Damn it all, if I hadn't pulled him away he may have murdered him. It wouldn't take much, would it?" said Ivan to Alyosha.

"God forbid!" cried Alyosha.

"Why should He forbid?" Ivan went on. "One reptile will devour the other. And serve them both right, too."

Alyosha trembled.

"Of course I won't let him be murdered, as I didn't just now. Stay here, Alyosha, I'll go for a turn in the yard. My head's aching."

Alyosha went to his father's bedroom and sat by his bedside for an hour. The old man opened his eyes and gazed for a long while at Alyosha, evidently remembering and thinking. All at once his face betrayed great excitement.

"Alyosha," he whispered fearfully, "where's Ivan?"

"In the yard. His head hurts. He's on the watch."

"Give me that looking-glass. It stands over there."

Alyosha gave him a little looking-glass that stood on the chest of drawers. The old man looked at himself in it; his nose was swollen, and on the left side of his forehead there was a large purple mark.

"What does Ivan say? Alyosha, my dear, my only son, I'm afraid of Ivan. I'm more afraid of Ivan than the other. You're the only one I'm not afraid of...."

"Don't be afraid of Ivan either. He's angry, but he'll defend you."

"What of the other? He's run to Grushenka. Tell me, was she here?"

"No one has seen her. It was a mistake. She has not been here."

"You know Mitya wants to marry her."

"She won't marry him."

"She won't on any account!"

The old man fairly shone with joy, as though nothing more comforting could have been said. In his delight he seized Alyosha's hand and pressed it warmly to his heart. Tears glittered in his eyes.

"I'll let you go back to the monastery. I was joking, don't be angry. Alyosha, comfort my heart. Tell me the truth!"

"You're still asking if she has been here?" Alyosha asked.

"No, no. I believe you. I'll tell you what it is: you go to Grushenka, or see her somehow; ask her; see for yourself, which she means to choose, him or me."

"If I see her I'll ask her," Alyosha said, turning red.

"No, she won't tell you," the old man said. "She's no good. She'll kiss you and say it's you she wants. She has no shame. You mustn't go!"

"No, father, and it wouldn't be right at all."

"Where was he sending you just now? He shouted 'Go'."

"To Katerina Ivanovna."

"For money? To ask her for money?"

"No. Not for money."

"He has no money; nothing. I'll settle down for the night, and think things out, and you can go. Perhaps you'll meet her. Only be sure to come tomorrow. I have a word to say to you. Will you come?"

"Yes."

"When you come, pretend you've come of your own accord to ask after me. Don't tell anyone I told you to. Don't say a word to Ivan."

"Very well."

"Goodbye, my angel. You stood up for me. I shall never forget it. I've a word to say to you tomorrow—but I must think about it."

"How do you feel now?"

"I shall get up tomorrow and go out, perfectly well!"

Crossing the yard Alyosha found Ivan sitting on the bench at the gateway.

He was writing something in his note-book. Alyosha told Ivan that their father had waked up, and had let him go back to sleep at the monastery.

"Alyosha, I should be glad to meet you tomorrow morning," said Ivan.

His friendliness was a complete surprise to Alyosha.

"I shall be at the Hohlakovs' tomorrow," answered Alyosha, "I may be at Katerina Ivanovna's, too, if I don't find her now."

"But you're going to her now, anyway? For that 'compliments and farewell,'" said Ivan smiling. "I think I understand his exclamations, and part of what went before. Dmitri has asked you to go to her and say that he takes his leave of her?"

"Brother, how will all this end between father and Dmitri?" asked Alyosha.

"One can't tell. Perhaps it may all die out. That woman is a beast. In any case we must keep the old man indoors and not let Dmitri into the house."

"Let me ask one thing more: has any man a right to look at other men and decide which is worthy to live?"

"Why bring in 'worth'? The matter is usually decided in men's hearts on other grounds more natural. And as for rights—who has not the right to wish?"

"Not for another man's death?"

"What if for another man's death? Why lie to one's self, since all men live so and can't help it. Are you thinking of what I said just now—that one snake will eat the other? Do you think I'd murder him?"

"What are you saying, Ivan? Such an idea never crossed my mind. I don't think Dmitri could do it, either."

"Thanks, if only for that," smiled Ivan. "Be sure, I will always defend him. But I keep my wishes to myself. Good-by."

They shook hands as never before. Alyosha felt his brother had taken the first step towards him, and that he did this with some motive.

Chapter X

Both Together

Alyosha left his father's house feeling even more exhausted and sad than when he entered it. His mind seemed shattered. He felt something bordering upon despair, which he had not known till then. Above all stood the fatal question: How would things end between his father and his brother? Only Dmitri could be made completely unhappy.

There were other people concerned too. Ivan made a step towards him, which was what Alyosha had long wanted. Yet, for some reason, it frightened him. That morning he had set out for Katerina Ivanovna's with the greatest unease; now he was hurrying as if expecting guidance from her. Yet to give her the message was more difficult than before. The matter of the three thousand was decided and Dmitri might now sink to any depth.

It was seven o'clock and getting dark as Alyosha entered the house in High Street. Alyosha knew Katerina Ivanovna lived with two aunts. It was said they gave way in everything to her, and that she only kept them as chaperons. Katerina Ivanovna herself gave way to no one but the general's widow, her benefactress, who had been kept by illness in Moscow, and to whom she wrote twice a week.

When Alyosha entered the hall, it was evident they were aware of his arrival. He heard the sound of footsteps and rustling skirts. Two or three women had run out of the room. Alyosha thought it strange his arrival should cause such excitement. He was led to the drawing-room, a large room elegantly furnished. It was rather dark. He made out a silk mantle on the sofa, and on a table in front of the sofa were two unfinished cups of chocolate. He had interrupted visitors. But at that instant the curtain was raised, and Katerina Ivanovna came in, holding out both hands to him with a radiant smile of delight.

"Thank God! You've come! I've been praying for you all day! Sit down."

It was with amazement that he felt now, as Katerina Ivanovna ran to him, that he had perhaps been utterly mistaken about her the first time he met her. This time her face beamed with good-nature and kindness. The "pride," which had struck him before, was betrayed now in a frank, generous energy.

"I was so eager to see you because I can learn from you the whole truth."

"I have come," said Alyosha confusedly, "I—he sent me."

"Ah, he sent you! I foresaw that. Now I know everything!" cried Katerina Ivanovna. "Wait a moment, Alexey Fyodorovitch, I'll tell you what I want from you. I want to know your impression of him. I want you to tell me plainly what you thought of him. That will be better than a personal explanation, as he does not want to come to me. Tell me every word of the message he sent you with."

"He told me to give you his best wishes—and say he would never come again."

"His best wishes? Was that his own expression?"

"Yes."

"Accidentally, perhaps, he made a mistake in the word?"

"No; he told me to repeat that word. He begged me not to forget to say so."

Katerina Ivanovna flushed hotly.

"Help me now, Alexey Fyodorovitch. Now I really need your help. I'll tell you what I think, and you say whether it's right or not. If he had sent me his compliments without insisting on your repeating the words, that would be the end of everything! But if he insisted on those words, if he told you not to forget them, then perhaps he was beside himself. He had made his decision and was frightened at it. He wasn't walking away from me, but leaping. The emphasis on that phrase may have been bravado."

"Yes, yes!" cried Alyosha warmly. "I believe that is it."

"And, if so, he's not altogether lost. I can still save him. Did he tell you anything about money—about three thousand rubles?"

"He did speak about it, and it's that more than anything that's crushing him. He lost his honor, he said, and nothing matters now," Alyosha answered, feeling hope there really might be a way of saving his brother.

"Do you know about it?"

"I've known it a long time; I heard long ago from Moscow that the money had not arrived. But I said nothing. My only object was that he should know to whom to turn, and who was his true friend. No, he won't recognize that; he looks on me merely as a woman. I've been in pain all week trying to think how to prevent him from being shamed to face me. He can tell God everything without shame. Why does he still not understand how much I am ready to bear for his sake? How dare he not know me after all that has happened? I want to save him. He wasn't afraid to be open with you. How is it I don't deserve the same?"

The last words she uttered in tears.

"I must tell you," Alyosha began, his voice trembling, "what happened just now between him and my father."

He described how Dmitri had sent him to get the money, how he had broken in, knocked his father down, and after that begged him to take his best wishes to her. "He went to that woman," Alyosha added softly.

"Do you suppose I can't put up with that? He won't marry her," she said. "It's passion, not love. He won't marry her because she won't marry him."

Again Katerina Ivanovna laughed strangely.

"He may marry her," said Alyosha sadly.

"He won't marry her, I tell you. That girl is an angel!" Katerina Ivanovna exclaimed with great warmth. "She is one of the most fantastic creatures. I know how entrancing she is, but I know, too, that she is kind and noble. You don't believe me? Agrafena Alexandrovna, my angel!" she cried suddenly. "Come in to us. This is Alyosha. He knows all about our affairs."

"I've only been waiting for you to call me," said a soft, sugary voice.

The curtain parted and Grushenka, smiling, came in.

Alyosha trembled. Here she was, that awful woman, the "beast," as Ivan called her. And yet one would have thought the creature standing before him most simple and ordinary, a good-natured, kind woman, handsome certainly, but no more so than other ordinary women! She was tall, though shorter than Katerina Ivanovna. She had a full figure, with noiseless movements softened to a peculiar over-sweetness, like her voice. Her feet made no sound on the floor.

She sank softly into a chair, rustling her silk dress, her milk-white neck and broad shoulders nestled in a shawl. She was twenty-two years old, and very white, with a pale pink color on her cheeks. Her face might be said to be too broad, and the lower jaw was set forward. Her upper lip was thin, but the lower lip was full, which gave her a pouting look. Her dark hair and eyebrows, and gray-blue eyes with their long lashes would have made any passer-by stop at the sight of her.

What struck Alyosha most in that face was its child-like good nature, a look in her eyes of childish delight. She came to the table smiling, as if expecting something. The light in her eyes gladdened the soul. There was something else in her he could not understand, which yet affected him. It was that animal-like movement, a cat-like noiselessness, as if she were seeking a prey and might leap upon it.

It was an ample body. Under the shawl could be seen full broad shoulders, and high, quite girlish, breasts. Though one could see that this fresh, youthful beauty would fade by thirty, would "spread"; that the face would become swollen, and wrinkles appear; the skin would grow coarse—it was the fleeting beauty of the moment.

Alyosha wondered with an unpleasant sensation why she spoke the way she did, and could not speak naturally. She must have felt there was a charm in the honey voice. It was, of course, only a bad habit that showed bad education and a false idea of good manners. Yet her way of speaking didn't fit with the childish and happy face, the joy in her eyes.

Katerina Ivanovna made her sit facing Alyosha, and kissed her several times on her smiling lips. She seemed quite in love with her.

"This is the first time we've met, Alexey Fyodorovitch," she said. "I wanted to know her, to go to her, and I'd no sooner expressed the wish than she came to me. I knew we should settle everything together. My heart told me—it would be a way out of the difficulty, and I was not wrong. Grushenka has explained everything."

"You did not turn me away, sweet young lady," said Grushenka.

"Don't dare to speak to me like that, you angel! Here, I must kiss your lower lip once more. It looks as though it was swollen, and now it will be even more so. Look how she laughs, Alexey Fyodorovitch! It does one's heart good to see."

"You make so much of me, dear lady; I am not worthy."

"Not worthy!" Katerina Ivanovna cried. "You know, Alexey Fyodorovitch, we have only been too ready to make every sacrifice for a man perhaps not worthy of our love. But there was another man, you know—an officer, too—we loved. He forgot us and married another. Now he is a widower and has written he is coming here to see us, and, do you know, we've loved none but him all this time! He will come and Grushenka will be happy again. For the past five years, did you know, she has been the most miserable of creatures. She has even, at times, would you believe it, had the thought of killing herself. It was only her old merchant who saved her."

"You defend me kindly, dear young lady," Grushenka said.

"Defend you! Is it for me to defend you? Grushenka, give me your hand. Look at that charming hand, Alexey Fyodorovitch! It has brought me happiness and has lifted me up, and I'm going to kiss it!"

Three times she kissed the rather fat, hand, of Grushenka, who held it out with a charming, musical little laugh.

"You shame me, kissing my hand, before Alexey Fyodorovitch."

"Do you think I meant to do that?" said Katerina Ivanovna. "Ah, my dear, how little you understand me!"

"Yes, and you, too, perhaps do not understand me. Maybe I'm not so good as I seem. I've a bad heart; I went after poor Dmitri Fyodorovitch just for fun."

"But now you'll save him. You gave me your word. You'll tell him you have long loved another man, who now offers you his hand."

"Oh, no! I didn't give my word on that. It was you kept saying it."

"But...," said Katerina Ivanovna, turning pale. "You promised—"

"Oh, no, I've promised nothing," Grushenka said softly in her honeyed. "You see, dear lady, what a terrible person I am. If I want to do a thing I do it. I may have made you some promise just now, though I don't remember it. But now I'm thinking I may take to Mitya again."

"But you said—," Katerina Ivanovna said faintly.

"What I might have said, I don't know. Or suppose I do? You speak with such passion that I might have completely forgotten myself. But, you know, I'm such a soft-hearted, silly creature. Only think what he's gone through for me! What if when I go home I feel sorry for him? If I think of all the suffering I have caused him. How can I help it if I change my mind?"

"I never expected—"

"Ah, how good you are! Perhaps you won't care for a silly creature like me, now you know my character. Give me your hand, dear, sweet lady," she said tenderly, taking Katerina Ivanovna's hand. "I'll kiss it as you did mine. You kissed mine three times; I must kiss yours three hundred more!"

She slowly raised the hands to her lips.

"She's perhaps too naïve," thought Katerina Ivanovna.

Grushenka seemed enthusiastic over the "sweet hand." She raised it to her lips, but then held it there.

"Do you know, sweet lady," she said in an even more sugary voice, "I think I won't kiss your hand, after all?"

And she laughed a little merry laugh.

"What's the matter with you?" said Katerina Ivanovna

"So you may remember you kissed my hand, but I didn't kiss yours," she said with a gleam in her eyes.

"Evil creature!" cried Katerina Ivanovna.

She flushed and leapt up from her seat.

Grushenka, too, got up, but slowly.

"I'll tell Mitya how you kissed my hand, but I didn't yours. He'll laugh!"

"Terrible woman! Go away!"

"For shame, young lady! That's not the way for you talk."

"You're a creature for sale!" screamed Katerina Ivanovna.

"For sale indeed! You used to visit gentlemen for money once; you brought your beauty for sale. You see, I know."

Katerina Ivanovna rushed at her, but Alyosha held her.

"Not a step, not a word! She'll go away—at once."

Katerina Ivanovna's two aunts ran in at her cry.

"I'll go," said Grushenka. "Alyosha, darling, see me home!"

"Go away—go away, hurry!" cried Alyosha.

"Alyosha, see me home! I've got a little story to tell you. I got up this scene for your benefit. See me home, you'll be glad."

Alyosha turned away, wringing his hands.

Grushenka ran from the house laughing.

Katerina Ivanovna went into a fit. She sobbed, and shook.

"I warned you," said her aunt. "I tried to prevent you. How could you do such a thing? You don't know these creatures."

"She's a tigress!" yelled Katerina Ivanovna. "Why did you hold me, Alexey Fyodorovitch? I'd have beaten her! She ought to be flogged in public on a scaffold!"

Alyosha withdrew towards the door.

"But, my God!" cried Katerina Ivanovna, clasping her hands. "How could he be so without honor! He told that creature what happened that day! 'You put your beauty up for sale, dear young lady.' She knows it! Your brother's evil!"

Alyosha wanted to say something, but couldn't.

"Go away, Alexey Fyodorovitch! Don't condemn me. Forgive me. I don't know what I shall do with myself now!"

Alyosha walked into the street, his head spinning. He almost wept.

He was overtaken by the maid.

"The young lady forgot to give you this letter from Madame Hohlakov; it's been left with us since dinner-time."

Alyosha took the envelope and put it in his pocket.

Chapter XI

Another Good Name Ruined

It was not quite a mile from the town to the monastery, the road at that hour deserted. Alyosha walked quickly. It was almost night and too dark to see anything clearly. He made out a figure under a willow at the cross-roads.

It rushed at him, shouting, "Your money or your life!"

"So it's you, Mitya," cried Alyosha, startled.

"You didn't expect me? I wondered where to wait for you. At last I thought of waiting here, for you had to pass here. But what's the matter?"

"Nothing, brother—it's the fright you gave me. Oh, Dmitri!" Alyosha began to cry.   "Father's blood! You almost killed him—and now—here—you're making jokes!"

"Well, what of it? It's not seemly—is that it? Not suitable in my position?"

"No—I only—"

"Look. You see what a dark night. I hid here under the willow, waiting for you, and suddenly thought, why go on in misery any longer, what is there to wait for? Here I have a willow, a handkerchief, a shirt; I can twist them into a rope. Why go on burdening the earth with my sinning? And then I heard you coming—it was as though something flew down to me. There is a man whom I love more than anyone in the world. I loved you so much at that moment I thought, 'I'll fall on his neck at once.' Then a stupid idea struck me, to scare you. Forgive me—it was nonsense.... What did she say? Was she furious?"

"No, not that.... There, Mitya. There—I found them both there."

"Both? Whom?"

"Grushenka at Katerina Ivanovna's."

Dmitri was struck dumb.

"Impossible!" he cried. "You're raving! Grushenka with her?"

Alyosha described all that happened, and his own sensations.

Dmitri listened in silence, but it was clear he understood it all. As the story went on, his face became gloomy. He scowled, clenched his teeth, and his fixed stare became still more rigid. Suddenly his angry face changed, his lips parted, and he broke into laughter.

"So she wouldn't kiss her hand! She ran away!" he exclaimed with delight. "So the other one called her a tigress! And said she ought to be flogged on a scaffold? That's just what I think. Let her be punished, but I must get better first. I understand the queen of nerve. She's magnificent! I'll run to her! Alyosha, don't blame me."

"But Katerina Ivanovna!" exclaimed Alyosha.

"I see her, too! I see right through her! What a thing to do! That's just like Katya, who was not afraid to face a coarse officer and risk a deadly insult to save her father! You say her aunt tried to stop her? That aunt is overbearing. So she tried to prevent Katya, but she wouldn't listen to her! Katya thinks she can overcome everything. She thought she could bewitch Grushenka. Do you think she kissed Grushenka's hand with a motive? No, she really was fascinated! Alyosha, how did you escape from those women?"

"Brother, you don't seem to know how you've insulted Katerina Ivanovna by telling Grushenka about that day. She flung it in her face just now that she had gone in secret to gentlemen to sell her beauty! Brother, what could be worse than that?"

Dmitri struck his head with his hand. He only now realized it, though Alyosha had just told him of Katerina Ivanovna's cry: "Your brother is evil!"

"Yes, perhaps, I really did tell Grushenka about that 'fatal day,' as Katya calls it. Yes, I remember! It was at Mokroe. I was drunk.... I was sobbing, kneeling and praying to Katya's image, and Grushenka understood it. She cried herself.... Damn it all! Then she cried, but now 'the dagger in the heart'! That's how women are."

He sank into thought.

"I am evil!" he said. "It doesn't matter whether I cried or not! Tell her I accept the fact that I am evil, if that's any comfort. Come, that's enough. It's no use talking! You go your way and I mine. I don't want to see you again except as a last resource."

He pressed Alyosha's hand and, as though tearing himself away, turned towards the town. Alyosha looked after him, unable to believe he would go away so abruptly.

"Alexey, one more confession!" he cried, returning. "There's a terrible disgrace in store for me. I'm a man without honor, but let me tell you that I've never done before anything that compares in baseness with the dishonor I bear this minute on my breast, here, which will come to pass, though I'm perfectly free to stop it. Well, I shan't. I told you everything just now, but I didn't tell you this. I can still give back half of my lost honor tomorrow. But I shan't. I shall carry out my base plan, and you can bear witness that I told you so. Good-by. Don't pray for me, I'm not worth it!"

He retreated, and Alyosha went on his way.

"I shall never see him again! What is he saying? Why, I shall see him tomorrow. I shall look him up. I shall make a point of it. What does he mean?"

He crossed the wood to Father Zossima's cell. The door was opened to him. He trembled as he went into his cell. There he found Porfiry and Father Païssy, who came every hour to inquire after Father Zossima. Alyosha learnt that he was getting worse. Even his usual talk could not take place that day.

"He is weaker," Father Païssy whispered as he blessed him. "It's difficult to rouse him. He woke for five minutes, sent his blessing to the brothers and begged their prayers for him. He intends to take the sacrament in the morning. He remembered you, Alexey. He asked whether you had gone away, and was told that you were in the town. 'I blessed him for that work,' he said, 'his place is there, not here, for a time.' He remembered you lovingly. But how is it he has decided you shall spend some time in the world? He must have seen something in your destiny! Understand, Alexey, that if you return to the world, it must be to do the duty laid upon you, and not for frivolous vanity and pleasure."

Father Païssy left. Alyosha had no doubt that Father Zossima was dying. He firmly decided that in spite of his promises to his father, the Hohlakovs, and Katerina Ivanovna, he would not leave the monastery next day, but would remain with his elder to the end. His heart glowed with love, and he blamed himself for having been able for one instant to forget him when he was on his deathbed. He went into Father Zossima's bedroom, knelt down, and bowed to the ground before the elder, who was asleep.

Alyosha returned to the other room and, taking off his boots, lay down on the sofa he used as a bed. He took off his monk's dress, which he used as a blanket. Before going to bed, he fell on his knees and prayed a long time. In his prayer he did not ask God to lighten his darkness, but only thirsted for the joyous emotion which always visited his soul after the praise of his evening prayer.

As he was praying, he felt in his pocket the little pink note the servant had handed him as he left Katerina Ivanovna's. He was troubled, but finished his prayer. Then, after a pause, he opened the envelope. In it was a letter to him, signed by Lise, the young daughter of Madame Hohlakov, who had laughed at him before the elder.

"Alexey Fyodorovitch," she wrote, "I am writing without anyone's knowledge, and I know how wrong it is. But I cannot live without telling you the feeling in my heart, and this no one but us two must know for a time. But how am I to tell you? Paper, they say, does not feel shame, but it's not true; it's turning red now, just as I am. Dear Alyosha, I love you, I've loved you from my childhood, since our Moscow days, and I shall love you all my life. My heart has chosen you, to unite our lives and pass them together till old age. Of course, on condition you leave the monastery. As for our age we will wait for the time fixed by law. By then I shall certainly be quite strong, walking and dancing.

"You see how I've thought of everything. There's only one thing I can't imagine: what you'll think of me when you read this. I'm always laughing and being naughty. I made you angry this morning, but I assure you before I took up my pen, I prayed to the Mother of God, and now I'm praying, and almost crying. My secret is in your hands. When you come tomorrow, I don't know how I shall look at you. Ah, Alexey, what if I can't restrain myself, and laugh when I look at you as I did today. You'll think I'm a mean girl making fun of you, and you won't believe my letter. I beg you, dear one, if you've any pity for me, when you come tomorrow don't look me straight in the face, for if I meet your eyes, it will be sure to make me laugh, especially as you'll be in that long gown. So when you come, don't look at me, look at mamma....

"Here I've written you a love-letter. Oh, dear, what have I done? Alyosha, don't hate me, and if I've done something terrible and wounded you, forgive me. Now the secret of my reputation, ruined perhaps forever, is in your hands. I shall certainly cry today. Good-by till our meeting, our *awful* meeting.—Lise.

"P.S.—Alyosha! You must, must, must come!—Lise."

Alyosha read the note through twice, thought a little, and laughed a soft, sweet laugh. He started. That laugh seemed to him sinful. But a minute later he laughed again just as softly and happily. He slowly replaced the note in the envelope, crossed himself, and lay down. The stirring in his heart passed at once.

"God, have mercy upon all of them, have all these unhappy and worried souls in Thy keeping, and set them in the right path. All ways are Thine. Save them according to Thy wisdom. Thou art love. Thou wilt send joy to all!"

Alyosha crossed himself and fell into peaceful sleep.

PART II

Book IV • Wounds

Chapter I

"You Must Go"

Alyosha was roused before daybreak. Father Zossima woke up feeling weak. His mind was quite clear; his face looked tired, yet bright and almost joyful.

"Maybe I shall not live through the coming day," he said to Alyosha.

He desired to confess and take the sacrament. The monks assembled and the cell gradually filled up. After the service was over the elder desired to kiss and take leave of every one. As the cell was so small the earlier visitors withdrew for others.

"I've been teaching you so many years," said the elder, "it's more difficult to hold my tongue than to talk, even now, in spite of my weakness," he joked, looking at those around him. He seemed anxious before death to say everything he had not said in his life.

"Love one another, Fathers," said Father Zossima. "Though we have shut ourselves within these walls, we are no holier than those outside, but on the contrary, by the fact of coming here each of us has confessed he is worse than all others.... Love God's people, let not strangers draw away the flock, for if you slumber in your slothfulness and pride they will come from all sides and draw away your flock. Expound the Gospel unceasingly. Do not love gold and silver. Have faith. Cling to the banner and raise it high."

When Alyosha left the cell, he was struck by the excitement among the monks. All were expecting some marvel after the elder's death. Alyosha was called to see Rakitin, who came with a letter from Madame Hohlakov. In it she told of an incident. Among the women who received Father Zossima's blessing the previous day, there was one who had asked whether she might pray for her son's soul, who had gone to Irkutsk and sent her no news for over a year.

Father Zossima had forbidden her to do so, saying that to pray for the living as though they were dead was wrong. He forgave her because of her ignorance, and added, "her son was certainly alive and he would either come himself very shortly, or send a letter, and that she was to go home and expect it." And "Would you believe it?" exclaimed Madame Hohlakov, "the prophecy has been fulfilled. Scarcely had the old woman reached home when they gave her a letter from Siberia. In it her son told her he was returning in three weeks."

Alyosha, after reading the letter, handed it to Father Païss. Even that austere man could not completely restrain himself.

"We shall see greater things!" broke from him.

"We shall see greater things yet!" the monks repeated.

Father Païssy begged them not to speak of the matter "till it be made more certain, seeing there is so much credulity among those of this world, and indeed this might well have chanced naturally," he added, as if to satisfy his conscience. But, within the hour the "miracle" was known to everyone.

When Father Zossima, feeling tired again, had gone back to bed, he thought of Alyosha as he was closing his eyes, and sent for him. Alyosha ran at once. The elder, opening his weary eyes, asked him: "Are your people expecting you, my son?"

Alyosha hesitated.

"Don't they need of you? Didn't you promise to see them today?"

"I did promise—to my father—my brothers—others too."

"You must go. I shall not die without your being by to hear my last word. To you I will say that word; it will be my last gift to you."

Alyosha immediately obeyed, though it was hard to go. But the promise he should hear his last word sent a thrill of rapture through him. He hurried that he might finish what   he had to do in town and return quickly. But Father Païssy, too, uttered some words of advice which moved and surprised him. He spoke as they left the cell together.

"Remember, young man," he began, "that the science of this world, which has become a great power, has analyzed everything divine handed down to us in the holy books. After this cruel analysis the learned of this world have nothing left of all that was sacred of old. But they have only analyzed the parts and overlooked the whole, and indeed their blindness is marvelous. Yet the whole still stands before their eyes, and the gates of hell shall not prevail against it. Has it not lasted nineteen centuries, is it not still a living, moving power in the individual soul and in the masses of people?

"It is still as strong and living even in the souls of those who do not believe, who have destroyed everything! For even those who have renounced Christianity still follow the Christian ideal, for neither in their hearts or minds have they been able to create a higher ideal of man and of virtue than that given by Christ. Remember this, young man, since you are being sent into the world by your dying elder. Maybe, remembering this great day, you will not forget my words from the heart, seeing you are young, and the world's temptations are great and beyond your strength. Well, now go, my orphan."

With these words Father Païssy blessed him.

As Alyosha left the monastery and thought them over, he suddenly realized that he had met a new and unexpected friend, a warm, loving teacher, in this monk who had before this treated him so gravely. It was as though Father Zossima had put him in this monk's care at his death, and "perhaps that's just what happened," Alyosha thought. The reflections he had just heard testified to the warmth of Father Païssy's heart.

Chapter II

At His Father's

Alyosha went to his father's. The old man was sitting alone at the table wearing slippers, looking through some accounts, when Alyosha went in. Though he had got up early and was trying to put a bold face on it, he looked tired and weak. His head was bandaged, his nose swollen, and bruises covered his face, giving it a mean, ugly look. The old man glanced with anger at him.

"The coffee is cold," he cried; "I won't offer you any. I've ordered nothing but fish soup today, and I don't invite any one to share it. Why have you come?"

"To find out how you are," said Alyosha.

"Besides, I told you to come. It's of no consequence. You need not have come. But I knew you'd come poking in directly."

As he was saying this, he got up and looked in the looking-glass at his nose. He began binding the red cloth on it more becomingly.

"Red's better. It's just like the hospital in a white one," he said. "Well, how are things over there? How is your elder?"

"He is very bad; he may die today," answered Alyosha.

But his father had not listened, and forgot his own question.

"Ivan's gone out," he said suddenly. "He is doing his utmost to carry off the woman Mitya's engaged to. That's what he is staying here for," he added.

"Surely he did not tell you so?" asked Alyosha.

"Yes, he did, three weeks ago. You don't suppose he came to murder me, do you? He must have had some object in coming."

"What do you mean? Why do you say such things?" said Alyosha.

"He doesn't ask for money, and he won't get a penny from me. I intend living as long as possible, and so I need every penny, and the longer I live the more I'll need it," he continued. "I can still pass for a man at five and fifty, but I want to pass for one for another twenty years. As I get older, you know, I shan't be a pretty object. The women won't come to me on their own, so I shall need money. You may as well know I mean to go on in my sins to the end. Your paradise is not to my taste, even if it exists. I believe I shall fall asleep and not wake up. You can pray for my soul if you like. If not, don't!"

Alyosha listened to him in silence.

"Ivan talked well yesterday, though we were drunk. Ivan is stuck-up, but he has no education. He smiles without speaking—that's what pulls him through. If he does speak, he gives himself airs. Your Ivan is up to no good! I'll marry Grushenka in a minute if I want to. If you have money, Alexey Fyodorovitch, you have only to want a thing and it's yours. That's what Ivan is afraid of. He's on the watch to keep me from getting married. That's why he is egging on Mitya to marry Grushenka. He hopes to keep Grushenka from me. If Mitya marries Grushenka, Ivan will carry off his rich woman, that's what he's counting on! He is no good, your Ivan!"

"How cross you are! It's because of yesterday."

"You say that," the old man said, "and I am not angry. But if Ivan said it, I should be angry. It is only with you I have good moments, otherwise I'm an ill-natured man."

"You are not ill-natured, but mixed up," said Alyosha.

"I meant this morning to get that ruffian Mitya locked up. Now I don't know what I shall decide. In these days fathers are looked down on, but even now the law does not allow you to drag your old father about by the hair, to kick him in the face in his own house, and tell him you are going to murder him."

"Then you don't mean to take proceedings?"

"Ivan talked me out of it. I don't care about Ivan, but there's another thing."

He went on in a whisper, though there was no one about to hear.

"If I send him to prison, she'll hear of it and run to see him. But if she hears he has beaten me, she may come to me. For that's her way. I know her through and through! Won't you have a drop of brandy? Take some cold coffee, and I'll pour a quarter of a glass of brandy into it."

"No, thank you. I'll take that roll if I may," said Alyosha, taking a roll and putting it in his pocket. "And you'd better not have brandy."

"You are quite right. Only one little glass..."

He opened the cup-board, poured a glass, and drank it. "That's enough. One glass won't kill me."

"You see you are in a better humor now," said Alyosha, smiling.

"I love you even without the brandy, but with mean people I am mean. Ivan is not going to Tchermashnya—why is that? He wants to spy on how much I give Grushenka if she comes. They are all no good! But I don't recognize Ivan. He's not one of us. As though I'd leave him anything! I shan't leave a will at all. And I'll crush Mitya like a bug. *Your* Mitya, for you love him. I am not afraid of your loving him. But if Ivan loved him I should be afraid. But Ivan loves nobody. People like Ivan are not our sort, my boy..... I had a silly idea in my head when I told you to come today; I wanted to find out from you about Mitya. If I were to hand him a thousand or two, would he agree to take himself off without Grushenka and give her up?"

"I'll ask him," said Alyosha. "If you give him three thousand…"

"That's foolish! Don't ask him! I've changed my mind. It was a bad idea. I won't give him a penny, I need my money myself," cried the old man. "I'll crush him like a bug. There's nothing for you to do here, you needn't stay. Is that woman of his, Katerina Ivanovna, going to marry him or not?"

"Nothing will make her leave him."

"You see how these fine young ladies love a no-good man. They are poor creatures, very different from—ah, if I had his youth and the looks I had then, what a man I'd be. But he shan't have Grushenka! I'll crush him!" His anger returned with the last words.

"You can go. There's nothing for you to do here today."

Alyosha went up to say good-by, and kissed him.

"What's that for?" The old man asked. "We shall see each other again, shan't we?"

"I didn't mean anything."

"Nor did I," said the old man. "Listen," he said. "Come again tomorrow and I'll have a fish soup for you, a fine one, not like today. Be sure to come!"

As soon as Alyosha left, he went to the cupboard and poured another half-glass.

"I won't have more!" he said, clearing his throat.

He locked the cup-board and put the key in his pocket, then went into his bedroom, lay down, and in one minute was asleep.

Chapter III

At the Hohlakovs'

When Alyosha reached Madame Hohlakov's house, she ran in to him.

"Did you get my letter about the new miracle?" she asked.

"Yes."

"Did you show it to every one? He restored the son to his mother!"

"He is dying today," said Alyosha.

"I heard. How I long to talk to you about this! And how sorry I am I can't see him! The whole town is excited. Do you know Katerina Ivanovna is here?"

"That's lucky," said Alyosha. "She told me I must see her."

"I heard what happened yesterday—the terrible behavior of that—creature. My goodness! I'm forgetting; your brother is here, not that dreadful brother but Ivan Fyodorovitch. They are having a serious talk. If you could only imagine what's passing between them—they are ruining their lives for no reason. But now I must speak of something else—why is Lise upset?"

"*Mama*, it's you who are upset now, not I," Lise's voice came through a crack of the door. She sounded as though she wanted to laugh but was trying to control it.

"And no wonder, Lise, your carrying-on will make me up-set, too. But she is so ill, Alexey Fyodorovitch, she has been so ill all night! I could hardly wait for the morning and for Herzenstube to come. He says he can make nothing of it. As you approached the house, she screamed, and insisted on being wheeled into this room."

"Mama, I didn't know he had come. It wasn't on his account."

"That's not true, Lise, Yulia ran to tell you that Alexey Fyodorovitch was coming."

"My darling mamma, it's not at all clever of you. But if you want to make up for it, tell Alexey Fyodorovitch he has shown his want of wit by coming to see us after what happened yesterday. They laugh at him."

"Lise, you go too far. I shall have to be firm with you. Who laughs at him? I am so glad he has come, I can't do without him. Oh, Alexey Fyodorovitch, I am so unhappy!"

"But what's the matter with you, mamma darling?"

"Your carrying-on, Lise, that awful night of fever, that awful Herzenstube! Everything, in fact.. Even that miracle! Oh, how it has upset me. And that tragedy in the drawing-room, it's more than I can bear. Will Father Zossima live till tomorrow? Oh, my God! What is happening to me? It's all nonsense. I forgot—"

And she hurried away.

"Now she is gone, I can speak; give me the letter I sent you yesterday, Alexey Fyodorovitch—be quick, for mamma will be back in a minute and I don't want—"

"I haven't got the letter."

"That's not true. I knew you would say that. You've got it in that pocket. I've been sorry about that joke all night. Give me back the letter at once."

"I left it at home."

"But you can't consider me as a little girl after that joke! I beg your pardon for that silliness, but you must bring me the letter today."

"I can't possibly, for I am going back to the monastery. I shan't see you for the next three or four days—for Father Zossima—"

"Four days, what nonsense! Listen. Did you laugh at me?"

"I didn't laugh at all."

"Why not?"

"Because I believed all you said."

"You are insulting me!"

"Not at all. As soon as I read it, I thought it would come to pass, for as soon as Father Zossima dies I am to leave the monastery. Then I shall finish my studies, and when you reach the legal age we'll be married. I shall love you. I couldn't find a better wife than you, and Father Zossima tells me I must marry."

"But I am a cripple, wheeled about in a chair," laughed Lise.

"I'll wheel you about myself, but I'm sure you'll get well by then."

"You are mad," she said, "to make all this out of a joke! Here's mamma. Mamma, how slow you are!"

"Oh, Lise, don't scream. Oh, my dear Alexey Fyodorovitch, what's killing me is no one thing in particular, but everything together, that's what is too much for me."

"That's enough, mama," Lise laughed gaily. "Would you believe it, mamma, on the way here he had a fight with the boys in the street. Isn't he a child himself? Is he fit to be married? For only fancy, he wants to be married, mamma. Just think of him married, wouldn't it be funny, wouldn't it be awful?"

And Lise kept laughing her thin giggle, looking slyly at Alyosha.

"But why married, Lise? What makes you talk of such a thing? It's quite out of place. Come, that's enough. Katerina Ivanovna has only just heard you are here, Alexey Fyodorovitch. She's dying to see you!"

"Mama, go to them yourself. He can't go just now, he hasn't much time."

"Not at all, I can go quite well," said Alyosha.

"What! You are going away? Is that what you say?"

"Well, when I've seen them, I'll come back and we can talk as much as you like. But I should like to see Katerina Ivanovna, for I am anxious to be back at the monastery."

"Mama, take him away. Alexey Fyodorovitch, don't trouble to come and see me afterwards, but go straight to your monastery. I didn't sleep all night."

"Lise, you're making fun, but I wish you would sleep!" cried Madame Hohlakov.

"I'll stay another three minutes, five, if you like," said Alyosha.

"Even five! Do take him away, mamma, he is a monster."

"Lise, you are crazy. Alexey Fyodorovitch, she is not herself today. I am afraid to cross her. The trouble one has with nervous girls! Perhaps she really will be able to sleep after seeing you. How quickly you have made her sleepy, and how fortunate!"

"Ah, mama, how sweetly you talk! I must kiss you for it, mama."

"And I kiss you too, Lise. Alexey Fyodorovitch," Madame Hohlakov began in a whisper. "You will see for yourself what's going on. It's the most fantastic scene. She loves your brother Ivan, but is doing her best to make herself believe she loves your brother Dmitri. It's too terrible! I'll go in with you and stay if they don't turn me out."

Chapter IV

A Wound in the Drawing-Room

In the drawing-room the conversation was over. Katerina Ivanovna was excited, though she looked firm. When Alyosha and Madame Hohlakov entered, Ivan Fyodorovitch stood up to take his leave. His face was pale, and Alyosha looked at him anxiously. During the preceding month it had been several times suggested to him that Ivan was in love with Katerina Ivanovna and that he meant "to carry her off" from Dmitri. Until quite lately the idea seemed terrible to Alyosha. He loved both his brothers, and dreaded such rivalry.

Meantime, Dmitri had said to him he was glad Ivan was his rival, and that it was a great help to him. In what way did it help him? To marry Grushenka? That Alyosha thought the worst thing possible. Besides, Alyosha had till the evening before believed that Katerina Ivanovna had a passion for Dmitri. He fancied, too, that she couldn't possibly love a man like Ivan, and that she loved Dmitri just as he was.

But during yesterday's scene with Grushenka another idea struck him. Madame Hohlakov had just uttered the word "wounding," which made him start, because waking at daybreak that night he had cried out "Wound," probably thinking of his dream, the scene at Katerina's. Now Alyosha was impressed by Madame Hohlakov's statement that Katerina Ivanovna was in love with Ivan, and only deceived herself through a sort of "wound," giving herself pain by thinking she loved Dmitri out of some fancied gratitude.

"Yes," he thought, "perhaps the truth lies in those words."

But in that case what was Ivan's position? Alyosha felt instinctively that a character like Katerina Ivanovna's must rule the roost, and she could only rule over someone like Dmitri, never a man like Ivan. No, Ivan could not be ruled, and if he was he would not be happy. Another idea, too, forced itself upon him: "What if she loved neither of them?" But his thoughts shamed him. "What do I know about love and women and how can I decide such questions?" Yet it was impossible not to think about it. This opposition was of great importance in his brothers' lives, and much depended on it.

"One reptile will devour the other," Ivan had said, speaking of his father and Dmitri. So Ivan looked upon Dmitri as a reptile. Was it since he had known Katerina Ivanovna? That phrase had escaped Ivan unawares yesterday, but that only made it more important. If he felt like that, what chance was there of peace? Were there, in fact, new grounds for hatred and hostility? And with which of them was Alyosha to sympathize?

He loved them both, but he might go astray, and Alyosha's heart could not endure uncertainty, because his love was always of an active character. If he loved anyone, he set to work at once to help him. And to do so he must know what he was aiming at; he must know for certain what was best for each. Instead, he found nothing but uncertainty on all sides. "It was lacerating," but what could he understand of it?

Seeing Alyosha, Katerina Ivanovna said quickly and joyfully to Ivan, who had already got up to go, "Stay another minute! I want to hear the opinion of this person whom I trust absolutely. Don't go away," she added, addressing Madame Hohlakov. She made Alyosha sit beside her, and Madame Hohlakov sit opposite, by Ivan.

"You are all my friends here," she began in a voice close to tears, and Alyosha's heart warmed to her. "You, Alexey Fyodorovitch, were witness yesterday of that awful scene. You did not see it, Ivan Fyodorovitch, he did. What he thought of me yesterday I don't know. I only know that if it happened again today, I should express the same feelings—the same words, the same actions. You remember my actions, Alexey Fyodorovitch; you checked me in one of them. I must tell you that I don't even know whether I still love *him*. Or feel *pity* for him. If I still loved him, perhaps I shouldn't be sorry for him now, but should hate him."

Her voice quivered, and tears glittered on her eyelashes.

"That girl is truthful and sincere," Alyosha thought. "She does not love Dmitri."

"That's true," cried Madame Hohlakov to Katerina.

"Wait, dear. I haven't told you the decision I came to last night. I feel that perhaps my decision is a terrible one—for me, but I foresee that nothing will induce me to change it. It will be so all my life. My dear, kind, ever-faithful and generous adviser, the one friend I have in the world, Ivan Fyodorovitch, approves and commends my decision."

"Yes, I approve of it," Ivan assented, in a quiet but firm voice.

"But I should like Alyosha, too, to tell me before my two friends whether I am right. Alyosha, my dear brother," she said again, taking his cold hand in her hot one, "I foresee that your decision, your approval, will bring me peace, in spite of my sufferings, for, after your words, I shall be calm and submit—I feel that."

"I don't know what you are asking," said Alyosha, flushing. "I only know I love you and wish for your happiness! But I know nothing about such affairs," he added.

"In such affairs, Alexey Fyodorovitch, the chief thing is honor, duty, and something higher—I don't know what. I sense this feeling in my heart, and it compels me. But it may all be put in two words. I've already decided, even if he marries that—creature," she began, "whom I never can forgive, *even then I will not abandon him*. From this time forward I will never abandon him!" she cried. "Not that I would keep running after him, or get in his way. Oh, no! I will go away to another town, but I will watch over him.

"When he becomes unhappy with that woman, and that is bound to happen, let him come to me and he will find a friend, a sister.... Only a sister, of course; but he will learn at least that that sister loves him and has sacrificed all her life to him. I will gain my point. I will insist on his knowing me and confiding in me, without reserve," she cried. "I will be a god to whom he can pray—and that, at least, he owes me for his treachery and for what I suffered yesterday. Let him see that all my life I will be true to him and the promise I gave him, in spite of his being untrue and betraying me. I will become nothing but a means for his happiness my whole life! That's my decision."

She had perhaps intended to express her idea with more dignity and naturalness, but her speech was hurried and crude. It was full of youthful impulsiveness; it betrayed that she was still smarting from yesterday's insult, and that her pride wanted satisfaction. She felt this herself. Her face darkened, an unpleasant look came into her eyes.

Alyosha saw it and felt a pang of sympathy. His brother Ivan made it worse by adding: "I've only expressed my own view. From anyone else, this would have been affected, but from you—no. Any other woman would have been wrong, but you are right. I don't know how to explain it, but I see that you are absolutely right."

Madame Hohlakov had not intended to interfere, but she could not stop herself.

"That's only for the moment. And what does it stand for? Yesterday's insult."

"Quite so," cried Ivan, annoyed at being interrupted. "In any one else this moment would be only due to yesterday's impression. But with Katerina Ivanovna's character, that moment will last all her life. What for anyone else would be only a promise is for her an everlasting duty. And she will be sustained by the feeling of this duty being fulfilled. Your life, Katerina Ivanovna, will henceforth be spent in painful brooding over your own feelings, your own suffering; but in the end that suffering will be softened and will pass into sweet contemplation of the fulfillment of a proud design. And this will at last be a source of complete satisfaction and will make you resigned to everything else."

This was said with malice, with no desire to conceal the irony.

"Oh, dear, how mistaken it all is!" Madame Hohlakov cried again.

"Alexey Fyodorovitch, speak. I want to know what you think!" Katerina Ivanovna cried, bursting into tears.

Alyosha got up from the sofa.

"It's nothing!" she went on through her tears. "I'm upset, I didn't sleep last night. But by the side of two such friends as you and your brother I feel strong—for I know—you two will never desert me."

"I am obliged to return to Moscow—perhaps tomorrow—and to leave you for a long time—it's unavoidable," Ivan said.

"Tomorrow—to Moscow! How fortunate!" she cried in a voice suddenly changed. There was no trace of her tears. Her change amazed Alyosha. Instead of a poor, insulted girl, weeping in "laceration," he saw a woman self-possessed and quite pleased, as though something agreeable had just happened.

"Oh, not fortunate that I am losing you, of course not," she corrected herself, with a charming smile. "Such a friend as you could not suppose I am not unhappy at losing you." She rushed at Ivan and, seizing his hands, pressed them warmly. "But what is fortunate is that you will be able in Moscow to see auntie and Agafya and tell them the horror of my present position. You will know how to do that. You can't think how wretched I was this morning wondering how I could write them that dreadful letter—for one can never tell such things in a letter. Now it will be easy for me to write, for you will see them and explain everything. Oh, how glad I am! I will run and write the letter."

She took a step to leave the room.

"And what about Alyosha and his opinion?" cried Madame Hohlakov. There was a sarcastic, angry note in her voice.

"I had not forgotten that," cried Katerina Ivanovna, stopping, "and why are you so antagonistic?" she added with bitter reproach. "What I said, I repeat. I must have his opinion. More than that, I must have his decision! As he says, so it shall be. You see how anxious I am for your words, Alexey Fyodorovitch.... But what's the matter?"

"I couldn't have believed it. I can't understand it!" Alyosha cried.

"What? What?"

"He is going to Moscow, and you cry out that you are glad. And you explain that you are not glad of that but sorry to be—losing a friend. But that was acting, too—you were playing a part—as in a theater!"

"In a theater? What do you mean?" exclaimed Katerina Ivanovna.

"Though you assure him you are sorry to lose a friend in him, you persist in telling him to his face that it's fortunate he is going," said Alyosha.

He was standing at the table and did not sit down.

"What are you talking about? I don't understand."

"I don't understand myself.... I know I am not saying it properly, but I'll say it all the same," Alyosha went on in a shaking voice. "What I see is that you don't love Dmitri at all ... and never have.... And Dmitri, too, has never loved you ... and only esteems you.... I really don't know how I dare to say all this, but someone must tell the truth ... for nobody here will tell the truth."

"What truth?" cried Katerina Ivanovna.

"I'll tell you," Alyosha went on hurriedly. "Call Dmitri; I will fetch him—and let him come here and take your hand and take Ivan's and join your hands. You're torturing Ivan because you love him—torturing him because you love Dmitri through 'self-laceration'—with an unreal love—."

Alyosha broke off and was silent.

"You...you...are a religious idiot—that's what you are!" Katerina Ivanovna snapped, her face white.

Ivan laughed and got up, hat in hand.

"You are mistaken, my good Alyosha," he said, an expression in his face Alyosha had never seen before—of youthful sincerity and strong feeling. "Katerina Ivanovna has never cared for me! She has known all the time that I cared for her—though I never said a word to her—she knew, but she didn't want me. I've never been her friend either, for she is too proud to need my friendship. She kept me at her side for revenge.

"She revenged with me and on me all the insults she has received from Dmitri ever since their first meeting. For even that first meeting has rankled in her heart as an insult—that's what her heart is like! She has talked to me of nothing but her love for him. I am going now; but, believe me, Katerina Ivanovna, you really love him. And the more he insults you, the more you love him—that's your 'laceration.'

"You love him just as he is; you love him for insulting you. If he reformed, you'd give him up at once and cease to love him. But you need him so as to contemplate your heroic fidelity and to reproach him for infidelity. And it all comes from your pride. I've loved you too much. I know I ought not to say this, it would be more dignified simply to leave, and it would be less offensive for you. But I am going away and shall never come back.... I don't want to sit beside a 'laceration.'... Good-by, Katerina Ivanovna; you can't be angry with me, for I am a hundred times more severely punished than you, if only by the fact that I shall never see you again. Good-by! I don't want your hand. You have tortured me too deliberately for me to be able to forgive you at this moment. I shall forgive you later, but not now."

He left the room without saying good-by even to his hostess, Madame Hohlakov.

Alyosha clasped his hands.

"Ivan!" he cried after him. "Come back! No, nothing will make him come back now! It's my fault. I began it! Ivan spoke angrily, and unjustly. He must come back," Alyosha exclaimed frantically.

Katerina Ivanovna went into the next room.

"You've done no harm. You behaved beautifully, like an angel," Madame Hohlakov whispered to Alyosha. "I will do all I can to prevent Ivan Fyodorovitch from going."

Her face beamed with delight, to the great distress of Alyosha.

Katerina Ivanovna had disappeared behind the curtain so quickly that Alyosha had not time to utter a word, though he wanted to speak. He longed to beg her pardon, to say he was to blame, for his heart was full and he could not bear to leave without it. But Madame Hohlakov took him by the hand and drew him along with her.

In the hall she stopped him again as before.

"She is proud, she is struggling with herself; but kind, charming, generous," she said in a whisper. "Oh, how I love her, and how glad I am again of everything! Dear Alexey Fyodorovitch, you didn't know, but I must tell you, that we all—both her aunts, I and all of us, Lise, even—have been hoping and praying for nothing for the last month but that she give up Dmitri, who does not care for her, and marry Ivan Fyodorovitch—such an excellent and cultivated young man, who loves her more than anything. We are in a regular plot to bring it about, and I am even staying on here on that account."

"She has been crying, and has been wounded again," cried Alyosha.

"Never trust a woman's tears, Alexey Fyodorovitch. I am never for the women in such cases. I am always on the side of the men."

"Mamma, you are spoiling him," Lise's voice cried from behind the door.

"No, it was my fault. I am terribly to blame," Alyosha repeated.

"Quite the contrary; you behaved like an angel."

"Mamma, how has he behaved like an angel?" Lise cried.

"I somehow fancied," Alyosha went on, ignoring Lise, "that she loved Ivan, and so I said that stupid thing.... What will happen now?"

"To whom?" cried Lise. "Mamma, you don't answer."

At this moment the maid ran in.

"Katerina Ivanovna is ill.... She is crying, acting crazy."

"What's the matter?" cried Lise. "Mamma, I shall go crazy"

"Lise, for mercy's sake, don't scream. At your age one can't know everything. Oh, mercy on us! I am coming.... Hysterics is a good sign, Alexey Fyodorovitch. That's just as it ought to be. As for Ivan Fyodorovitch's going away like that, it's her own fault.

But he won't go away. Lise, for mercy's sake, don't scream! Oh, yes; you are not screaming. It's I who am screaming. Forgive your mamma; but I am delighted! Did you see, Alexey Fyodorovitch, how young Ivan Fyodorovitch looked just now when he said all that? I thought he was so learned, and all of a sudden he behaved so warmly, and youthfully, and it was all so fine, like you.... But I must fly! Alexey Fyodorovitch. For mercy's sake, Lise, don't keep Alexey Fyodorovitch a minute. He will come back to you at once."

Madame Hohlakov ran off.

Before leaving, Alyosha would have opened the door to see Lise.

"On no account," cried Lise. "Speak through the door. How have you come to be an angel? That's what I want to know."

"For an awful piece of stupidity, Lise! Good-by!"

"Don't dare to go away like that!"

"Lise, I'll be back directly, but I have a great sorrow!"

He ran out of the room, grieved in a way he had seldom been before. He had rushed in like a fool, and meddled in what? In a love-affair. "What do I know about it? What can I tell about such things?" he said to himself. "Oh, shame is nothing; it is the punishment I deserve. The trouble is I shall have caused more unhappiness.... And Father Zossima sent me to reconcile and bring them together. What have I done?" Then he remembered how he had tried to join their hands, and he felt shame again.

Katerina Ivanovna's commission took him to Lake Street, and his brother Dmitri lived close by. Alyosha decided to go to him in any case before doing the other, though he had a feeling he would not find him. He suspected he would keep out of his way now, but he must find him. Time was passing: the thought of his dying elder had not left him.

Dmitri was not at home. The people of the house, an old cabinet-maker, his son, and his wife, looked with suspicion at Alyosha. "He hasn't slept here for the last three nights. Maybe he has gone away," the old man said.

Alyosha saw that he was answering as he had been told. When he asked whether he were not at Grushenka's or in hiding, all three looked at him in alarm. "They are fond of him and are doing their best for him," thought Alyosha.

Book V • Pro and Contra

Chapter I

The Engagement

Madame Hohlakov was the first to meet Alyosha. She was flustered. Katerina Ivanovna's hysterics had ended in a fainting fit, and she lay with her eyes turned up, delirious, and had a fever. They sent for Herzenstube, but he was not here yet. They were sitting in her room, waiting. She was unconscious now! This is serious," she added, as though nothing before had been serious. Alyosha began to describe his adventures, but she stopped him. She had not time to listen. She begged him to sit with Lise and wait for her there.

"Lise," she whispered, "has surprised me, dear Alexey Fyodorovitch, and touched me, too, and so my heart forgives her everything. As soon as you had gone, she felt bad for having laughed at you. She was ready to cry. She thinks a great deal of your opinion, Alexey Fyodorovitch. She said you were 'the greatest friend of her childhood'—think of that! Well, goodbye! I am so worried. Alexey Fyodorovitch, go to Lise, cheer her up. Lise," she cried, "I've brought you Alexey Fyodorovitch. He's not angry."

"Thank you, mamma. Come in, Alexey Fyodorovitch."

Alyosha went in.

Lise, evidently feeling shame, began talking of other things. Alyosha listened, but she saw perfectly well that he, too, looked

131

away, and was trying to talk of other things. In the old days, in Moscow, he had been fond of coming to her and describing his day. Sometimes they made day-dreams and wove whole romances together—usually cheerful and amusing ones. Now they both felt taken back to those days, two years before.

When he told her about helping someone, she cried, "Ah, Alexey Fyodorovitch, let us care for people as we would for the sick!"

"Let us, Lise; I am ready. Though I am not completely ready myself. I'm too often impatient and at other times I don't see things. It's different with you."

"I don't believe it! Alexey Fyodorovitch, how happy I am!"

"I am so glad you say so, Lise."

"Alexey Fyodorovitch, you are wonderfully good, but you are sometimes sort of formal.... And yet you are not a bit formal really. Go to the door, open it gently, and see whether mamma is listening," said Lise, in a nervous whisper.

Alyosha opened the door, and said no one was listening.

"Come here, Alexey Fyodorovitch," Lise went on, turning red. "Give me your hand—that's right. I have to make a confession, I didn't write to you yesterday as a joke, but in earnest," and she hid her eyes with her hand, shamed.

Suddenly she snatched his hand and kissed it three times.

"Ah, Lise, what a good thing!" cried Alyosha joyfully. "You know, I was perfectly sure you were in earnest."

"Upon my word!" She put aside his hand, but did not let go, turning red and laughing a happy laugh. "I kiss his hand and he says, 'What a good thing!'"

But her reproach was undeserved. Alyosha was greatly overcome.

"I should like to please you always, Lise, but I don't know how to do it."

"Alyosha, dear, you are cold and rude. He has chosen me as his wife and is quite settled about it. He is sure I was in earnest. What a thing to say!"

"Why, was it wrong of me to feel sure?" Alyosha asked, laughing.

"No, it was delightfully right," cried Lise, looking tenderly at him.

Alyosha stood still, holding her hand. Suddenly he kissed her on her lips.

"Oh, what are you doing?" cried Lise.

Alyosha was terribly shamed.

"Oh, forgive me if I shouldn't.... Perhaps I'm awfully foolish.... You said I was cold, so I kissed you.... But I see it was wrong."

Lise laughed, and hid her face in her hands.

"And in that dress!" she cried in the midst of her mirth.

She suddenly ceased laughing and became serious, almost stern.

"Alyosha, we must put off kissing. We are not ready for that yet, and we shall have a long time to wait," she said. "Tell me why you who are so clever choose a little idiot, an invalid like me? Alyosha, I am awfully happy, for I don't deserve you a bit."

"You do, Lise. I shall be leaving the monastery in a few days. If I go into the world, I must marry. I know that. *He* told me to marry. Whom could I marry better than you—and who would have me except you? I've been thinking it over. In the first place, you've known me from a child and you've a great many qualities I haven't. You are more light-hearted than I; above all, you are more innocent than I am. I have been brought into contact with many things already.... You don't know, but I, too, am a Karamazov. What does it matter if you do laugh and make jokes? Go on laughing. I am so glad you do."

"Alyosha, give me your hand. Why are you taking it away?" said Lise, her voice weak with happiness. "Listen, Alyosha. What will you wear when you come out of the monastery? What sort of suit? Don't laugh, it's very important to me."

"I haven't thought about the suit, Lise; but I'll wear whatever you like."

"I should like you to have a blue coat, a white waistcoat, and a soft gray felt hat.... Tell me, did you believe I didn't care for you when I said I didn't mean what I wrote?"

"No, I didn't believe it."

"Oh, you terrible person, what am I going to do with you?."

"You see, I knew that you—seemed to care for me, but I pretended to believe that you didn't care for me to make it—easier for you."

"That makes it worse! And better! Alyosha, I'm awfully fond of you. Before you came this morning, I tried my fortune. I decided I would ask you for my letter, and if you brought it out and gave it to me, it would mean you did not love me at all, that you felt nothing, and were simply a stupid boy, good for nothing, and that I am ruined. But you left the letter at home; that cheered me. You left it behind on purpose so as not to give it back, because you knew I would ask for it? Wasn't that it?"

"Lise, it was not so a bit. The letter is with me now, and was this morning."

Alyosha pulled the letter out, laughing, and showed it her at a distance.

"But I am not going to give it to you. Look at it from here."

"Why, then you told a lie? You, a monk, told a lie!"

"I told a lie if you like," Alyosha laughed. "I told a lie so as not to give you back the letter. It's very precious to me," he added. "It always will be, and I won't give it up!"

Lise looked at him joyfully.

"Alyosha," she whispered, "look at the door. Isn't mamma listening?"

"Isn't it better not to look? Why suspect your mother of meanness?"

"Meanness? It's her right to spy on her daughter!" cried Lise. "You may be sure, Alexey Fyodorovitch, that when I am a mother, if I have a daughter like myself, I shall certainly spy on her!"

"Really, Lise? That's not right."

"My goodness! What has meanness to do with it? If she were listening to an ordinary conversation, it would be meanness, but when her own daughter is shut up with a young man.... Alyosha, I shall spy on you when we're married, and I shall open all your letters and read them, so you may as well be prepared."

"Yes, of course, if so—" said Alyosha, "only it's not right."

"How contemptuous! Alyosha, dear, we won't quarrel the very first day. I'd better tell you the whole truth. Of course, it's very wrong to spy on people, and, of course, I am not right and you are, only I shall spy on you all the same."

"Do, then; you won't find out anything," laughed Alyosha.

"And, Alyosha, will you give in to me? We must decide that too."

"I'll be delighted to, Lise, and certain to, only not in the most important things. Even if you don't agree with me, I'll do my duty in the important things."

"That's right; but let me tell you I am ready to give in to you not only in the most important matters, but in everything. And I am ready to vow to do so now—and for all my life!" cried Lise. "And I'll do it gladly! What's more, I'll swear never to spy on you, never read one of your letters. For you are right. And though I shall be tempted to spy, I know that I won't, since you consider it dishonorable. You're my conscience now.... Alexey Fyodorovitch, why have you been so sad lately? I know you have a lot of anxiety and trouble, but you have some special grief besides, a secret one?"

"Yes, Lise, I have a secret one, too," answered Alyosha. "I see you love me, since you guessed that."

"What grief? Can you tell me?" asked Lise.

"I'll tell you later, Lise—afterwards," said Alyosha. "Now you wouldn't understand —and perhaps I couldn't explain it."

"I know your brothers and your father are worrying you, too."

"Yes, my brothers, too," said Alyosha.

"I don't like your brother Ivan, Alyosha," said Lise.

"My brothers are destroying themselves," he said, "my father, too. And they are destroying others with them. It's 'a primitive force,' as Father Païssy said. I don't know about that, I only know I, too, am a Karamazov.... Me a monk! You said so."

"Yes, I did."

"And perhaps I don't even believe in God."

"You don't believe?" said Lise quietly and gently. But Alyosha did not answer. There was something mysterious in these last words, giving him pain.

"And now on the top of it all, my friend, the best man in the world, is leaving the earth! If you knew, Lise, how bound up I am with him! And I shall be left alone.... I shall come to you, Lise.... For the future we'll be together."

"Yes! We shall be always together, all our lives! Kiss me, I allow you."

Alyosha kissed her.

"Now go. Christ be with you!" She made the sign of the cross over him. "Hurry back to *him* while he is alive. I've kept you cruelly. I'll pray today for him and you. Alyosha, we shall be happy! Shall we be happy?"

"I believe we shall, Lise."

Alyosha thought it better not to go in to Madame Hohlakov and was going out of the house without saying good-by to her. But no sooner had he opened the door than he found Madame Hohlakov standing before him. From the first word Alyosha guessed she had been waiting on purpose to meet him.

"Alexey Fyodorovitch, this is awful. This is all childish nonsense. I trust you won't dream—it's foolishness, nothing but foolishness!" she said at once.

"But don't tell her that," said Alyosha.

"Sensible advice from a sensible young man. Am I to understand you only agreed with her from compassion for her invalid state so you didn't hurt her?"

"Not at all. I was quite serious," Alyosha declared.

"To be serious about it is impossible, and in the first place I shall never be at home to you again, and I shall take her away, you may be sure of that."

"Why?" asked Alyosha. "We may have to wait another year or more."

"Alexey Fyodorovitch, that's true, and you'll have time to quarrel and separate a thousand times. But I am so unhappy! Though it's such nonsense, it's a great blow to me. So this is the explanation of her dreadful night and her hysterics! It means love to the daughter but death to the mother. I might as well be in my grave at once. And a more serious matter still, what is this letter she has written? Show it me at once!"

"There's no need. Tell me, how is Katerina Ivanovna now?"

"She has not regained consciousness. Her aunts are here; but they do nothing but sigh. Herzenstube came and was so alarmed I didn't know what to do for him. I nearly sent for a doctor to look after him. He was driven home in my carriage. On the top of it all, you and this letter! It's true nothing can happen for a year or more. In the name of all that's holy, in the name of your dying elder, show me that letter, Alexey Fyodorovitch. I'm her mother. Hold it in your hand, and I will read it so."

"No, I won't show it to you. Even if she said it was okay. I'm coming tomorrow, and we can talk, but now good-by!"

And Alyosha ran downstairs and into the street.

Chapter II

Smerdyakov with a Guitar

Alyosha had no time to lose. While saying goodbye to Lise, the thought struck him that he must find his brother Dmitri. It was getting late. His whole being longed to be at the monastery with his dying saint, but the need to see Dmitri out-weighed everything. The feeling that something terrible was about to happen grew stronger every hour. What would happen, and what he would say to his brother, he could not say.

"Even if the elder dies without me, I won't have to feel I might have saved something and did not. I shall be following his teaching."

His plan was to catch his brother unawares, to climb the fence into the garden, and sit in the summer-house. If Dmitri was not there, he would stay hidden, even if he had to wait till evening. If, as before, Dmitri were lying in wait for Grushenka to come, he would most likely come to the summer-house. Alyosha did not give much thought to the details of his plan, but resolved to act upon it, even if it meant not getting back to the monastery.

There was no one in the summer-house. Alyosha sat down and waited. Though the day was just as fine as yesterday, it seemed a terrible little place. There was a circle on the table left from the glass of brandy spilt the day before. He felt depressed. But he had not sat more than a quarter of an hour, when he heard the thrum of a guitar quite close. People were sitting, or had only just sat down, somewhere in the bushes not more than twenty yards away. Alyosha remembered that, on coming out of the summer-house the day before, he had seen a low garden-seat among the bushes on the left. People must be sitting on it now. A man suddenly began singing in a falsetto, playing the guitar.

The voice ceased.

A woman's voice asked bashfully, "Why haven't you been to see us for so long, Pavel Fyodorovitch? Do you look down upon us?"

"Not at all," answered the man politely. It was clear he had the best of the position, and that the woman was making advances.

"The man must be Smerdyakov," thought Alyosha. And the lady must be the daughter of the house, who has come from Moscow."

"I like verses if they rhyme," the woman said. "Do go on."

The man sang again:

"It was better last time," said the woman. "You sang 'If my darling be in health'; it was more tender. I suppose you've forgotten."

"Poetry is rubbish!" said Smerdyakov.

"Oh, no! I am very fond of poetry."

"So far as it's poetry, it's rubbish. Who ever talks in rhyme? If we talked in rhyme, we shouldn't say much. Poetry is no good, Marya Kondratyevna."

"How clever you are! How is it you know so much?"

The woman's voice was more and more insinuating.

"I could have known more if it had not been for my destiny. I am descended from a filthy beggar and have no father. They used to throw it in my teeth in Moscow. It had reached them from here, thanks to Grigory Vassilyevitch. Grigory blames me for rebelling against my birth, but I would have said okay to their killing me before I was born. They used to say in the market, and your mamma, too, that her hair was like a mat on her head, and that she was short of five foot by a wee bit. Why talk of a wee bit while she might have said 'a little bit'? She wanted to make it touching. From my childhood up, when I hear 'a wee bit,' I am ready to burst with rage. I hate Russia. I could have been a cadet in the army, or a young hussar."

"If you'd been a cadet in the army you wouldn't have talked like that, but would have drawn your sword to defend Russia."

"I don't want to be a soldier, Marya Kondratyevna; why have soldiers?"

"When an enemy comes, who is going to defend us?"

"There's no need of defense. In 1812 there was an invasion of Russia by Napoleon; it would have been a good thing if they had beaten us. A clever nation would have taken over a dull one. We would be different today."

"Are they so much better in their country? I wouldn't change a Russian I know of for three Englishmen," said Marya Kondratyevna.

"That's as one prefers."

"But you are just like a foreigner—a gentleman foreigner."

"If you care to know, the folks there and ours here are the same in their vice. They both steal, only there those who steal wear polished boots and here they live in filth. The Russian people want a beating, as Fyodor Pavlovitch says, though he is mad, and all his children."

"You said yourself you had such a respect for Ivan Fyodorovitch."

"But he said I was a stinking boot-licker. He is mistaken. If I had a certain sum in my pocket, I would have left here long ago. Dmitri Fyodorovitch is lower than any boot-licker in his behavior, in his mind, and in his poverty. He doesn't know how to do anything, and yet he is respected by everyone.

"I may be only a soup-maker, but with luck I could open a restaurant in Moscow. Dmitri Fyodorovitch is a beggar, but if he were to challenge the son of the first count in the country, he'd fight him. How is he better than I am? He's much less bright. Look at the money he's wasted!"

"A duel must be so dreadful," Marya Kondratyevna said, "and so brave. I'd give anything to see one! Two men facing off with guns in their hands, all to protect the honor of a lady!"

"It's all very well when you are firing at someone, but when he is firing at you, you'd feel pretty silly. You'd be glad to run."

"You don't mean you would run away?"

Smerdyakov did not reply. After a moment the guitar tinkled again, and he sang in the same falsetto. Then something unexpected happened. Alyosha sneezed. They were silent. Alyosha got up and walked towards them. He found Smerdyakov dressed up and wearing polished boots, his hair pomaded. The guitar lay on the garden-seat. The woman was the daughter of the house. She was young and was not too bad-looking.

"Will my brother Dmitri soon be back?" asked Alyosha.

Smerdyakov got up slowly; Marya Kondratyevna rose too.

"How am I to know? I'm not his keeper," answered Smerdyakov.

"But I simply asked whether you do know?" Alyosha said.

"I know nothing of his whereabouts and don't want to."

"But my brother said you'd promised to let him know all that goes on in the house, and if Agrafena Alexandrovna comes."

Smerdyakov turned a deliberate, unmoved glance upon him, and said, "How did you get in, since the gate was bolted?"

"I came in the back, over the fence, and went to the summer-house. I hope you'll forgive me," he said to Marya Kondratyevna.

"As though we could take it amiss in you!" said Marya, flattered by Alyosha's apology. "For Dmitri Fyodorovitch often goes to the summer-house in that way, and we don't always know he is here."

"I am anxious to find him, or learn where he is. It's important."

"He never tells us," lisped Marya Kondratyevna.

"Though I used to come here as a friend," Smerdyakov said, "Dmitri Fyodorovitch has pestered me in a merciless way, even here, by his questions about the master. 'What news?' he'll ask. 'What's going on in there now? Who's coming and going?' Twice he's threatened me with death."

"With death?" Alyosha exclaimed.

"Do you suppose he'd think much of that, with his temper, which you had a chance to observe yesterday? He says if I let Agrafena Alexandrovna in and she passes the night, I'll be the first to suffer for it. I am terribly afraid of him, and if I were not even more afraid of doing so, I would let the police know. God only knows what he might not do!"

"His honor said to him, 'I'll pound you to death!'" added Marya.

"Oh, if it's pounding, it's only talk," said Alyosha. "If I could meet him, I might speak to him about that, too."

"Well, the only thing I can tell you is this," said Smerdyakov. "I am here as an old friend and neighbor, and it would be odd if I didn't come. Though Ivan Fyodorovitch sent me first thing this morning to your brother's lodging in Lake Street with a message to Dmitri Fyodorovitch to dine with him at the restaurant in the market-place. I went, but didn't find Dmitri Fyodorovitch at home, though it was eight o'clock. 'He's been here, but is gone,' were the words of his landlady. It's as if there was an understanding between them. Perhaps at this moment he is in the restaurant with Ivan Fyodorovitch, for Ivan has not been home to dinner and Fyodor Pavlovitch dined alone an hour ago. But I beg you not to speak of me and of what I told you."

"Ivan invited Dmitri to the restaurant today?" said Alyosha.

"That's so."

"The Metropolis tavern in the market-place?"

"The very same."

"That's quite likely," cried Alyosha, excited. "Thank you, Smerdyakov; that's important. I'll go there at once."

"Don't betray me," Smerdyakov called after him.

"No, I'll go to the tavern as by chance. Don't be anxious."

"But wait a minute, I'll open the gate," cried Marya Kondratyevna.

"No, I'll get over the fence again."

What he heard made Alyosha greatly excited. He ran to the tavern. It was not possible for him to go in because of his monastic dress, but he could ask at the entrance for his brothers and call them down. But just as he reached the tavern, a window was flung open, and his brother Ivan called down to him:

"Alyosha, can you come up? I shall be awfully grateful."

"To be sure I can, only I don't quite know if in this dress—"

"But I'm in a room apart. Come up the steps; I'll meet you."

A minute later Alyosha was sitting beside his brother Ivan, who was dining alone.

Chapter III

The Brothers Make Friends

Ivan was in a room near the entrance, with waiters darting to and fro. The only other customer in the room was a retired military man drinking tea in a corner. But the usual bustle was going on in the other rooms. Alyosha knew that Ivan did not like taverns, so he must have come here, he reflected, to meet Dmitri.

"Shall I order you fish, soup, or anything? You don't live on tea alone, I should think," cried Ivan, delighted at having got hold of Alyosha.

"Let me have soup, and tea, I am hungry," said Alyosha.

"And cherry jam? You remember how you used to love cherry jam?"

"You remember that? Let me have jam too, I like it still."

Ivan rang for the waiter and ordered soup, jam, and tea.

"I remember everything, Alyosha, I remember you till you were eleven. I was nearly fifteen then. There's such a difference between the ages of fifteen and eleven that brothers are never companions at those ages. I don't know whether I was fond of you even. When I went away to Moscow for the first time, I never thought of you. Then, when you came to Moscow yourself, we only met once. Now, I've been here more than three months, and so far we have scarcely said a word to each other. Tomorrow

I'm going away, and I was just thinking how I could see you to say goodbye and then you passed."

"Were you very anxious to see me, then?"

"Very. I want to get to know you once for all, and I want you to know me. I believe it's best to get to know people just before leaving them. I've noticed how you've been looking at me these three months. There has been continual expectation in your eyes, and I can't endure that. That's why I've kept away from you. But in the end I've learned to respect you. You stand firm. You do, don't you? I like people who are firm like that whatever it is they stand by, even if they are such little fellows as you. Your expectant eyes ceased to annoy me, I grew fond of them. You seem to love me for some reason, Alyosha?"

"I do love you, Ivan. Dmitri says of you—Ivan is a tomb! I say of you, Ivan's a riddle. But I understand something in you I did not understand before."

"What's that?" laughed Ivan.

"You won't be angry?"

"Well?"

"That you are just as young as other young men of three and twenty, just a young, fresh, nice boy, green in fact! Now, have I insulted you?"

"On the contrary, I am struck by a coincidence," cried Ivan. "Would you believe it? Ever since that scene with her, I have thought of nothing else but my youthful greenness. Do you know I've been sitting here thinking to myself: that if I didn't believe in life, if I lost faith in the woman I love, lost faith in the order of things, if I were struck by every horror—still I should want to live and, having once tasted of the cup, I would not turn away from it till I had drained it!

"At thirty, though, I shall be sure to leave the cup, even if I've not emptied it, and turn away—where, I don't know. But till I am thirty, I know that my youth will triumph over everything—every disgust with life. I have a longing for life, and I go on living in spite of logic. Though I may not believe in the order of the universe, yet I love the sticky little leaves as they open in spring. I love the blue sky, I love some people, sometimes without knowing why. I love some great deeds done by men. Here they have brought your soup; eat it, it will do you good. It's first-rate. And I shall steep myself in my emotion. It's not a matter of intellect; it's loving with one's insides. One loves the first strength of one's youth. Do you understand, Alyosha?" Ivan laughed.

"I understand too well, Ivan. One longs to love with one's insides. You said that so well. I'm awfully glad you have such a longing for life," said Alyosha. "I think everyone should love life above all."

"Love life more than the meaning of it?"

"Love it no matter: it's only then one understands its meaning. Half your work is done. You love life; you've only to do the second half to be saved."

"You want to save me! What does your second half mean?"

"Why, one has to raise up your dead, who perhaps have not died after all. Come, let me have tea. I am so glad of our talk, Ivan."

"I see you are turned on. I am awfully fond of such faith from—novices. You are stead-fast, Alexey. Do you mean to leave the monks?"

"Yes, my elder sends me out into the world."

"We shall see each other then. We shall meet before I am thirty, when I shall begin to turn aside from the cup. Father doesn't want to turn aside till he is seventy, he dreams of hanging on to eighty in fact. He means it only too seriously, though he is a buffoon. He stands on a firm rock, too, his sensuality—though after we are thirty there may be not much else to stand on. But to hang on to seventy is nasty, better only thirty; one might keep 'a shadow of nobility' by deceiving oneself. Have you seen Dmitri today?"

"No, but I saw Smerdyakov," and Alyosha described his meeting.

Ivan listened anxiously, and questioned him.

"He begged me not to tell Dmitri he told me," added Alyosha. Ivan made a face.

"Are you making a face on Smerdyakov's account?" Alyosha asked.

"Yes. I certainly did want to see Dmitri; now there's no need."

"But are you really going so soon, brother?"

"Yes."

"What of Dmitri and father? How will it end?" asked Alyosha.

"You are always speaking of it! What have I to do with it? Am I my brother's keeper?" Ivan said angrily, but then he smiled. "Cain's answer about his murdered brother, wasn't it? Perhaps that's what you're thinking? Well, I can't stay here to be their keeper. I've finished what I had to do, and I am going. Do you think I'm jealous of Dmitri, that I've been trying to steal his beautiful Katerina? That's nonsense, I had business of my own. I finished it. I am going."

"At Katerina Ivanovna's?"

"Yes. I've released myself once for all. After all, what have I to do with Dmitri? I had my own business to settle with Katerina Ivanovna. Dmitri behaved as though there was an understanding between us. I didn't ask him to do it, but he handed her over to me and gave us his blessing. It's all too funny. Alyosha, if you only knew how light my heart is! Would you believe, it, I sat here eating my dinner and nearly ordered wine to celebrate my freedom. It's been going on nearly six months, and all at once I've thrown it off. I never guessed how easy it would be."

"You are speaking of your love, Ivan?"

"Of love, if you like. I fell in love with the young lady, I worried over her and she worried me. And all at once it ended! I spoke truly this morning , but I went away roaring with laughter. Would you believe it? It's the truth."

"You seem very merry about it now," said Alyosha.

"How could I tell that I didn't care for her a bit! And yet how she attracted me! How attractive she was just now when I made my speech! And she attracts me even now, yet how easy it is to leave her. Do you think I am boasting?"

"No, only perhaps it wasn't love."

"Alyosha," laughed Ivan, "don't talk about love, it's not right for you. How you rushed into the discussion this morning! I've forgotten to kiss you for it.... How she pained me! It certainly was a 'wound.' She knew I loved her! She loved me and not Dmitri," Ivan insisted. "Her feeling for Dmitri was simply self-wounding. All I told her was true, but the worst of it is, it may take her fifteen or twenty years to find out she doesn't care for Dmitri, and loves me, whom she pains, or perhaps she may never find it out. Well, it's better so; I can leave for good. By the way, how is she now? What happened after I departed?"

Alyosha told him she cried, and was now out of her mind.

"Isn't Madame Hohlakov laying it on?"

"I think not."

"I must find out. Nobody dies of that, though. God gave woman those emotions as a relief. I won't go to her at all. Why push myself forward again?"

"But you told her she had never cared for you."

"I did that on purpose. Alyosha, shall I call for some wine? Let us drink to my freedom. If only you knew how glad I am!"

"No, we had better not drink," said Alyosha. "Besides I feel sad."

"Yes, you've been sad for a long time, I've noticed it."

"Have you settled to go tomorrow morning, then?"

"Morning? I didn't say I should go in the morning.... But perhaps it may be the morning. Would you believe it, I dined here today only to avoid dining with the old man, I hate him so. I should have left long ago, so far as he is concerned. But why are you so worried about my going away? We've plenty of time before I go, forever, in fact!"

"If you are going away tomorrow, what do you mean by forever?"

"What does it matter?" laughed Ivan. "We've time enough for talk. Why do you look so surprised? Why have we met here? To talk of Katerina Ivanovna?"

"No."

"Then you know what for. It's different for other people; but we in our youth have to settle the eternal questions first. That's what we care about. While the old folks deal with practical questions. Why have you been looking at me in that way? To ask me, 'What do you believe, or don't believe?' That's what your eyes have been saying?"

"Perhaps," smiled Alyosha. "You are not laughing at me, Ivan?"

"Me laughing! I don't want to wound my little brother. Alyosha, look at me! Of course I am just such a boy as you are, only not a novice. And what have Russian boys been doing up till now, some of them, I mean. In this stinking tavern, for instance, they meet and sit in a corner. They've never met in their lives before and they won't meet again for forty years. And what do they talk? Of the eternal questions, of the existence of God and immortality. And those who do not believe in God talk of socialism or anarchism, of the change of all humanity, so that it all comes to the same. Isn't it so?"

"Yes, for real Russians the questions of God's existence and of immortality, as you say, come first, and so they should," said Alyosha, watching his brother with a smile.

"Well, Alyosha, it's sometimes unwise to be a Russian, but anything stupider than the way Russian boys spend their time one can hardly imagine. But there's one Russian boy called Alyosha I am awfully fond of."

"How nicely you put that in!" Alyosha laughed.

"Well, tell me where to begin, give your orders. The existence of God?"

"Begin where you like. You said yesterday at father's there was no God."

"I said that to tease you. But I've no objection to discussing it with you seriously. I want to be friends with you, Alyosha, for I have no friends and want to try it. Only fancy, perhaps I too accept God," laughed Ivan; "that's a surprise for you, isn't it?"

"Yes, of course, if you are not joking."

"Joking? I was told at the elder's yesterday I was joking. You know, dear boy, there was an old sinner in the eighteenth century who declared that, if there were no God, he would have to be invented. And man has actually invented God. And what's strange, what's marvelous, is not that God should really exist; the marvel is that such an idea, the idea of the necessity of God, could enter the head of such a savage beast as man. So holy it is, so touching, so wise and so great a credit to man. As for me, I've long resolved not to think whether man created God or God man. And I won't go through all the axioms on that subject. For what are we aiming at now? I am trying to explain as quickly as possible my essential nature, what manner of man I am, what I believe, and for what I hope. And therefore I tell you that I accept God.

"But you must note this: if God exists and really did create the world, then he created it according to the geometry of Euclid and the human mind, with only three dimensions in space. Yet there are philosophers who doubt that; they even dare to dream that two parallel lines, which according to Euclid can never meet on earth, may meet somewhere in infinity. I have come to the conclusion that, since I can't understand even that, I can't expect to understand God. I know that I have no faculty for settling such questions. I have a Euclidian earthly mind, and how could I solve problems that are not of this world? I advise you never to think about it either, my dear Alyosha, especially about God. All such questions are utterly inappropriate for a mind created with an idea of only three dimensions. And so I accept God, and what's more, I accept His wisdom, His purpose—which are utterly beyond our understanding.

"I believe in the underlying order and meaning of life; I believe in the eternal harmony in which they say we shall one day be blended. I believe in the Word to Which the universe is striving, and Which Itself was 'with God,' and Which Itself is God and so on to infinity. Yet would you believe it, in the final result I don't accept this world of God's, and though I know it exists, I don't accept it. It's not that I don't accept God, it's the world created by Him I cannot accept. I believe that in the world's finale, at the moment of eternal harmony, something so precious will come to pass that it will suffice for all hearts, and make it not only possible to forgive but to justify all that has happened—but though all that may come to pass, I don't accept it. Even if parallel lines meet and I see it myself, I shall say that they've met, but still I won't accept it. That's what's at the root of me, Alyosha; that's my creed. I began our talk as stupidly as I could, but I've led up to my confession, for that's all you want.

You didn't want to hear about God, but only to know what the brother you love lives by. And so I've told you."

"Why did you begin 'as stupidly as you could'?"

"To begin with, Russian conversations on such subjects are always carried on stupidly. And secondly, the stupider one is, the closer one is to reality. The stupider one is, the clearer one is. Stupidity is brief and artless, while intelligence wriggles and hides itself. Intelligence is a knave, but stupidity is honest and straightforward. I've led the conversation to my despair, and the more stupidly I have presented it, the better for me."

"You will explain why you don't accept the world?"

"That's what I've been leading up to. I don't want to turn you from your beliefs, perhaps I want to be healed by you."

Ivan smiled like a child. Alyosha never saw such a smile.

Chapter IV

Up-Rising

"I must make you a confession," Ivan began. "I have never understood how one can love one's neighbors. It's just one's neighbors, to my mind, one can't love. To love a man, he must be hidden, for as soon as he shows his face, love is gone."

"Father Zossima talked of that," observed Alyosha. "He, too, said that the face of a man often keeps many people not practiced in love from loving him. Yet there's a great deal of love in mankind, almost Christ-like love. I know that."

"Well, I know nothing of it. To my thinking, Christ-like love is a miracle impossible on earth. He was God, we are not. Suppose I, for instance, suffer. Another can never know my sufferings, because he is another and not I. What's more, a man is not ready to admit another's suffering. One can love one's neighbors in our thoughts, but at close quarters it's almost impossible. But enough of that. I simply wanted to show you my point of view. I meant to speak of the suffering of mankind generally, but let's confine ourselves to that of children. In the first place, children can be loved even at close quarters, even when they are dirty, or ugly. In the second, children are innocent.

"Are you fond of children, Alyosha? I know you are, and you will understand why I prefer to speak of them. If they suffer, they must suffer for their fathers' sins; but that reasoning I don't understand. The innocent must not suffer for another's sins! You may be surprised, Alyosha, but I am awfully fond of children. Children while they are quite little—up to seven, for instance—are so remote from grown-up people; they are different creatures. Why I am telling you all this, Alyosha? My head aches and I am sad."

"You speak strangely," said Alyosha, "as though not yourself."

"By the way, a Bulgarian I met," Ivan went on, "told me about the crimes by Turks in Bulgaria through fear of a general uprising. They burn villages, murder, outrage women and children, nail their prisoners by the ears to the fences, leave them till morning, and hang them—all sorts of things you can't imagine. They took pleasure in torturing children, too; cutting the unborn child from the mother's womb, and tossing babies in the air and catching them on the points of their bayonets before their mothers' eyes. Doing it before the mothers' eyes gave zest to the amusement. Artistic, wasn't it?"

"Brother, what are you driving at?" asked Alyosha.

"If the devil doesn't exist, man has created him in his own image."

"Just as he did God, then?" said Alyosha.

"It's wonderful how you turn my words against me," laughed Ivan. "Well, I'm glad. You asked what I was driving at. I am fond of collecting certain facts. The Turks have gone into my collection, but they are foreigners. I have specimens from home that are even better. You know we prefer beating—rods and scourges—that's what we do. Nailing ears is unthinkable for us, but the rod and the scourge we have always with us. A cultured gentleman and his wife beat their own child with a birch-rod, a girl of seven. The papa said he was glad that the birch was covered with twigs. 'It stings more,' he said.

"I know for a fact there are people who at every blow are worked up sensually. They beat for a minute, for five minutes, for ten minutes. The child screams. At last the child gasps, 'Daddy! Daddy!' By some unseemly chance the case was brought into court. The counsel protests in his client's defense. 'It's a simple thing,' he says, 'an everyday domestic event. A father corrects his child. To our shame, it is brought into court.' The jury, convinced by him, give a favorable verdict. The public roars with delight. Do you understand that, brother? Do you understand why this infamy is permitted? Without it, I am told, man could not have existed on earth, for he could not have known good and evil. Why should he know good and evil when it costs so much? The whole of knowledge is not worth that child's prayer to 'dear, kind God'! I say nothing of the sufferings of grown-up people! But these little ones! I am making you suffer, Alyosha. I'll leave off."

"Never mind. I want to suffer too," said Alyosha.

"I understand nothing," Ivan went on. "I don't want to understand. I want to stick to the fact. I made up my mind long ago not to understand. If I try to understand anything, I shall be false to the fact, and I have made up my mind to stick to the fact."

"Why are you trying me?" Alyosha cried. "Will you say what you mean?"

"Of course, I will; that's what I've been leading up to. You are dear to me, I don't want to let you go, and I won't give you up to your Zossima."

Ivan for a minute was silent, and his face became very sad.

"I took children only to make my case clearer. I cannot understand why the world is arranged as it is. With my pitiful understanding, all I know is that there is suffering and none are guilty; everything finds its level—but that's only Euclidian nonsense, I know that, and I can't consent to live by it! I must have justice I haven't suffered simply that I may manure the soil of future harmony for somebody else. I want to see with my own eyes the lamb lie down with the lion and the victim rise up and embrace his murderer. I want to be there when we understand what it has all been for. There are numbers of questions, but I've only taken the children, because in their case what I mean is so clear. If all must suffer to pay for eternal harmony, what have children to do with it?

"Oh, Alyosha, I am not going against the Church. I understand, of course, what an upheaval of the universe it will be when everything in heaven and earth blends in one hymn of praise and everything that lives and has lived cries aloud: 'Thou art just, O Lord, for Thy ways are revealed.' But what pulls me up is that I can't accept that harmony. Perhaps it may happen that if I live to that moment, or rise again to see it, I, too, may cry aloud with the rest, 'Thou art just, O Lord!' but I don't want to cry aloud then.

"While there is still time, I want to renounce the higher harmony altogether. It's not worth the tears of one tortured child! It's not worth it, because those tears must be atoned for, or there can be no harmony. But how are you going to atone for them? By their being avenged? What do I care for avenging them, since those children have already been tortured? I don't want more suffering. And if the sufferings of children go to swell the sum of sufferings necessary to pay for truth, then the truth is not worth such a price. I would rather be left with the suffering. And so I hasten to give back my entrance ticket, and if I am an honest man I am bound to give it back as soon as possible. And that I am doing. It's not God that I don't accept, Alyosha, I am only returning Him the ticket."

"That's rebellion," said Alyosha.

"Rebellion? I am sorry you call it that," said Ivan. "One can hardly live in rebellion, and I want to live. Imagine you are creating human destiny with the object of making men happy in the end, giving them peace at last, but it is essential to torture to death only one tiny creature—a baby, for instance—and to found that edifice on its tears, would you consent to be the architect on those conditions?"

"No, I wouldn't," said Alyosha.

"And would men for whom you are building it accept their happiness on the foundation of the blood of a little victim?"

"No, I can't admit it. Brother," said Alyosha. "You said just now is there a being in the whole world who would have the right to forgive and could forgive? There is a Being and He can forgive everything, because He gave His blood for all. You have forgotten Him. It is to Him they cry, 'Thou art just, O Lord, for Thy ways are revealed!'"

"Ah! The One without sin! I have not forgotten Him; on the contrary I've been wondering how it was you did not bring Him in before, for all arguments on your side put Him first. Isn't that Father Païssy's teaching?"

"Father Païssy did once say something rather the same...."

"It's all nonsense, Alyosha. It's no business of mine. I told you, all I want is to live on to thirty, and then ... dash the cup to the ground!"

"But the little sticky leaves, the blue sky, the woman you love! How will you live, how will you love them?" Alyosha cried. "With such a hell in your heart and head, how can you live? You will kill yourself, you can't endure it!"

"There is strength to endure everything," Ivan said.

"What strength?"

"The strength of the Karamazovs—the strength of their baseness."

"To sink into sin, to stifle your soul with corruption?"

"Only perhaps till I am thirty I shall escape it, and then—"

"How will you escape it? That's impossible with your ideas."

"In the Karamazov way, again."

"'Everything is lawful,' is that it?"

Ivan scowled, and all at once turned pale.

"Ah, you've caught up yesterday's phrase, which Dmitri so naïvely paraphrased! Yes, if you like, 'everything is lawful'"

Alyosha looked at him in silence.

"I thought going away I would have you, at least," Ivan said with feeling; "but now I see there is no place for me even in your heart. The truth, 'all is lawful,' I won't renounce it—will you renounce me for it?"

Alyosha got up, went to him, and softly kissed him on the lips.

"Thank you, Alyosha. But get up, it's time we were going."

They went out, but stopped when they reached the entrance.

"Listen, Alyosha," Ivan began, "if I'm really able to care for the sticky little leaves I shall only love them remembering you. It's enough for me that you are somewhere, and I shan't lose my desire for life yet. Is that enough for you? Take it as a declaration of love if you like. And now you go to the right, I to the left. It's enough, even if I don't go away tomorrow and we meet again.

"Don't say a word more on these subjects. I beg you. And about Dmitri too, I ask you especially never speak to me again," he added. "It has all been said! And I'll make you one promise in return. When at thirty, I want to 'dash the cup to the ground,' wherever I may be I'll come to have one more talk with you. It will be interesting to have a look at you, to see what you'll be by that time. Go now to your Pater Seraphicus, he is dying. If he dies without you, you will be angry with me for having kept you. Good-by, kiss me once more; now go."

Ivan turned and went his way without looking back. It was just as Dmitri had left Alyosha the day before. The strange resemblance flashed through his mind in distress and sadness.

He waited a little, looking after his brother, then turned and almost ran to the monastery. It was nearly dark, and he felt frightened; something new was growing in him for which he could not account. The wind had risen again, and the ancient pines murmured gloomily as he entered the woods.

"Pater Seraphicus—he got that name from somewhere— where?" he wondered. "Poor Ivan, when shall I see you again? Here is the hermitage. Yes, Pater Seraphicus will save me— forever!"

Several times afterwards he wondered how he could, on leaving Ivan, so completely forget his brother Dmitri, though he had that morning so firmly resolved to find him and not to give up doing so, even should he be unable to return to the monastery that night.

Chapter V

For a While a Very Obscure One

Ivan, on parting from Alyosha, went home to Fyodor Pavlovitch's. He was overcome by depression. He had often been depressed before, and there was nothing surprising that when he had broken off with everything and was preparing to make a new start. He would again be as solitary as ever, and though he had great expectations he couldn't say what they were. He had a fear of the unknown, but what worried him was something else.

"Is it loathing for my father's house?" he wondered. "Quite likely; I am so sick of it; and though it's the last time I shall cross its threshold, still I loathe it.... But it's not that. Is it the parting with Alyosha and the conversation I had? For so many years I've been silent, not wishing to speak, and all of a sudden I say stuff like that."

What made his depression so irritating was that it had a kind of external character. Some person or thing seemed to be standing out somewhere. Feeling cross and ill-humored, he arrived home and suddenly, about fifteen paces from the garden gate, he guessed what it was. On a bench in the gateway Smerdyakov was sitting enjoying the evening. At the first glance Ivan knew that he was on his mind, and that he loathed him.

"Is it possible that a creature like that can worry me so much?"

Ivan had come to feel an intense dislike for the man, a growing feeling that was almost hatred. When he first came he felt differently. Then he had taken an interest in Smerdyakov, and thought him very original. He encouraged him to talk; they discussed philosophical questions, and even how there could have been light on the first day when the sun, moon, and stars were only created on the fourth day. But Ivan soon saw that Smerdyakov was looking for something different. He began to betray a boundless vanity.

Grushenka had come on the scene, and there had been the scandals with his brother Dmitri—they discussed that, too. But though Smerdyakov always talked of that with great excitement, it was impossible to know what he desired to come of it. There was, in fact, something surprising in his thinking. Smerdyakov was always asking indirect but obviously questions he had given some thought to, but what his object was he did not explain. What irritated Ivan most was the familiarity which Smerdyakov began to show. Not that he forgot himself and was rude; on the contrary, he always spoke with respect, yet he had obviously begun to think there was some sort of understanding between them.

With a feeling of disgust, Ivan tried to pass in at the gate without speaking or looking at Smerdyakov. But Smerdyakov rose from the bench, and from that action alone Ivan knew he wanted to talk to him. Ivan looked at him and stopped, and the fact that he did stop, instead of passing by, as he meant to, drove him to fury. With anger he looked at Smerdyakov's sickly face, the little curls combed forward.

"Get away, you fool. What have I to do with you?" was on the tip of his tongue, but to his surprise he heard himself say, "Is my father still sleeping?"

He asked the question softly, and again to his own surprise, sat on the bench. For an instant he felt almost frightened. Smerdyakov stood facing him.

His honor is still asleep," he said. "I am surprised at you."

"Why are you surprised at me?" Ivan asked, doing his best to check himself, but realizing he was feeling intense curiosity.

"Why don't you go to Tchermashnya, sir?" Smerdyakov asked.

"Why should I go to Tchermashnya?" Ivan asked in surprise.

Smerdyakov was silent again.

"Fyodor Pavlovitch has so begged you to," he said at last.

"Damn you! Say what you want!" Ivan cried angrily.

Smerdyakov pulled himself up, but with the same little smile.

"Nothing, sir—but just by way of conversation."

Another silence followed. Ivan knew he ought to show anger, and Smerdyakov seemed to be waiting to see if he would be angry or not.

At last Ivan moved to get up. Smerdyakov seized the moment.

"I'm in an awful position, Ivan Fyodorovitch. I don't know what to do."

Ivan Fyodorovitch sat down again.

"They are both crazy," Smerdyakov said. "I'm speaking of your parent and your brother Dmitri. Fyodor Pavlovitch keeps worrying me every minute, 'Has she come? Why hasn't she come?' and so on up till midnight. And if Agrafena Alexandrovna doesn't come, he will be at me again tomorrow morning—as though I were to blame for it. On the other side it's no better. As soon as it gets dark, your brother appears with his gun in his hands. 'Look out, you rogue, you soup-maker,' he says. "If you miss her and don't let me know she's been—I'll kill you.' In the morning, he, too, begins worrying me to death. 'Why hasn't she come? Will she come soon?' And he, too, thinks me to blame because she hasn't come. Every day they get angrier, until I sometimes think I shall kill myself."

"Why have you meddled? Why did you spy for Dmitri?"

"How could I help it? I kept quiet, not daring to answer; but he picked me to be his servant. He had only one thing to say: 'I'll kill you, if you miss her,' I feel certain, sir, that I shall have a long fit tomorrow."

"What do you mean by 'a long fit'?"

"A fit lasting several hours, or perhaps a day or two. Once it went on for three days. I fell from the garret that time. The struggling ceased and then began again, and for three days I couldn't come back to my senses. Fyodor Pavlovitch sent for Herzenstube, and he put ice on my head.... I might have died."

"But they say one can't tell with epilepsy when a fit is coming. What makes you say you will have one tomorrow?" Ivan asked.

"That's just so. You can't tell beforehand."

"Besides, you fell from the garret then."

"I climb to the garret every day. I might fall tomorrow. If not, I might fall down the cellar steps. I go into the cellar every day, too."

Ivan took a long look at him.

"You're not making sense. Do you mean to pretend to be ill tomorrow for three days?"

Smerdyakov, looking at the ground and grinning, said: "If I were able to play such a trick, I should have a perfect right to use such a means to save myself from death. For even if Agrafena Alexandrovna comes to see his father while I am ill, his honor can't blame a sick man for not telling him."

"Hang it all!" Ivan cried, his face working with anger, "why are you always worried for your life? All my brother's threats are only words and mean nothing. He won't kill you; it's not you he'll kill!"

"He'd kill me first of all, like a fly. But even more than that, I'm afraid I'll be accused of helping him when he does something crazy to his father."

"Why should you be taken for helping him?"

"Because I let him know the signals as a great secret."

"What signals? Whom did you tell? Speak more plainly!"

"I have a secret with Fyodor Pavlovitch," Smerdyakov said. "As you know, he has for several days past locked himself in as soon as night comes on. Of late you've been going upstairs to your room early every evening, and yesterday you did not come down at all, so perhaps you don't know how carefully he has begun to lock himself in. Grigory Vassilyevitch does not come, because I wait upon him. That's how it's been arranged since this to-do with Agrafena Alexandrovna began. At night I don't get to sleep till midnight, but am on the watch, waiting for Agrafena Alexandrovna.

"For the last few days he's been on edge expecting her. He says she's afraid of Dmitri Fyodorovitch, 'and so,' says he, 'she'll come the back-way, late at night. You look out for her,' says he, 'till midnight; and if she does come, knock at my door or the window from the garden. Knock twice, gently, then three times quickly,' says he. 'I shall understand at once that she has come, and will open the door to you.' Another signal he gave me in case anything not expected happens. First, two knocks, then, another louder. He'll understand that something has happened and that I must see him, and will open so I can speak to him.

"But Dmitri Fyodorovitch might come, too, so I must let him know he is near. His honor is awfully afraid of Dmitri Fyodorovitch, so that even if Agrafena Alexandrovna had come and were locked in with him, and Dmitri Fyodorovitch turns up, I should be bound to let him know, knocking three times. The first signal of five knocks means Agrafena Alexandrovna has come, while the second of three knocks means 'something important to tell you.' No one knows these signals but myself and his honor, so he'd open the door without   calling out. Well, those signals are now known to Dmitri Fyodorovitch, too."

"How are they known? You told him? How dared you tell him?"

"It was through fright. How dare I keep it back? Dmitri Fyodorovitch kept saying every day, 'You are lying to me, you are hiding something from me! I'll break both your legs for you.' So I told him those secret signals that he might see how devoted I am to him, and might be satisfied that I was not lying to him."

"If you think he'll use those signals to get in, don't let him."

"But if I am laid up with a fit, how can I prevent him coming in?"

"How can you be sure you'll have a fit? Are you laughing at me?"

"How could I dare laugh at you? I am in no laughing humor. I feel I am going to have a fit. Fright alone will bring it on."

"But if you are laid up, Grigory will be on the watch. Let Grigory know; he will be sure not to let him in."

"I should never dare to tell Grigory Vassilyevitch the signals without orders from my master. As for Grigory Vassilyevitch hearing him and not admitting him, he has been ill since yesterday, and Marfa Ignatyevna intends to give him medicine. It's a very strange remedy of hers. It's strong. She has the secret of it, and always gives it to Grigory Vassilyevitch three times a year when his legs are so bad he can hardly walk. Then she takes a towel, wets it with the stuff, and rubs his back for half an hour till it's quite red and swollen. What's left in the bottle she gives him to drink; but not quite all, for she leaves some for herself. And as they never take strong drink, they both drop asleep at once and sleep sound a long time. When Grigory Vassilyevitch wakes up he is perfectly well, but Marfa Ignatyevna always has a headache. So, if Marfa Ignatyevna carries out what she intends tomorrow, they won't hear anything. They'll be asleep."

"What a run-around! And it all seems to happen at once, as though it were planned. You'll have a fit and they'll both be out of it," cried Ivan. "You're trying to arrange it!" broke from him.

"How could I? And why should I, when it all depends on Dmitri and his plans? If he means to do anything, he'll do it; but if not, I shan't do anything."

"Why should he go to father if Agrafena Alexandrovna won't?" Ivan went on, white with anger. "You say that yourself, and all the while I've felt sure it was the old man's fancy, and the creature won't come to him. Why should Dmitri break in if she doesn't come?"

"You know yourself why he'll come. Your brother will come simply because he is in a rage or suspects something on account of my illness, and he'll run in, as he did yesterday, to see whether she hasn't escaped him. He is aware, too, that Fyodor Pavlovitch has an envelope with three thousand rubles in it. On it is written, 'To my angel Grushenka, if she will come,' to which he added, 'for my little chicken.' There's no knowing what that might do."

"That's not so!" cried Ivan. "Dmitri wouldn't steal money and kill to do it. He might have killed father yesterday, but he won't steal."

"He is in great need of money, Ivan Fyodorovitch. You don't know," Smerdyakov said. "He looks on that three thousand as his own. He said so himself. 'My father still owes me three thousand.' Besides that, there is something else. It's certain that Agrafena Alexandrovna will force him, if she cares to, to marry her—the master himself, I mean. And of course she may care to in the end.

"All I've said is that she won't come, but maybe she's looking for more than that—I mean to be mistress here. I know that Samsonov, her merchant, was laughing with her about it, telling her it would not be a bad thing to do. She's got plenty of sense. She won't marry a beggar like Dmitri Fyodorovitch. So think about it, Ivan Fyodorovitch; neither Dmitri Fyodorovitch nor you, or your brother, Alexey Fyodorovitch, would have anything after the master's death, for Agrafena Alexandrovna would marry him simply to get hold of his money. But if your father were to die now, there'd be some forty thousand for sure, even for Dmitri Fyodorovitch, whom he hates so, for he has no will...."

Ivan felt himself trembling.

"Then why," he cut in, "do you think I ought to go to Tchermashnya? What did you mean by that? If I go away, you see what will happen here."

"Exactly so," said Smerdyakov, watching Ivan.

"What do you mean by 'exactly so'?"

"I spoke because I felt sorry for you. If I were in your place I should simply throw it all up...rather than stay on in such a position," said Smerdyakov.

They were both silent.

"You seem to be perfectly crazy, and up to no good, too."

Ivan rose. He was about to pass through the gate, but turned to Smerdyakov. In a sudden fit, he bit his lip, clenched his fists, and, in another minute, would have flung himself on Smerdyakov. The latter noticed it and shrank back. But the moment passed, and Ivan turned in silence to the gate.

"I am going away tomorrow, if you care to know—in the morning. That's all!" he said angrily, wondering afterwards what need there was to say that.

"It's the best thing you can do," Smerdyakov said. "You can always be sent for from Moscow, if anything should happen here."

Ivan stopped and turned quickly. A change had passed over Smerdyakov, too. All his familiarity and carelessness had disappeared. His face expressed attention and respect, but he also seemed afraid.

"And couldn't I be sent for from Tchermashnya—if anything happens?"

"From Tchermashnya, too ... you could be sent for," Smerdyakov said.

"But Moscow is farther. Is it to save money on the fare, or to save my going so far out of my way that you insist on Tchermashnya?"

"Exactly so ..." said Smerdyakov.

He looked at Ivan with a smile, and made ready to draw back. But to his surprise Ivan laughed, and went through the gate.

Chapter VI

"Always Worth While Speaking to a Clever Man"

Meeting Fyodor Pavlovitch in the drawing-room, Ivan shouted, "I'm going up to my room. Good-by!" and passed by, trying not to look at his father. Such a display of hate was a surprise even to Fyodor Pavlovitch. The old man wanted to tell him something and had come to meet him in the drawing-room, but, receiving this greeting, he stood in silence, watching his son go upstairs.

"What's the matter with him?" he asked Smerdyakov, who followed Ivan.

"Angry about something. Who can tell?" Smerdyakov said.

"Let him be angry. Bring the tea-maker, and look sharp! No news?"

Then followed questions such as Smerdyakov had just complained of to Ivan, all relating to his expected visitor. Half an hour later the house was locked, and the old man was wandering through the rooms in excited expectation of hearing every minute the knocks agreed upon. Now and then he peered into the darkness.

It was very late, but Ivan was still awake. There were no thoughts in his brain but something vague, and he was intensely excited. He felt he had lost his bearings, and he was fretted by all sorts of strange and surprising desires; for instance, he suddenly had a sharp desire to go into the lodge and beat Smerdyakov. On the other hand, he was more than once that night overcome by a terror which paralyzed him. Hatred rankled in his heart, as though he meant to avenge himself on some one. He even hated Alyosha, and at moments hated himself. Of Katerina Ivanovna he almost forgot to think, and wondered at it afterwards, especially as he remembered that when he told her he would go away next day to Moscow, he heard a whisper in his heart, "That's nonsense, you are not going, and it won't be so easy to tear yourself away as you think."

Remembering that night long afterwards, Ivan recalled with repulsion how he got up from the sofa, opened the door, and went out on the staircase and listened to Fyodor Pavlovitch stirring below. He listened with a strange curiosity, holding his breath. Why he had done this he could not say. He felt no hatred for his father at that moment, but was simply curious to know why he was walking about and what he must be doing. He imagined him peeping out of the dark windows, listening for someone to knock. About two o'clock when everything was quiet, and even Fyodor Pavlovitch had gone to bed, Ivan got into bed, and fell into a deep, dreamless sleep.

He woke early, when it was broad daylight, and, opening his eyes, was surprised to feel himself vigorous. He jumped up and dressed quickly; then dragged out his trunk and began packing. He smiled at the thought that everything was helping his departure. Though he had said the day before that he was leaving next day, yet he remembered that he had no thought of departure when he went to bed, or, at least, had not dreamed that his first act in the morning would be to pack his trunk.

At last his trunk and bag were ready. It was nine o'clock when Marfa Ignatyevna came in and asked, "Where will you take your tea, in your room or downstairs?" He looked almost cheerful, but there was something hurried and scattered about him. Greeting his father affably, even inquiring after his health, he announced he was starting off in an hour to return to Moscow, and begged him to send for the horses. His father heard this with no sign of surprise, and showed no regret at losing him. Instead, he flew into a flutter, recalling some important business of his own.

"What a fellow you are! Not to tell me yesterday! Never mind; we'll manage it all the same. Do me a great service, my dear boy. Go to Tchermashnya on the way."

"I'm sorry, I can't. It's eighty miles to the railway and the train starts for Moscow at seven o'clock tonight. I can only just catch it."

"You'll catch it tomorrow. Go to Tchermashnya. It won't put you out much! If I hadn't something to keep me here, I would run over myself. But here I ... it's not the time for me to go now.... You see, I've two pieces of copse land there. Last year I just missed a purchaser who would have given twelve. There's no getting anyone here to buy it. But the priest at Ilyinskoe wrote Thursday that a merchant called Gorstkin, a man I know, had turned up. He says he will give me eleven thousand for the woods. But he'll only be here for a week, so you must go at once and make a bargain with him."

"Well, you write to the priest; he'll make the bargain."

"He has no eye for business. This Gorstkin looks like a peasant, but he is a liar. Sometimes he tells such lies that you wonder why he is doing it. He told me the year before last that his wife was dead, and there was not a word of truth in it. His wife never died, she is alive to this day and gives him a beating twice a week. So what you have to find out is whether he is lying when he says he wants to buy it."

"I shall be no use in such a business. I have no eye either."

"I will tell you the signs by which you can judge Gorstkin. I've done business with him before. You must watch his beard. If his beard shakes when he talks and he gets cross, it's all right. But if he strokes his beard with his left hand and grins—he is trying to cheat you. Don't watch his eyes—watch his beard! He's called Gorstkin, though his real name is Lyagavy; but don't call him so, he will be offended. If you and he come to an understanding, write at once. You need only write: 'He's not lying.' Hold out for eleven thousand; one thousand you can knock off, but not more. It's not easy to find a purchaser, and I'm in desperate need of money. Only let me know it's serious, and I'll run over and fix it up. I'll snatch the time somehow. Will you go?"

"I can't spare the time. You must excuse me."

"Come, you might oblige your father. I shan't forget it. You've no heart, any of you. What's a day or two to you? Where are you going now—to Venice? Venice will keep another two days. I would have sent Alyosha, but what use is Alyosha in a thing like that? I send you because you are clever. You know nothing about timber, but you've got an eye. All that is wanted is to see whether the man is in earnest. Watch his beard—if his beard shakes you know he is in earnest."

"You force me to go to that damned Tchermashnya, then?"

Fyodor Pavlovitch did not catch the hate, but he caught the smile.

"Then you'll go? I'll scribble the note for you at once."

"I don't know whether I shall go. I don't know. I'll decide on the way."

"Decide now! If you settle the matter, write me a line; give it to the priest and he'll send it to me. The priest will lend you horses back to the station."

The old man was quite delighted. He wrote the note and sent for the horses. He was quite unmoved by the parting with

Ivan, and seemed at a loss for something to say. Only when accompanying his son out on to the steps, the old man began to fuss about. He would have kissed him, but Ivan quickly held out his hand.

His father saw it, and instantly pulled himself up.

"Well, good luck!" he said. "You'll come again?"

Ivan got into the carriage.

"Good-bye, Ivan! Don't be too hard on me!" the father called.

The whole household came out to take leave—Smerdyakov, Marfa and Grigory. Ivan gave them ten rubles each. As he seated himself in the carriage, Smerdyakov jumped up to arrange the rug.

"You see ... I am going to Tchermashnya," broke from Ivan.

As the day before, the words seemed to drop of themselves.

"It's a true saying then that 'it's always worth while speaking to a clever man,'" answered Smerdyakov, looking at him.

The carriage rolled away. Nothing was clear in Ivan's soul, but he looked eagerly around him at the fields, the hills, the trees, at a flock of geese flying overhead in the bright sky. All of a sudden he felt very happy. He tried to talk to the driver, but realized he was not catching anything, not even his answer.

"Why is it worth while speaking to a clever man? What did he mean?" Ivan wondered. That thought he couldn't shake. "Why did I say I was going to Tchermashnya?"

At Volovya station, Ivan got out of the carriage, and the drivers stood round him bargaining over the journey of twelve miles to Tchermashnya. He told them to harness the horses. He went into the station house, looked round, and went back to the entrance.

"I won't go to Tchermashnya. Is it too late to reach the railway by seven?"

"We shall just do it. Shall we get the carriage out?"

"At once. Will any one of you be going to the town tomorrow?"

"To be sure. Mitri here will."

"Can you do me a service, Mitri? Go to my father's, Fyodor Karamazov, and tell him I haven't gone to Tchermashnya. Can you?"

"Of course. I've known Fyodor Pavlovitch a long time."

"Here's something for you; I dare say he won't give you anything," said Ivan.

"You may depend on it." Mitri laughed, too. "Thank you, sir. I'll be sure to do it."

At seven o'clock Ivan got into the train and set off to Moscow.

"Away with the past. I've done with the old world, and may I have no news from it. To a new life, new places and no looking back!"

But instead of delight his soul was filled with bad thoughts, and his heart with pain. He was thinking all the night.

Only at daybreak, approaching Moscow, did he rouse himself.

"I am no good," he whispered to himself.

Fyodor Pavlovitch was well satisfied at having seen his son off. For two hours he felt almost happy, and sat drinking brandy. Then something happened which was very unpleasant for everyone, and completely upset Fyodor Pavlovitch. Smerdyakov went to the cellar for something and fell down the steps.

Fortunately, Marfa Ignatyevna was in the yard and heard him. She did not see the fall, but heard his scream—the strange, peculiar scream, long familiar to her—the scream of the epileptic in a fit. They could not tell whether the fit had come on him while he was descending the steps, so that he must have fallen unconscious, or whether it was the fall that caused the fit. They found him at the bottom of the cellar steps in convulsions, foaming at the mouth. At first they thought he had broken a bone—but "God preserved him," as Marfa Ignatyevna expressed it.

It was difficult to get him out of the cellar. They asked the neighbors to help, and managed it somehow. Fyodor Pavlovitch himself helped. The sick man did not come to his senses; the convulsions ceased for a time, but then began again, and everyone concluded that the same thing would happen as a year before.

In the evening, Fyodor Pavlovitch sent for Doctor Herzenstube. He concluded that the fit was a violent one and might have serious consequences, but by tomorrow morning, if the remedies were unavailing, he would try something else. The invalid was taken to the lodge, to a room next to Grigory's and Marfa Ignatyevna's.

Fyodor Pavlovitch had one misfortune after another that day. Marfa Ignatyevna cooked the dinner, and the soup, compared with Smerdyakov's, was "no better than dish-water," and the fowl was so dry it was impossible to chew it. In the evening there was more trouble; he was informed that Grigory, who had not been well for the last three days, was completely laid up by his lumbago. Fyodor Pavlovitch finished his tea early and locked himself in the house. He was in terrible excitement and suspense. That evening he reckoned on Grushenka's coming; he had received from Smerdyakov that morning an assurance "that she had promised to come without fail."

The old man's heart throbbed with excitement; he paced up and down his empty rooms listening. He had to be on the alert. Dmitri might be on the watch for her, and when she knocked on the window the door must be opened at once. She must not be a second in the passage, for fear—God forbid!—she should be frightened and run away. Fyodor Pavlovitch had much to think of, but never had his heart been steeped in such voluptuous hopes. This time he could say almost certainly that she would come!

PART III

Book VI • Alyosha

Chapter I

Father Zossima and His Visitors

When Alyosha went into his elder's cell, he was astonished. Instead of a sick man at his last gasp, he saw Father Zossima sitting up, bright and cheerful, surrounded by visitors with whom he was having a conversation.

It was beginning to get dark, and the room was lit by lamps and candles. Seeing Alyosha in the doorway, Father Zossima smiled at him joyfully and held out his hand, saying, "Welcome, my quiet one. I knew you would come."

Alyosha went up to him, bowed before him, and wept.

"Come, don't weep over me yet," Father Zossima said, laying his hand on him. "Get up, my dear boy. Let me look at you. Have you been home and seen your brother?"

It seemed strange to Alyosha that he asked so confidently about one of his brothers only—but which one?

"I have seen one of my brothers," answered Alyosha.

"I mean the elder one, to whom I bowed down."

"I only saw him yesterday and could not find him today," said Alyosha.

"Hurry to find him tomorrow. Perhaps you may still have time to prevent something terrible. I bowed down to the great suffering in store for him."

After that he was silent and seemed to be thinking.

"Father, your words are not clear. What is this suffering in store for him?"

"I seemed to see something terrible yesterday ... as though his whole future were in his eyes. I was struck with fear at what he is preparing for himself. Once or twice in my life I've seen such a look in a man's face ... showing, as it were, his fate, and that fate, sadly, came to pass. I sent you to him, Alexey, for I thought your brotherly face would help him. Because of it you will go forth from these walls, but will live like a monk in the world. You'll have many enemies, but even they will love you. Life will bring you many ills, but you will find your happiness in them, and will bless life.

"My life is ending, but every day left me I feel how my earthly life is in touch with a new, approaching life, the nearness of which sets my soul quivering with rapture, my mind glowing, and my heart weeping with joy. Fathers, forgive me and don't be angry that, like a little child, I've been babbling of what you already know. I only speak from rapture, and forgive my tears, for I love the Bible. The thing is so simple that sometimes one is even afraid to put it into words for fear of being laughed at, and yet how true it is! One who does not believe in God will not believe in God's people. He who believes in God's people will see His Holiness, though he had not believed till then. And what is the use of Christ's words, unless we set an example? The people is lost without the Word of God, for it is thirsty for the Word and for all that is good.

"Fathers and teachers, look at those who set themselves above the people of God, has not God's image and His truth been distorted in them? The spiritual world, the higher part of man's being, is thrown away. The world has announced a new freedom, but what follows from this? In the rich, isolation and the death of the higher feelings; in the poor, envy and murder. They say the world is getting more united as it overcomes distance and sets thoughts flying through the air. But put no faith in such a union. In viewing freedom as the satisfaction of desires, men distort their own nature. They live only for luxury and show. We see the same among those who are not rich; the poor drown their unsatisfied needs and envy in drink. Is such a man free? What becomes of man if he is a slave to the desires he has created for himself? He is isolated, and has no care for others.

"The monastic way is different. Obedience, fasting and prayer, only through them   lays the way to true freedom. I cut off my unnecessary desires, I subdue my pride and correct it with obedience, and with God's help I attain freedom and joy. We shall see which will best further the cause of brotherly love. It is not we, but they, who are in isolation. Take care of the common man. That's your duty as monks, for the common man has God in his heart.

"Remember that you cannot be a judge of anyone. For no one can judge a criminal until he recognizes that he, too, is just such a criminal. If you can take upon yourself the crime of the criminal, take it at once, suffer for him, and let him go without blaming him. Work without ceasing. If you remember in the night as you go to sleep, 'I have not done what I ought to have done,' rise up at once and do it. If the people around you will not hear you, fall down before them and beg their forgiveness. And if you cannot speak to them in their bitterness, serve them in silence and in humility.

"If the evil-doing of men moves you to anger, put aside such feelings. Go at once and seek suffering for yourself, as though you were yourself guilty. Accept that suffering and your heart will find comfort; you will understand that you too are guilty, for you might have been a light to the evil-doers. If you had been a light, perhaps the evil-doer might have been saved by your light.

And even though your light is shining, yet men not saved by it, hold firm and doubt not the power of the light. Believe that if they were not saved, they will be saved in the future. And if they are not saved in the future, then their sons will be saved, for your light will not die even when you are dead. Seek no reward, for great is your reward on earth, the joy that is only given to the good. Fear not the great or mighty, but be wise and serene. Love all men, love everything. Water the earth with the tears of your joy. Don't be ashamed of that joy, for it is a gift of God that is not given to many, but only to the elect."

The elder's death came unexpectedly. Though those gathered about him knew his death was near, it was difficult to imagine it would come so suddenly. His friends, seeing him talking so cheerfully, were convinced there was a change for the better. Even five minutes before his death it was impossible to see it coming. He seemed suddenly to feel a sharp pain in his chest, turned pale, and pressed his hands to his heart. Though suffering, he looked at them with a smile, sank slowly to his knees, bowed his face to the ground, stretched out his arms as though in joy, and quietly gave himself up to God.

Chapter II

A Critical Moment

It was a bright, clear day, and many of the visitors were wandering about the graves scattered around the hermitage. As he walked among them, Father Païssy remembered Alyosha and that he had not seen him since the night.

He had no sooner thought of him than he noticed him in the farthest corner of the hermitage, sitting on a tombstone, his face to the wall. He seemed to be hiding behind the tombstone. Father Païssy saw that he was weeping quietly, his face hidden in his hands, and that his whole frame was shaking with sobs.

Father Païssy stood over him.

"Enough, dear son," he said at last. "Why do you weep? Rejoice and weep not. This is the greatest of his days. Think where he is now, at this moment!"

Alyosha looked at him, his face swollen with crying.

"Maybe it is well," said Father Païssy; "weep if you must, Christ has sent you those tears. They are a relief to you and will serve to gladden your heart," he added, moving away quickly for fear that he too might weep.

Meanwhile time was passing; the services for the dead followed in due course. Father Païssy again took his place by the coffin reading the Gospel.

Before dawn, they laid Father Zossima's body in the coffin and brought it into the front room. Some moments later the bell rang for service, and all who were there crossed themselves.

Father Païssy let Father Iosif read in his place and went out. At that moment Alyosha passed him, hurrying away.

Alyosha quickly turned away, and from his look alone Father Païssy guessed what a great change was taking place in him at that moment.

Father Païssy watched him attentively.

"Where are you hastening? The bell calls to service," he asked.

Alyosha gave no answer.

"Are you leaving us? Without asking leave, without asking a blessing?" Alyosha cast a smile and strange look at the Father to whom his former guide, his beloved elder, had confided him as he lay dying. Still without speaking, he waved, and with rapid steps walked towards the gates.

"You will come back again!" said Father Païssy softly.

It is true that the elder, being so long been accepted by him as his ideal, all his young strength and energy could not but turn towards that ideal, even to forgetting "everyone and everything." On that terrible day he entirely forgot his brother Dmitri, about whom he had been so anxious; he had forgotten other things, too, that he had intended to do.

Something strange came to Alyosha's mind at this fatal moment. It was the impression left by the conversation with Ivan, which now haunted him. It was not that his faith had been shaken. He loved his God and believed in Him always. Yet, though not clear, an evil impression left by his talk with Ivan the day before came back to him.

It had begun to get dusk when Rakitin, crossing the wood to Father Zossima's cell, noticed Alyosha lying face down on the ground under a tree.

"You here, Alexey?" he called. "Can you have—" he began, but broke off.

He had meant to say, "Can you have come to this?"

Alyosha did not look up, but a slight move let Rakitin know he heard him.

"What's the matter?" he went on. "I've been looking for you. You disappeared. What foolery is this?"

Alyosha raised his head and sat up. There was suffering in his face.

"Do you know your face is quite changed? There's none of your famous mildness in it now. Are you angry with some one? Have you been ill-treated?"

"Let me alone," said Alyosha.

"So that's how we're feeling! You can shout at people like other mortals. That is a come-down. Alyosha, you surprise me."

Alyosha gazed a long while with his eyes half closed at Rakitin, and there was a sudden look in his eyes ... but not of anger with Rakitin.

"I'm not rebelling against my God; I simply 'don't accept His world.'"

"How do you mean, you don't accept His world? What are you saying?"

Alyosha did not answer.

"Come, enough of this. Have you had anything to eat today?"

"I don't remember.... I think I have."

"You need keeping up, to judge by your face. It makes one sorry to look at you. You didn't sleep all night either, I hear. And then all this to-do here. Most likely you've had nothing to eat but bread. I've sausage in my pocket; only you won't eat sausage...."

"Give me some."

"I say! You *are* going it! Why, it's a regular up-rising! Well, my boy, we must make the most of it. Come to my place.... I shouldn't mind a drop of vodka, I'm tired to death. Vodka is going too far for you, I suppose ... or ...?"

"Give me some vodka, too."

"You surprise me, brother!" Rakitin looked at him. "Well, one way or another, vodka or sausage, this is a chance that mustn't be missed."

Alyosha got up in silence and followed Rakitin.

"If your brother Ivan could see this—wouldn't he be surprised! By the way, he set off to Moscow this morning, did you know?"

"Yes," answered Alyosha, and the thought of his brother Dmitri came to him. But only for a minute before fading.

"Your brother Ivan declared once that I was an open-minded fool with no abilities. Once you, too, could not resist letting me know that I was without honor. Well! I should like to see what your abilities and sense of honor will do for you now. Let's go to town. I ought to go to Madame Hohlakov's. I've written to tell her everything that happened."

He stopped and, taking Alyosha by the shoulder, made him stop, too.

"Do you know, Alyosha," he said, a new thought having come to him, though he was afraid to say it aloud, so difficult he still found it to believe in the strange and unexpected mood in which he found Alyosha. "Do you know where we had better go?" he brought out.

"I don't care ... where you like."

"Let's go to Grushenka? Will you come?" said Rakitin, with some daring.

"Let's go to Grushenka," Alyosha answered at once.

"Well! I say!" Rakitin cried. Seizing Alyosha by the arm, he led him along the path, afraid he would change his mind. "How glad she will be!" he added.

But it was not to please Grushenka he was taking Alyosha to her. He did nothing without the possibility of gain for himself. Also, he had a desire to see Alyosha's fall "from the saints to the sinners."

"So the critical moment has come," he thought with glee, "and we shall catch it on the hop, for it's just what we want."

Chapter III

An Onion

Grushenka lived in the busiest part of town, in a small wooden lodge in the courtyard of the house of the widow Morozov. The widow led a secluded life with two unmarried nieces, also elderly women. She had no need to let her lodge, but everyone knew she had taken Grushenka as a lodger solely to please her kinsman, the merchant Samsonov.

Four years had passed since the old man brought the slim, delicate, shy, and sad girl of eighteen from the chief town of the province. Little was known of her. There were rumors she had been at seventeen "done wrong" by someone, who had gone away and married, leaving Grushenka poor and shamed. Now, after four years, the little orphan had become a plump, rosy beauty, a woman of determined character, proud and able to take care of herself. She had a good head for business and had put together a little fortune.

There was one point on which all agreed. She was not easily approached, and except for her aged protector there was not one man who could boast of her favors during those four years. Many had tried, but failed. It was known, too, that this strong-willed person had shown marked abilities in making money. She had for some time past, in partnership with old Karamazov, purchased bad debts for next to nothing and made from them ten times their value.

The old widower Samsonov, a man of large fortune, was stingy. He tyrannized over his grown-up sons, but for the last year, having been ill and lost the use of his legs, he had fallen greatly under the influence of his protégée. Grushenka succeeded in freeing herself, while she established in him a belief in her fidelity. The old man, now dead, had had a large business in his day, and was miserly and hard as flint. Though Grushenka's hold upon him was strong, he did not settle any fortune on her, but he gave her a small sum.

"You are a woman with brains," he said to her when he gave her the eight thousand rubles, "and you must look after yourself; except your yearly allowance as before, you'll get nothing more from me to the day of my death, and I'll leave you nothing in my will."

He kept his word, and left everything to his sons, whom, with their wives and children, he had treated all his life as servants. Grushenka was not even mentioned in his will. But he had helped with advice to increase her capital, and he put business in her way.

When Fyodor Pavlovitch, who first met her over business, ended by falling madly in love with her, old Samsonov thought it was very funny. But when Dmitri came on the scene, the old man stopped laughing and gave Grushenka firm advice: "If you have to choose between the father or son, choose the old man, but make sure he'll marry you and settle some fortune on you before you do. You'll get nothing out of the son."

Many knew of the quarrel between the Karamazovs, father and son, the object of which was Grushenka, but scarcely anyone knew what really her attitude to them was. She lived very cheaply and her surroundings were anything but rich. Her living quarters consisted of three rooms furnished with old furniture belonging to her landlady.

It was quite dark when Rakitin and Alyosha entered her rooms. Grushenka was lying on her back on the sofa in her drawing-room, her hands behind her head. She was dressed as though expecting someone, in a black silk dress with a lace on her head. Over her shoulders was a shawl pinned with a huge gold pin. She lay as though tired and weary, her face rather pale and her lips and eyes hot.

The appearance of Rakitin and Alyosha caused some excitement. From the hall they heard Grushenka leap up from the sofa and cry out, "Who's there?"

The maid at once called back to her: "It's not he, only other visitors."

"What can be the matter?" said Rakitin, leading Alyosha into the room.

Grushenka was standing by the sofa, still alarmed. She was not easy till she recognized her visitors.

"Ah, it's you, Rakitin? You quite frightened me. Whom have you brought? Good heavens, you have brought him!" she exclaimed, recognizing Alyosha.

"Do send for candles!" said Rakitin, with the easy air of a close friend.

"Candles... of course, candles.... Fenya, fetch a candle.... Well, what a moment to bring him!" she said, turning to the looking-glass to fix her hair.

She seemed displeased.

"Haven't I managed to please you?" asked Rakitin.

"You frightened me, Rakitin, that's what." Grushenka turned with a smile to Alyosha. "Don't be afraid of me, my dear Alyosha, you cannot think how glad I am to see you. But you frightened me; I thought it was Mitya breaking in. I told him I was going to spend the evening with my old man, and should be there till late counting up his money. Mitya believes I am there, but I came back and have been sitting here, expecting some news. Fenya, run out to the gate to see whether the captain is to be seen! Perhaps he is spying, I am terribly frightened."

"There's no one there, Agrafena Alexandrovna, I've just looked out."

"Are the shutters fastened, Fenya? And we must draw the curtains! He'd rush in at once if he saw a light. I am afraid of your brother Mitya, Alyosha."

Grushenka, though she was alarmed, seemed happy about something.

"Why are you so afraid of Mitya today?" inquired Rakitin. "I should have thought you were not timid with him, you'd twist him round your little finger."

"I am expecting priceless news, so I don't want Mitya at all. I don't feel he believed I would stay at Kuzma Kuzmitch's. He must be in ambush now, in Fyodor Pavlovitch's garden, watching for me. And if he's there, he won't come here, so much the better! But I really have been to Kuzma Kuzmitch's, Mitya escorted me there. I told him I should stay till midnight, and I asked him to be sure to come at midnight to fetch me home. He went away and I sat ten minutes with Kuzma Kuzmitch, then came back here again."

"And why are you so dressed up?"

"I'm expecting a message. If it comes, I shall gallop away and you will see no more of me. That's why I'm dressed up."

"And where are you galloping to?"

"If you know too much, you'll get old too soon."

"I've never seen you like this. You're dressed as if you're going to a ball."

"Much you know about balls," she responded.

"And do you know much about them?"

"I have seen a ball. The year before last, Kuzma Kuzmitch's son was married and I looked on from the gallery. Do you suppose

I want to be talking to you, Rakitin, while a prince like this is standing here! Alyosha, my dear boy, I can't believe my eyes. Good heavens, can you have come to see me! Though this is not the moment to have come, I am awfully glad to see you. Sit down on the sofa, here, my bright young moon. If only you had brought him yesterday, Rakitin, or the day before! But I am glad as it is!"

She sat beside Alyosha on the sofa, looking at him with delight. Her eyes glowed, her lips laughed. Alyosha had not expected to see such a kind expression in her face. He had hardly met her till the day before, and had formed an alarming idea of her. He was greatly surprised to find her altogether different. Her whole manner seemed changed for the better since yesterday. There was scarcely any trace of that mawkish sweetness in her speech. Everything was simple and good-natured, her gestures rapid and direct.

"Dear me, how everything comes together today!" she said. "Why I am so glad to see you, Alyosha, I couldn't say! If you ask me, I couldn't tell you."

"Come, don't you know why you're glad?" said Rakitin, grinning. "You used to be always pestering me to bring him, you'd some object, I suppose."

"I had a different object once, but now that's over. I want you to have something nice. I am so good-natured now. You sit down, too, Rakitin. Look, Alyosha, he's sitting there opposite us, so offended that I didn't ask him to sit down before you. Rakitin is such a one to take offense! Don't be angry, Rakitin, I'm kind today. Why are you so depressed, Alyosha? Are you afraid of me?"

"He'd sad. His elder…" said Rakitin.

"Be quiet! Let me sit on your knee, Alyosha." She jumped, laughing, on his knee, her right arm about his neck. "I'll cheer you up, my pious boy. Will you let me sit on your knee? You won't be angry? If you tell me, I'll get off?"

Alyosha did not speak. He sat afraid to move. He heard her words, "If you tell me, I'll get off," but he did not answer. The grief in his heart swallowed up every sensation that might have been aroused. Yet in spite of his sorrow, he could not help wondering at a new and strange sensation in his heart.

This woman, this "dreadful" woman, had no terror for him now. On the contrary, this woman, dreaded above all women, sitting now on his knee, holding him in her arms, aroused in him now a quite different, unexpected feeling, a feeling of intense and pure interest without a trace of his former terror. That was what surprised him.

"You've talked nonsense enough," cried Rakitin, "you'd much better give us some champagne. You owe it me!"

"Yes, I really do. Do you know, Alyosha, I promised him champagne on top of everything if he'd bring you? I'll have some too! Fenya, bring us the bottle Mitya left! Though I am so stingy, I'll stand a bottle, not for you, Rakitin, you're a toadstool, but he is a falcon! And though my heart is full of something very different, I'll drink with you."

"But what is the matter with you? And what is this message, may I ask, or is it a secret?" Rakitin put in, doing his best not to notice the snubs.

"It's not a secret," Grushenka said, her voice suddenly anxious, turning towards Rakitin, and drawing a little away from Alyosha, though she still sat on his knee with her arm round his neck. "My officer is coming, Rakitin."

"I heard he was coming, but is he so near?"

"He is at Mokroe; he'll send a messenger from there; I got a letter from him today. I am expecting the messenger any minute."

"You don't say so! Why at Mokroe?"

"That's a long story, I've told you enough."

"Mitya'll be up to something now—I say! Does he know or doesn't he?"

"Of course he doesn't! If he knew, there would be murder. But don't remind me of Dmitri Fyodorovitch, he has bruised my heart. And I don't want to think of that at this moment. I can think of Alyosha here, I can look at Alyosha ... smile at me, dear, smile at my foolishness, at my pleasure.... Ah, he's smiling! How kindly he looks at me! And you know, Alyosha, I've been thinking all this time you were angry with me, because of the day before yesterday, because of that young lady. I was a cur, that's the truth.... But it's a good thing it happened. It was a horrid thing, but a good thing too."

Grushenka smiled dreamily, and a little cruel line showed in her smile.

"Mitya told me she screamed that I 'ought to be flogged.' I did insult her dreadfully. She sent for me, she wanted to make a conquest of me.... No, it's a good thing it ended like that.. "But I am still afraid of your being angry."

"That's true," Rakitin put in. "Alyosha, she is really afraid of a chicken like you."

"He is a chicken to you, Rakitin ... because you've no conscience! I love him with all my soul, that's how it is! Alyosha, do you believe I love you with all my soul?"

"Ah, you shameless woman! She is declaring you her lover, Alexey!"

"Well, what of it, I love him!"

"And what about your officer? And the priceless message from Mokroe?"

"That is quite different."

"That's a woman's way of looking at it!"

"Don't you make me angry, Rakitin." Grushenka said hotly. "This is quite different. I love Alyosha in a different way.

It's true, Alyosha, I had designs on you before. For I am a terrible, physical creature. But at other times I've looked upon you as my conscience. I've kept thinking 'how any one like that must despise a nasty thing like me.' I have thought of you a long time in that way, Alyosha, and Mitya knows; I've talked to him about it. Mitya understands. Would you believe it, I sometimes look at you and feel shamed.... How and when I began to think about you like that, I can't say...."

Fenya came in and put a tray with a bottle and three glasses of wine on the table.

"Here's the champagne!" cried Rakitin. "You're excited, Agrafena Alexandrovna, and not yourself. When you've had a glass of champagne, you'll be ready to dance. Eh, they can't even do that properly," he added, looking at the bottle. "The old woman's poured it out in the kitchen and the bottle's been brought in warm and without a cork."

He took a glass, emptied it at one gulp, and poured himself another.

"One doesn't often stumble upon champagne," he said. "Alyosha, take a glass! What shall we drink to? The gates of paradise? Take a glass, Grushenka, too."

She took a glass; Alyosha took his, tasted it, and put it back.

"No, I'd better not," he smiled gently.

"And you bragged!" cried Rakitin.

"Well, if so, I won't either," said Grushenka, "I really don't want any. You can drink the whole bottle, Rakitin. If Alyosha has some, I will."

"What a touching sentiment!" said Rakitin; "and she's sitting on his knee, too! He's got something to grieve over. He is rebelling against his God and ready to eat sausage...."

"How so?"

"His elder died today, Father Zossima, the saint."

"So Father Zossima is dead," cried Grushenka. "Good God, I did not know!" She crossed herself devoutly. "Goodness, what have I been doing, sitting on his knee like this at such a moment!"

She instantly slipped off his knee and sat on the sofa.

Alyosha bent a wondering look at her and a light dawned in his face.

"Rakitin," he said in a firm voice; "don't taunt me with having rebelled against God. I don't want to feel angry with you, so you must be kinder, too, I've lost a treasure such as you have never had. You'd much better look at her—do you see how she has pity on me? I came here to find a wicked soul—I felt drawn to evil because I was base and evil myself, and I've found a true sister, I've found a treasure—a loving heart. She had pity on me.... Agrafena Alexandrovna, I am speaking of you. You've raised my soul from the depths."

Alyosha's lips were quivering.

"She has saved you, it seems," laughed Rakitin. "And she meant to get you in her clutches, do you realize that?"

"Stay, Rakitin." Grushenka jumped up. "Hush, both of you. I'll tell you all about it. Hush, Alyosha, your words make me shamed, for I am bad and not good—that's what I am. And you hush, Rakitin, because you are telling lies. I had the idea of getting him in my clutches, but now you are lying, it's all different. Don't let me hear anything more."

All this Grushenka said with extreme emotion.

"They are both crazy," said Rakitin, looking at them with amazement. "I feel as though I were in a madhouse. They'll begin crying in a minute."

"I shall begin to cry," said Grushenka. "He called me his sister and I shall never forget that. Only let me tell you, Rakitin, though I am bad, I did give away an onion."

"An onion? You are really are crazy."

Rakitin wondered at their enthusiasm, and was annoyed. Though sensitive about everything that concerned himself, he was very thick-skinned as regards the feelings of others.

"You see, Alyosha," Grushenka turned to him with a nervous laugh. "I was boasting when I told Rakitin I had given away an onion, but it's not to boast I tell you about it. It's a nice story. I used to hear it when I was a child from Matryona, my cook. It's like this. "Once upon a time there was a wicked peasant woman who died, leaving not a single good deed behind. The devils caught her and plunged her into the lake of fire. Her guardian angel wondered what good deed of hers he could remember to tell to God.

"'She once pulled up an onion in her garden,' said he, 'and gave it to a beggar.' And God answered: 'Take that onion then, hold it out to her in the lake, and let her take hold and be pulled out. And if you can pull her out of the lake, let her come to Paradise, but if the onion breaks, then the woman must stay where she is.' The angel ran to the woman and held out the onion. 'Come,' said he, 'catch hold and I'll pull you out.' And he began cautiously pulling her out. He had just pulled her out, when the other sinners in the lake, seeing she was being saved, caught hold of her to be pulled out with her. But she was a very wicked woman and began kicking them.

"'I'm to be pulled out, not you. It's my onion, not yours.'

"As soon as she said that, the onion broke. And the woman fell into the lake and is burning there to this day. That's the story, Alyosha; I know it by heart, for I am that wicked woman. I boasted to Rakitin that I had given away an onion, but to you I'll say: 'I've done nothing but give away one onion all my life, that's the only good deed I've done.' So don't praise me, Alyosha, don't think me good, I am bad, I am a wicked woman and you shame me if you praise me. I must confess everything. Alyosha. I was so anxious to get hold of you that I promised Rakitin twenty-five rubles if he would bring you to me.

She went to the table, opened a drawer, and took from it a twenty-five ruble note.

"What nonsense! What nonsense!" cried Rakitin.

"Take it. Rakitin, I owe it you, there's no fear of your refusing it, you asked for it." And she threw the note to him.

"Likely I should refuse it," said Rakitin. "That will come in very handy; fools are made for wise men's profit."

"Now hold your tongue, Rakitin, what I am going to say now is not for your ears. Sit in that corner and keep quiet. You don't like us, so hold your tongue."

"What should I like you for?" Rakitin said, not concealing his ill-humor.

He put the note in his pocket, shamed at Alyosha's seeing it. He had reckoned on receiving his payment later, without Alyosha's knowing. Now, losing his temper, he said:

"One loves people for a reason, but what have either of you done for me?"

"You should love people without a reason, as Alyosha does."

"How does he love you? How has he shown it that you make such a fuss?"

Grushenka said with heat: "Hush, Rakitin, you know nothing about us! And don't dare speak to me like that again. How dare you be so familiar!

"Sit in that corner and be quiet! And now, Alyosha, I'll tell you the whole truth., that you may see what a wretch I am! I wanted to ruin you, that's the truth. I wanted to so much that I bribed Rakitin to bring you. And why did I want to do such a thing? I've looked at you a hundred times before today; I began asking everyone about you. Your face haunted me. 'He despises me,' I thought; 'he won't even look at me.' I wondered at being so frightened of a boy.

"I'll get him in my clutches and laugh at him. I was full of anger. Would you believe it, nobody dares talk or think of coming to Agrafena Alexandrovna with any evil purpose. Old Kuzma is the only man I have anything to do with here. But looking at you, I thought, I'll get him in my clutches and laugh at him. You see what a spiteful cur I am, and you called me your sister! And now that man who wronged me has come; I sit here waiting for a message from him. And do you know what that man has been to me?

"Five years ago, when Kuzma brought me here, I used to sit here sobbing; I used to lie awake all night, thinking: 'Where is he now, the man who wronged me? If only I could see him again, I'd pay him out!' At night I used to lie sobbing into my pillow in the dark; I used to tear my heart and gloat over my anger. 'I'll pay him back!' That's what I used to cry out in the dark. And when I thought he was laughing at me, or had forgotten me, I would fling myself on the floor, melt into helpless tears, and lie there shaking till dawn.

"In the morning I'd get up spiteful, ready to tear the whole world to pieces. I began saving money, I became hard-hearted, grew stout—grew wiser, would you say? No, no one knows it, but when night comes, I lie sometimes as I did five years ago, clenching my teeth and crying all night, thinking, 'I'll pay him out!' Do you hear? Well then, now you understand me. A month ago a letter came—he was coming, he was a widower, he wanted to see me. It took my breath away; I thought: 'If he comes and whistles to me, I shall creep back to him like a beaten dog.' I couldn't believe myself. Am I so abject? I've been in such a rage all this month that I am worse than I was five years ago.

"Do you see now, Alyosha, what a violent creature I am? I have shown you the truth! I played with Mitya to keep me from running to that other. Hush, Rakitin, I am not speaking to you. Before you came in, I was lying here brooding, deciding my whole future, and you can never know what was in my heart. Alyosha, tell your young lady not to be angry with me for what happened.... Nobody in the whole world knows what I am going through, and no one ever can know....For perhaps I shall take a knife with me today, I can't decide ..."

At this "tragic" phrase Grushenka broke down, hid her face in her hands, flung herself on the sofa pillows, and sobbed like a little child.

Alyosha got up and went to Rakitin.

"Misha," he said, "don't be angry. She hurt you, but you heard what she said just now? How much can one endure? You must be merciful."

Alyosha said this at the prompting of his heart. If Rakitin had not been there, he would have spoken to the air. But Rakitin looked at him ironically and Alyosha stopped.

"You were so primed with your elder's teaching last night that now you have to let it off on me, Alexey, man of God!" said Rakitin, with a smile of hatred.

"Don't talk of the dead, Rakitin—he was better than anyone in the world!" cried Alyosha with tears in his voice. "I didn't speak to you as a judge but as the lowest of the judged. What am I beside her? I came here seeking my ruin.' But she, after five years in torment, as soon as any one says a word from the heart to her—it makes her forgive everything!

"The man who wronged her has come back and sends for her, and she forgives him, and hastens to meet him. I am not like that. I don't know whether you are, Misha, but I am not. It's a lesson to me.... She is more loving than we.... Have you heard her speak before of what she just told us? If you had, you'd have understood her long ago ... and the person insulted the other day must forgive her, too! She will, when she knows ... This soul is not yet at peace ... there is a treasure in that soul...."

Alyosha stopped to catch his breath. In spite of his ill-humor Rakitin looked at him with astonishment. He had never expected such a tirade from him.

"She's found someone to plead her cause! Why, are you in love with her? Agrafena Alexandrovna, our monk's in love with you, you've made a conquest!" he cried.

Grushenka lifted her head from the pillow and looked at Alyosha with a tender smile on her tear-stained face.

"Let him alone, Alyosha, my angel; you see what he is, not a person for you to speak to." She turned to Rakitin. "I meant to beg your pardon for being rude to you, but now I won't. Alyosha, come to me, sit down here."

She beckoned to him with a smile. "Tell me," she said, taking him by the hand and peeping into his face, smiling. "Do I love that man or not? The man who wronged me? Before you came, that's what I kept asking my heart. Decide for me, Alyosha, it shall be as you say. Am I to forgive him or not?"

"But you have forgiven him already," said Alyosha, smiling.

"Yes, I really have," Grushenka said. "What an abject heart! To my abject   heart!" She took a glass from the table, emptied it at a gulp, and flung it on the floor. The glass broke with a crash. A little cruel line came into her smile.

"Perhaps I haven't forgiven him," she said, menace in her voice. "Perhaps my heart is only getting ready to forgive. I shall struggle with my heart. You see, Alyosha, I've grown to love my tears.... Perhaps I only love my resentment...."

"Well, I shouldn't care to be in his shoes," said Rakitin.

"Well, you won't be, Rakitin, you'll never be in his shoes. You shall black my shoes, that's the place for you. You'll never get a woman like me, and he won't either, perhaps."

"Won't he? Then why are you dressed up like that?" said Rakitin.

"Don't taunt me with dressing up, Rakitin, you don't know all that is in my heart! If I choose to tear off my finery, I'll tear it off ," she cried. "You don't know what that finery is for! Perhaps I shall see him and say: 'Have you ever seen me look like this before?' He left me a thin cry-baby of seventeen. I'll sit by him, fascinate him, and work him up. 'Do you see what I am like now?' I'll say to him; 'well, and that's enough for you, my dear sir, there's many a slip between cup and lip!' That may be what the finery is for, Rakitin. I'm angry and full of hate, Alyosha, I'll tear off my finery, I'll destroy my beauty, I'll scorch my face, slash it with a knife, and turn beggar, if I choose. If I choose, I'll send Kuzma back all he has ever given me, and go out cleaning houses for the rest of my life. You think I wouldn't do it, Rakitin? I would, only don't exasperate me ... I'll send him about his business, I'll snap my fingers, he shall never see me again!"

She uttered the last words in a scream, but broke down again, hid her face in her hands, buried it in the pillow, and shook with sobs.

Rakitin got up.

"It's time we left," he said, "it's late; we shall be shut out."

Grushenka leapt up from her place.

"You don't want to go, Alyosha!" she cried. "What are you doing to me? You've stirred up my feelings, tortured me, and now you'll leave me to face this night alone!"

"He can hardly spend the night with you! Though if he wants to, let him! I'll go alone," Rakitin said.

"Quiet, evil tongue! You never said such words to me as he has."

"What has he said to you so special?" asked Rakitin.

"I can't say, I don't know. I don't know what he said to me, it went straight to my heart; he has wrung my heart.... He is the first, the only one who has pitied me, that's what it is. Why did you not come before, you angel?"

She fell on her knees before him.

"I've been waiting all my life for someone like you, I knew that someone like you would come and forgive me. I believed that, nasty as I am, someone would really love me, not only with a shameful love!"

"What have I done to you?" said Alyosha, bending over her with a smile, gently taking her by the hands; "I only gave you a tiny little onion, that' all!"

He was moved to tears himself as he said it.

At that moment there was a noise in the passage as someone came in.

Grushenka jumped up, alarmed.

Fenya ran into the room, crying out: "Mistress darling, a messenger has come. A carriage from Mokroe for you, Timofey the driver, with three horses, they are putting in fresh horses.... A letter, here's the letter, mistress."

A letter was in her hand and she waved it in the air while she talked.

Grushenka snatched the letter from her and carried it to the candle. It was only a note, a few lines. She read it in one instant.

"He has sent for me," she cried. "He whistles! And I crawl back!"

For an instant she stood as though hesitating; the blood rushed to her head.

"I will go," she cried. "Five years of my life! Good-by, Alyosha, my fate is sealed. Go, leave me, don't let me see you again! Grushenka is flying to a new life.... Don't you remember evil against me. I may be going to my death!"

She left them and ran into her bedroom.

"Well, she has no thoughts for us now!" said Rakitin. "Let's go, or we may hear that female cry again. I am sick of all these tears and cries."

Alyosha let himself be led out. In the yard was a covered cart. Horses were being taken out of the shafts; men were running to and fro with lanterns. Fresh horses were being led in at the gate. But when Alyosha and Rakitin reached the bottom of the steps, Grushenka's bedroom window was opened, and she called:

"Alyosha, give my greetings to Mitya and tell him not to remember evil against me. Tell him, too, in my words: 'Grushenka has fallen to a scoundrel, and not to you, noble heart.' And add, too, that Grushenka loved him only one hour—let him remember that hour all his life—say, 'Grushenka tells you to!'"

She ended in a voice full of sobs. The window was shut with a slam.

"H'm!" growled Rakitin, laughing, "She murders your brother Mitya and then tells him to remember it all his life! What nerve!"

Alyosha made no reply. He walked beside Rakitin, lost in thought. Rakitin felt a twinge, as though he had been touched on an open wound. He expected something different by bringing Grushenka and Alyosha together.

"He is a Pole, that officer of hers," he began, "and he is not an officer now. He served in the customs in Siberia, somewhere on the Chinese frontier, some little beggar of a Pole, I expect. Lost his job, they say. He's heard now that Grushenka has saved a little money, so he's turned up again."

Again Alyosha seemed not to hear. Rakitin could not control himself.

"Well, so you've saved the sinner?" he laughed. "Have you turned the Magdalene into the true path? Driven out the seven devils?"

"Hush, Rakitin," Alyosha answered with an aching heart.

"So you despise me now for those twenty-five rubles? I've sold my friend, you think. But you are not Christ, you know, and I am not Judas."

"Oh, Rakitin, I assure you I'd forgotten about it," cried Alyosha.

This was the last straw for Rakitin.

"Damn you all!" he cried. "Why the devil did I take you up? I don't want to know you from this time forward. Go alone, there's your road!"

And he turned into another street, leaving Alyosha alone in the dark.

Chapter IV

Alyosha Leaves the Monastery

It was late when Alyosha returned to the hermitage. He opened the door and went into the elder's cell, where his coffin was standing. There was no one there but Father Païssy, reading the Gospel over the coffin. Though he heard Alyosha come in, he did not turn.

Alyosha began to pray. He saw the coffin before him, the hidden dead figure so precious to him, but the grief of the morning was no longer in his soul. Fragments of thought floated through him, yet there reigned in him a sense of the wholeness of all—something comforting. He longed to pour out his thankfulness and love.... Instead he listened to Father Païssy.

Alyosha fell asleep on his knees, but now he got up and with three rapid steps went to the coffin. Father Païssy raised his eyes for an instant from his book, but looked away again at once, seeing that something strange was happening to the boy.

Alyosha gazed for half a minute at the coffin, at the motionless man in the coffin with the icon on his breast. Then suddenly he turned and went out. He went quickly down the steps; his soul, overflowing with rapture, yearned for openness.

The vault of heaven, full of soft, shining stars, stretched above him. The Milky Way ran in pale streams to the horizon. The fresh, still night enfolded the earth. The autumn flowers, in the beds round the house, were sleeping till morning. The silence of earth seemed to melt into the silence of the heavens.

Alyosha stood gazing, and suddenly threw himself on the earth. He did not know why he embraced it. He could not have told why he longed to kiss it. But he did it, sobbing and watering it with his tears, and vowed passionately to love it forever.

"Water the earth with the tears of your joy and love those tears," echoed in his soul.

What was he weeping over?

In his joy he was weeping over those stars which were shining to him from the abyss of space, and he was not ashamed of that joy. There seemed to be threads from all those many worlds of God linking his soul to them, and it was trembling in contact with other worlds. He longed to forgive everyone for everything, and to beg forgiveness—not for himself, but for all men, for all and for everything.

"And others are praying for me too," echoed in his thoughts. With every instant he felt that something as firm as that vast heaven had entered into him. It was as though an idea had seized rule over his mind—and it was for all his life.

He had fallen on the earth a weak boy, but he rose a man; he felt it at the very moment of his joy. Never, all his life, would Alyosha forget that minute.

"Someone visited me in that hour," he used to say.

Within three days he left the monastery as his elder had wished.

Book VII • Mitya

Chapter I

Kuzma Samsonov

Dmitri, to whom Grushenka had left her greetings, knew nothing of what had happened to her, and was in a state of great anxiety. Alyosha had not been able to find him the morning before, and he had not met Ivan at the tavern.

He spent those days rushing in all directions. Though Grushenka had loved him for an hour, yet she tortured him cruelly. The worst of it was he could never tell what she meant to do. He was persuaded that Fyodor Pavlovitch would offer Grushenka lawful wedlock, but did not believe the old man would gain his object for three thousand rubles. But it never occurred to him to think of the "officer," the other man in Grushenka's life.

It is true that of late Grushenka had been very silent about it. Yet he knew of a letter she received a month ago from her seducer, but he simply did not believe in a suitor who suddenly turned up after five years. Also, in the "officer's" first letter the possibility of a visit was vague. Grushenka told him nothing of what had passed later; so by degrees he forgot the officer's existence.

With a sinking heart he expected Grushenka's decision, that suddenly she would say to him: "Take me, I'm yours forever," and he would marry her and they would begin a new life somewhere. If only it were not for these people, his circumstances, this cursed place—he would enter on a new path. But all this could only be if the *happy* solution occurred. There was still the possibility she might say: "Go away. I have come to terms with Fyodor Pavlovitch. I am going to marry him."

Up to the last hour Mitya didn't know what would happen. He watched and spied in agony, while preparing himself for the happy solution. But for that ending a different anxiety arose. If she were to say to him: "I'm yours; take me away," where would he get the money? All sources of revenue from Fyodor Pavlovitch had ceased. Grushenka had money, but Mitya wanted to begin their new life at his own expense.

He made up his mind to return Katerina Ivanovna that three thousand *first of all*. This decision was reached after his interview with Alyosha two days before. Dmitri felt it would be better "to murder and rob someone than fail to pay my debt to Katya. I'd rather be thought a robber and murderer than that Katya should have the right to say I deceived her and stole her money to run away with Grushenka!"

He kept hoping the three thousand would come to him of itself somehow, as though it might drop from heaven. He had the most fantastic ideas. One was the idea of going to Samsonov, Grushenka's protector, to propose a "scheme" to him, and by means of it get the sum he needed. Of the commercial value of his scheme he had no doubt; he was only uncertain how Samsonov would look at it. For some reason he was sure that the old man, at death's door, would not object to Grushenka marrying a man "she could depend on".

Mitya looked on Grushenka's past as something completely over. Once Grushenka told him she loved him and would marry him, it would be the beginning of a new life. As for Kuzma Samsonov, Dmitri saw him as a man who had exercised a fateful influence in Grushenka's remote past, and was now completely done with. Besides, it was known to everyone the old man was a wreck whose relations with Grushenka were now paternal.

After Mitya's conversation with Alyosha at the cross-roads, he hardly slept, and at ten o'clock the next morning he was at the house of Samsonov, a large and gloomy old house of two stories. When he was informed of the arrival of the "captain," he refused to see him. But Mitya sent his name up again. The old man again refused to see him. Mitya had foreseen this and brought pencil and paper with him. He wrote: "On most important business concerning Agrafena Alexandrovna," and sent it up to the old man. After a little thought, Samsonov told the lad to take the visitor to the drawing-room.

When the old man appeared, Mitya jumped up. The old man stood dignified and straight, and Mitya felt at once that he had looked him through and through. Samsonov bowed and motioned him to a chair. Leaning on his son's arm, he lowered himself on the sofa opposite, groaning painfully. Mitya, seeing his painful exertions, felt insignificant in his presence.

"What is it you want of me, sir?" asked the old man.

Mitya leapt up, but sat down again.

"Most honored sir, Kuzma Kuzmitch, you have no doubt heard of my disputes with my father, Fyodor Pavlovitch Karamazov, who stole my inheritance.... Grushenka might have told you about it... I beg your pardon, Agrafena Alexandrovna... a lady for whom I have the highest respect."

So Mitya began, breaking down at the first sentence.

Three months ago, he said, he consulted "Pavel Porneplodov. You have perhaps heard of him? He's a lawyer. He knows you ... spoke of you in the highest terms." This Korneplodov, after questioning him and inspecting the documents he brought (Mitya was vague about these), reported they certainly might proceed against his father in regard to the village of Tchermashnya, which ought to have come to Mitya from his mother. He told Mitya he might count on as much as six or even seven thousand rubles from Fyodor Pavlovitch, as Tchermashnya was worth at least twenty-five, or "thirty thousand rubles."

"Kuzma Kuzmitch, and would you believe it, I didn't get seventeen from that man!"

Mitya had thrown the business up for the time, he said, knowing nothing about the law, but on coming here was struck dumb by a cross-claim made upon him (here Mitya went vague again), "so will not you, excellent and honored Kuzma Kuzmitch, be willing to take up my claims against that monster, and pay me a sum of only three thousand. You see, you cannot, in any case, lose over it. On the contrary, you may make six or seven thousand instead of three." Above all, he wanted this concluded that very day.

"I'll do the business with you at a notary's, or whatever it is ... in fact, I'm ready to do anything.... I'll hand over all the deeds ... whatever you want, sign anything ... and we could draw up the agreement at once ... and if it were only possible.... You could pay me that three thousand, and so would save me from ... for an honorable action.... For I cherish the most honorable feelings for a certain person, whom you know well and care for as a father. I would not have come otherwise. So as you see...."

"You see, sir, business of that sort's not in our line," said Kuzmitch. "There's the court, and the lawyers—it's a perfect misery. But there is a man here you might apply to."

"Good heavens! Who is it? You're my salvation, Kuzma Kuzmitch!"

"He is a peasant who does business in timber. His name is Lyagavy. He's been haggling with Fyodor Pavlovitch for the last year over your copse at Tchermashnya. They can't agree on the price, maybe you've heard? Now he's come back again and is staying with the priest at Ilyinskoe, about twelve miles from the Volovya station. He wrote to me asking my advice. Fyodor Pavlovitch means to go and see him himself. So if you were to get there first and make Lyagavy the offer you've made me, he might possibly—"

"A brilliant idea!" Mitya interrupted. "He's the very man. He's haggling with him for it, and here he would have all the documents entitling him to the property itself!"

Mitya suddenly laughed, startling Samsonov.

"How can I thank you, Kuzma Kuzmitch?" cried Mitya.

"Don't mention it," said Samsonov.

"You've saved me!"

"No need of thanks."

"I'll fly there. I'm afraid I've over-taxed your strength. I shall never forget it."Mitya seized his hand to press it, but there was an evil gleam in the old man's eye. Mitya drew back his hand, but at once blamed himself for his mistrust.

"It's because he's tired," he thought.

"For her sake, Kuzma Kuzmitch! You understand, it's for her!"

He bowed and walked to the door without looking back.

"Everything was on the verge of ruin and my guardian angel saved me," he was thinking. And if such a business-man as Samsonov suggested this course, then ... then success was assured. He would fly off immediately.

"I'll be back before night, and the thing is done," thought Mitya. He could imagine nothing but that the advice was practical "from a man with an understanding of business, with an understanding of this Lyagavy." Or—the old man was laughing at him.

When Mitya had gone, Kuzma Kuzmitch, white with rage, turned to his son and told him see to it that that beggar never be let in again. He did not utter a threat. But even his son, who often saw him enraged, trembled with fear.

Chapter II

Lyagavy

He must drive at full speed and had not the money for horses. All he had left was forty pennies. He had a silver watch at home, which he carried to a watch-maker in the market-place, who gave him six rubles for it. He seized his six rubles and ran home, where he borrowed three rubles from the people of the house. In his excitement he told them his fate would be decided that day, and of the scheme he had put before Samsonov.

Having thus collected nine rubles, he sent for horses to take him to Volovya station.

Though radiant with the thought he would at last solve all his difficulties, as he drew near Volovya station he trembled at the thought of what Grushenka might be doing in his absence. What if she made up her mind to go to Fyodor Pavlovitch?

"I must get back tonight," he said as he jolted along, "and I dare say I shall have to bring this Lyagavy back here ... to draw up the deed."

So mused Mitya, though his dreams were not to be carried out. To begin with he was late; taking a short cut from Volovya station turned out to be eighteen miles instead of twelve. And he did not find the priest at home at Ilyinskoe but had to look for him. And though Lyagavy had been staying with the priest, he was now at Suhoy Possyolok, staying the night in the forester's cottage, as he was buying timber there. At Mitya's request to take him to Lyagavy, and by so doing "save him," the priest finally agreed.

Mitya began talking to him of his plans, asking advice in regard to Lyagavy. The priest listened attentively but gave little advice. He turned off Mitya's questions with: "I don't know. I can't say," and so on. When Mitya began to speak of his quarrel with his father, it alarmed the priest, as he was in some way dependent on Fyodor Pavlovitch. However, he asked with surprise why he called the peasant-trader Gorstkin, Lyagavy, and explained that, though the man's name really was Lyagavy, he was never called so, as he would be grievously offended, and that he must call him Gorstkin.

Mitya was surprised, and explained that that was what Samsonov called him. On hearing this, the priest dropped the subject, though he would have done well to put into words his doubt whether, if Samsonov had called the peasant Lyagavy, there was not something wrong. But Mitya had no time to pause over such trifles. Only when they reached Suhoy Possyolok did he realize they had come not one mile, but at least three.

They went into the hut. The forester lived in one half, and Gorstkin lodged in the other. They went into that room and lighted a candle. The hut was overheated. On the table was a samovar that had gone out, a tray with cups, an empty rum bottle, a bottle of vodka partly full, and some half-eaten crusts of bread. The visitor himself lay stretched out on the bench with his coat crushed up under his head for a pillow, snoring heavily.

Mitya stood wondering what to do.

"Of course I must wake him. My business is too important," he said.

But the priest and the forester stood in silence, giving no opinion.

Mitya began trying to wake him, but the sleeper did not wake.

"He's drunk," Mitya decided. "Good Lord! What am I to do?"

He pulled him by the arms and legs and shook him, yet he only succeeded in getting the drunken man to utter grunts and curses.

"You'd better wait a little," the priest said, "for he's not in a fit state."

"He's been drinking the whole day," the forester said.

"Good God!" cried Mitya. "If only you knew how important it is to me!"

"You'd better wait till morning," the priest repeated.

"Till morning? That's impossible!"

He was about to attack the sleeping man again, but realized it was useless.

The priest said to him very reasonably that if he succeeded in wakening the man, he would still be drunk and not able to hold a conversation. "Your business is important," he said, "so you'd certainly better put it off till morning."

With a gesture of despair Mitya agreed.

"Father, I will stay here with a light. As soon as he wakes I'll begin. I'll pay you for the light," he said to the forester, "and the night's lodging. But Father, I don't know what we're to do with you. Where will you sleep?"

"I'm going home. I'll take his horse," he said, indicating the forester.

So it was settled. The priest rode off on the forester's horse, delighted to escape, though wondering uneasily whether he ought to inform Fyodor Pavlovitch of this curious incident, "or he may hear of it, be angry, and withdraw his favor."

The forester and Mitya sat on the bench to "catch the favorable moment," as Mitya expressed it. He was terribly dejected and could reach no conclusion. The candle burnt dimly; it became close in the overheated room. He saw the garden of his father's house, the door open, Grushenka running in, and he leapt up from the bench. He went to the sleeping man and looked in his face. It was a long face, with flaxen curls, and a thin, reddish beard. From the pocket of waistcoat pocket peeped the chain of a silver watch. Mitya looked at him with hatred. What was humiliating was that, after making sacrifices and utterly worn out, he should, with business of such urgency, be standing over this dolt on whom his whole fate depended, while he snored away.

"How dishonorable it all is!" cried Mitya.

His head began to ache. "Should he give up and go away?" he wondered. "No, I'll wait till tomorrow. What else did I come for? Besides, I've no means of going. How am I to get away from here now? Oh, the idiocy of it!"

He sat without moving and fell asleep. He seemed to have slept for two hours or more, when he was waked by his head aching so he could have screamed. It was a long time before he waked fully and understood what had happened. The room was full of fumes from the stove. The drunken peasant still lay snoring, the candle about to go out. Mitya staggered across the passage into the forester's room. The forester waked at once.

"But he's dead, he's dead! What am I to do?" cried Mitya.

The forester went with him, and they threw open the doors and a window.

"It'll be all right, now," the forester said.

He went back to sleep, leaving Mitya the lantern. Mitya fussed about the drunken peasant for half an hour, wetting his head, resolving not to sleep all night. But he was so worn out that when he sat down for a moment, he closed his eyes and slept like the dead.

It was late when he woke. The sun was shining in the two little windows of the hut. The curly-headed peasant was sitting on the bench with his coat on. He had another bottle in front of him. The other one had been finished and the new one was half empty.

Mitya saw at once that the peasant was drunk again. He went to him and stared at him. The peasant slyly watched him.

"Excuse me, I...you've most likely heard from the forester why I'm here. I'm Dmitri Karamazov, the son of old Karamazov whose woods you're buying."

"That's a lie!" said the peasant.

"A lie? You know Fyodor Pavlovitch?"

"I don't know any of Fyodor Pavlovitches," said the peasant.

"You're bargaining with him for the woods. Do wake up, and collect yourself. Father Pavel of Ilyinskoe brought me here. You wrote to Samsonov; he sent me to you."

"You're l-lying!" Lyagavy blurted out again.

Mitya's legs went cold.

"For mercy's sake! It isn't a joke! You're drunk, perhaps. Yet you can speak and understand ... or else ... I understand nothing!"

"You're a painter!"

"For mercy's sake! I'm Dmitri Karamazov. I have an offer to make you concerning the copse!"

The peasant stroked his beard.

"No, you've contracted for the job and turned out a scoundrel!"

"I assure you you're mistaken," cried Mitya, wringing his hands.

The peasant stroked his beard and screwed up his eyes.

"No, you tell me the law that allows roguery. You're a scoundrel! D'you hear?"

Mitya stepped back. Something seemed to hit him on the head. In an instant he grasped it all. He stood stupefied, wondering how he could have yielded to such folly. "Why, the man's dead drunk and will go on drinking for a week; what's the use of waiting here? And what if Samsonov sent me here on purpose? Oh, God, what have I done?"

The peasant sat watching him and grinning.

Another time Mitya might have killed the fool in a fury, but now he felt as weak as a child. He went to the bench and took up his coat. Not finding the forester in his room, he took fifty pennies from his pocket and put them on the table for his night's lodging.

Coming out of the hut he saw nothing but forest. He walked, not knowing which way to turn. Hurrying there with the priest, he had not noticed the road. He walked along a narrow path, aimless, without heeding where he was going. He got out of the forest somehow, and a vista of bare fields stretched as far as the eye could see.

"What despair! What death all round!" he said.

He was saved by an old merchant who was being driven across country in a hired trap. When he overtook him, Mitya asked the way, and it turned out the old merchant, too, was going to Volovya. After some discussion Mitya got into the trap.

Three hours later they arrived at Volovya, and Mitya ordered horses to drive home, but suddenly realized he was hungry. While the horses were being harnessed, he ate an omelet, plus a huge hunk of bread and a sausage, and swallowed three glasses of vodka.

His spirits grew lighter. He flew towards the town, urging on the driver, and made a new plan to get the "cursed" money. "I'll settle it today." And if it had not been for the thought of Grushenka and of what might have happened to her, he would have become quite cheerful again.... But the thought of her stabbed him to the heart, like a sharp knife.

At last they arrived, and he at once ran to Grushenka.

Chapter III

Gold Mines

This was the visit of Mitya of which Grushenka spoke to Rakitin with such terror. She was expecting the "message," and was relieved that Mitya had not been to see her. She hoped that "please God he won't come till I'm gone," and he suddenly burst in on her.

To get him off her hands she suggested he should walk with her to Samsonov's, where she said she must "settle his accounts," but at the gate she made him promise to come at twelve o'clock to take her home.

Mitya was delighted at it being so arranged. If she was at Samsonov's she could not be going to Fyodor Pavlovitch's.

After leaving her at the gate he rushed home.

"Now I must hurry and find out from Smerdyakov whether anything happened there last night, whether she went to Fyodor Pavlovitch!" he said to himself.

Before he reached his lodging, jealousy surged up again. The first thing to do was to get at least a small loan of money. The nine rubles was almost all gone. He had dueling pistols in a case, which he had not pawned till then because he prized them. In the tavern he had met a young official who was very fond of weapons.

Mitya went straight to him and offered to pawn his pistols to him for ten rubles. The official, delighted, tried to get him to sell them outright. But Mitya would not consent, so the man gave him ten rubles. Mitya then rushed towards Fyodor Pavlovitch's by the back way to get hold of Smerdyakov.

From Marya Kondratyevna (the woman living near Fyodor Pavlovitch's) he learned of Smerdyakov's illness—his fall, his fit, the doctor's visit, and Fyodor Pavlovitch's anxiety.

"Who'll keep watch? Who'll bring me word?"

He began questioning the women whether they had seen anything the evening before. They quite understood what he was trying to find out, and assured him no one had been there. He would certainly have to keep watch today, but where? Here or at Samsonov's gate? He decided he must be on the lookout both here and there. Meanwhile he had to carry out the plan he had made on the journey back. He was sure of its success, but he must not delay acting on it. He resolved to sacrifice an hour.

"In an hour I shall know everything, and settle everything. But first to Samsonov's. I'll make sure Grushenka's there, come back here till eleven, then go to bring her home."

He flew home, combed his hair, brushed his clothes, and went to Madame Hohlakov's to borrow three thousand from her, convinced she would not refuse. He knew she didn't like him and, for some reason, desired that Katerina Ivanovna should throw him over and marry Ivan. But that morning in the cart a brilliant idea struck him:

"If she is so anxious I should not marry Katerina Ivanovna, why should she refuse me the money that would make it possible for me to leave Katya forever?"

His "plan" was based, as before, on the offer of his rights to Tchermashnya as security for the debt. Mitya gave himself up to this new idea with great hope. Yet, when he mounted the steps of Madame Hohlakov's he felt a shiver of fear. He saw that this was his last hope, that nothing else was left but to "rob and murder someone for the money."

It was half-past seven when he rang the bell.

At first fortune seemed to smile upon him.

As soon as he was announced he was received with great rapidity. As soon as he entered the drawing-room, the lady of the house herself ran in and declared: "I was expecting you!"

"That is certainly wonderful, madam," said Mitya, "but I have come to you on a matter of great importance.... for me, that is, madam, and I hurried—"

"I know you've come on important business, Dmitri Fyodorovitch; you couldn't help coming, after all that has passed with Katerina Ivanovna; you couldn't, that's a certainty."

"The realism of life, madam, that's what it is. But allow me to explain—"

"Dmitri Fyodorovitch. You've heard that Father Zossima is dead?"

"No, madam, it's the first I've heard of it."

The image of Alyosha rose to his mind.

"Last night, and only imagine—"

"Madam," said Mitya, "I can imagine nothing except that I'm desperate, and if you don't help me, everything will come to grief. Excuse me, but I'm in a fever—"

"I know you're in a fever. You could hardly fail to be. Whatever you may say, I already know. I have long been thinking over your destiny, studying it...."

"Madam," said Mitya, trying to be polite, "I feel that if you are watching over my destiny in this way, you will help me in my ruin, and so allow me to explain to you the plan with which I have come to you ... and what, madam—"

"Don't explain it. It's of secondary importance. As for help, you're not the first I have helped, Dmitri Fyodorovitch. You ask for a certain sum, three thousand, but I can give you much more. I will save you, Dmitri Fyodorovitch."

Mitya started from his seat.

"Madam, will you really be so good! Good God, you've saved me! You have saved a man from death, from a bullet.... My eternal gratitude—"

"I will give you infinitely more than three thousand!" she cried.

"But I don't need so much. I only need three thousand, and I can give security for that sum. I propose a plan which—"

"Enough, Dmitri Fyodorovitch, it's said and done." Madame Hohlakov cut him short. "I have promised to save you, and I will. What do you think of the gold mines?"

"Gold mines, madam? I have never thought anything about them."

"I have thought of them for you. I have been watching you. I've watched you a hundred times as you've walked past, saying to myself: That's a man of energy who ought to be at the gold mines. From your walk I concluded: that's a man who would find gold."

"From my walk, madam?"

"Yes, from your walk. You surely don't deny that character can be told from one's walk, Dmitri Fyodorovitch? Science supports the idea. I'm all for science and realism. After all this business with Father Zossima, I want to devote myself to practical things!"

"But, madam, the three thousand you promised to lend me—"

"It is yours, Dmitri Fyodorovitch," Madame Hohlakov cut in at once. "The money is as good as in your pocket, not three thousand, but three million, in less than no time. I'll make you a present of the idea: you shall find gold mines, and make millions—"

"Madam!" Dmitri interrupted with an uneasy feeling. "I shall perhaps follow your advice.... I shall perhaps set off...to the gold-mines.... I'll come and see you again about it...but now, that three thousand you so generously...oh, that would set me free, and if you could today...you see, I haven't a minute to lose—"

"Enough, Dmitri Fyodorovitch!" Madame Hohlakov interrupted. "The question is, will you go to the gold mines or not? Answer yes or no."

"I will go, madam, afterwards.... I'll go where you like...but now—"

"Wait!" cried Madame Hohlakov.

Jumping up and running to a bureau with numerous little drawers, she pulled out one drawer after another, desperately looking for something.

"The three thousand," thought Mitya, his heart racing, "and without any formalities...that's doing things in style! She's a fine woman, if only she didn't talk so much!"

"Here!" cried Madame Hohlakov, running back joyfully to Mitya.

It was a tiny silver icon on a cord.

"This is from Kiev, Dmitri Fyodorovitch," she went on, "from the relics of the Holy Martyr, Varvara. Let me put it on you and dedicate you to a new life."

She actually put the cord round his neck and began arranging it.

"Now you can set off," she said.

"Madam, I am so touched. I don't know how to thank you... but...if only you knew how precious time is to me.... That sum of money, for which I shall be indebted to you.... Madam, since you are so kind," Mitya exclaimed, "let me tell to you...though, of course, you've known it a long time...that I love.... I've been false to Katya Ivanovna.... I've done her wrong, but I fell in love with another woman...a woman you, madam, perhaps, look down on, but whom I cannot leave—"

"Leave it all, Dmitri Fyodorovitch," Madame Hohlakov said. "Especially women. Gold mines are your goal, and there's no place for women there. Afterwards, when you come back rich, you will find the girl of your heart, a modern girl of education and advanced ideas. By that time the dawning woman question...."

"Madam, that's not the point at all."

"Yes, it is, Dmitri Fyodorovitch, just the thing you're yearning for. I am not at all opposed to the present woman movement. People don't know that side of me.... Good Heavens, what is the matter!"

"Madam!" cried Mitya, jumping up and clasping his hands before her. "You will make me weep if you delay what you have so generously—"

"Oh, do weep, Dmitri Fyodorovitch! That's a noble feeling... such a path lies open to you! Tears will ease your heart, and later you will return to share—"

"But allow me!" Mitya cried. "For the last time I beg you, tell me, can I have the sum you promised me today; if not now, when?"

"What sum, Dmitri Fyodorovitch?"

"The three thousand you promised me so generously—"

"Three thousand? Rubles? Oh, no, I haven't got three thousand." Mitya was stunned.

"Why, just now ... you said it was as good as in my hands—"

"Oh, no, you didn't understand me, Dmitri Fyodorovitch. I was talking of the gold mines. It's true I promised you more, but I meant the gold mines."

"But the money? The three thousand?" Mitya exclaimed.

"Oh, if you meant money, I haven't a penny, Dmitri Fyodorovitch. And if I had, I wouldn't give it to you. I never lend money. Also, I wouldn't give it to you because I like you and want to save you. The gold mines…!"

"Oh, the devil!" roared Mitya, bringing his fist down on the table.

"Aie! Aie!" cried Madame Hohlakov.

Alarmed, she flew to the other end of the room. Mitya strode out of the house!

He walked like one possessed, beating himself on the breast. What those blows upon his breast meant, *on that spot*, was, for the time, a secret which was known to no one in the world. That secret meant for him more than disgrace; it meant ruin, suicide. He had determined, if he did not get the three thousand to pay his debt to Katerina Ivanovna, and so remove from his breast *that spot*, the shame he carried, it was the end. His last hope vanished, he burst out crying like a child.

He walked, not knowing what he was doing, wiping away his tears with his fist. In this way he reached the square, then became aware he had stumbled against something. He heard a piercing wail from an old woman whom he had almost knocked down.

"Good Lord, you almost killed me! Look where you're going"

"Why, it's you!" cried Mitya, recognizing the old woman in the dark.

It was the old servant who waited on Samsonov.

"Who are you, sir?" said the old woman. "I don't know you in the dark."

"You live at Kuzma Kuzmitch's. You're the servant there?"

"Just so, sir, I was only running out to Prohoritch's…."

"Tell me, my good woman, is Agrafena Alexandrovna there now?" said Mitya. "I saw her to the house some time ago."

"She has been there, sir. She stayed a little while, and went off again."

"What? Went away?" cried Mitya. "When did she go?"

"As soon as she came. She only stayed a minute."

"You're lying, damn you!" roared Mitya.

"Aie! Aie!" shrieked the old woman, but Mitya had vanished.
He ran to Grushenka's, but she had left for Mokroe.

Fenya was sitting with her grandmother, the cook, in the
kitchen when "the captain" ran in. Fenya uttered a piercing
shriek on seeing him.

"You scream?" roared Mitya, "where is she?"

Without giving the terror-stricken Fenya time to utter a
word, he cried, "Fenya, for Christ's sake, tell me, where is she?"

"I don't know, Dmitri Fyodorovitch, I don't know. You may
kill me but I can't tell you. She went out with yourself not long
ago—"

"She came back!"

"Indeed she didn't. By God I swear she didn't come back."

"You're lying!" shouted Mitya. "From your terror I know
where she is."

He rushed away.

Fenya in her fright was glad she had got off so easily. But
she noticed, as he ran, he grabbed from the table a brass mortar,
with a small brass pestle in it, not much more than six inches
long. Mitya already had opened the door with one hand when,
with the other, he snatched up the pestle, and thrust it in his
side-pocket.

"Oh, Lord! He's going to murder some one!" cried Fenya.

Chapter IV

In The Dark

"Where could she be except at Fyodor Pavlovitch's? She must have run straight to him from Samsonov's. The whole intrigue is evident." It all rushed through his mind. He did not run to Marya Kondratyevna's. "There was no need to go there ... they would run and tell directly.... Marya Kondratyevna was clearly in the plot, Smerdyakov too!"

He formed another plan: he ran the long way round to Fyodor Pavlovitch's house, to the deserted alley at the back, with, on one side the fence of a neighbor's garden, on the other the strong high fence that ran all round Fyodor Pavlovitch's garden. Here he chose the place, apparently, where Lizaveta had climbed over: "If she could climb over it," he thought, "surely I can." He jumped up, caught hold of the top of the fence, then he pulled himself up and sat astride it. He could see the windows.

"Yes, the old man's bedroom is lighted. She's there!"

He leapt from the fence into the garden and walked softly over the grass in the garden, avoiding the trees and shrubs. It took him five minutes to reach the lighted window. The door from the house into the garden was shut. He hid behind the bushes.

"I must wait now," he thought, "to reassure them, in case they heard my footsteps and are listening ... if only I don't cough or sneeze."

He waited two minutes, his heart beating, scarcely breathing. Then, noiselessly, he raised himself on tiptoe. Fyodor Pavlovitch's bedroom lay open before him. It was not a large room, and was divided in two by a red screen.

"Behind the screen is Grushenka," came into Mitya's mind" He watched Fyodor Pavlovitch, who was wearing his new striped-silk dressing-gown with a silk cord. A clean shirt of linen with gold studs peeped out under the collar.

"He has got himself up," thought Mitya.

His father was standing near the window, lost in thought. Suddenly he jerked up his head, listened a moment and, hearing nothing, went to the table, poured out half a glass of brandy from a decanter and drank it off. Then he uttered a deep sigh, walked carelessly to the looking-glass, raised the bandage on his forehead and began examining his bruises.

"He's alone," thought Mitya, "in all probability he's alone."

Fyodor Pavlovitch moved away from the looking-glass, turned to the window, and looked out. Mitya instantly slipped into the shadow. Fyodor Pavlovitch moved away from the window. "He's looking for her out of the window, so she's not there," thought Mitya.

He slipped back and fell to gazing in at the window again.

The old man was sitting at the table, apparently disappointed. At last he put his elbow on the table and laid his cheek against his hand.

"He's alone!" Mitya repeated. "If she were here, he would be different."

Strange to say, he was irked that she was not here.

"It's not that she's not here," he thought to himself, "but that I can't tell for certain whether she is or not."

Mitya's mind was quite clear; he took in everything to the slightest detail. But a feeling of misery, of uncertainty, was growing in his heart.

"Is she here or not?"

The angry doubt filled his heart. Making up his mind, he knocked on the window the signal the old man had agreed upon that meant "Grushenka is here!"

The old man jerked up his head and, jumping up, ran to the window.

Mitya slipped away into the shadow.

Fyodor Pavlovitch opened the window and thrust his head out.

"Grushenka, is it you?" he called. "Where are you, my angel?"

He was agitated and breathless.

"He's alone." Mitya decided.

"Where are you?" cried the old man again, thrusting his head out farther, gazing in all directions. "Come here, I've a little present for you. Come...."

"He means the three thousand," thought Mitya.

"But where are you? Are you at the door? I'll open it directly."

The old man almost climbed out of the window, peering to the right toward the door into the garden, trying to see in the darkness. In another second he would have run out to open the door without waiting for Grushenka's answer.

Mitya looked at him from the side without stirring. The old man's profile that he loathed so, his pendent Adam's apple, his hooked nose, his lips that smiled in greedy expectation, were all lit up by the slanting lamplight.

A fury of hatred surged up in Mitya's heart: "There he was, his rival, the man who had tormented him, had ruined his life!" It was a rush of that furious anger of which he had spoken to Alyosha four days ago in answer to his question, "How can you say you'll kill our father?" He had said, "I don't know." Then had added: "Perhaps I shall not kill him, perhaps I shall. I'm afraid he'll be so loathsome to me. That's what I'm afraid of, that's what may be too much for me."

This repulsion was growing unendurable. Mitya was beside himself.

He suddenly pulled the brass pestle out of his pocket.

———————

"God was watching over me," Mitya said afterwards. Grigory woke up and. after a moment, sat up in bed. Then he got up and dressed. Perhaps he was uneasy at the thought of sleeping while the house was unguarded. Smerdyakov, exhausted by his fit, lay in the next room. Marfa Ignatyevna did not stir.

"The stuff's been too much for the woman," Grigory thought, glancing at her. He went out on the steps, only intending to look out from there, for he was hardly able to walk, the pain in his back and his leg was so bad. But he remembered he had not locked the gate into the garden. Limping with pain, he went into the garden. The gate stood wide open. Perhaps he fancied something or heard a sound. He saw his master's window open.

"What's it open for? It's not summer now," thought Grigory.

He caught a glimpse of something in the garden. Forty paces in front of him a man was running in the dark, a shadow moving very fast.

"Good Lord!" cried Grigory.

Forgetting the pain in his back, he hurried to catch the running figure. It went towards the bath-house, ran behind it, and rushed to the fence. Grigory followed, reaching the fence at the moment the man was climbing over it. Grigory cried out, and clutched his leg in his two hands.

Yes, his foreboding had not deceived him. He recognized him.

"Father-killer!" he shouted, so loud that all the neighbors could hear. But he had not time to shout more, for he fell at once, as though struck by lightning.

Mitya jumped back and bent over the fallen man. In Mitya's hands was the metal tool. He flung it in the grass, but it fell on the path. For some seconds he examined the figure before him. The old man's head was covered with blood.

Mitya put out his hand and felt it.

He was anxious to make sure he had not broken the old man's skull, but had simply stunned him. But the blood was flowing, and in a moment Mitya's fingers were covered with it.

He took his handkerchief and, putting it to the old man's head, tried to wipe the blood from his face. The handkerchief was instantly soaked with blood.

"Good heavens! What am I doing?" he thought. "If I've broken his skull, how can I find out now? And what difference does it make? If I've killed him, I've killed him.... "You've come to grief, old man, so there you must lie!"

He climbed back over the fence into the lane and fell to running—the handkerchief soaked with blood crushed in his fist. He shoved it into his coat pocket and flew back again to the widow Morozov's house.

After Mitya left it that evening, Fenya had rushed to the chief porter and begged him "not to let the captain in again." The porter promised, but went upstairs to his mistress, who had sent for him. Meeting his nephew on the way up, he told him to take his place, but forgot to mention "the captain."

Mitya, running up to the gate, knocked. The lad instantly recognized him, for Mitya had more than once tipped him. Opening the gate, he let him in, and told him with a smile that "Agrafena Alexandrovna is not at home now."

"Where is she then, Prohor?" asked Mitya, stopping short.

"She set off this evening, some two hours ago, with Timofey, to Mokroe."

"What for?" cried Mitya.

"That I can't say. To see some officer. Horses were sent to fetch her."

Mitya left him and ran like a madman to Fenya.

Chapter V

A Sudden Decision

Fenya was sitting in the kitchen with her grandmother; they were both just going to bed. Relying on the chief porter, they had not locked themselves in. Mitya ran in, pounced on Fenya, and seized her by the throat.

"Speak! Where is she? With whom is she at Mokroe?" he roared.

Both the women squealed.

"Aie! I'll tell you, Dmitri Fyodorovitch, darling, I'll tell you everything, I won't hide anything, "said Fenya. "She's gone to Mokroe, to her officer."

"What officer?" cried Mitya.

"To the one she used to know, who threw her over five years ago."

Mitya withdrew his hands from her throat, pale as death. His eyes showed he realized it all, and guessed the whole position. Poor Fenya was not in a condition to know if he understood or not. She remained sitting on the trunk, trembling, holding her hands out as though trying to defend herself. And to make matters worse, both his hands were covered with blood.

Mitya sank on a chair next to Fenya. Everything was clear as day: that officer, he knew about from Grushenka herself. So, for a whole month, this had been going on, a secret from him, and he had never thought of him!

He grew cold with terror. But suddenly, as gently and mildly as a child, he began speaking to Fenya as though he had he had not just scared her to death. He questioned her in detail, and though the girl looked wildly at his blood-stained hands, she, too, with wonderful readiness, answered every question as though eager to put the whole truth before him.

She explained every detail, eager to be of the utter service to him. She described the whole of that day in great detail, the visit of Rakitin and Alyosha, how she, Fenya, had stood on the watch, how the mistress had set off, and how she had called out of the window to Alyosha to give him, Mitya, her greetings, and tell him "remember forever how she had loved him for an hour."

Hearing of the message, Mitya smiled; there was color on his cheeks.

At the same moment Fenya said to him, not afraid now, "Look at your hands, Dmitri Fyodorovitch. They're bloody!"

"Yes," answered Mitya, looking at his hands and at once forgetting them.

He sank into silence again. Twenty minutes had passed; his first fears were over, but evidently some new idea had taken hold of him. He rose, smiling.

"What has happened to you, sir?" said Fenya, pointing to his hands again.

Mitya looked at his hands again.

"That's blood, Fenya," he said, looking at her strangely. "That's human blood. My God! Why was it shed? But...Fenya...there's a fence here. At dawn tomorrow, when the sun rises, Mitya will leap over it.... You don't understand, never mind.... You'll hear tomorrow...and now, good-by. I won't stand in her way. I'll step aside. Live, my joy.... You loved me for an hour. Remember Mityenka Karamazov forever.... She used to call me Mityenka, remember?"

With those words he left and, ten minutes later, went in to Pyotr Ilyitch Perhotin, the young official with whom he had pawned his guns. It was now half-past eight, and Pyotr Ilyitch had just put his coat on to go to play billiards.

Seeing blood on his face, he cried, "Good heavens! What is the matter?"

"I've come for my guns," said Mitya. "I brought you the money. I'm in a hurry, Pyotr Ilyitch, please hurry."

Pyotr Ilyitch was even more surprised when he saw the roll of bank-notes in Mitya's hand. Mitya had walked in holding them in his out-stretched hand.

"What's the matter with you?" cried Pyotr Ilyitch, looking at him. "How is it you're covered with blood? Have you had a fall? Look at yourself!"

He took him by the elbow and led him to the glass.

Seeing his blood-stained face, Mitya made an angry face.

"That's the end!" he said, pulling the handkerchief from his pocket.

But the handkerchief was soaked with blood, too. It had not merely began to dry, but was a stiff ball that could not be pulled apart.

Mitya threw it on the floor.

"Oh, damn it!" he said. "Haven't you a rag ... to wipe my face?"

"So you're only stained, not wounded? You'd better wash. Here's a wash-stand. I'll pour you out some water."

"A wash-stand? That's all right ... but where am I to put this?"

He held up his roll of notes as though it were for Pyotr Ilyitch to decide.

"In your pocket, or on the table here. They won't be lost."

"In my pocket? Yes, all right.... But that's foolish," he cried, as though suddenly coming to. "Look, let's first settle that business of the guns. Give them back to me. Here's your money ... I need them...and haven't a minute to spare."

Taking the top note from the roll, he held it out to Pyotr Ilyitch.

"But I haven't change enough. Haven't you less?"

"No," said Mitya, turning over the notes. "They're all alike."

Again he looked at Pyotr Ilyitch.

"How have you grown so rich?" the latter asked. "Wait, I'll send my boy to Plotnikov's, they close late—to see if they won't change it. Here, Misha!"

"To Plotnikov's shop—first-rate!" cried Mitya.

He turned to the boy as he came in.

"Misha, here, run to Plotnikov's and tell them that Dmitri Fyodorovitch sends his greetings, and will be there directly.... Tell them to have wine, three dozen bottles, ready and packed to take to Mokroe."

The boy turned to go out.

"Stay, Misha," he cried. "Tell them to put in cheese, pies, smoked fish, ham, and everything they've got, up to the value of a hundred rubles, or a hundred and twenty as before.... But wait: don't let them forget dessert: sweets, pears, watermelons, two or three or four—no, one's enough, and chocolate, candy, toffee; in fact, everything I took to Mokroe before, three hundred rubles' worth with the wine...just the same as it was before. And remember, Misha, if you are called Misha—his name is Misha, isn't it?"

"Wait a minute," Protr Ilyitch said, uneasy, "you'd better go yourself. He'll get it mixed up."

"He will, I see he will! Misha, I was going to kiss you for doing it.... If you don't make a mistake, there's ten rubles for you, run along, hurry.... Wine's the chief thing. And drinks, too...all I had then.... They know what I had then."

"But listen!" Pyotr Ilyitch cut in. "Let him change the money and tell them not to close, and you go tell them.... Give him your note. Be off, Misha!"

Pyotr Ilyitch seemed to hurry Misha off on purpose, because the boy stood with his mouth and eyes wide open, understanding little of Mitya's orders, and gazing with terror at his blood-stained face and fingers.

"Well, now come and wash," said Pyotr Ilyitch sternly. "Put the money on the table or else in your pocket.... That's right, come along. Take off your coat."

Helping him with his coat, he cried: "Your coat's covered with blood, too."

"That...it's not the coat. It's only a little on the sleeve.... And that's only here where the handkerchief lay. It must have soaked through. I must have sat on it at Fenya's, and the blood's come through," Mitya explained.

Pyotr Ilyitch listened, and made a face.

"You must have been up to something, maybe fighting," he said.

They began to wash. Pyotr Ilyitch held the jug and poured the water. Mitya scarcely soaped his hands. But the young official made him soap them again and rub them more. He seemed to exercise more sway over Mitya as time went on.

"Look," he said, "you haven't got your nails clean. Rub your face; here, by your ear.... Will you go in that shirt? The cuff is covered with blood."

"Yes, it's all bloody," said Mitya, looking at the cuff.

"Then change your shirt."

"I haven't time..." Mitya went on, drying his face and hands and putting on his coat. "I'll turn up at the cuff. It won't be seen under the coat....!"

"What have you been up to? Have you been fighting with someone?" Pyotr Ilyitch asked him. "Or killing, perhaps?"

"Don't be foolish!" said Mitya.

"Why 'foolish'?"

"Don't worry," said Mitya. He suddenly laughed. "I knocked down an old woman in the market-place just now."

"An old woman?"

"An old man!" cried Mitya, looking Pyotr Ilyitch in the face and laughing.

"Fool! An old woman, an old man.... Have you killed someone?"

"We made it up. We had a row—and made it up. We parted friends. He's forgiven me.... He's sure to have forgiven me by now...if he got up he wouldn't have"—Mitya paused—"damn him, Pyotr Ilyitch!"

"What do you want to go picking quarrels with every one for? You've been fighting, and now you're rushing off raise hell—that's you all over!"

"Yes! Give me the guns. I should like to have a chat with you, dear boy, but I haven't the time. And there's no need, it's too late. Where's my money?"

"You put it on the table ... Here it is. Money's like dirt to you. Here are your guns. At six o'clock you pledged them for ten rubles, and now you've got thousands. Two or three I should say."

"Three, you bet," laughed Mitya, stuffing the notes into his trousers.

"You'll lose it like that. Have you found a gold mine?"

"The gold mines?" Mitya shouted at the top of his voice, roaring with laughter. "Would you like to go to the mines, Perhotin? There's a lady here who'll put up three thousand for you if only you'll go. She did it for me, she's so fond of gold mines. Do you know Madame Hohlakov?"

"I don't know her, but I've heard of her. Did she really give you three thousand? Did she really?" said Pyotr Ilyitch, eyeing him.

"As soon as the sun rises tomorrow, you go to her, this Madame Hohlakov, and ask her whether she put up that three thousand. Try and find out."

"I don't know on what terms you are...since you say it so surely, I suppose she did. You've got the money in your hand, but instead of going to the mines you're spending it.... Where are you really off to now?"

"Mokroe."

"I don't understand you!"

"Am I drunk?"

"Not drunk, but worse."

"I'm drunk in love, Pyotr Ilyitch! But that's enough!"

"What are you doing, loading the gun?"

"I'm loading the gun."

Opening the gun-case, Mitya took the powder horn and carefully poured powder into the gun and rammed in the charge. Then he took the bullet and, before putting it into the gun, held it in two fingers in front of the candle.

"Why are you looking at the bullet?" asked Pyotr Ilyitch.

"It's going into my brain, so it's interesting to see it. But that's enough," he added, putting in the bullet and driving it home.

"Pyotr Ilyitch, my dear fellow, that's all foolish! Give me a piece of paper."

"Here's some paper."

"No, a clean piece, writing-paper. That's right."

Taking a pen from the table, Mitya rapidly wrote two lines, folded the paper, and thrust it in his pocket. He put the guns in the case, locked it, and kept it in his hand. Then he looked at Pyotr Ilyitch with a thoughtful smile.

"Now, let's go."

"Where are we going? No, wait a minute.... Are you thinking of putting that bullet in your brain, perhaps?" Pyotr Ilyitch asked uneasily.

"I was fooling about the bullet! I want to live. I love life! You may be sure of that. Dear Pyotr Ilyitch, do you know how to step aside?"

"What do you mean by 'stepping aside'?"

"Making way for a dear creature, and for one I hate. To let the one I hate become dear—that's what it means! To say to them: God bless you, go your way, pass on, while I—"

"While you—?"

"That's enough, let's go."

"Upon my word. I'll tell someone to prevent your going there," said Pyotr Ilyitch, looking at him. "What are you going to Mokroe for now?"

"There's a woman there, a woman. That's enough for you."

"Listen, though you're an animal I've always liked you.... I feel anxious."

"Thanks, old fellow. I'm an animal you say. That's what I'm always saying. Beasts! Why, here's Misha! I was forgetting him."

Misha ran in with the change, and said everyone was busy at the Plotnikovs': "They're carrying down the bottles; it will all be ready at once."

Mitya handed ten rubles to Pyotr Ilyitch, then tossed ten rubles to Misha.

"Don't do that!" cried Pyotr Ilyitch. "I won't have it. Put your money away.

It will come in handy tomorrow, but I dare say you'll be coming to me to borrow ten rubles again. Don't put the notes in your side-pocket? You'll lose them!"

"I say, my dear fellow, let's go to Mokroe together."

"What should I go for?"

"Let's open a bottle and drink to life! I want to drink, and especially to drink with you. I've never drunk with you, have I?"

"Very well, we can go to the 'Metropolis.' I was just going there."

"I haven't time. Let's drink at Plotnikovs'. Shall I ask you a riddle?"

"Ask away."

Mitya took the piece of paper out of his pocket, unfolded it, and showed it to him. In a large hand was written: "I punish myself for my whole life!"

"I'll speak to someone, I'll go now," said Pyotr Ilyitch, reading the note.

"You won't have time, dear boy, come and have a drink!"

Plotnikov's shop was at the corner. They were waiting for Mitya. They remembered how he bought, a few weeks ago, wine and goods to the value of several hundred rubles. They remembered that then, as now, he had had a bundle of hundred-ruble notes in his hand, and threw them about without trying to deal.

The story was told all over the town that, driving off with Grushenka to Mokroe, he had "spent three thousand in one night, and had come back without a penny." He had picked up a troop of gypsies, who for two days got money out of him while he was drunk. People used to tell, laughing at him, how he had given wine to the common folk, and feasted the village women and girls on sweets and pies. Though to laugh at Mitya to his face was risky, there was much laughter behind his back, especially in the tavern when he told them all he got out of Grushenka was "permission to kiss her foot, which was all she allowed."

By the time Mitya and Pyotr Ilyitch reached the shop they found a cart with three horses harnessed, and with Andrey, the driver, waiting for Mitya. In the shop they had almost entirely finished packing one box, and were only waiting for Mitya's arrival to nail it shut and put it in the cart.

Pyotr Ilyitch was shocked. "Where did it come from so soon?" he asked.

"I met Andrey as I ran to you, and told him to drive straight to the shop. There's no time to lose. Shall we be very late, Andrey?"

"They'll only get there an hour before us, if even that," Andrey replied.

"Fifty rubles for vodka if we're only an hour behind them."

Though Mitya hurried about seeing after things, he gave his orders in a mixed up way. Pyotr Ilyitch found it necessary to come to the rescue.

"Four hundred rubles' worth, not less than four hundred rubles' worth, just as it was then," commanded Mitya. "Four dozen wine, not a bottle less."

"What do you want with so much? Stay!" cried Pyotr Ilyitch. "What's this box? What's in it? Surely there isn't four hundred rubles' worth here?"

The shop-men explained with great politeness that the first box contained only half a dozen bottles of wine, and only "the most important articles," such as savories, sweets, toffee, etc. The main part of the goods ordered would be sent off, as on the previous occasion, in a special cart also traveling at full speed, so it would arrive not more than an hour later than Dmitri Fyodorovitch himself.

"Not more than an hour! Put in more toffee. The girls are so fond of it."

"The toffee is all right. But what do you want with four dozen wine? One would be enough, "said Pyotr Ilyitch. He began concerning himself, asking for a bill, and refused to be satisfied. But he only succeeded in saving a hundred.

"Well, you may go to the devil!" cried Pyotr Ilyitch. "What's it to do with me? Throw away your money, since it cost you nothing."

"This way, my economist, this way, don't be angry." Mitya drew him into a room at the back of the shop. "They'll give us a bottle here. We'll taste it. Pyotr Ilyitch, come with me. You're a nice fellow, the sort I like."

Mitya sat on a chair before a table. Pyotr Ilyitch sat opposite, the wine appeared, and oysters were suggested.

"We don't need anything," cried Pyotr.

"Do you know, friend," Mitya said, "I never have liked this lack of order."

"Who does? Three dozen of wine for the common folk!"

"That's not what I mean. I'm talking of a higher order. There's no higher order. But...that's all over. There's no need to be sorry about it. It's too late!"

"You're making no sense, not puns! I keep thinking of your guns."

"That's all foolish, too! Drink. I love life. I've loved life too much. Enough! Let's drink to life, dear boy. Why am I pleased with myself? I'm not a good man, but I'm satisfied with myself. I bless the creation. I'm ready to bless God and His creation directly, but ... I must kill one noxious insect for fear it should crawl and spoil life for others.... Let's drink to life. What can be more precious than life? Nothing! To life, and to a queen of queens!"

"Let's drink to life and to your queen, too, if you like."

They drank a glass each. Although Mitya was excited, yet he was sad, too.

"Misha...come here, drink a glass to Phœbus, the golden-haired, of tomorrow morn...."

"What are you giving it him for?" cried Pyotr Ilyitch, angry.

"Yes, let me! I want to!"

Misha emptied the glass, bowed, and ran out.

"He'll remember it afterwards," Mitya said. "Woman, I love woman! What is woman? The queen of creation! My heart is sad, Pyotr Ilyitch."

Pyotr Ilyitch listened in silence. Mitya, too, was silent for a while.

"Dmitri Fyodorovitch, won't you come now?" called Andrey at the door.

"Are you ready? A few last words and—Andrey, a glass of vodka at starting. That box" (the one with the guns) "put it under my seat. Goodbye, Pyotr Ilyitch, don't remember evil against me."

"But you're coming back tomorrow?"

"Of course."

"Will you settle the bill now?" cried the waiter, springing forward.

Mitya pulled the bundle of notes out of his pocket, picked out three hundred rubles, threw them on the counter, and ran out of the shop.

Every one followed him out, bowing and wishing him good luck.

Andrey, coughing from the brandy, jumped up on the box. But Mitya was only just taking his seat when, to his surprise, he saw Fenya before him.

She ran up panting and, with a cry, plumped down at his feet.

"Dear good Dmitri Fyodorovitch, don't harm my mistress. It was I told you about it.... Don't murder him, he came first, he's hers! He'll marry her now. That's why he came back. Dmitri Fyodorovitch, don't take a creature's life!"

"So that's it, is it? You're off there to make trouble!" said Pyotr Ilyitch. "Now, it's all clear. Dmitri Fyodorovitch, give me your guns at once."

"The guns? I'll throw them in the pool on the road," Mitya answered.

"Fenya, get up. Mitya won't hurt anyone, the silly fool won't hurt anyone again. But I say, Fenya," he shouted after taking his seat. "I hurt you just now. Forgive me and have pity on me, forgive a bad man.... But it's all the same now. Andrey, look alive, fly along, full speed!"

Andrey whipped up the horses, and the bells began ringing.

"Good-bye, Pyotr Ilyitch! My last tear is for you!"

"He's not drunk, but he keeps talking like a crazy man," Pyotr Ilyitch thought as he watched him go. He had half a mind to stay and see the cart packed with the remaining wines and goods, knowing they would deceive Mitya. But, angry, he turned away with a curse and went to play billiards.

The game cheered him. He played a second game, and suddenly began telling one of the players that Dmitri Karamazov had come in for some cash again—three thousand rubles, and had gone to Mokroe to spend it with Grushenka.

This news roused great interest. They all spoke of it with a strange gravity.

"Three thousand? But where can he have got three thousand?"

The story of Madame Hohlakov's present was received with skepticism.

"Hasn't he robbed his old father?—that's the question."

"Three thousand! There's something odd about it."

"He boasted he would kill his father; we all heard him. And it was three thousand he talked about ..."

Pyotr Ilyitch listened. But he became short in his answers. He said not a word about the blood on Mitya's face and hands, though he had meant to. They began a third game, and gradually the talk about Mitya died away. By the end of the third game, Pyotr Ilyitch put down his cue and left.

When he reached the market-place he stood still. He realized that what he wanted was to go to Fyodor Pavlovitch's and find out if anything had happened.

"On account of some foolish talk—as it's sure to turn out—am I going to wake up the house and make a scene? Is it my business to look after them?"

In a very bad humor he went home. But suddenly he remembered Fenya.

"I ought to have questioned her just now," he thought. "I should have heard everything."

The desire to speak to her became so pressing that when he was almost home he turned and went to the house where Grushenka lived. He knocked. The sound of the knock in the silence of the night sobered him.

No one answered; everyone in the house was asleep.

"And I shall be making a to-do!" he thought. But instead of going away he fell to knocking again with all his might, filling the street with noise.

"Not coming? Well, I will knock them up!" he said, angry at himself.

At the same time he redoubled his knocks on the gate.

Chapter VI

"I Am Coming, Too!"

Dmitri Fyodorovitch sped along the road. It was more than twenty miles to Mokroe, but the horses galloped so swiftly the distance might be covered in an hour and a quarter. The motion made Mitya feel. The air was fresh and cool, with stars in the sky. His heart ached for his queen, to whom he was to look on for the last time. He felt no envy, no hostility, for he who was her first lover.

"Here there was no room for dispute: it was her right and his; this was her first love which, after five years, she had not forgotten; she had loved him only for those five years. Step aside, Mitya, make way! Even if he had not appeared, everything would be over ..."

These words would roughly have expressed his feelings, if he had been capable of reasoning. His plan of action had arisen without reasoning. At Fenya's first words, it had sprung from feeling. Yet, it seemed strange to him to think he had written his own death sentence: "I punish myself," and the paper was in his pocket, the pistol loaded; he had already resolved how, next morning, he would meet the first warm ray of the sun.

There was one moment when he felt an impulse to stop Andrey, jump out of the cart, pull out his gun, and make an end of it without waiting for the dawn. But that moment flew by like a spark. The horses galloped on, and as he drew near his goal, the thought of her took more and more possession of him, chasing away the fearful images. How he longed to look upon her, if only for a moment!

"She's now with *him*," he thought, "now I shall see what she looks like with him, her first love, and that's all I want."

Never had this woman, who was such a fateful influence in his life, aroused such love in his breast, such a feeling so tender!

"I shall be as nothing before her," he said in a rush of joy.

They galloped nearly an hour. Mitya was silent, and though Andrey usually was talkative, he did not say a word. He only whipped up his horses.

Suddenly Mitya cried out in anxiety: "Andrey! What if they're asleep?"

This thought fell upon him like a blow. It had not occurred to him before.

"It may well be that they're gone to bed by now, Dmitri Fyodorovitch."

Mitya frowned as though in pain. Yes, indeed...he was rushing there... with such feelings...while they were asleep. Anger surged up in him.

"Drive on, Andrey! Whip them up!" he cried. "Maybe they're not in bed!"

Andrey said, after a pause, "Timofey said they were a lot of them there—"

"A lot of them? Who are they?" cried Mitya, up-set.

"Well, Timofey said they're all gentle-folk. Two from our town—and two strangers, maybe more. I didn't ask. They're playing cards, Timofey said."

"Cards?"

"Maybe they're not in bed if they're at cards. It's not more than eleven."

"Quicker, Andrey!" Mitya cried again.

"May I ask you something, sir?" said Andrey. "I'm afraid of angering you."

"What is it?"

"Fenya threw herself at your feet and begged you not to harm her mistress, so you see, sir—It's I am taking you there...forgive me, sir...maybe it's wrong—"

Mitya suddenly seized him by the shoulders from behind.

"Are you a driver?" he asked.

"Yes, sir."

"Then you know that one has to make way. What would you say to a driver who wouldn't make way for anyone, but just drove on and crushed people? No, a driver mustn't run over people. One can't spoil people's lives. If you have spoilt a life—punish yourself.... If you've ruined anyone's life—punish yourself."

"That's right, Dmitri Fyodorovitch, you're quite right, one mustn't crush or torment a man, or any kind of creature, for everyone is created by God. Take a horse, for instance, for some folks, even among us drivers, nothing will restrain them, they force it along."

"To hell?" Mitya interrupted, and laughed. "Andrey, whip up the left!"

"So you see, sir, who it is hell for," said Andrey, whipping the horses, "but though you're quick-tempered, sir, yet God will forgive you for your kind heart."

"And you, do you forgive me, Andrey?"

"What should I forgive you for, sir? You've never done me any harm."

"No, for everyone, here on the road, will you forgive me for every one?"

"Oh sir! I feel afraid of driving you, your talk is so strange."

But Mitya did not hear. He was praying: "Lord, receive me, and do not condemn me, for I love Thee, Lord. I am a wretch, but I love Thee. If Thou send me to hell, I shall love Thee there, and from there I shall cry out I love Thee. But let me love to the end.... Here and now for just five hours ... till the first light of day ... for I love the queen of my soul ... I love her and I cannot help loving her. I shall fall before her and say, 'You are right to pass on and leave me. Farewell and don't fret yourself about me!'"

"Mokroe!" cried Andrey, pointing ahead with his whip.

Through the dark loomed a black mass of buildings. The village of Mokroe numbered two thousand, but at that hour all were asleep.

"Drive on, Andrey!" Mitya exclaimed.

"They're not asleep," said Andrey, pointing with his whip to the Plastunovs' inn, at the entrance to the village. The windows were brightly lit.

"They're not asleep," Mitya repeated happily. "Hurry, Andrey! Set the bells ringing! Let all know that I have come!"

Andrey lashed the team and pulled them up, steaming, at the high flight of steps. Mitya jumped out of the cart just as the innkeeper, on his way to bed, peeped out from the door, curious to see who had arrived.

"Trifon Borissovitch, is that you?"

The innkeeper rushed down the steps and up to the guest with delight.

"Dmitri Fyodorovitch, your honor! Do I see you again?"

Trifon Borissovitch was a peasant of middle height, with a fat face. His expression was severe, especially with the common folk of Mokroe, more than half whom worked lands he owned in payment of debts. But in spite of the thousands he had saved, Trifon Borissovitch liked to empty the pockets of a drunken guest, and remembered that not a month ago he had made two if not three hundred rubles out of Dmitri, when he had come with Grushenka.

"Dmitri Fyodorovitch, dear sir, we see you once more!"

"Stay, Trifon Borissovitch," began Mitya, "first, where is she?"

"Agrafena Alexandrovna?" The inn-keeper understood at once. "She's here, too ..."

"With whom?"

"A Pole, to judge from his speech. He sent the horses for her from here; and there's another with him, a friend of his. They're dressed like civilians."

"Well, are they feasting? Have they money?"

"Poor sort of a feast. Nothing to boast of, Dmitri Fyodorovitch."

"Nothing to boast of? And who are the others?"

"Two gentlemen from Tcherny who are putting up here. One's a young gentleman, but I've forgotten his name ... and I expect you know the other, a gentleman called Maximov. He's with a young gentleman."

"Is that all?"

"Yes."

"Stay, Trifon Borissovitch. What of her? How is she?"

"Oh, she's only just come. She's sitting with them."

"Is she cheerful? Is she laughing?"

"I think not. She seems dull."

"The Pole—the officer?"

"He's not young, and he's not an officer. It's the young gentleman that's with Maximov ... I've forgotten his name."

"Kalganov."

"That's it, Kalganov!"

"All right. I'll see for myself. Are they playing cards?"

"They have been playing, but now they're drinking tea."

"Stay, Trifon Borissovitch, I'll see for myself. Are the gypsies here?"

"You can't have the gypsies now, Dmitri Fyodorovitch. The authorities sent them away. But we've people that play the fiddle in the village."

"Send for them!" cried Mitya. "And get the girls together as you did then, Marya especially, Stepanida, too, and Arina. Two hundred rubles for a chorus!"

"For a sum like that I can get all the village together, though by now they're asleep. Are the common folk worth such kindness, Dmitri Fyodorovitch, or the girls either? I'll get my daughters up for nothing, let alone a sum like that. They've only just gone to bed, I'll give them a kick and set them singing for you. You gave the peasants champagne—"

For all his pretended concern for Mitya, Trifon Borissovitch had hidden half a dozen bottles of wine on that last occasion, and had picked up a hundred-ruble note under the table and kept it.

"Trifon Borissovitch, I spent more than one thousand last time I was here."

"I well remember. You must have left three thousand behind you."

"Well, I've come to do the same again, do you see?"

He held up his roll of notes.

"Listen. In an hour's time the wine will arrive, savories, pies, and sweets—bring them all up at once. That box Andrey has has got is to be brought up, too. Open it and hand out wine. And we must have the girls, Marya especially."

He turned to the cart and pulled out the box of pistols.

"Here, let's settle. Here's fifteen rubles for the drive, and fifty for vodka...for your readiness, for your love.... Remember Karamazov!"

"I'm afraid, sir," said Andrey. "Give me five rubles extra, but more I won't take. Trifon Borissovitch, bear witness. Forgive my foolish words..."

"What are you afraid of?" asked Mitya. "Well, go to the devil, if that's it!" he cried, throwing him five rubles. "Now, Trifon Borissovitch, take me up quietly and let me first get a look at them, so that they don't see me."

Trifon Borissovitch did his bidding. Leading him into the hall, he went himself into the first large room next to that in which the visitors were sitting, and took the light away. Then he quietly led Mitya to a corner in the dark where he could watch the company without being seen. But Mitya did not look long, and, indeed, he could not see them; he saw her, his heart throbbed, and all was dark before his eyes.

She was sitting side-ways to the table in a low chair, and beside her, on the sofa, was the pretty youth, Kalganov. She was holding his hand and laughing, while he, not looking at her, was speaking to Maximov across the table. Maximov was laughing. On the sofa sat *he*, relaxed, smoking a pipe.

Mitya had an impression of a stout, broad-faced, short little man, who was angry about something. His friend, on a chair by the sofa, struck Mitya as tall, but he could make out nothing more. He caught his breath. He could not bear it; he put the gun-case on a chest, and with a throbbing heart walked into the room.

"Aie!" shrieked Grushenka, the first to notice him.

Chapter VII

The First and Rightful Lover

Mitya walked up to the table and said in a loud voice, "Gentlemen, I...I'm all right! Don't be afraid! I—there's nothing wrong," he said, turning to Grushenka, who had shrunk back towards Kalganov. "I'm coming, too. I'm here till morning. May I stay with you till morning?" he asked the fat little man on the sofa.

The latter said severely: "*Panie*, we're private. There are other rooms."

"Why, it's you, Dmitri Fyodorovitch!" said Kalganov. "Sit down."

"Delighted to see you, dear...fellow, I always thought a lot of you," Mitya said with joy, holding out his hand across the table.

"How tight you shake! You've broken my fingers," laughed Kalganov.

"He always shakes like that," Grushenka put in, sure from Mitya's face he was not going to make a scene, though she watched him with uneasiness. She was impressed by something about him, but the last thing she expected was that he would come in and speak like this at such a moment.

"Good evening," Maximov said.

Mitya rushed up to him, too.

"Good evening. You're here, too! How glad I am to find you here! Gentlemen, I—I flew here.... I wanted to spend my last hour, in this room ... where I, too, adored...my queen.... Forgive me, *panie*," he cried, don't be afraid, it's my last night! Let's drink to our understanding. I brought this with me." (He pulled out his bundle of notes.) "Allow me, *panie*! I want to have music, singing, as before. Then I'll go away and there'll be no more of me."

He was almost choking. There was so much he wanted to say, but strange noises were all that came from him. The Pole gazed at him, at the bundle of notes in his hand, looked at Grushenka, and was in evident perplexity.

"If my suverin lady is permitting—" he began.

"What does 'suverin' mean?" interrupted Grushenka. "I can't help laughing at the way you talk. Sit down, Mitya, what are you talking about? Don't frighten us, please. If you won't, I'm glad to see you ..."

"Me frighten you?" cried Mitya. "Go your way, I won't stop you!"

He surprised them all, and no doubt himself as well, by flinging himself on a chair and bursting into tears, turning his head to the wall.

"Come, what a fellow you are!" cried Grushenka. "That's just how he comes to see me—he begins talking, and I can't make out what he means. He's cried like that before! It's shameful! Why are you crying? *As though you had anything to cry for!*" she added.

"I ... I'm not crying.... Well, good evening!"

He turned round in his chair and laughed.

"Well, there you are.... Cheer up!" Grushenka said. "I'm glad you've come, Mitya, do you hear! I want him to stay here with us," she said to the company, though her words were obviously meant for the man sitting on the sofa. "I wish it! And if he goes away I shall too!" she added with flashing eyes.

"What my queen commands is law!" said the Pole, kissing Grushenka's hand. "I beg you, *panie*, to join our company," he added to Mitya.

Mitya, seemed about to give another speech, but said, "Let's drink, *panie*."

Everyone laughed.

"Do you hear, Mitya," she went on. "It's nice you brought wine. I want some myself. And best of all, you've come, too. We were all so dull. You want to party again? Put your money in your pocket. Where did you get such a lot?"

Mitya had been all this time holding the roll of notes on which the eyes of all, especially the Poles', were fixed. As he stuffed them into his pocket, the inn-keeper brought in an opened bottle of wine and glasses.

Mitya seized the bottle, but didn't seem to know what to do with it.

Kalganov took it from him and poured out the champagne.

"Another bottle!" Mitya cried to the inn-keeper, and, forgetting to clink glasses with the Pole, whom he had invited to drink, he drank off his glass.

His whole look changed. The serious expression left his face, and a child-like look came into it. He became gentle and looked happily at everyone, with a nervous laugh and the expression of a dog who has done wrong but been forgiven. He looked at Grushenka, laughing, and brought his chair close to her.

He had gained some idea of the Poles, though no definite idea of them yet. The Pole on the sofa struck him by his look of dignity and his Polish accent; and, above all, by his pipe. "Well, what of it? It's a good thing he's smoking a pipe," he thought. The Pole's puffy face, with its tiny nose and thin, pointed mustaches, had not so far stirred the faintest doubts in Mitya. He was not even struck by the Pole's wig.

"I suppose it's all right since he wears a wig," he went on to himself. The other Pole, who was staring insolently at the company and listening with silent contempt, impressed Mitya by his great height. "If he stood up he'd be six foot three," he thought. It occurred to him this Pole must be the friend of the other."

Grushenka's mood and tone of words he failed to grasp. All he understood, with a thrilling heart, was that she was kind to him, that she had forgiven him, and made him sit by her. He was beside himself with delight, watching her sip her wine. The silence of the company struck him, however.

"Why are we sitting here Why don't you do something?" he asked.

"Maximov was talking foolishly and we were laughing," Kalganov said.

Mitya stared at Kalganov and then at Maximov.

"He's talking foolishly?" he laughed, seeming delighted.

"Yes. Would you believe it, he says that all our officers in the twenties married Polish women. That's foolish, isn't it?"

"Polish women?" repeated Mitya happily.

Kalganov was aware of Mitya's attitude to Grushenka, but that did not interest him; what he was interested in was Maximov. He had come with him, and met the Poles here at the inn for the first time. Grushenka he knew before, but she had not taken to him. Here, however, she looked at him with liking: before Mitya's arrival, she had been making much of him, but he seemed not to be moved by it. He was twenty, with a fair-skinned face and thick hair. He had beautiful blue eyes, with an intelligent and sometimes even deep expression.

"I've been taking him about with me for the last four days," he went on. "Ever since your brother, do you remember, shoved him off the carriage and sent him flying. That made me take an interest in him. I took him into the country, but he keeps talking such rot I'm ashamed to be with him."

"The gentleman has not seen Polish ladies, and says what is impossible," the Pole with the pipe said.

"But I was married to a Polish lady myself," said Maximov.

"You were talking about the officers. Were you an officer?" put in Kalganov. "Was he a cavalry officer?" cried Mitya, turning to each as he spoke.

"No, you see," Maximov said to him. "What I mean is that those pretty Polish ladies...when one of them dances with a Uhlan, she jumps on his knee like a kitten...and the *pan*-father and *pan*-mother look on and allow it. Next day the Uhlan comes and offers her his hand.... That's how it is!" Maximov ended.

"The *pan* is a *lajdak*!" the tall Pole said.

Mitya's eye was caught by his huge boot, with its dirty sole. The dress of both looked greasy.

"Well, now it's *lajdak*! What's he complaining about?" said Grushenka.

"*Pani* Agrippina, what the gentleman saw in Poland were servant girls, not ladies of good birth," the Pole with the pipe said to Grushenka.

"You can be sure of that," the tall Pole said.

"Let him talk! It makes it cheerful," Grushenka said, cross.

"I'm not stopping them, *pani*," said the Pole in the wig.

"No, no. The Polish gentleman spoke the truth." Kalganov got excited again. "He's never been in Poland, so how can he talk about it? You weren't married in Poland, were you?"

"No. A Uhlan brought her to Russia, my future wife, with her mamma and her aunt. He brought her from Poland and gave her to me. He was a lieutenant in our unit, a very nice young man. He meant to marry her himself. But he didn't because she turned out to be lame."

"So you married a lame woman?" cried Kalganov.

"Yes. They deceived me at the time, and concealed it. I thought she was hopping; she kept hopping.... I thought it was for fun."

"So pleased she was going to marry you!" yelled Kalganov.

"Yes. But it turned out to be quite different. After we were married, she confessed, and asked forgiveness. 'I once jumped over a puddle when I was a child,' she said, 'and injured my leg'!"

Kalganov went off into the most childish laughter, almost falling on the sofa. Grushenka, too, laughed. Mitya was at the pinnacle of happiness.

"Do you know, that's the truth," said Kalganov to Mitya; "and he's been married twice; it's his first wife he's talking about. His second wife ran away, and is alive now."

"Is it possible?" said Mitya, turning to Maximov with astonishment.

"Yes. She ran away. I've had that experience," Maximov said. And what was worse, she'd had all my property made over to her. 'You're an educated man,' she said to me. 'You can always get your living.' A bishop once said to me: 'One of your wives was lame, but the other was light-footed.'!"

"Listen," cried Kalganov, "if he's telling lies—and he often is—he's only doing it to amuse us. There's no harm in that, is there? I sometimes like him. He's awfully low, but it's natural to him. Some people are low from self-interest, but he's so from nature."

"What o'clock is it, *panie*?" the Pole with the pipe asked his tall friend.

The other shrugged. Neither of them had a watch.

"Why not talk? Let other people talk. Mustn't other people talk because you're bored?" Grushenka flew at him.

Something for the first time flashed upon Mitya's mind.

This time the Pole answered with unmistakable irritability.

"*Pani*, I didn't oppose it. I didn't say anything."

"All right then. Tell us your story," Grushenka said to Maximov.

"There's nothing to tell, it's all so foolish," answered Maximov.

"But what were you beaten for?" cried Kalganov.

"My education. People can thrash one for anything," Maximov concluded.

"That's enough! That's stupid, I don't want to listen," Grushenka said.

Mitya started, and at once left off laughing. The tall Pole rose, and with the haughty air of a man out of his element began pacing from corner to corner.

"Ah, he can't sit still," said Grushenka.

Mitya began to feel anxious. He noticed, besides, that the Pole on the sofa was looking at him with an irritable expression.

"*Panie!*" cried Mitya, "let's drink! And the other *pan*, too!."

He pulled three glasses towards him, and filled them with champagne.

"To Poland, *panovie*, I drink to your Poland!" cried Mitya.

"I shall be delighted, *panie*," said the Pole on the sofa with dignity.

"And the other *pan*, what's his name? Drink!" Mitya urged.

"Pan Vrublevsky," put in the Pole on the sofa.

Pan Vrublevsky came up to the table, swaying as he walked.

"To Poland, *panovie!*" cried Mitya, raising his glass. "Hurrah!"

All three drank. Mitya seized the bottle and again poured out three glasses.

"Now to Russia, *panovie*, and let us be brothers!"

"Pour out some for us," said Grushenka; "I'll drink to Russia, too!"

"So will I," said Kalganov.

"And I would, too ... to Russia, the old grandmother!" said Maximov.

"All! All!" cried Mitya. "Trifon Borissovitch, some more bottles!"

The other three bottles Mitya brought were put on the table. Mitya filled the glasses.

"To Russia!" he shouted again. Grushenka tossed off her glass at once.

The Poles did not touch theirs.

"How's this, *panovie*?" cried Mitya, "won't you drink?"

Pan Vrublevsky raised his glass and said: "To Russia before 1772."

"Come, that's better!" cried the other Pole, and they emptied their glasses.

"You're fools, you *panovie*," broke suddenly from Mitya.

"*Panie!*" shouted both the Poles, setting on Mitya like a couple of cocks.

Pan Vrublevsky was especially furious.

"Can one help loving one's own country?" he shouted.

"Be silent! I won't have any quarreling!" cried Grushenka, stamping her foot. Her eyes were shining. The effects of the glass she had just drunk were apparent.

Mitya was alarmed.

"*Panovie*, forgive me! It was my fault, I'm sorry."

"Hold your tongue! Sit down, you stupid!" Grushenka scolded.

Every one sat down, silent, looking at one another.

"Gentlemen, I was the cause of it all," Mitya began, unable to make anything of Grushenka. "Why are we sitting here? What shall we do to amuse ourselves again?"

"It's certainly anything but amusing!" Kalganov said.

"Let's play faro again, as we did just now," Maximov said.

"Faro? Splendid!" cried Mitya. "If only the *panovie*—"

"It's lite, *panovie*," the Pole on the sofa responded.

"That's true," assented Pan Vrublevsky.

"Lite? What do you mean by 'lite'?" asked Grushenka.

"Late, *pani*! 'A late hour' I mean," the Pole on the sofa explained.

"It's always late with them. They never do anything!" Grushenka shrieked. "They're dull, so they want others to be dull. Before you came, Mitya, they were just as silent."

"My goddess!" cried the Pole on the sofa, "I see you're not well-disposed to me, that's why I'm gloomy. I'm ready, *panie*," added he, addressing Mitya.

"Begin, *panie*," Mitya said, pulling his notes from his pocket and laying two hundred-ruble notes on the table. "I want to lose a lot to you. Take your cards."

"We'll have cards from the landlord, *panie*," said the little Pole gravely.

"That's much the best way," chimed in Pan Vrublevsky.

"From the landlord? I understand, let's get them from him. Cards!" Mitya shouted.

The landlord brought in a new, unopened pack and told Mitya that the girls were getting ready, and that the people with the instruments would be here soon; but the cart with the provisions had not yet arrived. Mitya ran into the next room to give orders, but only three girls had arrived, and Marya was not there yet. He did not know what orders to give and why he had run out. He only told them to take out of the box the presents for the girls, the sweets, toffee and candy.

"And vodka for Andrey!" he cried. "I was rude to Andrey!"

Maximov, who had followed him, touched him on the shoulder.

"Give me five rubles," he whispered. "I'll stake something, too!"

"Capital! Splendid! Take ten, here!"

He took the notes from his pocket and picked out one for ten rubles.

"And if you lose that, come again," Mitya said.

"Very good," Maximov whispered joyfully, and ran back.

Mitya, too, returned, apologizing for having kept them waiting. The Poles were already seated and had opened the pack. They looked much more amiable.

"To your places, gentlemen," cried Pan Vrublevsky.

"I'm not playing anymore," said Kalganov, "I've lost fifty rubles to them."

"The *pan* had no luck, perhaps he'll be lucky this time," the Pole said.

"How much in the bank? asked Mitya.

"That's up to you, *panie*, a hundred, two hundred, whatever you want."

"A million!" laughed Mitya, but checked himself. "Forgive me, *panie*, I stake ten rubles, the knave leads."

"And I put a ruble on the queen of hearts!" said Maximov.

Mitya won. The ruble won, too.

"A corner!" cried Mitya.

"I'll bet another ruble, a 'single' stake," Maximov said, hugely delighted.

"Lost!" shouted Mitya. "A 'double' on the seven!"

The seven too was trumped.

"Stop!" cried Kalganov.

"Double! Double!"

Mitya doubled his stakes, and each time he doubled the stake, the card he doubled was trumped by the Poles. The ruble stakes kept winning.

"On the double!" shouted Mitya furiously.

"You've lost two hundred, *panie*. Will you stake another hundred?" the Pole on the sofa asked.

"What? Lost two hundred already? Then another two hundred!"

Pulling his money out of his pocket, Mitya was about to fling two hundred rubles on the queen, but Kalganov covered it with his hand.

"That's enough!" he shouted in a ringing voice.

"What's the matter?" Mitya stared at him.

"That's enough! I don't want you to play anymore!"

"Why?"

"Because I don't. Hang it, come away."

Mitya gazed at him in astonishment.

"Give it up, Mitya. He's right. You've lost a lot as it is," said Grushenka, a curious note in her voice. Both the Poles rose from their seats, deeply offended.

"Are you joking, *panie*?" said the short man, looking severely at Kalganov.

"How dare you!" Pan Vrublevsky, too, growled at Kalganov.

"Don't dare to shout like that," cried Grushenka. "You turkey-cocks!"

Mitya looked at each of them in turn. But something in Grushenka's face struck him, and something new flashed into his mind—a strange new thought!

"*Pani* Agrippina," the little Pole was beginning, flushed with anger, when Mitya went up to him and slapped him on the shoulder.

"Most illustrious, two words with you."

"What do you want?"

"In the next room, I've words to say to you, pleasant words you'll be glad to hear."

The little *pan* was taken aback and looked fearfully at Mitya. He agreed, however, on condition that Pan Vrublevsky went with them.

"The bodyguard? Let him come, I want him, too!" cried Mitya.

"Where are you going?" asked Grushenka anxiously.

"We'll be back in a moment," answered Mitya.

There was a boldness, a sudden confidence, shining in his eyes.

He led the Poles into the bedroom on the right, where the trunks and packages were kept, and there were two large beds. There was a lit candle on a small table. The small man and Mitya sat down to this table, while Vrublevsky stood beside them.

The Poles looked severe but inquisitive.

"What can I do for you, *panie*?" lisped the little Pole.

"Well, look here, *panie*, I won't keep you long. There's money for you," he pulled out his notes. "Would you like three thousand? Take it and go your way."

The Pole gazed open-eyed at Mitya, with a searching look.

"Three thousand, *panie*?" He exchanged glances with Vrublevsky.

"Three, *panovie*, three! Listen, *panie*, I see you're a sensible man. Take three thousand and go to the devil, and Vrublevsky with you. But at once, and forever. You understand, *panie*r. Here's the door, you go out of it. What have you got there, a fur coat? I'll bring it out to you. They'll get the horses out, and then—good-by, *panie*!"

Mitya waited an answer with assurance. He had no doubts.

A determined look came into the Pole's face.

"And the money, *panie*?"

"The money, *panie*? Five hundred rubles now for the journey, as a first installment, and two thousand five hundred tomorrow, in town—on my honor, I'll get it, I'll get it at any cost!" cried Mitya.

The Poles exchanged glances again. The short man's look was dark.

"Seven hundred, not five hundred, this minute, cash!" Mitya added, sensing something wrong. "What's the matter, *panie*? Don't you trust me? I can't give you the whole three thousand now. If I give it, you may come back tomorrow.... Besides, it's at home, in town," said Mitya, his hopes sinking at every word. "Upon my word, the money's there, hidden."

A great sense of personal dignity showed itself in the little man's face.

"For shame!" and he said, and spat on the floor.

Pan Vrublevsky spat too.

"You do that," said Mitya, seeing with despair that all was over, "because you hope to make more out of Grushenka? You're up to no good!"

"This is a mortal insult!"

The little Pole turned red and left the room as though unwilling to hear another word. Vrublevsky went after him, and Mitya followed. He was afraid of Grushenka, afraid that the *pan* would at once raise an outcry. And so he did. The Pole walked into the room and took a theatrical attitude before Grushenka.

"*Pani* Agrippina, I have received a mortal insult!" he exclaimed.

Grushenka suddenly lost all patience, as though they had wounded her.

"Speak Russian!" she cried, "not another word of Polish! You used to talk Russian. You can't have forgotten it in five years."

She was red with anger.

"*Pani* Agrippina—"

"My name's Agrafena, Grushenka, speak Russian or I won't listen!"

The Pole drew himself up with dignity and said in broken Russian: "Agrafena, I came here to forget the past and forgive—"

"Forgive? To forgive me?" Grushenka cut him short, jumping up.

"Just so, *pani*, I'm forgiving. I was shocked when your lover Pan Mitya offered me three thousand in the other room to leave you.

"He offered you money for me?" cried Grushenka. "Is it true, Mitya? How dare you? Am I for sale?"

"*Panie!*" yelled Mitya, "she's pure. I have never been her lover!"

"How dare you defend me to him?" shrieked Grushenka. "It wasn't virtue kept me pure, and it wasn't that I was afraid of Kuzma, but that I might hold up my head when I met him and tell him he's no good. He refused the money?"

"He took it!" cried Mitya; "only he wanted to the whole three thousand at once, and I could only give him seven hundred straight off."

"I see: he heard I had money, and came here to marry me!"

"*Pani* Agrippina!" cried the little Pole. "I'm—a knight—a nobleman, not a *lajdak*. I came here to make you my wife and I find you a different woman."

"Go back where you came from! I'll tell them to turn you out and you'll be turned out," cried Grushenka in a fury. "I've been a fool to have been miserable these five years! And this isn't he at all! Was he like this? It might be his father! Where did you get your wig? He used to laugh and sing to me.... And I've been crying for five years, damned fool, shameless I was!"

She sank back in her chair and hid her face in her hands. At that instant the chorus began singing in the room on the left—a rollicking dance song.

"A Sodom!" Vrublevsky roared. "Landlord, send those women away!"

The landlord who, hearing the quarrelling, had been for some time past looking in at the door, entered the room and cried to Vrublenvksy, "What are you shouting for? D'you want to tear your throat?"

"Animal!" bellowed Pan Vrublevsky.

"Animal? And what sort of cards were you playing with just now? I gave you a pack and you hid it. You played with marked cards! I could send you to Siberia for that; it's the same as using false money...."

Going to the sofa, he thrust his fingers between the back and the cushion and pulled out a new pack of cards.

"Here's my pack, not opened!"

He held it up, showing it to all in the room.

"From where I stood I saw him slip my pack away and put his in place of it—you're a cheat and not a gentleman!"

"And I twice saw the *pan* change a card!" cried Kalganov.

"Shame on you!" cried Grushenka, rising. "Good Lord, he's come to that!"

"I thought so, too!" said Mitya.

But before he had uttered the words, Vrublevsky shook his fist at Grushenka, shouting: "You loose woman!"

Mitya flew at him, clutched him in both hands, lifted him in the air, and carried him into the room on the right from which they had just come.

"I've laid him on the floor, there," he said, returning, gasping. "He's struggling, the scoundrel! But he won't come back, no fear of that!"

He closed one half of the folding doors, and holding the other ajar called to the little Pole: "Most illustrious, will you be pleased to retire as well?"

"My dear Dmitri Fyodorovitch," said Trifon Borissovitch, "make them give you the money you lost. It's as good as stolen from you."

"I don't want my fifty rubles back," Kalganov declared.

"I don't want my two hundred, either," cried Mitya, "I wouldn't take it for anything! Let him keep it as a consolation."

"Bravo, Mitya! You're a trump, Mitya!" cried Grushenka with fierce anger.

The little *pan*, red with fury but still mindful of his dignity, was making for the door, but he stopped and said to Grushenka:

"*Pani*, if you want to come with me, come. If not, good-by."

Swelling with indignation and importance, he went to the door. This was a man of character: he had so good an opinion of himself that after all that had passed that he still thought she would marry him.

Mitya slammed the door after him.

"Lock it," said Kalganov. But the key clicked on the other side, locking it.

"That's capital!" exclaimed Grushenka. "Serve them right!"

Chapter VIII

Madness

What followed was almost an orgy. Grushenka was the first to call for wine. "I want to drink. I want to be quite drunk, as we were before. Do you remember, Mitya, do you remember how we made friends here last time!"

Mitya himself was almost delirious.

But Grushenka was continually sending him away from her.

"Go and enjoy yourself. Dance and make merry," she kept exclaiming.

And Mitya hastened to obey.

The next room was divided in two by curtains, behind which was a huge bed with a feather mattress and a pile of pillows. Grushenka settled herself at the door in an easy chair to watch the dancing and singing. The girls and the band with fiddles came, too, and at last the cart arrived with the food and wines.

Mitya busied himself running about. People began coming into the room to look on, with the hope of another party such as they had before. Mitya remembered their faces, greeting and embracing everyone. He opened the bottles and poured out wine, though only the girls were eager for the wine. The men preferred hard drinks. Mitya had hot chocolate made for the girls, and ordered three tea pots to be kept boiling to provide tea for everyone.

It became noisy, but Mitya was in his element, and the wilder it became, the more his spirits rose. If the visitors had asked him for money he would have given away his notes right and left. This was probably why Trifon Borissovitch kept hanging about Mitya. He seemed to have given up all idea of going to bed; he drank only one glass of punch, and kept a sharp look-out on Mitya's interests, making sure he did not to give cigars, Rhine wine, or money to the peasants.

Mitya remembered Andrey and had punch sent out to him. Kalganov did not want to drink, and did not care for the girls' singing; but after he had a couple glasses of wine he became lively, laughing and praising the music and songs. Maximov, drunk, never left his side. Grushenka, too, was getting drunk.

Pointing to Kalganov, she said to Mitya: "What a dear boy he is!"

Mitya, delighted, ran to kiss Kalganov and Maximov.

Great were his hopes! She had said nothing yet, and seemed purposely to refrain from speaking. But she looked at him from time to time with passion in her eyes. At last she gripped his hand and drew him to her.

"How was it you came just now? I was frightened. So you wanted to give me up to him, did you? Did you really want to?"

"I didn't want to spoil your happiness!" Mitya said.

But she did not need his answer.

"Well, go and enjoy yourself. Don't cry, I'll call you back again."

He ran away, and she listened to the singing and looked at the dancing, though her eyes followed him wherever he went. In another quarter of an hour she would call him once more and again he would run back to her.

"Come, sit beside me, tell me how you heard of my coming here?"

Mitya began telling her all about it, often looking sad.

"Why are you sad?" she asked.

"I left a man ill there. I'd give anything to know he was all right!"

"Well, never mind. So you meant to shoot yourself tomorrow! What a silly boy! What for? I like such reckless fellows as you," she said in her honey voice. "So you would go to any length for me? Did you really mean to shoot yourself tomorrow? Wait a little. Tomorrow I may have something to say to you. I won't say it today, but tomorrow. You'd like it to be today? No, I don't want to today. Go along now and have fun."

Once, however, she called him, puzzled and uneasy.

"Why are you still sad?" she said. "Though you're kissing everyone and shouting, I see something. Be merry. I'm merry. I love somebody here. Guess who it is. Ah, look, my boy has fallen asleep, poor dear, he's drunk."

She meant Kalganov. He had dropped asleep for a moment, sitting up. But he was not merely drowsy from drink; he felt suddenly down-cast. It was the whole scene. The girls' songs gradually became coarse and more reckless. And the dances were as bad. Two girls dressed up as bears rolled on the ground.

"Well, let them!" said Grushenka, happy. "When they do get a day to enjoy themselves, why shouldn't folks be happy?"

Kalganov looked as though he had been wiped with dirt. "They're beasts," he said, moving away. "It's the games they play when it's light all night in summer." And, almost as though it were personal, he declared he was bored, sat down on the sofa, and immediately fell asleep.

"Look how pretty he is," said Grushenka, taking Mitya to him. "I was combing his hair just now; his hair's so thick...."

Bending over him tenderly, she kissed his forehead.

Kalganov instantly opened his eyes and asked where Maximov was?

"So that's who you want." Grushenka laughed. "Mitya, find Maximov."

Maximov, it appeared, could not tear himself away from the girls, only running away from time to time to pour himself a glass of wine. His face and nose were red, his eyes moist. He ran up and said he was going to dance.

"Go with him, Mitya, I'll watch from here," said Grushenka.

Maximov danced his dance. But no one admired it. It consisted of nothing but skipping and hopping, and at every skip he slapped his foot.

Kalganov did not like it at all, but Mitya kissed the dancer.

"Thanks. You're tired perhaps? Would you like some sweets? A cigar?"

"A cigarette."

"Don't you want a drink?"

"I'll just have some wine.... Have you any candies?"

"Yes, there's a heap of them on the table there. Choose one, my dear soul!"

"I like one with vanilla ... for old people."

"No, brother, we've none of that sort."

"I say," the old man bent down to whisper in Mitya's ear. "That girl there, little   Marya! How would it be if you were to help me make friends with her?"

"So that's what you're after! No, brother, that won't do!"

"I'd do no harm to anyone," Maximov said.

"Oh, all right. They only come here to dance and sing, you know. But damn it all, wait a bit! Eat, drink, and be merry. Don't you want money?"

"Later on, perhaps," smiled Maximov.

"All right...."

Mitya's head was burning. He went outside to the balcony which ran round the building, overlooking the court-yard. The fresh air made him feel better. He stood in a corner, and suddenly clutched his head in his hands. His thoughts, his senses came together into a whole and threw a fearful, terrible light!

"If I'm to shoot myself, why not now?" he thought. "Why not go for the guns, and here, in this dark corner, make an end?"

He stood undecided. A few hours earlier, dashing here, he was chased by the theft he had committed, and that blood! But it was easier for him then. Then everything was over: he had lost her. His death sentence seemed necessary. But now? Now one terror had ended: that first lover had vanished. In her eyes he could see now whom she loved. Now he had everything to make him happy ... but he could not go on living!

"God! Restore to life the man I knocked down at the fence! Let this fearful cup pass from me! But what if the old man's alive? The shame of the other disgrace I would wipe away. I would restore the stolen money. I'd give it back; I'd get it somehow."

Yes, there was a ray of light in his darkness. He started to run back to the room—to her, his queen forever! Was not one moment of her love worth all the rest of life, even the agonies of disgrace? This question clutched at his heart. But as he turned from the balcony into the passage, he came upon the landlord, Trifon Borissovitch, who looked gloomy and worried, and evidently had come to find him.

"What is it, Trifon Borissovitch? Are you looking for me?"

"No, sir." He seemed not at ease. "Why should I be looking for you?"

"Why do you look so glum? You're not angry, are you? What's the time?"

"It'll be three o'clock. Past three, it must be."

"We'll leave off soon. We'll leave off."

"Don't mention it; it doesn't matter. Keep it up as long as you like...."

"What's the matter with him?" Mitya wondered.

He ran back to the room where the girls were dancing. But she was not there. She was not in the blue room either; there was no one but Kalganov asleep on the sofa. Mitya peeped behind the curtain—she was there. She was sitting in the corner on a trunk, her head and arms on the bed close by, crying bitterly.

Seeing Mitya, she beckoned him to her, and grasped his hand tightly.

"Mitya, I loved him, you know. How I loved him these five years! But did I love him or only my anger? No, him! It's a lie that it was my anger. Mitya, I was only seventeen; he was so kind to me, so merry; he used to sing to me…. And now, Lord, it's not the same man. Even his face is not the same. I shouldn't have known him. I drove here with Timofey, and all the way I was thinking how I should meet him, what I should say, how we should look at one another. My soul was faint, and all of a sudden it was just as though he had emptied a pail of dirty water over me. He talked to me like a school-master, so grave and learned. I was struck dumb. I sat staring at him, wondering why I couldn't say a word. It must have been his wife that ruined him; you know he threw me up to get married. Mitya, how shameful it is! Oh, Mitya, I'm so ashamed!"

Again she burst into tears, but clung tight to Mitya's hand.

"Mitya, darling, don't go away. I want to say one word to you," she whispered, and suddenly raised her face to him. "Tell me, who it is I love? I love one man here. Who is that man? That's what you must tell me."

A smile lit up her face swollen with weeping, her eyes shining in the half darkness.

"A falcon flew in, and my heart sank. 'Fool! That's the man I love!' That's what my heart whispered. You came in and all grew bright. What's he afraid of? I wondered. For you were frightened. It's not them he's afraid of—it's only me. So Fenya told you how I called to Alyosha out of the window that I'd loved Mityenka for one hour, and that I was going to love ... another. Mitya, how could I be such a fool as to think I could love any-one after you? Do you forgive me, Mitya? Do you love me?"

She jumped up and held him with both hands.

Mitya, dumb with rapture, gazed into her eyes, at her face, her smile, and clasped her tightly in his arms and kissed her passionately.

"You will forgive me for having tormented you? It was through spite I tormented you all. It was for spite I drove the old man out of his mind.... Do you remember how you drank at my house one day and broke the wine-glass? I remembered that and I broke a glass today and drank 'to my vile heart.' Mitya, my falcon, kiss me hard, that's right. If you love, then love! I'll be your slave now, for the rest of my life. It's sweet to be a slave. Kiss me! Beat me, do what you will with me.... I deserve to suffer. Wait...."

She thrust him away.

"Go along, Mitya, I'll come and have wine, I want to be drunk, I'm going to get drunk and dance!" She tore herself away and disappeared behind the curtain.

Mitya followed like a drunken man.

"Yes, come what may—whatever happens now, for one minute I'd give the whole world," he thought. Grushenka did, in fact, toss off a glass of champagne at one gulp, and became at once very tipsy. She sat down in the same chair as before, with a smile on her face, her cheeks glowing, her lips burning, her eyes moist; there was a passionate appeal in her eyes. Even Kalganov felt a stir at the heart and went to her.

"Did you feel how I kissed you when you were asleep just now?" she said. "I'm drunk now, that's what it is.... And aren't you drunk? And why isn't Mitya drinking? Why don't you drink, Mitya? I'm drunk, and you don't drink...."

"I am drunk with you! And now I'll be drunk with wine, too."

He drank another glass, which made him completely drunk, although till that moment he had been quite sober. From that moment everything turned about him. He walked, laughed, talked, without knowing what he was doing. He went up to her, sat beside her, gazed at her, listened to her....

She became talkative, calling everyone to her, and beckoned to different girls out of the chorus. When the girl came up, she either kissed her, or made the sign of the cross over her. In another minute she might have cried. She was greatly amused by the "little old man," as she called Maximov. He ran up every minute to kiss her hand, and finally danced again, singing a song of his own.

"Give him something, Mitya," said Grushenka. "Give him a present, he's poor, you know. Ah, the poor, the insulted! Do you know, Mitya, I shall go into a nunnery. No, I really shall one day. Alyosha said something to me today that I shall remember all my life.... Yes.... But today let us dance. I want to play today. God will forgive us. If I were God, I'd forgive every one. 'Forgive me, good people, a silly wench.' I'm a beast, that's what I am. But I want to pray. I gave a little onion. Wicked as I've been, I want to pray. Mitya, let them dance, don't stop them. Everyone in the world is good. Every one—even the worst of them. The world's a nice place. Come, I've something to ask you, everyone: Why am I so good? You know I am good. I'm very good...."

So Grushenka babbled on, more and more drunk. At last she announced she was going to dance, too. She got up from her chair, staggering.

"Sh-h! Mitya, why don't they come? Let everyone come. Call them in, too, that are locked in. Why did you lock them in? Tell them I'm dancing."

Mitya walked with a drunken swagger to the locked door, and knocked.

"Hi, you ... Podvysotskys! Come, she's going to dance. She calls you."

"*Lajdak!*" one of the Poles shouted.

"You're a *lajdak* yourself! You're a little no-good, that's what you are."

"Leave off laughing at Poland," said Kalganov.

He too was drunk.

"Be quiet, boy! If I call him no good, it doesn't mean that I called all Poland so. One *lajdak* doesn't make a Poland. Be quiet, my pretty boy."

"Why won't they make friends?" said Grushenka, and went to dance.

The chorus broke into "Ah, my porch, my new porch!"

Grushenka threw her head back, half opened her lips, waved her handkerchief, and suddenly, almost falling, stood still in the middle of the room.

"I'm weak...." she said in an exhausted voice. "Forgive me.... I'm weak."

She bowed to the chorus, and then began bowing in all directions.

"I'm sorry.... Forgive me.... Mitya, take me away," said Grushenka.

Mitya lifted her in his arms, and carried her through the curtains.

"Well, now I'll go," thought Kalganov. Walking out of the blue room, he closed the door after him. But the orgy went on and grew louder.

Mitya laid Grushenka on the bed and kissed her on the lips.

"Don't touch me...." she said in an imploring voice. "Don't touch me, till I'm yours. I've told you I'm yours, but don't touch me.... With them here, so close, you mustn't. He's here. It's nasty here...."

"I'll obey! I won't think of it...I worship you!" said Mitya. "It's nasty here."

Still holding her in his arms, he sank on his knees by the bedside.

"I know, though you're a brute, you're generous," Grushenka said. "It must be honorable...let us be good, not brutes...take me away, far away, do you hear? I don't want it to be here, but far away...."

"Yes!" said Mitya, pressing her in his arms. "I'll take you and we'll fly away.... Oh, I'd give my whole life for one year only to know about that blood!"

"What blood?" asked Grushenka.

"Nothing," said Mitya. "Grusha, you wanted to be honest, but I'm a thief. I've stolen money from Katya....a disgrace!"

"From Katya, from that young lady? No, you didn't steal it. Give it back, take it from me.... Why make a fuss? Now everything mine is yours. What does money matter? We shall waste it anyway.... Folks like us are bound to waste money. We'd better go and work the land. I want to dig the earth with my hands. We must work. I won't be your mistress, I'll be your slave, I'll work for you. We'll go to the young lady and bow down to her together, so that she may forgive us, and then we'll go away. And if she won't forgive us, we'll go anyway. Take her her money and love me.... Don't love her any more. If you love her, I shall strangle her.... I'll put out her eyes...."

"I love you. I love only you. I'll love you in Siberia...."

"Why Siberia? Never mind. I don't care...we'll work...there's snow in Siberia.... I love driving in the snow...and must have bells.... Do you hear, there's a bell ringing? Where is that bell ringing? ... Now it's stopped." She closed her eyes, exhausted, and fell asleep.

There had certainly been the sound of a bell in the distance, but the ringing had ceased. Mitya let his head sink on her breast. He did not notice that the bell had ceased ringing, nor did he notice that the songs had ceased, and that instead of singing and clamor there was absolute stillness in the house.

Grushenka opened her eyes.

"What's the matter? Was I asleep? Yes ... a bell ... I've been asleep and dreamt I was driving over the snow with bells. I was with someone I loved, with you. Far, far away. I was holding you and kissing you, nestling close to you. I was cold, the snow glistened.... It was as though I was not on earth. I woke up, and my dear one is close to me!"

"Close to you," murmured Mitya, kissing her dress, her bosom, her hands.

Suddenly he had a strange fancy: it seemed to him she was looking straight before her, not at him, not into his face, but over his head.

"Mitya, who is that looking at us?" she whispered.

Mitya turned, and saw that someone had, in fact, parted the curtains and seemed to be watching them. And not one person alone.

He jumped up and walked quickly to the intruder.

"Here, come to us," said a voice, speaking not loudly, but firmly.

Mitya passed to the other side of the curtain. The room was filled with people, but not those who had been there before. A shiver ran down his back. He recognized them. That tall, stout old man in the coat and cap was the police captain, Mihail Makarovitch. And that "consumptive-looking" dandy, "who always has such polished boots"—was the deputy prosecutor. And that small young man wearing glasses.... Mitya forgot his name though he knew him: he was the "investigating lawyer" who had only lately come to the town. And those fellows with the brass plates, why are they here? And those other two ... peasants.... And at the door was Kalganov, with Trifon Borissovitch....

"Gentlemen! What's this for?" began Mitya, but suddenly, as though beside himself, not knowing what he was doing, he cried aloud, at the top of his voice: "I under—stand!"

The young man wearing glasses came forward and began hurriedly:

"We have to make...in brief, I beg you to come this way.... It's imperative you give an explanation."

"The old man!" cried Mitya. "The old man and his blood! I understand." He almost fell on a chair close by.

"You understand? He understands! Monster and parricide! Your father's blood cries out against you!" the old captain of police roared.

He was beside himself, red in the face and quivering all over.

"This is impossible!" cried the young man. "Mihail Makarovitch, this won't do! I beg you'll allow me to speak. I should never have expected such behavior from you...."

"This is delirium, gentlemen," cried the captain. "Look at him: drunk, at this time of night, in the company of a fallen woman, and the blood of his father on his hands!"

"I beg you most earnestly, Mihail Makarovitch, to restrain yourself," the prosecutor said, "or I shall be forced to resort to—"

The lawyer did not allow him to finish. He turned to Mitya, and said in a loud voice: "Ex-Lieutenant Karamazov, it is my duty to inform you that you are charged with the murder of your father, Fyodor Pavlovitch Karamazov...."

He said something more, and the prosecutor, too, but though Mitya heard them he did not understand them. He stared at them all with wild eyes.

Book VIII • The Preliminary Investigation

Chapter I

The Beginning of Perhotin's Official Career

Pyotr Ilyitch Perhotin, knocking at the locked gates of the widow Morozov's house, was finally heard. Fenya, still excited by the fright of two hours before, was frightened again on hearing the knocking. She fancied it must be Dmitri Fyodorovitch.

She ran to the house-porter and begged him not to open the gate. But the porter, who had already been woken, had gone to the gate and, after questioning Pyotr Ilyitch and learning he wanted to see Fenya on "important business," had admitted him.

Pyotr Ilyitch Perhotin questioned her and at once learnt the most vital fact, that when Dmitri Fyodorovitch had run out to look for Grushenka, he had picked up a pestle, and when he returned, it was not with him, and his hands had blood on them.

"The blood was simply dripping from him!" Fenya exclaimed.

Pyotr Ilyitch had seen those hands stained with blood. What he now had to decide was where Dmitri Fyodorovitch had run with the pestle, to Fyodor Pavlovitch's or not. Though he had turned up nothing positive, he was sure Dmitri Fyodorovitch could have gone only to his father's.

"When he came back," Fenya added excitedly, "I told him the whole story, and asked him, 'Why have you got blood on your hands? He said it was human blood, and that he had just killed someone. He ran off like a mad man. I thought, He'll go to Mokroe and kill my mistress. I ran out to beg him not to kill her."

Fenya's old grandmother backed her story and, after asking more questions, Pyotr Ilyitch left the house more up-set than when he had entered it. The best thing to do, he decided, would be to go to Fyodor Pavlovitch's to find out whether anything had happened, and if so, what; and only go to the police when he knew for sure.

But the night was dark, Fyodor Pavlovitch's gates were strong, and he would have to knock again. His acquaintance with Fyodor Pavlovitch was the slightest. What if, after they opened to him, nothing had happened? Fyodor Pavlovitch, in his jeering way, would tell the story all over town, how a stranger called Perhotin, had broken in upon him at midnight to ask if he had been killed.

It would make a scandal. Yet the feeling was so strong that he set off again, not to Fyodor Pavlovitch's but to Madame Hohlakov's. He decided that if she denied giving Dmitri Fyodorovitch three thousand rubles, he would go to the police captain, but if she admitted giving him the money, he would go home and let the matter rest till morning.

It was, of course, perfectly evident that there was even more likelihood of causing scandal by going at eleven o'clock at night to a fashionable lady and rousing her from bed to ask her a strange question, than by going to Fyodor Pavlovitch. But uneasiness possessed him, driving him on against his will.

"I will get to the bottom of it," he repeated.

It was eleven o'clock when he entered Madame Hohlakov's house. He was admitted into the yard, but, in response to his inquiry whether the lady was still up, the porter could give no answer, except that she was usually in bed by that time.

"Ask at the top of the stairs," the porter said, "if the lady wants to receive you."

When Pyotr Ilyitch went up, the footman was unwilling to take in his name, but finally called a maid. Pyotr Ilyitch politely but insistently begged her to inform her lady that an official living in the town named Perhotin had called on business, and that if it were not of the greatest importance he would not have come.

"Tell her in those words," he told the girl.

She went away while he waited in the entry. Madame Hohlakov was in her room, though not asleep. She had been up-set ever since Mitya's visit, and had a feeling she would not get through the night without a headache. She was surprised on receiving the message from the maid, but declined to see him. But this time he was obstinate. He told the maid to say that "he had come on business of the greatest importance, and that Madame Hohlakov might regret it later if she refused to see him now."

The maid, gazing at him in wonder, took his message again to Madame Hohlakov, who was impressed. She thought a little, asked what he looked like and, when the maid he was "very well dressed, young and so polite," Madame Hohlakov decided to see him.

She put on a shawl and had "the official" wait in the drawing-room. When she went to meet him, she had a firm look and, without asking him to sit down, began at once with the question: "What do you want?"

"You, madam, on a matter concerning someone we both know, Dmitri Fyodorovitch Karamazov," Perhotin began.

He had hardly uttered the name when she interrupted him in a fury.

How much longer am I to be worried by that awful man?" she cried. "And how dare you, sir, dare to disturb a lady who is a stranger to you, in her own house at such an hour! And to force yourself upon her to talk of a man who came here, to this very room, only three hours ago, to murder me, and went stamping out as no one should leave a decent house. Let me tell you, sir, I shall complain to the authorities. Kindly leave me at once...."

"Murder! He tried to murder you, too?" exclaimed Perotin.

"Why, has he killed somebody else?"

"If you would kindly listen, madam, I'll explain it all in a few words," answered Perhotin. "At five o'clock this afternoon Dmitri Fyodorovitch borrowed ten rubles from me. Yet at nine o'clock, he came to see me with a bundle of hundred-ruble notes in his hand, his hands and face covered with blood. When I asked where he got the money, he said he got it from you so he could go to the gold mines...."

Madame Hohlakov assumed a pained but excited expression.

"Good God! He must have killed his old father!" she cried. "I have never given him money! Oh, run! Don't say another word! Save the old man ... run to his father ... run!"

"Excuse me, madam, you did not give him money? You remember it for a fact?"

"No! I refused to give it to him, for he would not have thanked me for it. He ran out in a fury. He rushed at me, but I slipped away...."

"Excuse me, I...."

"Run, you must save the poor old man from an awful death!"

"But if he has killed him already?"

"Good heavens, yes! Then what do you think we must do?"

She made Pyotr Ilyitch sit down and sat facing him. Briefly, Pyotr Ilyitch told her the history of the affair, that part of it at least which he had witnessed. He told her, too, about his visit to Fenya and about the pestle.

"Would you believe it," the lady shouted, "I knew this would happen! How often I've looked at that awful man and thought he will end by murdering me. Now it's happened ... that is, he hasn't murdered me but only his own father. And to think how near I was to death! He cursed me and flew away! What shall we do?"

Pyotr Ilyitch rose and said he was going to the police captain to tell him all about it, and leave him to do what he thought fit.

"Oh, he's an excellent man! Mihail Makarovitch, I know him. Of course, he's the person to go to. How practical you are, Pyotr Ilyitch! How well you have thought of everything! I should never have thought of it in your place!"

"Especially as I know the police captain, too," observed Pyotr Ilyitch, who continued to stand, obviously anxious to escape.

"Be sure," she went on, "to come back and tell me what you find out ... what comes to light ... how they'll try him ... and what will happen to him.... We have no capital punishment, have we? Be sure to come, even if it's three o'clock at night. Tell them to wake me.... Good heavens, I shan't sleep! Shouldn't I come with you?"

"No. But if you would write three lines in your own hand that you did not give Dmitri Fyodorovitch money, it might be of use.".

"To be sure!" Madame Hohlakov said. "I'm amazed at your good sense. Are you in the service here? I'm delighted to think you are!"

Still talking, she wrote on half a sheet of notepaper these lines: "I've never in my life lent to Dmitri Fyodorovitch Karamazov, three thousand rubles. I swear by all that's holy! K. HOHLAKOV.

"Here's the note!" she said. "Go. It's a noble deed you do!"

She made the sign of the cross over him, and saw him to the door.

"How grateful I am to you for having come to me first! How is it I haven't met you before? I shall feel flattered at seeing you at my house in the future. I'm so pleased you're living here! Such practical ability! If there's anything I can do, believe me ... oh, I love young people! Young people are the foundation of our suffering country...."

But Pyotr Ilyitch had already run away or she would not have let him go so soon. Yet Madame Hohlakov had made a rather agreeable impression on him, which softened his anxiety at being drawn into such an unpleasant affair.

"She's by no means so elderly," he thought, "on the contrary I should have taken her for her daughter."

As for Madame Hohlakov, she was enchanted by the young man.

"Such sense! In so young a man! And all that with such manners and appearance! People say the young people of today are no good for anything, but here's an example!"

So she simply forgot this "dreadful affair," and it was only as she was getting into bed, that, recalling "how near death she had been," exclaimed: "Ah, it is awful, awful!"

But she fell at once into a sound sleep.

Chapter II

Anxiety

The police captain, Mihail Makarovitch Makarov, was a widower whose widowed daughter lived with him, with her two unmarried daughters. Though he had a narrow education and lacked an understanding of the limits of his power, he did his work as well as any other. What mistakes he made were not so much from lack of brains but from carelessness, for he was always in too much of a hurry to get at things.

"I have the heart of a soldier, not a civilian," he used to say.

Pyotr Ilyitch knew he would meet some visitors at Mihail Makarovitch's, for the police captain entertained often. As it happened, the prosecutor and the district doctor, Varvinsky, a young man who had only just settled in town, were playing cards at the police captain's.

Ippolit Kirillovitch, the prosecutor, was about five and thirty. Though vain, he had a good intellect and a kind heart. All that was wrong with him was that he had a better opinion of himself than he deserved. Also, he leaned toward psychology, a study of crime and the criminal.

Nikolay Parfenovitch Nelyudov, the investigating lawyer, a charming young man who had settled in the town two months before, was sitting in the next room with the ladies. He was adept at teasing; and the ladies had christened him "the naughty man," at which he seemed to be delighted. He was short and delicate-looking, and wore a number of rings. When engaged in official duties, he became grave, as though realizing his position. He had a special gift for dealing with murderers and common criminals.

Still, Pyotr Ilyitch was shocked when he got to the police captain's. He saw everyone he knew, but they had all laid down their cards and were standing and talking. He was met with the news that old Fyodor Pavlovitch really had been murdered that evening, in his own house, and robbed. The news had only just reached them.

Marfa Ignatyevna, the wife of old Grigory who had been knocked senseless, was sleeping soundly in her bed, and might well have slept till morning after the drink she had taken. But all of a sudden she woke up, no doubt roused by a fearful epileptic scream from Smerdyakov, who was lying in the next room. That scream always preceded his fits.

Terrified, Marfa Ignatyevna ran half-awake to Smerdyakov's room. But it was dark there, and she could only hear him beginning to struggle. Then she herself screamed and was going to call her husband, but suddenly realized that when she got up he was not beside her in bed. He must have gone out—but where? She ran to the steps and called. She heard nothing but groans in the garden.

"Just as with Lizaveta Smerdyastchaya!" she thought.

She went down the steps and saw the garden gate was open.

"He must be out there, poor dear," she thought.

She went to the gate and heard Grigory weakly calling her.

"Lord, preserve us!" Marfa Ignatyevna cried, running toward the voice. That was how she found Grigory, not by the fence, but twenty paces off. It appeared he had crawled away on coming to himself, and probably had been a long time getting so far. She saw he was covered with blood, and screamed at the top of her voice.

Grigory said weakly, "He's murdered his father. Go get someone."

Seeing her master's window open and a candle in the window, she ran there and began calling him. Peeping in at the window, she saw Fyodor Pavlovitch lying on his back on the floor, his dressing-gown and shirt soaked with blood. The candle on the table lit his dead face. Terror-stricken, she rushed to the gate and ran to the neighbor, Marya Kondratyevna. Both mother and daughter were asleep, but they woke at Marfa's screaming and knocking.

Marfa managed to tell them the main fact, and to beg for help. It happened that Foma had come back from his wanderings and was staying the night with them. They got him up and all three ran to the scene of the crime.

"Someone screamed, then it was silent," Marya Kondratyevna said as they ran to where Grigory lay. The two women, with the help of Foma, carried him to the lodge. They lit a candle and saw that Smerdyakov was no better, that he had convulsions, his eyes fixed in a squint, foam flowing from his lips.

They moistened Grigory's forehead with water.

Revived, he asked immediately, "Is the master murdered?"

Foma and the women ran to the house and saw this time that not only the window, but the door to the house was open. They were afraid to go in "for fear anything should happen."

When they returned to Grigory, the old man told them to go to the police captain. Marya Kondratyevna ran there and told everyone at the party what had happened, only minutes before Pyotr Ilyitch. Thus, his story came, not as a theory, but by a witness who had seen the body.

It was resolved to act right away. The deputy police inspector was told to take four witnesses, enter Fyodor Pavlovitch's house, and open an inquiry on the spot. The district doctor insisted on accompanying him, the prosecutor, and the lawyer. Fyodor Pavlovitch was found to be quite dead, his skull battered in.

But with what? Most likely with the same weapon with which Grigory had been attacked. Grigory, to whom all possible medical assistance was given, described in a weak voice how he had been knocked down. They looked with a lantern and found the pestle.

There were no signs of disturbance in the room where Fyodor Pavlovitch was lying. But by the bed behind the screen they found an envelope. On it was written: "A present of three thousand rubles for my angel Grushenka, if she is willing to come." Below was added: "For my little chicken." The envelope had been torn open and the money removed. Beside it on the floor lay a piece of narrow pink ribbon.

One piece of Pyotr Ilyitch's evidence made a great impression on the prosecutor and the investigating magistrate, his idea that Dmitri Fyodorovitch would shoot himself by day-break, that he had spoken of it, had taken the pistols, loaded them before him, written a letter, put it in his pocket, etc. When Pyotr Ilyitch, though still unwilling to believe in it, threatened to tell someone to prevent the suicide, Mitya had answered, grinning: "You'll be too late." So they must hurry to Mokroe before the criminal shot himself.

"That's clear!" said the prosecutor, excited. "That's just the way with mad fellows like that: 'I shall kill myself tomorrow, so I'll make merry till I die!'"

The story of Dmitri buying the wine and provisions excited the prosecutor more. But all was delayed by the inquiry, the search, and formalities in the house of Fyodor Pavlovitch. So, two hours before starting, they sent on ahead to Mokroe the officer of the rural police, Mavriky Mavrikyevitch Schmertsov, who had arrived in the town the morning before to get his pay.

He was instructed to avoid raising the alarm, but to keep constant watch over the "criminal" till the arrival of the proper authorities. And he did as he was told, keeping his name and mission to himself, and giving no one but his old acquaintance, Trifon Borissovitch, the slightest hint of his secret business.

He had spoken to him just before Mitya met the landlord in the balcony, looking for him in the dark, and noticed at once a change in Trifon Borissovitch's face and voice. So neither Mitya nor anyone else knew he was being watched. The box with the pistols had been carried off by Trifon Borissovitch and put in a safe place.

It was almost four o'clock, almost sunrise, when the police captain, the prosecutor, the investigating lawyer, and other officials drove up in two carriages. The doctor had remained at Fyodor Pavlovitch's to make a post-mortem the next day on the body. He was particularly interested in the condition of Smerdyakov.

"Such violent and protracted epileptic fits, recurring continually for twenty-four hours," he said, "are rarely met with, and are of interest to science," he declared to his companions. They remembered him saying Smerdyakov could not last the night.

Chapter III

Sufferings, the First Ordeal

Mitya, looking wildly at the people round him and not understanding what was said to him, got up, threw up his hands, and shouted: "I'm not guilty of my father's blood.... I meant to kill him. But I'm not guilty."

He hardly said this before Grushenka rushed from behind the curtain and flung herself at the police captain's feet.

"It was my fault! My wickedness!" she cried. "He did it through me. I tortured him and drove him to it. I tortured that poor old man that's dead, too, in my wickedness, and brought him to this! It's my fault!"

"Yes, it's your fault! You harlot!" shouted the captain.

The prosecutor seized hold of him.

"This is not allowed, Mihail Makarovitch!" he cried. "You are not helping the inquiry.... You're ruining the case...."

"Follow custom!" cried Nikolay Parfenovitch, "Or it's impossible!"

"Judge us together!" Grushenka cried. "Punish us together. I will go with him if it's to death!"

"Grusha, my life!" Mitya fell on his knees beside her and held her in his arms. "Don't believe her," he cried. "She's not guilty of anything!"

He was dragged away from her, and she was led out.

When he recovered himself he was sitting at the table. Behind him stood men with metal plates. Facing him on the other side of the table sat Nikolay Parfenovitch, the investigating lawyer.

"Drink some water. It will calm you. Don't be frightened," he kept saying.

On Mitya's left the prosecutor was seated, and on his right a young man in a shabby hunting-jacket, with ink and paper before him. This was the secretary of the investigating lawyer.

"Drink some water," said the investigating lawyer softly.

"I have, gentlemen, I have ... come, crush me, punish me, decide my fate!" cried Mitya, staring at the investigating lawyer.

"You declare you're not guilty of your father's death?" asked the lawyer.

"I am guilty of the blood of another old man but not of my father's. And I weep for it! I killed the old man and knocked him down.... But it's hard to have to answer for that murder with a terrible murder of which I am not guilty.... It's a terrible accusation. But who has killed my father? Who can have killed him if I didn't?"

"Yes, who can have killed him?" the lawyer began, but Ippolit Kirillovitch, the prosecutor, glancing at him, addressed Mitya.

"You need not worry yourself about the old servant, Grigory Vassilyevitch. He is alive and has recovered, in spite of the terrible blows he received, according to his own and your evidence. There seems no doubt he will live."

"He's alive?" cried Mitya. "Lord, I thank Thee for the miracle."

He crossed himself three times.

"From Grigory we've received evidence concerning you that…"

The prosecutor would have continued, but Mitya jumped up.

"One minute, gentlemen, for God's sake; I will run to her—"

"It's quite impossible," Nikolay Parfenovitch almost shrieked.

Mitya was seized by the men with the metal plates and sat down.

"What a pity! I wanted to see her for one minute; I wanted to tell her that it has been washed away, that blood that was weighing on my heart, and that I'm not a murderer! Gentlemen, she is to be my wife!" he said. "Oh, thank you, gentlemen! In one minute you have given me new life! That old man used to carry me in his arms. He used to wash me in the tub when I was a baby three years old, he was like a father to me!"

"And so you—" the investigating lawyer began.

"Allow me, gentlemen, allow me one minute more," said Mitya, covering his face with his hands. "Let me have a moment to think, let me breathe, gentlemen. All this is horribly upsetting!"

"Drink a little more water," said Nikolay Parfenovitch.

Mitya took his hands from his face and laughed. His eyes were confident. He seemed completely transformed, his whole bearing changed; he was once more the equal of these men, as though they were at some social gathering.

"You're a most skillful lawyer, I see, Nikolay Parfenovitch," cried Mitya, "but I can help you now. Gentlemen, I feel like a new man, and don't be offended at my addressing you so simply. I don't pretend to be on equal terms with you. I understand why I am sitting here. There's a horrible suspicion ... hanging over me ... if Grigory has given evidence.... But to business, gentlemen, I am ready. Since I know I'm innocent, we can put an end to it in a minute. Can't we?"

Mitya spoke as though he took his listeners to be his best friends.

"For the present, we will write that you deny the charge brought against you," said Nikolay Parfenovitch, and bending down to the secretary he dictated what to write.

"You want to write that down? Well, I give my full consent, only... write this. Of disorderly conduct I am guilty, of violence on a poor old man I am guilty. And there is something else at the bottom of my heart of which I am guilty, too—but that you need not write down; that's my personal life, gentlemen. It doesn't concern you. But of the murder of my father I'm not guilty. I will prove it to you, and you'll be convinced...."

"Be calm, Dmitri Fyodorovitch," said the lawyer. "Before we go on, I should like, if you consent, to hear you confirm the statement that you disliked your father, Fyodor Pavlovitch, that you were involved in continual disputes with him. A quarter of an hour ago, you said you wanted to kill him: 'I didn't kill him,' you said, 'but I wanted to.'"

"Did I exclaim that? That may be so, gentlemen! Yes, unhappily, I did want to kill him ... many times I wanted to ... unhappily!"

"You wanted to. Would you consent to explain what motives led you to such a hatred for your parent?"

"What is there to explain, gentlemen?" Mitya shrugged his shoulders. "I have never concealed my feelings. All the town knows. Only lately I declared them in Father Zossima's cell.... And the same day, in the evening, I beat my father. I nearly killed him, and I swore I'd come again and kill him. I've been shouting it aloud for the last month, anyone can tell you that!

"But feelings, gentlemen, are another matter. You see"—Mitya made a face—"it seems to me that about feelings you've no right to question me. That's my private affair, yet ... since I haven't concealed my feelings in the past ... I won't make a secret of it now. You see, I understand, gentlemen, that there are terrible facts against me. I told everyone I'd kill him, and now, all of a sudden, he's been killed. So it must have been me!

"I can make allowances for you, gentlemen. I'm struck all of a heap myself, for who can have murdered him, if not I? That's what it comes to, isn't it? If not I, who can it be? Where was he murdered? How was he murdered? How, and with what?" he asked.

"We found him in his study, lying on his back, with his head beaten in," said the prosecutor.

"That's horrible!"

Mitya shook and hid his face in his hands.

"We will continue," said Nikolay Parfenovitch. "So what was it that caused this hatred? You have said in public, I believe, that it was based upon jealousy?"

"Well, yes, jealousy. And not only jealousy."

"Disputes about money?"

"Yes, about money, too."

"There was a dispute about three thousand rubles, I think, which you claimed as part of your inheritance?"

"Three thousand! More," cried Mitya; "more than six thousand, more than ten. I told everyone so. But I made up my mind to let it go at three thousand. I was desperately in need of three thousand ... so the bundle of notes for three thousand that I knew he kept under his pillow, ready for Grushenka, I considered as simply stolen from me. Yes, gentlemen, I looked upon it as mine, as my own property...."

The prosecutor looked significantly at the investigating lawyer.

"We will return to that subject later," said the lawyer. "You will allow us to note that point and write down that you looked upon that money as your own?"

"Write it down, by all means. I know that's another fact that tells against me, but I'm not afraid of facts. Do you know, gentlemen, you take me for a different sort of man from what I am. You're dealing with a man of the highest honor; above all—a man who's done a lot of nasty things, but has always been, and still is, honorable at bottom. I don't know how to express it. That's just what's made me wretched all my life, that I yearned to be honorable. And yet all my life I've been doing filthy things like all of us, gentlemen ... that was a mistake, like me alone!... My head aches." His brows contracted in pain. "You see, gentlemen, I couldn't bear the look of him, there was something in him that was ignoble, impudent, trampling on everything sacred, something sneering and loathsome. But now that he's dead, I feel differently."

"How do you mean?"

"I don't feel differently, but I wish I hadn't hated him so."

"You feel sorry?"

"No, not sorry, don't write that. I'm not much good myself, I'm not very beautiful, either, so I had no right to consider him ugly. That's what I mean."

Saying this Mitya became sad.

At that moment another unexpected scene followed. Though Grushenka had been removed, she was only in the room next but one from the one in which the examination was going on. She was sitting there with no one by her but Maximov, who was terribly depressed and scared, clinging to her side as though for security. At their door stood one of the peasants with a metal plate on his breast.

Grushenka was crying.

Suddenly her grief was too much for her. She jumped up and, with a wail of sorrow, rushed out of the room to her Mitya, so unexpectedly that they had not time to stop her. Mitya, hearing her cry, jumped up with a yell and rushed to meet her, not knowing what he was doing. But they were not allowed to come together, though they saw one another. He was seized by the arms. He struggled and tried to tear himself away. It took three or four men to hold him. She was seized too, and he saw her stretching out her arms, crying, as they led her away.

When the scene was over, he came to himself, sitting in the same place as before, crying out: "What do you want with her? Why do you torment her? She's done nothing!"

The lawyers tried to soothe him.

About ten minutes later Mihail Makarovitch came hurriedly into the room, and said in an excited voice to the prosecutor: "She's been removed, she's downstairs. Will you allow me to say one word to this unhappy man, gentlemen?"

"By all means, Mihail Makarovitch," said the investigating lawyer. "In the present case we have nothing against it."

"Listen, Dmitri Fyodorovitch, my dear fellow," began the police captain with a look of warm, almost fatherly, feeling on his face. "I took Agrafena Alexandrovna downstairs, and confided her to the care of the landlord's daughters, and that old fellow Maximov. I calmed her. I impressed on her that you have to clear yourself, so she mustn't hinder you, or depress you, or you may lose your head and say the wrong thing.

"She understood. She's a sensible girl, my boy, a good-hearted girl. She would have kissed my hands, begging help for you. She sent me to tell you not to worry about her. I must go, my dear fellow, and tell her that you are comforted and calm. So you must be calm, you understand? I was unfair to her; she is a gentle soul, and not to blame for anything. What am I to tell her, Dmitri Fyodorovitch? Will you sit quietly now and be calm?"

The good-natured police captain said much that was not permitted, but Grushenka's suffering had touched his heart.

Mitya jumped up and rushed towards him.

"Forgive me, gentlemen, allow me!" he cried. "You've the heart of an angel, Mihail Makarovitch, I thank you. I will be calm.

Tell her that I am quite cheerful knowing she has a guardian like you. I'll be done with all this directly, and as soon as I'm free, I'll be with her. Gentlemen," he said to the lawyers, "now I'll tell everything. We'll finish this directly.

"Gentlemen, that woman is the queen of my heart. If only you knew! Did you hear her cry, 'I'll go to death with you'? And what have I, a penniless beggar, done for her? Why such love for me? How can an ugly brute like me deserve such love that she is ready to go to exile with me? And how she fell down at your feet for my sake! And yet she's proud and has done nothing! How can I help adoring her, and rushing to her? Gentlemen, forgive me! But now I am comforted."

He sank back in his chair and, covering his face with his hands, burst into tears. But they were happy tears. The old police captain seemed much pleased, the lawyers also. They felt the examination was passing into a new phase.

"Now, gentlemen, I am at your service. If it were not for these trivial details, we should understand one another in a minute. But, I declare, we must have confidence in each other, or there'll be no end to it. To business, gentlemen, and don't tease me with trifles. Only ask me about facts and what matters."

So spoke Mitya. The questioning began again.

Chapter IV

The Second Ordeal

"You don't know how you encourage us, Dmitri Fyodorovitch, by your readiness to answer," said Nikolay Parfenovitch. "And you have made a very just remark about the mutual confidence without which it is impossible to get on in cases of such importance. We, on our side, will do everything in our power in conducting the case. You approve, Ippolit Kirillovitch?" he asked, turning to the prosecutor.

"Undoubtedly," replied the prosecutor somewhat coldly.

Nikolay Parfenovitch felt marked respect for Ippolit Kirillovitch, the prosecutor. He was almost the only one who put faith in Ippolit Kirillovitch's talents as a psychologist. On the other hand, young Nikolay Parfenovitch was the only person the prosecutor liked. They had come to an understanding about the present case. And as they sat at the table, the sharp-witted junior caught every indication on his senior colleague's face.

"Gentlemen, only let me tell my story without trivial questions and I'll tell you everything," said Mitya.

"Excellent! Thank you. But before we listen to your views, will you allow me to inquire as to another little fact of great interest to us? I mean the ten rubles you obtained yesterday on the security of your pistols from your friend, Pyotr Ilyitch Perhotin."

"I pledged them, gentlemen, for ten rubles. What more? As soon as I got back to town I pledged them."

"You got back to town? Then you had been out of town?"

"Yes, I went a journey of forty miles into the country. Didn't you know?"

The prosecutor and Nikolay Parfenovitch exchanged glances.

"Well, how would it be if you began your story with all you did yesterday, from the morning onwards? Allow us, for instance, to inquire why you were absent from town, and when you left and when you came back."

"You should have asked me like that from the beginning," said Mitya, "and, if you like, we won't begin from yesterday, but from the morning of the day before; then you'll understand how, why, and where I went. I went the day before yesterday, gentlemen, to a merchant of the town called Samsonov to borrow three thousand rubles on safe security. It was a pressing matter, gentlemen."

"Allow me to interrupt you," the prosecutor put in politely. "Why were you in such pressing need for just that sum, three thousand?"

"Gentlemen, you needn't go into details, how, when and why—why just so much money, and all that rigmarole. It'll run to three volumes, and you'll want an epilogue!"

Mitya said all this with the good-natured but impatient familiarity of a man who is anxious to tell the whole truth and is full of the best intentions.

"Gentlemen!"—he corrected himself—"don't be angry with me for my restlessness. Don't think I'm drunk. I'm quite sober. And I've my own dignity to keep up, too. I am, after all, in the position of a criminal, and it's your business to watch me. I can't expect you to pat me on the head for what I did to Grigory.

"But you puzzle God Himself with such questions. I shall get mixed up, if you go on like this. I ask you, gentlemen, to drop that method of questioning. You can put peasants off their guard like that, but I know the tricks. I've been in the service, too. You forgive my openness?" he cried good-naturedly.

Nikolay Parfenovitch listened, and laughed, too. Though the prosecutor did not laugh, and kept his eyes fixed on Mitya as though anxious not to miss the least syllable, the slightest movement, the smallest twitch of his face.

"That's how we've treated you from the start," said Nikolay Parfenovitch. "We haven't tried to put you out by asking how you got up in the morning and what you had for breakfast. We began, indeed, with questions of the greatest importance."

"I understand. I appreciate your present kindness. We three are gentlemen, so let everything be on the footing of mutual confidence between educated, well-bred people. Allow me to look upon you as my best friends. That's no offense to you, is it?"

"Not at all. You've expressed it well," said Nikolay Parfenovitch.

"Then enough of those trivial questions, gentlemen!" cried Mitya. "Or there's simply no knowing where we shall get to!"

"I will follow your sensible advice entirely," the prosecutor broke in. "I don't withdraw my question, however. It is vitally important for us to know exactly why you needed precisely three thousand."

"Why I needed it? Oh.... Well, it was to pay a debt."

"A debt to whom?"

"That I refuse to answer, gentlemen. Not because I can't, or it would be damaging, for it's a small matter, but—I won't because it's a matter of principle: that's my private life, and I won't allow any going into my private life. Your question has no bearing on the case, and what has nothing to do with the case is my private affair. I wanted to pay a debt of honor, but to whom I won't say."

"Allow me to make a note of that," said the prosecutor.

"By all means. Write down I think it not honorable to say."

"Allow me to caution you, sir, and remind you again, if you are unaware of it," the prosecutor began sternly, "that you have a perfect right not to answer questions put to you now, and we on our side have no right to extort an answer from you if you decline to give it for one reason or another. That is entirely a matter for your personal decision. But it is our duty to explain the degree of injury you will be doing yourself by refusing to give this or that piece of evidence. I beg you to continue."

"Gentlemen, I'm not angry. I..." Mitya said. "Well, gentlemen, you see, that Samsonov to whom I went then ..."

Mitya was anxious not to omit the slightest detail. At the same time he was in a hurry to get it over. But as he gave his evidence it was written down, and they had time to pull him up.

Mitya disliked this, but submitted. He did exclaim from time to time, "That's enough to make an angel out of patience!" Or, "Gentlemen, it's no good your irritating me." But he preserved his good-humor.

He told how Samsonov had made a fool of him two days before. The sale of his watch for six rubles to get money for the journey was something new to the lawyers. They were greatly interested, and even, to Mitya's up-set, thought it should be written down as a second proof that he had hardly a penny at the time.

Little by little Mitya began to speak less politely.

After describing his journey to see Lyagavy, the night spent in the stifling hut, and so on, he came to his return to the town. Here he began, without being particularly urged, to give a minute account of the agonies of jealousy he endured on Grushenka's account.

He was heard with silent attention. They inquired into the circumstance of his having a place of ambush in Marya

Kondratyevna's house at the back of Fyodor Pavlovitch's garden to keep watch on Grushenka, and of Smerdyakov's bringing him information. They laid stress on this, and noted it down.

The coldness with which the investigating lawyer and the prosecutor stared at him as he told his story up-set him at last.

"That boy, Nikolay Parfenovitch, and that sickly prosecutor are not worth my confidences," he thought. "It's base of me to do it." But he pulled himself together to go on.

When he came to his visit to Madame Hohlakov, he regained his spirits and wished to tell a little story of that lady which had nothing to do with the case. But the investigating lawyer stopped him, and suggested he pass on to "more essential matters."

He described his despair when leaving Madame Hohlakov's, and how he thought he'd "get three thousand if he had to murder someone," they stopped him and noted it down." Mitya let them write without protest. At last he reached the point when he learned Grushenka had deceived him and returned from Samsonov's as soon as he left her there, though she said she would stay.

"If I didn't kill Fenya then, gentlemen, it was only because I hadn't time," broke from him. That, too, was written down. Mitya waited sadly, and was beginning to tell how he ran into his father's garden, when the investigating lawyer stopped him, and, opening a case that lay on the sofa, brought out the pestle.

"Do you recognize this?" he asked.

"Oh, yes," he laughed. "Of course I recognize it. Let me have a look at it.... Damn it, never mind!"

"You've forgotten to mention it," said the lawyer.

"I wouldn't have concealed it from you. Do you suppose I could have managed without it? It simply escaped my memory."

"Please tell us how you came to arm yourself with it."

"Certainly, gentlemen."

And Mitya described how he took the pestle and ran.

"What was your object in arming yourself with it?"

"What object? No object. I just picked it up and ran off."

"What for, if you had no object?"

Mitya's anger flared He stared at "the boy" and smiled angrily. He felt shame at having told "such people" about his jealousy.

"Bother the pestle!" broke from him.

"But still—"

"Oh, to keep off dogs ... Because it was dark...."

"Have you ever on previous occasions taken a weapon with you when you went out, since you're afraid of the dark?"

"Damn it, gentlemen! There's no talking to you!" cried Mitya. Turning to the secretary he said, red with anger, he said, "Write down at once...'that I snatched up the pestle to go and kill my father ... Fyodor Pavlovitch...by hitting him on the head with it!' Well, now are you satisfied, gentlemen?" he said, glaring.

"We quite understand that you made that statement just now because you are angry with us and with the questions we have been asking you, which you do not consider important, though they are, in fact, essential," the prosecutor remarked dryly.

"Yes, I took the pestle.... What does one pick things up for at such moments? I don't know. I picked it up and ran—that's all. Move on, or I won't tell you anymore."

He sat with his elbows on the table and gazed at the wall, struggling with his feelings. He wanted to get up and declare he wouldn't say another word.

"You see, gentlemen," he said at last, controlling himself, "I listen to you and am having a dream...a dream I have sometimes.... It's always the same dream...someone is hunting me, someone I'm afraid of ... he's hunting me in the dark, in the night ... tracking me, and I hide somewhere from him, behind a door or cupboard, and the worst of it is he always knows where I am, but pretends not to know to stretch out my agony, to enjoy my terror.... That's just what you're doing now. It's just like that!"

"Is that the sort of dream you have?" asked the prosecutor.

"Yes, it is. Why don't you write it down?" said Mitya, smiling.

"No; no need to. But still you do have curious dreams."

"It's not a question of dreams now, gentlemen—this is real life! I'm a wolf and you're the hunters. Well, hunt him down!"

"You're wrong to make such..." began Nikolay Parfenovitch.

"No, I'm not wrong!" Mitya flared up again, though he grew more good-humored at every word. "You may not trust a criminal or a man on trial tortured by your questions, but an honorable man—no! You have no right... but—Well, shall I go on?"

"If you'll be so kind," answered Nikolay Parfenovitch.

Chapter V

The Third Ordeal

Though Mitya spoke sullenly, it was evident he was trying more than ever not to miss a single detail. He told them how he leapt over the fence into his father's garden; how he went up to the window; told them all that had passed under the window. He described the feelings that troubled him in the garden when he longed so to know whether Grushenka was there or not. But, strange to say, the lawyers listened now with a sort of reserve, looked coldly at him, and asked few questions.

"They're angry and offended," Mitya thought. "Well, bother them!"

When he described how he decided to make the "signal" to his father that Grushenka had come so that he should open the window, the lawyers paid no attention to the word "signal," as though they failed to grasp the meaning of the word. Then, coming to the moment when, seeing his father peering out of the window, his hatred flared up and he pulled the pestle out of his pocket, he suddenly stopped short

"Well?" said the lawyer. "You pulled out the weapon and ... what happened?"

"Why, then I murdered him ... hit him on the head and cracked his skull.... I suppose that's your story. That's it!"

His eyes suddenly flashed. All his smothered anger flamed up.

"Our story?" repeated Nikolay Parfenovitch. "Well—and yours?"

Mitya was a long time silent.

"My story, gentlemen, is this," he began softly. "Whether it was someone's tears, or my mother prayed to God, or an angel kissed me, I don't know. But I rushed from the window and ran to the fence. My father was alarmed, and for the first time he saw me and cried out, then sprang back from the window. And then Grigory caught me."

At that point he raised his eyes and looked at his listeners. They were staring at him with unruffled attention. Indignation seized him.

"Why, you're laughing at me, gentlemen!" He broke off.

"What makes you think that?" asked Nikolay Parfenovitch.

"You don't believe one word I've said—that's why! I understand, of course, that I have come to the vital point. The old man's lying there now with his skull broken, while I—after describing how I wanted to kill him, and how I snatched up the pestle—but ran from the window. As though one could believe a fellow on his word!"

He swung round on his chair so that it creaked.

"And did you notice," asked the prosecutor, as though not seeing that Mitya was upset, "when you ran away from the window if the door into the garden was open?"

"No, it was not open."

"It was not?"

"It was shut. Wait a bit!" He seemed suddenly to bethink himself. "Why, did you find the door open?"

"Yes, it was open."

"Who could have opened it if you did not yourselves?" cried Mitya.

"The door stood open and your father's murderer undoubtedly went in at that door, and, having accomplished the crime, went out by the same door," the prosecutor said. "That is clear. The murder was committed in the room and *not through the window*. There can be no doubt of that."

Mitya was absolutely dumbfounded.

"But that's impossible!" he cried. "I didn't go in.... The door was shut the whole time I was in the garden. I only stood at the window and saw him through the window. That's all.... I remember. And if I didn't, it would be just the same. I know it, for no one knew the signals except Smerdyakov, and me, and the dead man. And he wouldn't have opened the door without the signals."

"What signals?" asked the prosecutor, instantly losing all trace of his dignity. He scented an important fact of which he knew nothing, and was filled with dread that Mitya might not disclose it.

"So you didn't know!" Mitya looked at him with a malicious smile. "What if I won't tell you? How could you find out? No one knew the signals except Smerdyakov, my father, and me. It's an interesting fact. There's no knowing what you might build on it.

"But take comfort, gentlemen, I'll reveal it," he said. "You don't know the man you have to deal with! For I'm a man of honor and you—are not."

The prosecutor took this without a word. He was trembling with impatience to hear the new fact. Mitya told them about the signals invented by Fyodor Pavlovitch for Smerdyakov. He told them what every tap on the window meant, tapped the signals on the table, and when Nikolay Parfenovitch said he supposed he, Mitya, had tapped the signal that "Grushenka has come" when he tapped to his father, he answered, "Yes."

"So now build up your tower," Mitya broke off, turning away.

"No one knew the signals but your dead father, you, and Smerdyakov? No one else?" Nikolay Parfenovitch asked again.

"Yes. The valet Smerdyakov, and Heaven. Write down about Heaven. That may be of use. Besides, you will need God yourselves."

They had already begun writing it down. But while they wrote, the prosecutor said, as though it were a new idea: "But if Smerdyakov also knew these signals and you deny all responsibility for the death of your father, was it not he, perhaps, who knocked the signal agreed upon to get your father to open, and ... committed the crime?"

Mitya turned upon him a look of deep hatred.

"You've caught the fox," commented Mitya at last; "you've got the beast by the tail. I see through you, Mr. Prosecutor. You thought, of course, that I should jump at that, and shout with all my might, 'Yes! It's Smerdyakov; he's the murderer.' Confess!"

But the prosecutor did not confess. He held his tongue.

"You're wrong. I'm not going to shout 'It's Smerdyakov,'" said Mitya.

"And you don't even suspect him?"

"Why, do you suspect him?"

"He is suspected, too."

"Listen," Mitya brought out. "From the beginning, almost from the moment when I ran out to you from behind the curtain, I've had Smerdyakov in my mind. I've been sitting here shouting that I'm innocent, and thinking of Smerdyakov. In fact, I, too, thought of Smerdyakov just now; but it's not his doing."

"Do you suspect anyone else?" Nikolay Parfenovitch asked.

"I don't know anyone it could be, but ... not Smerdyakov,"

"What makes you so sure it's not he?"

"Because Smerdyakov is a man of the lowest character. He has the heart of a chicken. When he talked to me, he always trembled for fear I should kill him, though I never raised my hand to him. He fell at my feet and cried; he kissed these boots, begging me 'not to frighten him.' He's a chicken—sickly, epileptic, weak-minded—a child of eight could thrash him.

"It's not Smerdyakov, gentlemen. He doesn't care for money; he wouldn't take my presents. Besides, what motive had he? Also, he's very likely his son. Do you know that?"

"We have heard that story about Smerdyakov. But you are your father's son, too, you know; yet you yourself told everyone you meant to murder him."

"That's a thrust! And a nasty one! It's base of you to say that to my face, because I told you myself. I not only wanted to murder him, but I might have done it. What's more, I went out of my way to tell you I nearly murdered him. But I didn't; that's what you're not taking into account. And that's why it's base. I didn't kill him!"

He was almost choking.

"And what has he told you, gentlemen—Smerdyakov, I mean?" he added after a pause. "May I ask that question?"

"You may ask any question," the prosecutor replied, "any question relating to the facts of the case, and we are, I repeat, bound to answer every inquiry you make. We found the servant Smerdyakov lying unconscious in his bed, in an epileptic fit. The doctor who was with us told us he may not live out the night."

"Well the devil must have killed him," broke from Mitya.

"We will come back to this later," Nikolay Parfenovitch said. "Now, would you like to continue your statement?" Mitya went on with his story. But he was evidently depressed. He was exhausted, and shaken. To make things worse, the prosecutor angered him, as though intentionally, with interruptions about "trifling points."

Scarcely had Mitya described how, sitting on the wall, he had struck Grigory on the head with the pestle, and how he had then jumped down to look at him, when the prosecutor stopped him to ask him to describe exactly how he was sitting on the wall. Mitya was surprised.

"I was sitting like this, one leg on one side, one on the other."

"And the pestle?"

"The pestle was in my hand."

"Not in your pocket? Was it a violent blow you gave him?"

"It must have been a violent one. Why do you ask?"

"Would you mind showing us how you moved your arm, and in what direction?"

"You're making fun of me, aren't you?" asked Mitya.

Mitya turned, sat astride his chair, and swung his arm.

"This was how I struck him! How I knocked him down!"

"Thank you. May I ask you to tell us why you jumped down?"

"I jumped down to look at the old man. I don't know why!"

"Though you were excited and were running away?"

"Yes, though I was excited and running away."

"You wanted to help him?"

"Yes, perhaps I did want to help him.... I don't remember."

"You didn't quite know what you were doing?"

"I remember every detail. I jumped down to look at him, and wiped his face with my handkerchief."

"We have seen it. Did you hope to restore him?"

"I don't know. I wanted to make sure if he was alive or not."

"You wanted to be sure? Well, what then?"

"I couldn't decide. I ran away thinking I'd killed him."

"Good," said the prosecutor. "That's all I wanted. Proceed."

It never entered Mitya's head to tell them he had jumped back from pity and, standing over the figure, had uttered words of regret: "Now you've done it old man. I'm sorry. You'll have to live with it."

The prosecutor could only draw one conclusion: that the man had jumped back "to see whether the *only* witness of his crime were dead; that he must therefore have been a man of great strength, coolness, and foresight even at such a moment."

He was satisfied: "I've provoked the fellow by 'trifles' and he has said more than he meant to."

With painful effort Mitya went on.

But this time he was pulled up immediately.

"How came you to run to the servant, Fedosya Markovna, with your hands covered with blood, and your face, too?"

"I didn't notice the blood at all at the time," answered Mitya.

"That's quite likely. It does happen sometimes."

The prosecutor exchanged glances with Nikolay Parfenovitch.

"I simply didn't notice. You're quite right there, prosecutor," Mitya said.

Next came the account of Mitya's decision to "step aside" and make way for the happiness of Grushenka. But he could not make up his mind to open his heart to them as before. He disliked speaking of "the queen of his soul" before these persons "who were on him like bugs." So, in response to their questions he answered: "Well, I made up my mind to kill myself. What had I left to live for? Her first rightful lover had come back, the man who wronged her but who'd hurried back after five years to atone for the wrong with marriage.... So I knew it was all over for me.... And behind me disgrace, and that blood—Grigory's.... What had I to live for? So I went to redeem the pistols I had pledged, and to put a bullet in my brain tomorrow."

"And a grand feast the night before?"

"Yes, a grand feast the night before. Damn it all, gentlemen! Do hurry and finish. I meant to shoot myself not far from here. I'd planned to do it at five o'clock in the morning. And I had a note in my pocket that I wrote at Perhotin's when I loaded my pistols. Here's the letter. Read it!" He took it from his pocket and flung it on the table.

The lawyers read it with curiosity, and added it to the papers.

"And you didn't even think of washing your hands at Perhotin's? You were not afraid then of arousing suspicion?"

"What suspicion? Suspicion or not, I should have galloped here just the same, and shot myself at five o'clock, and you wouldn't have been in time to do anything. If it hadn't been for what's happened to my father, you would have known nothing about it, and wouldn't have come here. Oh, it's the devil murdered father, it was through the devil you found it out so soon. How did you manage to get here so quick?"

"Mr. Perhotin informed us that when you came to him you held in your blood-stained hands ... a bundle of hundred-ruble notes"

"That's true, gentlemen. I remember it."

"Now, one little point presents itself. Can you tell us," Nikolay Parfenovitch began with extreme gentleness, "where you got so much money, when it appears from the facts that you had not been home?"

"No, I didn't go home," answered Mitya, perfectly composed.

"Allow me then to repeat my question," Nikolay Parfenovitch went on, as though inching up to the subject. "Where were you able to obtain such a sum all at once, when by your own confession, at five o'clock the same day you—"

"I was in want of ten rubles and pledged my pistols with Perhotin, and then went to Madame Hohlakov to borrow three thousand, which she wouldn't give me, and so on, and all the rest of it," Mitya said. "Yes, gentlemen, I was in want of money, and suddenly thousands turned up. You're afraid, 'What if he won't tell us where he got it?' Well, I'm not going to tell you, gentlemen. You'll never know," said Mitya.

The lawyers were silent for a moment.

"You must understand, Mr. Karamazov, that it is of vital importance for us to know," said Nikolay Parfenovitch softly and gently.

"I understand; but still I won't tell you."

The prosecutor, too, intervened, reminding the prisoner he was at liberty to refuse to answer questions if he thought it to his interest, and so on. But in view of the damage he might do himself by his silence—

"And so on, Gentlemen, enough! I've heard that before," Mitya said. "I can see for myself how important it is, that it's the vital point, and still I won't say."

"What's it to us? You're harming yourself," said Nikolay Parfenovitch nervously.

"Gentlemen," said Mitya, lifting his eyes, "I had an idea from the first that we should come to a dead-end at this point. But when I began to give my evidence, it was still far away; and I was so simple that I began with the idea of mutual confidence existing between us. Now I see that such confidence is out of the question, for we were bound to come to this stumbling-block. Now there's an end of it! But I don't blame you. You can't believe it all simply on my word. I understand that."

He sat in sad silence.

"Couldn't you, without giving up your resolve to be silent about the chief point, could you not give us some hint as to the motives which make you to refuse to answer at a crisis so full of danger to you?"

Mitya smiled sadly.

"I'm much more good-natured than you think, gentlemen. I'll tell you the reason why and give you that hint, though you don't deserve it. I won't speak of that, gentlemen, because it would be a stain on my honor. The answer to the question where I got the money would expose me to far greater disgrace than the murder and robbing of my father, if I had done so. That's why I can't tell you. Are you going to write that down?"

"Yes, we'll write it down," said Nikolay Parfenovitch.

"You ought not write that about 'disgrace.' I needn't have told you. I made you a present of it, so to speak, and you pounce upon it at once. Oh, well, write what you like," he said with disgust. "I'm not afraid of you, I can still hold up my head before you."

"And can't you tell us the nature of that disgrace?"

"No, it's over, don't trouble yourselves. It's not worth soiling one's hands. I have soiled myself enough. You're not worth it.... Enough. I'm not going on."

This was said with such finality that Nikolay Parfenovitch did not insist, but from Ippolit Kirillovitch's eyes he saw he had not given up.

"Can you at least tell us what sum you had when you went into Mr. Perhotin's?"

"I can't tell you that."

"You spoke to Mr. Perhotin, I believe, of having received three thousand from Madame Hohlakov."

"Perhaps I did. Enough, gentlemen. I won't say how much I had."

"Will you be so good then as to tell us how you came here and what you did since you arrived?"

"You might ask the people about that. But I'll tell you if you like."

He proceeded to do so, briefly. Of the raptures of his love he said nothing, but told them he gave up his decision to shoot himself because of "new things in the case." He told the story without going into details. And this time the lawyers did not worry him much.

"We shall verify all that. We will come back to it during the examination of the witnesses, which will, of course, take place in your presence," said Nikolay Parfenovitch. "And now allow me to request you to lay on the table everything in your possession, especially all the money you still have about you."

"My money, gentlemen? Certainly. I understand. I'm surprised you haven't inquired about it before. It's true I couldn't get away anywhere. But here's my money—count it—take it. That's all, I think."

He turned it out his pockets. They counted the money, which amounted to eight hundred and thirty-six rubles, and forty pennies.

"And is that all?" asked the investigating lawyer.

"Yes."

"You stated just now that you spent three hundred rubles at Plotnikovs'. You gave Perhotin ten, your driver twenty, here you lost two hundred, then...."

Nikolay Parfenovitch reckoned it all up. Mitya helped him readily. They recollected every penny and included it in the reckoning.

"With this eight hundred you must have had about fifteen hundred?"

"I suppose so," snapped Mitya.

"How is it they all say there was much more?"

"Let them say it."

"But you said it yourself."

"Yes, I did, too."

"We will compare all this with the evidence of other persons not yet examined. Don't be anxious about your money. It will be taken care of and be given back to you at the conclusion of... what is beginning...if it appears, or is proved you have the right to it. Well, and now...."

Nikolay Parfenovitch got up, and told Mitya it was his duty to make a minute and thorough search "of your clothes and everything else...."

"By all means, gentlemen. I'll turn out all my pockets, if you like."

And he did, in fact, begin turning out his pockets.

"It will be necessary to take off your clothes, too."

"Undress? Damn it! Won't you search me as I am! Can't you?"

"It's impossible, Dmitri Fyodorovitch. You must remove your clothes."

"As you like," Mitya said gloomily; "only, please, not here, but behind the curtains. Who will search them?"

"Behind the curtains, of course."

Nikolay Parfenovitch bent his head in agreement.

Chapter VI

The Prosecutor Catches Mitya

Mitya could never have conceived that anyone could behave like that to him. Worst of all, there was something humiliating in it. It was nothing to take off his coat, but he was asked to undress further. From pride he gave in without a word. "Well, must I take off my shirt, too?" he asked, but Nikolay Parfenovitch did not answer. He was busy with the prosecutor examining the coat, the trousers, and the cap.

"I ask you for the second time—need I take off my shirt or not?"

"We will tell you what to do," Nikolay Parfenovitch said.

Meantime a consultation was going on between the lawyers. There turned out to be on the coat a huge patch of blood, dry, and stiff. There were bloodstains on the trousers, too. Nikolay Parfenovitch, in the presence of the witnesses, passed his fingers along the collar, the cuffs, and the seams of the coat and trousers, looking for money.

"He treats me not as an officer but as a thief," Mitya said to himself.

"Excuse me," cried Nikolay Parfenovitch, noticing that the cuff of Mitya's shirt was turned in and covered with blood, "what's that, blood?"

"Yes," Mitya said.

"That is, what blood? ... and why is the cuff turned in?"

Mitya told him how he got the sleeve stained with blood looking after Grigory, and had turned it inside when he was washing his hands.

"You must take off your shirt, too. That's important as evidence."

Mitya flushed red with rage.

"What, am I to stay naked?" he shouted.

"Don't be disturbed. We will arrange something. Take off your socks."

"You're joking? Is that really necessary?"

"We are in no mood for joking," answered Nikolay Parfenovitch.

"Well, if I must—" said Mitya.

Sitting on the bed, he took off his socks. He felt awkward. All were clothed while he was naked, and strange to say, when he was undressed he felt somehow guilty in their presence, and was almost ready to believe himself that he was inferior to them. It was a misery to him to take off his socks. They were very dirty, and so were his underclothes, and now everyone could see. What was worse, he hated his feet. All his life he thought his big toes hideous. And now they would all see them.

"Would you like to look else-where if you're not shamed to?"

"No, there's no need at present."

"Well, am I to stay naked like this?" he added angrily.

"Yes, that can't be helped for the time.... You can wrap yourself in a quilt from the bed, and I ... I'll see to all this."

All the things were shown to the witnesses. The report of the search was drawn up, and at last Nikolay Parfenovitch went out, and the clothes were carried out after him. Ippolit Kirillovitch went out, too.

Mitya was left alone with the peasants. He wrapped himself in the quilt. He felt cold. His bare feet stuck out, and he couldn't pull the quilt, which was small, over them enough so as to cover them.

Nikolay Parfenovitch seemed to be gone a long time.

"He thinks of me as a puppy," thought Mitya. "That rotten prosecutor has gone, too. No doubt my nakedness disgusts him!"

Mitya imagined his clothes would be returned to him. But Nikolay Parfenovitch came back with different clothes, brought in by one of the common folk.

"Here are clothes for you," he said, well satisfied with his mission. "Mr. Kalganov has kindly provided these for this emergency. You can keep your own socks and underclothes."

Mitya flew into a passion.

"I won't have other people's clothes!" he cried, "give me my own!"

"It's impossible!"

"Give me my own. Damn Kalganov and his clothes!"

It was a long time before they were able to quiet him down. They impressed upon him the fact that his clothes, being stained with blood, must be "included with the other evidence," and they "had not the right to let him have them now ... till the outcome of the case."

Mitya subsided into a dull silence and dressed himself with Kalganov's clothes. He observed as he put them on that the clothes were better than his old ones, and he disliked "gaining by the change." The coat was tight. "Am I to be dressed like a fool for your amusement?"

They said he was exaggerating, that Kalganov was only a little taller, so only the trousers were a little too long. But the coat turned out to be really tight in the shoulders.

"Damn it! I can hardly button it," Mitya said. "Be so good as to tell Kalganov that I didn't ask for his clothes, and it's not my doing that they've dressed me up like a clown."

"He understands that, and is sorry...I mean, not sorry to lend you his clothes, but sorry about all this business," said Nikolay Parfenovitch.

"Confound his sorrow! Well, am I to go on sitting here?"

He was asked to go back to the "other room."

Mitya went in, scowling with anger and trying not to look at anyone. Dressed in another man's clothes, he felt disgraced, even in the eyes of the common folk, and of Trifon Borissovitch, whose face appeared in the doorway, and disappeared immediately.

"He's come to look at me dressed up," thought Mitya.

He sat on the same chair as before.

"What now? Are you going to flog me? That's all that's left," he said to the prosecutor. He would not turn to Nikolay Parfenovitch. "He looked too closely at my socks, and turned them inside out on purpose to show everyone how dirty they were!"

"Well, now we must begin the examination of witnesses," said Nikolay Parfenovitch, as though in reply to Mitya's question.

"Yes," said the prosecutor thoughtfully.

"We've done what we could in your interest, Dmitri Fyodorovitch," Nikolay Parfenovitch went on, "but having received from you a refusal to explain the source from which you obtained the money found upon you, we are, at the present moment—"

"What is the stone in your ring?" Mitya interrupted, pointing to a ring on the prosecutor's finger.

"Ring?" repeated Nikolay Parfenovitch with surprise.

"Yes...on your middle finger, what stone is that?" Mitya persisted.

"That stone is called a smoky topaz," Nikolay Parfenovitch said, smiling. "Would you like to look at it? I'll take it off ..."

"No, don't take it off," cried Mitya, suddenly angry with himself. "There's no need. Damn it! Gentlemen, you've sullied my heart! Can you suppose I would conceal it from you if I had really killed my father? No, that's not Dmitri Karamazov. If I were guilty, I shouldn't have waited for your coming, but should have killed myself before this! The man who opened the door to my father and killed him, robbed him. Who was he? I'm racking my brains. But it was not Dmitri Karamazov, and that's all I can tell you."

Mitya uttered his monologue as though he were determined to be absolutely silent for the future. When he ceased speaking, the prosecutor said, as though it were the most ordinary thing: "Oh, about the open door of which you spoke just now, we may as well inform you of a very interesting piece of evidence of the greatest importance. It was given by Grigory, the old man you wounded.

"On his recovery, he stated that *before* he noticed you running in the dark from the open window, he glanced to the left and saw the door open—that door which you stated had been shut the whole time you were in the garden. I will not conceal from you that Grigory himself bears witness that you must have run from that door, though, of course, he did not see you do so, since he only noticed you first some distance away."

Mitya leapt up from his chair.

"Nonsense!" he yelled. "It's a barefaced lie. He couldn't have seen the door open because it was shut. He's lying!"

"I consider it my duty to repeat that he is firm in his statement. He does not waver. We've cross-examined him several times."

"It's false! It's either an attempt to slander me," Mitya shouted. "Or he's raving from loss of blood. He must have fancied it when he came to....."

"Yes, but he noticed the open door, not when he came to after his injuries, but as soon as he went into the garden from the lodge."

"It's false! It can't be! He's slandering me from spite.... He couldn't have seen it ... I didn't come from the door," gasped Mitya.

The prosecutor turned to Nikolay Parfenovitch.

"Confront him with it," he said.

"Do you recognize this object?"

Nikolay Parfenovitch laid upon the table a thick official envelope. It was empty, and open at one end.

Mitya stared at it.

"It...it must be that envelope of my father's, the envelope that contained the three thousand rubles...and if there's inscribed on it, allow me, 'For my little chicken' ... yes—three thousand!" he shouted, "three thousand, do you see?"

"Of course, we see. But we didn't find the money in it. It was empty, lying on the floor by the bed, behind the screen."

For some seconds Mitya stood as though thunderstruck.

"Gentlemen, it's Smerdyakov!" he shouted. "It's he who's murdered him! He's robbed him! No one else knew where the old man hid the envelope. It's Smerdyakov!"

"But you, too, knew of the envelope and that it was under the pillow."

"I never knew. This is the first time I've seen it. I only heard of it from Smerdyakov He was the only one who knew where the old man kept it hidden, I didn't know ..."

Mitya was completely breathless.

"But you told us yourself the envelope was under your father's pillow. You said it was under the pillow, so you must have known it."

"We've got it written down," confirmed Nikolay Parfenovitch.

"It's absurd! I'd no idea it was under the pillow. And perhaps it wasn't.... It was just a guess that it was under the pillow. What does Smerdyakov say? Have you asked him where it was? I told you without thinking that it was under the pillow, and now you—you know how one says the wrong thing, without meaning it. Only Smerdyakov.... He didn't even tell me where it was! It's his doing; there's no doubt about it, he murdered him, that's as clear as daylight now," Mitya said. "You must arrest him at once.... He must have killed him while I was running away and while Grigory was unconscious, that's clear now.... He gave the signal and father opened to him ... for no one but he knew the signal, and without the signal father would never have opened the door...."

"But you're forgetting the circumstance," the prosecutor said, still speaking with the same restraint, though with a note of triumph, "that there was no need to give the signal if the door already stood open when you were there, in the garden...."

"The door," said Mitya, and he stared speechless at the prosecutor. "Yes, the door! It's a nightmare! God is against me!" he exclaimed.

"Come," the prosecutor went on, "you can judge for yourself, Dmitri Fyodorovitch. On the one hand we have the evidence of the open door from which you ran out, a fact which overwhelms you and us. On the other side your persistent silence with regard to the source of the money you obtained so suddenly, when only three hours earlier you pledged your pistols for the sake of ten rubles! In view of these facts, what are we to believe? And don't accuse us of being 'scoffing people' who are incapable of believing in the generous impulses of your heart.... Try to see our position ..."

Mitya turned pale.

"Very well!" he exclaimed. "I will tell you my secret. I'll tell you where I got the money! I'll reveal my shame, that I may not have to blame myself or you hereafter."

"Believe me, Dmitri Fyodorovitch," put in Nikolay Parfenovitch, in a voice of almost pathetic delight, "every sincere and complete confession on your part may, later on, have an immense influence in your favor, and may, indeed, moreover—"

The prosecutor gave him a slight shove under the table.

Chapter VII

Mitya's Great Secret. Received with Hisses

"Gentlemen," Mitya began, "I want to make a full confession: that money was *my own*."

The lawyers' faces lengthened. They hadn't expected that.

"How do you mean?" asked Nikolay Parfenovitch, "when at five o'clock on the same day, from your own confession—"

"Damn five o'clock on the same day! That's nothing to do with it! That money was my own, stolen by me...it was fifteen hundred rubles, I had it on me all the time."

"But where did you get it?"

"I took it off my neck, gentlemen ... it was here, round my neck, sewn up in a rag. It's a month since I put it round my neck...to my shame and disgrace!"

"And from whom did you...take it?"

"You mean, 'steal'? Speak plainly. Yes, I stole it last night."

"Last night? But you said it was a month since you ... got it?"

"Yes. I stole it from her, Katerina Ivanovna, to whom I was once engaged. Do you know her?"

"Yes, of course."

"She's a noble creature. But she has hated me ever so long, and with good reason!"

"Katerina Ivanovna!" Nikolay Parfenovitch exclaimed.

"Oh, don't take her name in vain! It's wrong of me to bring her into it. Yes, I've seen that she hated me. But enough. I need only tell you that she sent for me a month ago, gave me three thousand rubles to send off to her sister in Moscow, and I ... it was just at that fatal moment in my life when I ... well, in fact, when I'd just come to love another. She's sitting below now, Grushenka. I carried her off here to Mokroe, and wasted in two days half that damned three thousand; the other half I kept round my neck. But yesterday I spent it. What's left of it, eight hundred rubles, is in your hands now."

"Excuse me. When you were here a month ago you spent three thousand, not fifteen hundred, everybody knows that."

"Who knows? Who counted the money?"

"You told everyone you spent exactly three thousand."

"True. I told the whole town. And here, at Mokroe, too, everyone reckoned it was three thousand. Yet I didn't spend three thousand, but fifteen hundred. And the other fifteen hundred I sewed into a little bag. That's where I got that money yesterday...."

"This is almost miraculous," said Nikolay Parfenovitch.

"Allow me to ask," said the prosecutor, "have you informed anyone of this before?"

"I told no one."

"That's strange. Do you mean absolutely no one?"

"Absolutely no one."

"Why did you make such a secret of it? You told us it was 'disgraceful,' though, in my view at least, it's only an act of the greatest recklessness and not so disgraceful.... Even admitting it was highly discreditable, still, that's not 'disgraceful.' There are indications, too, if I am not mistaken, that you confessed this to someone, I mean that the money was Katerina Ivanovna's, and so it's surprising that, to the present moment, you have made such a secret of it.... It's not easy to believe it could cost you such distress to confess such a secret...."

The prosecutor ceased speaking. He did not conceal his anger.

"It's not the fifteen hundred that's the disgrace, but that I put it apart from the rest of the three thousand," said Mitya.

"Why?" asked the prosecutor. "What is there disgraceful in your having set aside half of the three thousand? Your taking the three thousand is more important than what you did with it. And by the way, for what purpose did you set apart that half?"

"The purpose is the whole point!" cried Mitya. "I was calculating, and to calculate in such a case is vile ... and that vileness has been going on a whole month."

"It's incomprehensible."

"Perhaps it is. Attend to what I say. I appropriate three thousand entrusted to me and spend it on a spree. Say I spend it all, and next morning I go to her and say, 'Katya, I've done wrong, I squandered your three thousand.' Is that right? No, it's not right—it's not honest, and it's cowardly. I'm a beast, with no more self-control than a beast, but I'm not a thief! I squandered it, but I didn't steal it.

"Follow me carefully: I spend fifteen hundred of the three thousand. Next day I take half that to her: 'Katya, take this fifteen hundred from me, I'm a beast, and no good, for I've wasted half the money, and I shall waste this, too, so keep me from temptation!'

"What of that alternative? I should be a beast and no good, but not altogether a thief, or I should not have brought back what was left, but have kept that, too. She would see at once that since I brought back half, I would pay back what I'd spent. In that case I should be no good, but not a thief!"

"I admit that there's a certain distinction," said the prosecutor. "But it's strange that you see such a vital difference."

"Yes, I see a vital difference! Every man may be a scoundrel, but not everyone can be a thief. And a thief is lower than a scoundrel, that's my conviction. Listen, I carry the money about me a whole month, I may make up my mind to give it back tomorrow, and I'm a scoundrel no longer, but I cannot make up my mind, though every day wanting to, and yet for a whole month I can't bring myself to it. Is that right to your thinking?"

"Certainly, that's not right, that I can understand," answered the prosecutor. "But let us give up all discussion of these subtleties and, if you will be so kind, get back to the point. And the point is that you have still not told us, although we've asked you, why, in the first place, you halved the money, throwing away one half and hiding the other? What did you mean to do with that fifteen hundred? That I must know, Dmitri Fyodorovitch."

"Yes, of course!" said Mitya. "Forgive me, I'm not explaining the chief point, or you'd understand in a minute, for it's the motive that's the disgrace! It was all to do with the old man, my dead father. He was always after Agrafena Alexandrovna, and I was jealous; I thought she was hesitating between me and him.

"So I kept thinking every day, suppose she were to make up her mind all of a sudden, and say to me, 'I love you, not him; take me to the other end of the world.' And I had only forty pennies, what could I do? I'd be lost. You see, I didn't understand her then, I thought she wanted money, and that she wouldn't forgive my poverty. So I counted out half of that three thousand, sewed it up in the little bag before I was drunk, and went off to get drunk on the rest. That was base!"

Both the lawyers laughed aloud.

"I should have called it sensible not to have spent it all," laughed Nikolay Parfenovitch, "for, after all, what does it amount to?"

"Why, I stole it, that's what it amounts to! You horrify me by not seeing that! Every day I had that fifteen hundred round my neck, I said to myself, 'You're a thief!' That's why I've been so savage all this month, because I felt I was a thief. I couldn't make up my mind. I didn't dare even tell Alyosha about that fifteen hundred, I felt such a scoundrel.

"While I carried it I said to myself every hour: 'No, Dmitri Fyodorovitch, you may yet not be a thief.' Why? Because I might go and pay back that fifteen hundred to Katya. Only yesterday I made up my mind to tear it off my neck. And it was only when I did that I became a thief, and a dishonest man. Why? Because I destroyed my dream of going to Katya and saying, 'I'm a scoundrel, but not a thief!' Do you understand now?"

"What made you decide to do it yesterday?" Nikolay Parfenovitch asked.

"Because I had condemned myself to die at five o'clock this morning. I thought it made no difference whether I died a thief or a man of honor. But I see it's not so. What tortured me most has not been the thought I'd killed the old servant, and was in danger of Siberia just when my love was being rewarded. That did torture me, but not so much as knowing that I had torn that money off my breast and spent it, and had become a thief! Gentlemen, I tell you, it's impossible not only to live a scoundrel, but to die a scoundrel."

Mitya was pale. His face had a haggard look.

"I am beginning to understand you, Dmitri Fyodorovitch," the prosecutor said. "But all this, if you'll excuse my saying so, is a matter of nerves. Why, for instance, should you not have saved yourself such misery by returning that fifteen hundred to the lady who entrusted it to you? And after confessing your errors to her, why could you not have asked her to lend you the sum needed for your expenses, which she would certainly not have refused you in your distress, especially if it had been with the security you offered to Madame Hohlakov?"

Mitya turned red.

"You can't be speaking in earnest?" he said angrily.

"I assure you I'm in earnest.... Why do you imagine I'm not?"

"How base that would have been! Gentlemen, you are torturing me! You must know I had that plan myself! Yes, gentlemen, I, too, had that thought, all this month, so that I was on the point of deciding to go to Katya—tell her of my treachery, and beg for money to run away with the other, the rival who hated and insulted her! Are you mad!"

"Mad I am not, but I did speak in haste ... of that feminine jealousy ... if there could be such in this case, as you assert ... yes, perhaps there is something of the kind."

"But that would have been infamous!" Mitya brought his fist down on the table. "That would have been filthy beyond everything! Do you know, she might have given me that money, to show her contempt for me. And I'd have taken the money and, for the rest of my life ... oh, God! Forgive me, gentlemen, I'm making such an outcry because I've had that thought in my mind only the day before yesterday, that night when I was having all that bother with Lyagavy, till that happened ..."

"Till what happened?" put in Nikolay Parfenovitch.

But Mitya did not hear it.

"I have made you an awful confession," Mitya said gloomily. "You must appreciate it, and what's more, you must respect it, for if not, then you've no respect for me, and I shall die of shame at having confessed it to men like you! Oh, I shall shoot myself! Yes, I see already that you don't believe me. What, you want to write that down, too?" he cried.

"Yes, what you said just now," said Nikolay Parfenovitch, "that up to the last hour you were still thinking of going to Katerina Ivanovna to beg that sum from her. That's an important piece of evidence for us, Dmitri Fyodorovitch, for the case ... and for you."

"Have mercy, gentlemen! Don't write that. I've torn my heart apart, and you are fingering the wounds.... Oh, my God!"

He hid his face in his hands.

"Don't worry," the prosecutor said, "everything that is written down will be read over to you afterwards, and what you don't agree to we'll change as you like. But now I'll ask you one little question for the second time. Has no one heard from you of that money you sewed up? That is almost impossible to believe."

"No one, I told you before, or you've not understood anything!"

"Very well, this matter is bound to be explained, and there's plenty of time. We have perhaps a dozen witnesses that you spread it abroad, and even shouted almost everywhere about the three thousand you'd spent, not fifteen hundred. And now, too, you gave many people to understand you brought three thousand with you."

"You've got not dozens, but hundreds of witnesses, that have heard it!" cried Mitya.

"Well, all bear witness to it. And that *all* means something."

"It means nothing. I talked rot, and everyone just repeated it."

"But what need had you to 'talk rot,' as you call it?"

"From bravado perhaps ... at having wasted so much money.... To try and forget the money I had sewn up, perhaps ... yes, that was why ... damn it ... how often will you ask me that question? Well, I told a fib, and that was the end of it. Once I said it I didn't care to correct it. Why does a man tell lies sometimes?"

"That's difficult to decide," said the prosecutor. "Tell me, though, was that 'amulet' on your neck a big thing?"

"No, not big."

"How big, for instance?"

"If you fold a hundred-ruble note in half, that would be the size."

"You'd better show us the remains of it. You must have them."

"What nonsense! I don't know where they are."

"Excuse me: where and when did you take it off your neck? According to your own evidence you didn't go home."

"When I was going from Fenya's to Perhotin's, on the way I tore it off my neck and took out the money."

"In the dark?"

"What should I want a light? I did it with my fingers in one minute."

"Without scissors, in the street?"

"Why scissors? It was an old rag, torn in a minute."

"Where did you put it afterwards?"

"I dropped it there."

"Where was it, exactly?"

"In the market-place! The devil knows where. Why must you know?"

"That's extremely important, Dmitri Fyodorovitch. It would be evidence in your favor. Don't you understand? Who helped you to sew it up?"

"No one helped me. I did it myself."

"Where did you get the material, the rag in which you sewed it?"

"Are you laughing at me?"

"Not at all. We're in no mood for laughing, Dmitri Fyodorovitch."

"I don't know where I got the rag—somewhere, I suppose."

"I should have thought you couldn't have forgotten it?"

"It's true, I don't remember. I might have torn a bit off my linen."

"That's interesting. We might find tomorrow the shirt or whatever it is from which you tore the rag. Was it, cloth or linen?"

"Goodness only knows what it was. Wait a bit.... I believe I sewed it up in a cap of my landlady's."

"In your landlady's cap?"

"Yes. I took it from her."

"How did you get it?"

"I remember taking a cap for a rag, perhaps to wipe my pen. I took it without asking because it had no worth. I sewed the notes up in it."

"And you remember that for certain now?"

"No. I think it was in the cap. What does it matter?"

"In that case your landlady will remember the thing was lost?"

"No, she didn't miss it. It was an old rag, not worth a penny."

"And where did you get the needle and thread?"

"I'll stop now. I won't say more. Enough!" said Mitya, angry.

"It's strange that you should have so completely forgotten where you threw the pieces in the market-place."

"Give orders for the market-place to be swept tomorrow, and perhaps you'll find it," said Mitya. "Enough, gentlemen! I see you don't believe me! It's my fault, not yours. I ought not to have been so ready to confess. Why did I degrade myself? It's a joke to you. I see that from your eyes. You led me on. Damn you!"

He hid his face in his hands. The lawyers were silent. A minute later he raised his head and looked at them, his face expressing complete despair. But they had to finish what they were about. They had to begin examining the witnesses.

It was by now eight o'clock in the morning. The lights had been turned off. Mihail Makarovitch and Kalganov, who had been continually in and out of the room while the questioning was going on, had now both gone out again. The lawyers, too, looked tired. It was a wretched morning, the rain streamed down in bucketfuls.

"May I look out the window?" Mitya asked Nikolay Parfenovitch.

"Oh, as much as you like," the latter replied.

Mitya went to the window. The rain lashed against its little greenish panes. He could see the muddy road just below the house, and farther away, in the rain and mist, a row of poor, black huts. He thought of what he had planned when the sun rose.

"Perhaps it would be even better on a morning like this," he thought.

Suddenly he turned to his questioners.

"Gentlemen," he cried, "I see I am lost! But she? Tell me about her, I beg you. Surely she need not be ruined with me? She's innocent, she was out of her mind when she cried last night 'It's all my fault!' She's done nothing! I've been grieving over her all night.... Can't you tell me what you're going to do with her now?"

"You can set your mind at rest, Dmitri Fyodorovitch," the prosecutor said. "We have, so far, no grounds for interfering with the lady. I trust it may be the same later in the case.... We'll do everything in our power. Set your mind completely at rest."

"Gentlemen, I thank you. I knew you were honest, straight-forward people in spite of everything. You've taken a load off my heart.... Well, what are we to do now?"

"We must examine the witnesses without delay. That must be done in your presence and therefore—"

"Shall we have some tea first?" said Nikolay Parfenovitch.

They decided that if tea were ready downstairs they would have a glass, then "go on," putting off their proper breakfast until a more favorable opportunity.

Tea was ready below and was soon brought up. Mitya was exhausted. He could hardly hold his head up, and from time to time everything seemed to be dancing before his eyes. "A little more and I shall begin raving," he said to himself.

Chapter VIII

The Evidence of the Witnesses. The Babe

The examination of the witnesses began. The main point was the three thousand rubles: did Mitya spend it at Mokroe on the first occasion, and was it three thousand or fifteen hundred? And, again, did he spend three thousand or fifteen hundred yesterday? All the evidence turned out to be against Mitya. And some facts went against his story.

The first witness was Trifon Borissovitch. He was not in the least shamed as he stood before the lawyers. He had, on the contrary, an air of severe anger with the accused, which gave him an appearance of truthfulness and personal dignity. He said little, waited to be questioned, and answered exactly. He bore witness that the sum spent a month before could not have been less than three thousand.

"What a lot of money he flung away on the gypsy girls alone! I dare-say he wasted a thousand on them alone."

"I don't believe I gave them five hundred," Mitya cut in. "It's a pity I didn't count the money at the time, but I was drunk...."

"More than a thousand went on them, Dmitri Fyodorovitch," said Trifon Borissovitch. "You threw it about every which way, and they picked it up. They've been driven away from here, or maybe they'd bear witness themselves how much they got from you. I saw it in your hands myself—count it I didn't, that's true enough—but by the look of it I should say it was far more than fifteen hundred...."

As for what was spent yesterday, he said Dmitri Fyodorovitch told him, as soon as he arrived, that he had brought three thousand with him.

"Surely I didn't declare that, Trifon Borissovitch?" said Mitya.

"You did, Dmitri Fyodorovitch. You said it before Andrey. Andrey himself is still here. Send for him. And in the hall, when you were treating the chorus, you shouted out you would leave your sixth thousand here—with what you spent before."

The evidence as to the "sixth" thousand made a strong impression on the lawyers. They were delighted with this new way of reckoning. They questioned the peasants, the driver, and Kalganov. The peasants and driver all confirmed Trifon Borissovitch's evidence. The lawyers noted with special care Andrey's account of the conversation he had with Mitya on the road: "'Where,' says Dmitri Fyodorovitch, 'am I going, to heaven or to hell, shall I be forgiven in the next world?'"

The psychological Ippolit Kirillovitch heard this with a smile, and recommended these remarks as to where Dmitri Fyodorovitch would go be "included in the case."

Kalganov, when called, spoke to the lawyers as though he had never met them before. He began by saying "he knew nothing about it and didn't want to." But it appeared he had heard of the "sixth" thousand. He "didn't know" how much money Mitya had in his hands. He backed up the information that the Poles had cheated at cards. But he stated that, after the Poles had been turned out, Mitya's position with Agrafena Alexandrovna improved, and she said she loved him. He spoke of Agrafena Alexandrovna with respect, as though she was a lady of the best society. Ippolit Kirillovitch examined him at length, and only from him learnt what made up Mitya's "romance" on that night.

Mitya did not once pull Kalganov up.

The Poles, too, were examined. Though they had gone to bed in their room, they had not slept all night, and when the police arrived they hastily dressed and got ready, realizing that they would certainly be sent for. They gave their evidence with dignity, though not without some uneasiness. The little Pole was a retired official who had served as a veterinary surgeon. His name was Mussyalovitch. Pan Vrublevsky, they discovered, was a dentist with no degree.

Although Nikolay Parfenovitch asked the questions, they gave their answers to Mihail Makarovitch, Pan Colonel, to them the most important person. But after being corrected several times by Mihail Makarovitch himself, they grasped that they had to address their answers to Nikolay Parfenovitch. It turned out they could speak Russian quite correctly, except for their accent.

Of his relations with Grushenka, past and present, Pan Mussyalovitch spoke proudly and warmly, so that Mitya was roused and said he would not allow those "no good so-and-so's" to speak like that in his presence! Pan Mussyalovitch at once called attention to the words "no good" and begged it should be put down in the record.

Mitya was filled with rage.

"He's no good! You can put that down. And put down, too, that, in spite of the 'rules' I still declare he's no good!" he cried.

Though Nikolay Parfenovitch did insert this in the record, he showed great tact. After reprimanding Mitya, he cut short all further inquiry into the romantic aspect of the case, and quickly passed to what was essential. One piece of evidence given by the Poles roused special interest: how Mitya tried to buy off Pan Mussyalovitch, offering him three thousand rubles to resign his claims, seven hundred down, the rest "to be paid next day."

He had sworn at the time that he had not the whole sum with him at Mokroe, but that his money was in the town. Mitya said hotly that he had not said that he would be sure to pay him the remainder next day. But Pan Vrublevsky confirmed the statement, and Mitya finally admitted it must have been as the Poles said.

The prosecutor pounced on this piece of evidence. It seemed to establish for the prosecution that half, or a part, of the three thousand that had come into Mitya's hands might really have been left somewhere in Mokroe. This would explain why only eight hundred rubles were to be found in Mitya's hands. This circumstance had been the one piece of evidence which, insignificant as it was, had so far told in Mitya's favor.

Now this piece of evidence had broken down. In answer to the prosecutor's inquiry where he would have got the remaining two thousand three hundred rubles, since he denied having more than fifteen hundred, Mitya replied he meant to offer the "little chap," not money, but a formal deed to his rights to the village of Tchermashnya, those rights which he had offered to Samsonov and Madame Hohlakov.

The prosecutor smiled at the "innocence of this subterfuge."

"And you imagine he would have accepted such a deed as a substitute for two thousand three hundred rubles in cash?"

"He certainly would have accepted it," Mitya declared. "Why, he might have grabbed not two thousand, but four or six, for it. He would have put his lawyers on to the job, and might have got, not three thousand, but the whole property out of the old man."

The evidence of Pan Mussyalovitch was entered, then they let the Poles go. The incident of the cheating at cards was hardly touched upon. Nikolay Parfenovitch was too well pleased with them, and did not want to bring up trifles. There had been drinking and disorder enough that night.... So the two hundred rubles stayed in the Poles' pockets.

Then old Maximov was summoned. He came in timidly, looking depressed. He had, all this time, taken refuge below with Grushenka, sitting dumbly beside her, "now and then blubbering over her and wiping his eyes," as Mihail Makarovitch described afterwards. So that she herself began trying to comfort him.

The old man at once confessed that he had done wrong, that he had borrowed "ten rubles" from Dmitri Fyodorovitch, and was ready to pay it back. To Nikolay Parfenovitch's direct question had he noticed how much money Dmitri Fyodorovitch held in his hand, as he must have been able to see the sum when he took the note from him, he declared, surely, that there was twenty thousand.

"Have you ever seen so much as twenty thousand before, then?" inquired Nikolay Parfenovitch with a smile.

"To be sure I have, not twenty, but seven, when my wife mortgaged my little property. She'd only let me look at it from a distance, boasting of it. It was a very thick bundle, all rainbow-colored notes. And Dmitri Fyodorovitch's were rainbow-colored...."

He was not kept long. At last it was Grushenka's turn. Nikolay Parfenovitch was worried about the effect her appearance might have on Mitya, and said a few words of caution to him, but Mitya bowed his head in silence, giving him to understand "that he would not make a scene." Mihail Makarovitch himself led Grushenka in.

She entered with a stern and gloomy face that looked almost composed, and sat down quietly on the chair offered by Nikolay Parfenovitch. She was pale, and seemed cold, and wrapped herself closely in her shawl. She was suffering from a slight fever—the first symptom of the long illness which followed that night. Her grave air, her direct earnest look and quiet manner, made a very favorable impression on everyone. Nikolay Parfenovitch was even a bit "fascinated." He admitted himself, when talking about it afterwards, that only then had he seen "how handsome she was," for, though he had seen her before, he looked upon her as something of a "harlot."

"She has the manners of the best society," he said, gossiping later.

As she entered the room, Grushenka glanced for an instant at Mitya, who looked at her uneasily. But her face reassured him at once. After the usual inquiries and warnings, Nikolay Parfenovitch asked her, hesitating, but in the most courteous manner, on what terms she was with the retired lieutenant, Dmitri Fyodorovitch Karamazov.

To this Grushenka firmly and quietly replied: "He was a friend. He came to see me as an acquaintance during the last month."

To further questions she answered plainly and frankly that, though "at times" she thought him attractive, she had not loved him, but had won his heart as well as his old father's "in my nasty spite." She saw that Mitya was jealous of Fyodor Pavlovitch, but that only amused her. She had never meant to go to Fyodor Pavlovitch, but was simply laughing at him. I had no thoughts for either of them all this last month. I was expecting another man, who had wronged me. But I think, she said in conclusion, "that there's no need for you to inquire about that, or for me to answer you, for that's my own affair."

Nikolay Parfenovitch dismissed the "romantic" aspect of the case and passed to the serious one, the question of the three thousand rubles. Grushenka confirmed the statement that three thousand rubles had certainly been spent on the first party at Mokroe, and, though she had not counted the money herself, she heard it was three thousand from Dmitri Fyodorovitch's own lips.

"Did he tell you that alone, or before someone else, or did you only hear him speak of it to others in your presence?" the prosecutor inquired.

Grushenka replied that she had heard him say so before other people, and had heard him say so when they were alone.

"Did he say it to you alone once, or several times?" inquired the prosecutor, and learned that he had said it several times.

Ippolit Kirillovitch was well satisfied with this evidence.

Further examination brought out the fact that Grushenka knew, too, where that money had come from, and that Dmitri Fyodorovitch had got it from Katerina Ivanovna.

"Did you ever hear that the money spent a month ago was not three thousand, but less, and that Dmitri Fyodorovitch had saved half that sum for his own use?"

"No, I never heard that," answered Grushenka.

She said further that Mitya often told her he hadn't a penny.

"He was always expecting to get some from his father," said Grushenka.

"Did he never say... casually, perhaps" Nikolay Parfenovitch put in, "that he intended to make an attempt on his father's life?"

"He did say so," admitted Grushenka.

"Once or several times?"

"He mentioned it several times, always in anger."

"And did you believe he would do it?"

"No, I never believed it," she said. "I had faith in him."

"Gentlemen, allow me," cried Mitya, "to say one word to Agrafena Alexandrovna."

"You can speak," Nikolay Parfenovitch assented.

"Agrafena Alexandrovna!" Mitya stood. "Have faith in God and in me. I am not guilty of my father's murder!"

Having uttered these words, Mitya sat down again. Grushenka stood up and crossed herself devoutly. "Thank be to Thee, O Lord," she said, in a voice of emotion, then turned to Nikolay Parfenovitch and added: "As he has spoken now, believe it! I know him. He'll say anything as a joke or from obstinacy, but he'll never deceive you against his conscience. He's telling the whole truth, you may believe it."

"Thanks, Agrafena Alexandrovna, you've given me fresh courage," Mitya cried.

As to the money spent the previous day, she said she did not know what sum it was, but had heard him tell several people that he had three thousand. As to where he got the money, she said he told her he had "stolen" it from Katerina Ivanovna, and that she replied he hadn't stolen it and must pay it back the next day.

On the prosecutor's asking her if the money he said he had stolen from Katerina Ivanovna was what he had spent yesterday, or what he squandered here a month ago, she said he meant the money spent a month ago, and that that was how she understood him.

Grushenka was released, and Nikolay Parfenovitch told her she might return to the town and that if he could be of any assistance to her, with horses for example, he—

"I thank you," said Grushenka, bowing to him, "I'm going with this old gentleman, I am driving him back to town with me, and meanwhile, if you'll allow me, I'll wait below to hear what you decide about Dmitri Fyodorovitch."

Mitya was calm and looked more cheerful, but only for a moment. He felt down because of his physical weakness; his eyes were closing with fatigue. The examination of the witnesses over, they went on to a final change in the proceedings. Mitya moved from his chair to the corner and lay down on a large chest covered with a rug.

He was almost asleep when he heard close beside him Grushenka's tender voice, thrilling with emotion, say, "I'm coming with you. I won't leave you now for the rest of my life, I'm coming with you." His heart glowed, he struggled towards the light, and he longed to live.

"What! Where?" he exclaimed, opening his eyes and sitting up, as though he had awakened from a fainting spell, smiling brightly. Nikolay Parfenovitch was standing over him, suggesting he should hear the procedures read aloud and sign it.

Mitya guessed that he had been asleep an hour or more, but he did not hear Nikolay Parfenovitch. He was suddenly struck by the fact that there was a pillow under his head, which hadn't been there when he lay back, exhausted.

"Who put that pillow under my head? Who was so kind?" he cried, tears in his voice, as though some great kindness had been shown him.

He never found out who this was; perhaps one of the peasants, or Nikolay Parfenovitch's secretary, had thought to put a pillow under his head; but his whole soul quivered with tears. He went to the table and said he would sign whatever they liked.

"I've had a good dream, gentlemen," he said, with joy in his face.

Chapter IX

They Carry Mitya Away

When the papers were signed, Nikolay Parfenovitch read the "Committal" to the prisoner setting forth the charges that, having examined the accused, who pleaded not guilty but has brought forward nothing in his defense, while the witnesses testified against him, has ruled that, to prevent him from evading pursuit and judgment, he be detained in such-and-such a prison, which he hereby notifies to the accused. In brief, Mitya was informed that he was a prisoner and would be driven to the town and there shut up.

Mitya listened attentively, and only shrugged his shoulders.

"Well, gentlemen, I don't blame you. I'm ready.... I understand there's nothing else for you to do."

Nikolay Parfenovitch told him gently that he would be taken by the police officer, Mavriky Mavrikyevitch....

"Stay," Mitya said, feeling the need to address all in the room.

"Gentlemen, we're all monsters, and I am the lowest! I've sworn to change my ways, and every day I've done the same filthy things. Such men as I need a blow to catch them and bind them by a force. Never should I have risen of myself! I accept the charge against me, and the public shame. I want to suffer, and by suffering I shall be made whole. But for the last time, I am not guilty of my father's blood. I accept my punishment, not because I killed him, but because I meant to kill him. Good-by,

350

gentlemen, don't be angry with me for having shouted at you during the examining. In another minute I shall be a prisoner, but now, for the last time as a free man, Dmitri Karamazov offers you his hand."

His voice trembled as he stretched out his hand, but Nikolay Parfenovitch, with a sudden movement, hid his hands behind his back. "The inquiry is not yet over," he said, embarrassed.

"We will continue it in the town. I, for my part, am ready to wish you all success...in your defense. As a matter of fact, Dmitri Fyodorovitch, I tend to regard you as more unfortunate than guilty. All of us here, if I may be so bold, are ready to recognize that you are, at bottom, a man of honor, but one who has been carried away by passion to far too great a degree...."

"You are good and humane, may I see *her* to say 'good-by' for the last time?"

"Certainly, though it's impossible except in the presence of..."

"Oh, well, if it must be so, it must!"

Grushenka was brought in, but the farewell was brief. She made a bow to Mitya and said, "I have told you I am yours, and I will be yours. I will follow you wherever they send you. Farewell; you are guiltless, though you've been your own undoing."

Her lips quivered, and tears flowed.

"Forgive me, Grusha, for ruining you, too, with my love."

Mitya would have said something more, but broke off and went out. He was at once surrounded by men who kept a constant watch on him.

At the foot of the steps two carts stood in readiness. Mavriky Mavrikyevitch, a sturdy, thick-set man with a wrinkled face, was annoyed about something, and was shouting angrily.

He asked Mitya to get into the cart with excessive surliness.

"When I stood him drinks in the tavern, he had a different face," thought Mitya.

At the gates there was a crowd of people. All stared at Mitya.

"Forgive me at parting, good people!" Mitya shouted.

"Forgive us too!" he heard two or three voices cry.

"Good-bye to you, too, Trifon Borissovitch!"

But Trifon Borissovitch did not turn round. He was too busy shouting about some-thing. It appeared that everything was not yet ready in the second cart, in which two constables were to accompany Mavriky Mavrikyevitch. The peasant who had been ordered to drive the second cart was pulling on his smock, saying it was not his turn to go, but Akim's. But Akim was not to be seen. They ran to look for him.

"What do we want a second cart for?" Mitya put in. "Let's start with the one, Mavriky Mavrikyevitch. I won't run away from you, old fellow?"

"I'll trouble you, sir, to learn how to speak to me. I'm not 'old fellow' to you, and you can keep your advice for another time!" Mavriky Mavrikyevitch said.

Mitya was reduced to silence. He flushed. A moment later he felt cold. The rain had ceased, but the sky was still overcast, and a keen wind was blowing in his face.

"I've taken a chill," thought Mitya.

At last Mavriky Mavrikyevitch got into the cart, sat down heavily, and, as though without noticing, squeezed Mitya into the corner.

"Good-bye, Trifon Borissovitch!" Mitya shouted again.

But Trifon Borissovitch stood proudly, both hands behind his back, staring straight at Mitya with a stern and angry face, and made no reply.

"Good-by, Dmitri Fyodorovitch, good-by!" Mitya heard.

It was the voice of Kalganov, who had darted out. Running up to the cart, he held out his hand to Mitya. Mitya had time to seize and press it.

"Good-by, dear fellow! I shan't forget your generosity," he cried.

The cart moved and their hands parted.

Kalganov ran back, sat in a corner, hiding his face in his hands, and burst out crying.

"What are these people? What can men be after this?" he exclaimed in despair. At that moment he had no desire to live. "Is it worth it?" he exclaimed in his grief.

PART IV

Book IX • Ivan

Chapter I

At Grushenka's

Alyosha went to the widow Morozov's house to see Grushenka, who had sent Fenya to him early in the morning with a message to come. Questioning Fenya, Alyosha learned that her mistress had been distressed since the previous day. During the two months that had passed since Mitya's arrest, Alyosha had called frequently to take messages for Mitya.

Three days after Mitya's arrest, Grushenka took ill and was ill for nearly five weeks. She was thinner and a little sallow, though she had for the past two weeks been well enough to go out. But to Alyosha her face was even more attractive than before, and he liked to meet her eyes. They had developed a look of firmness and intelligent purpose. There were also signs of a spiritual transformation in her.

There was scarcely a trace of her former frivolity. It seemed strange to Alyosha, too, that in spite of the calamity that had overtaken her—engaged to a man who had been arrested for a terrible crime, and the inevitable sentence hanging over Mitya, she had not lost her cheerfulness. There was a soft light in the once proud eyes, though at times they gleamed with the old fire when she was visited by one disturbing thought—of Katerina Ivanovna, of whom Grushenka had raved when she lay in delirium.

Alyosha knew that she was very jealous of her. Yet Katerina Ivanovna had not once visited Mitya in prison, though she might have done it whenever she liked. Which made a difficult problem for Alyosha, for he was the only person to whom Grushenka opened her heart, and from whom she was always asking advice.

Full of anxiety, he entered her lodging.

She had returned from seeing Mitya half an hour before, and from the rapid movement with which she leapt up from her chair to meet him he saw that she had been expecting him. A pack of cards lay on the table. A bed had been made up on the leather sofa, and Maximov lay, half-reclining, on it, wearing a dressing-gown and cotton nightcap. He was evidently ill and weak.

When the homeless old man returned with Grushenka from Mokroe two months before, he stayed on, and Grushenka, who was in terrible grief and in the first stage of fever, almost forgot his existence. Suddenly she chanced to look at him: he laughed a pitiful laugh. She called Fenya and told her to give him something to eat. All that day he sat in the same place without stirring. When it got dark, Fenya asked her mistress:

"Is the gentleman going to stay the night?"

"Yes; make him a bed on the sofa," answered Grushenka.

Grushenka had learned he had nowhere to go, that Kalganov "told me he wouldn't receive me again and gave me five rubles."

"Well, God bless you, you'd better stay, then," she said.

Her smile wrung the old man's heart and he shed grateful tears. So he stayed with her. He did not leave the house even when she was ill. Fenya and the cook did not turn him out, but went on serving him meals and making up his bed on the sofa. Grushenka grew used to him, and coming back from seeing Mitya, she would sit down and begin talking to him to keep from thinking of her sorrow.

The old man turned out to be a good story-teller, so that at last he became necessary to her. Grushenka saw scarcely any one else besides Alyosha, who did not come every day and never stayed long. Her old merchant lay seriously ill, and he did, in fact, die a week after Mitya's trial. Three weeks before his death, feeling the end approaching, he made his sons, their wives and children, come upstairs to him. He gave strict orders to his servants not to admit Grushenka and to tell her if she came, "The master wishes you long life and happiness and tells you to forget him."

But Grushenka sent almost every day to ask after him.

"You've come at last!" she cried to Alyosha. "Maximushka's been scaring me that perhaps you wouldn't come. How I need you! Sit down. Will you have coffee?"

"Yes, please," said Alyosha, sitting down at the table. "I am very hungry."

"Fenya, coffee," cried Grushenka. "It's been ready a long time. And bring some little pies, and mind they are hot. Do you know, we've had a storm over those pies today? I took them to the prison for him, and he would not eat them. He flung one of them on the floor and stamped on it. So I said to him: 'I shall leave them with the warder; if you don't eat them, it will be because of your spite!' With that I went away. We quarreled again, would you believe it? Whenever I go we quarrel."

Grushenka said this all at once. Maximov looked on the floor.

"What did you quarrel about this time?" asked Alyosha.

"I didn't expect it. Only fancy, he is jealous of the Pole. 'Why are you keeping him?' he asked. He is jealous all the time!"

"But he knew about the Pole before?"

"Yes, but there it is. He has known about him from the beginning, but today he began scolding about him. I'm ashamed to repeat what he said. Silly fellow! Rakitin went in as I came out. Perhaps Rakitin is egging him on. What do you think?"

"He loves you, that's what: he loves you so much. And now he is worried."

"I should think he might be, with the trial tomorrow. I went to say something about tomorrow, for I dread to think what's going to happen. You say he is worried, but how worried I am! And he talks about the Pole! He's too silly!"

"My wife was terribly jealous over me, too," Maximov put in.

"Jealous of you?" Grushenka laughed. "Of whom could she have been jealous?"

"Of the servant girls."

"Hold your tongue, Maximushka, I am in no laughing mood; I feel angry. Don't eye the pies. I shan't give you any; they are not good for you, and I won't give you any vodka either. I have to look after him, too, just as though I kept an almshouse."

"I don't deserve your kindness. I am a worthless creature," said Maximov tearfully. "You'd do better to spend your kindness on people of more use than me."

"Everyone is of use, Maximushka, and how can we tell who's of most use? If only that Pole didn't exist. He's taken it into his head to fall ill, too. I've been to see him. And I shall send him some pies. I hadn't sent him any, but Mitya accused me of it, so now I shall send some! Ah, here's Fenya with a letter! Yes, it's from the Poles—begging again!"

Pan Mussyalovitch had sent an extremely long letter in which he begged her to lend him three rubles. In the letter was enclosed a receipt for the sum, with a promise to repay it within three months. Grushenka had received many such letters from her former lover during the time of her convalescence. The first letter from them was a long one, written on large notepaper and with a big family crest on the seal. It was so obscure that she put it down before she had read half, unable to make head or tail of it.

It was followed next day by another in which Pan Mussyalovitch begged her for a loan of two thousand rubles.

A series of letters had followed—one every day—each as self-important as the one before, but the amount asked for gradually grew less, to a hundred rubles, then twenty-five, ten. Finally she received a letter in which they begged her for only one ruble and included a receipt signed by both. Grushenka, feeling sorry for them, at dusk went round to their lodging. She found them in great poverty, without food or fuel, without cigarettes, in debt to their landlady.

The two hundred rubles they had taken from Mitya at Mokroe had disappeared. Grushenka was surprised at their meeting her with such self-assertion, and the most high-flown speeches. She laughed, and gave her former admirer ten rubles. Then, laughing, she told Mitya of it and he was not in the least jealous. But ever since, the Poles had attached themselves to Grushenka, and daily sent requests for money, and she sent them small sums. And that day Mitya had decided to be jealous.

"Like a fool, I stopped in to see them for a minute on the way to see Mitya, for he is ill, too, my Pole," Grushenka began. "I was laughing, telling Mitya about it. 'Fancy,' I said, 'my Pole had the happy thought to sing his old songs to me to the guitar. He thought I would be touched and marry him!' Mitya leapt up and swore.... So, there, I'll send them the pies! Fenya, is it that little girl they've sent? Here, give her three rubles and pack a dozen pies and tell her to take them. Alyosha, be sure to tell Mitya I sent the pies."

"I wouldn't tell him for anything," said Alyosha.

"You think he is unhappy about it? He's jealous on purpose. He doesn't care."

"On purpose?" asked Alyosha.

"You are silly, Alyosha. You know nothing about it, with all your cleverness. I am not offended that he is jealous of a girl like me. I would be offended if he were not. I have a fierce heart, too. I can be jealous myself. Only what offends me is that he doesn't love me at all. I tell you he is jealous *on purpose*. Am I blind? He began talking to me of that woman, Katerina, saying she was this and that, how she had ordered a doctor from Moscow for him; how she had ordered the best counsel, too. So he loves her if he'll praise her to my face! He's treated me badly, so he attacked me, to make out I am in fault. 'You were with your Pole before me, so I can't be blamed for Katerina,' that's what it amounts to. He wants to throw the whole blame on me. He attacked me on purpose—"

Grushenka could not finish saying what she would do. She sobbed violently.

"He doesn't love Katerina Ivanovna," said Alyosha firmly.

"Well, whether he loves her or not, I'll soon find out," said Grushenka. Her face was distorted. Alyosha saw that from being mild and serene, it had become spiteful.

"Enough of this foolishness," she said. "It's not for that I sent for you. Alyosha, darling—what will happen tomorrow? That's what worries me! It's only me it worries! No one cares about it. Are you thinking about it even? Tomorrow he'll be tried. Tell me, how will he be tried? You know it's the valet killed him! Can they condemn him in place of the valet and will no one stand up for him? They haven't troubled the valet at all."

"He's been severely cross-examined," said Alyosha, "but everyone came to the conclusion it was not he. Now he is lying very ill. He has been ill ever since that attack."

"Couldn't you go to that lawyer and tell him the whole thing? He's been brought from Petersburg for three thousand rubles."

"We gave him the three thousand together—Ivan, Katerina Ivanovna and I—but she paid two thousand for the doctor from Moscow. The lawyer Fetyukovitch would have charged more, but the case has become known all over Russia. He agreed to come more for the glory, because the case is so well-known."

"Did you talk to him?" Grushenka put in.

"He listened and said nothing. He told me he had already formed his opinion. But he promised to consider my words."

"Consider! They're thieves! Why did she send for the doctor?"

"As an expert. They want to prove Mitya's mad and killed his father when he was out of his mind; but Mitya won't agree to that."

"That would be the truth if he had killed him!" cried Grushenka. "He was mad then, and that was my fault! But, of course, he didn't do it! They are all against him. Even Fenya's evidence went to prove he did it. And the people at the shop and the tavern, too, heard him say so! They are all against him."

"Yes, there's a fearful amount of evidence," Alyosha said.

"And Grigory Vassilyevitch sticks to his story that the door was open—there's no shaking him. I talked to him myself. He's rude about it, too."

"That's the strongest evidence they have," said Alyosha.

"As for Mitya's being mad, he certainly seems like it now," Grushenka began. "Do you know, Alyosha, I go to him every day and wonder at him. Tell me, what do you suppose he's always talking about? He talks and talks and I can make nothing of it. 'I am not a murderer, but I must go!' What that meant I couldn't tell. I cried when he said it, because he said it so nicely. He cried himself, and kissed me. What did it mean, Alyosha?"

"Rakitin's been seeing him lately," said Alyosha. "Those ideas sound like his. I didn't see Mitya yesterday. I'll see him today."

"No, it's not Rakitin; it's his brother Ivan Fyodorovitch. He's been seeing him, that's what it is," Grushenka began, and stopped.

Alyosha gazed at her with surprise.

"Ivan's been to see him? Mitya told me he hasn't been once."

"What a girl I am! Blurting things out!" exclaimed Grushenka. "Stay, Alyosha, hush! Since I've said so much I'll tell the whole truth—he's been to see him twice, the first time when he arrived from Moscow; the second time was a week ago. He told Mitya not to tell you about it, not to tell anyone."

Alyosha sat deep in thought. The news evidently up-set him.

"Ivan doesn't talk to me of Mitya's case," he said slowly. "He's said very little to me these last two months. And whenever I go to see him, he seems angry at my coming, so I've not been to him for weeks. If he was there a week ago ... there certainly has been a change in Mitya this week."

"There has been a change," Grushenka agreed. "They have a secret! Mitya told me, and such a secret he can't rest. Before then he was cheerful—but now, when he shakes his head like that, and strides about the room and keeps pulling at the hair, I know there is something on his mind!"

"But you said he was worried."

"Yes, he is worried and yet cheerful. He is irritable for a minute and then cheerful again. You know, Alyosha, I am constantly wondering at him—with this awful thing hanging over him, he sometimes laughs at such trifles."

"And did he really tell you not to tell me about Ivan?"

"Yes, he told me, 'Don't tell him.' It's you that Mitya's most afraid of. Because it's a secret. Alyosha, go to him and find out what their secret is and come tell me," Grushenka begged him. "Set my mind at rest that I may know the worst."

"You think it's something to do with you? If it were, he wouldn't have told you there was a secret."

"I don't know. Perhaps he wants to tell me, but doesn't dare."

"What do you think yourself?"

"What do I think? It's the end for me, that's what I think. They all three have been plotting my end, for Katerina's in it. It's all Katerina. She is this and that, and that means that I am not. He tells me that to warn me. He is going to throw me over, that's the secret. They've planned it together, the three of them—Mitya, Katerina, and Ivan Fyodorovitch. A week ago he told me that Ivan was in love with Katerina. Did he tell me the truth or not? Tell me, tell me the worst."

"I won't tell you a lie. Ivan does not love Katerina Ivanovna."

"That's what I thought! He is lying to me! And he was jealous of me just now so as to put the blame on me. He can't disguise what he is doing.... But I'll give it to him! 'You believe I did it,' he said. He said that to me. God forgive him! You wait; I'll make it hot for Katerina at the trial! I'll tell everything then!"

Again she cried bitterly.

"This I can tell you for certain, Grushenka," Alyosha said, getting up. "First, that he loves you more than anyone in the world, and you only, believe me. The second is that I don't want to worm his secret out of him, but if he'll tell me of himself, I shall tell him I promised to tell you. Then I'll come and tell you. Only ... I fancy Katerina Ivanovna has nothing to do with it, and that the secret is about something else."

Alyosha shook hands with her. Grushenka was still crying. He saw that she put little faith in his consolation, but she was better for having spoken to him. He was sorry to leave her in such a state, but he had a great many things to do.

Chapter II

The Wounded Foot

The first thing Alyosha had to do was at Madame Hohlakov's, and he hurried there to get it over and not be late for Mitya. Madame Hohlakov had been slightly ailing for the last three weeks: her foot had swollen up, and though she was not in bed, she lay all day half-reclining on the couch in her boudoir.

Alyosha had not called for four days and he was in a hurry to go straight to Lise, as it was with her he had to speak, for Lise had sent a maid to him the day before, asking him to come to her "about something very important." But while the maid took his name in to Lise, Madame Hohlakov heard of his arrival, and sent to beg him to come to her.

Alyosha reflected that it was better to accede to the mamma's request, or else she would be sending down to Lise's room every minute he was there. Madame Hohlakov, lying on her couch, was smartly dressed, and in a state of nervous excitement.

She greeted Alyosha with cries of rapture.

"It's ages since I've seen you! Ah, but you were here only four days ago. You have come to see Lise. I'm sure you meant to slip into her room without my seeing you. If you only knew how worried I am about her! But of that later, though it's the most important thing. Dear Alexey Fyodorovitch, I trust you implicitly with my Lise. Since the death of Father Zossima—God rest his soul! I look upon you as a monk, though you're charming in your new suit. Forgive me for sometimes calling you Alyosha; an old woman like me may take liberties.

"The important thing is I shouldn't forget what is important. Please remind me of it yourself. As soon as my tongue runs away with me, you just say 'the important thing?' But how do I know now what is of most importance? Ever since Lise took back her promise to marry you, you've realized that it was only the playful fancy of a sick child—thank God, she can walk now! That new doctor Katya sent for from Moscow for your unhappy brother, who will be here tomorrow— But why speak of tomorrow?

"I am ready to die at the very thought of tomorrow. Ready to die of curiosity.... That doctor was with us yesterday and saw Lise.... I paid him fifty rubles for the visit. But that's not the point. You see, I'm mixing everything up. I'm in such a hurry. Why am I in a hurry? It's awful how I seem to be unable to understand anything. Everything seems mixed up. I'm afraid you are so bored you will jump up and run away, and that will be all I shall see of you. Goodness! Why are we sitting here and no coffee?"

Alyosha made haste to thank her, and said that he had only just had coffee.

"Where?"

"At Agrafena Alexandrovna's."

"At....at that woman's? Ah, it's she who has brought ruin on everyone. I know nothing about it though. They say she has become a saint, though it's rather late for that. She had better have done it before. What use is it now? Hush, Alexey Fyodorovitch, for I have so much to say to you that I am afraid I shall tell you nothing. This awful trial...I shall certainly go. I shall be carried there in my chair; besides I can sit up. And I am a witness. How shall I speak? I don't know what to say. One has to take an oath?"

"Yes; but I don't think you will be able to go."

"I can sit up. This trial, this savage act, and then they are all going to Siberia, some are getting married, and all this so quickly, everything's changing, and at last—nothing. All grow old and have death to look forward to. Well, so be it! I am weary. This Katya has disappointed all my hopes. Now she is going to follow your brother to Siberia, and your other brother is going to follow her and live in the nearest town, and they will all torment one another.

"It drives me out of my mind. Worst of all—the publicity. The story has been told a million times in all the papers. Would you believe it, there's a paragraph that says I was 'a dear friend' of your brother's— Just fancy!"

"Impossible! Where was the paragraph? What did it say?"

"I'll show you. I got the paper and read it yesterday. Here, in the Petersburg *Gossip*. The paper began coming out this year. I am awfully fond of gossip, and I take it in, and now—this is what gossip comes to! Here it is, this passage. Read it."

She handed Alyosha a newspaper page from under her pillow.

She seemed overwhelmed and mixed. The paragraph was typical, and must have been a shock to her, but, fortunately, she was unable to keep her mind on any one subject at that moment, and so might race off to something else and quite forget the newspaper.

Alyosha was well aware that news of the terrible case had spread all over Russia. And what wild rumors about his brother, about the Karamazovs, and about himself he had read! One paper had even stated that he had gone into a monastery and become a monk in horror at his brother's crime. Another stated that he and Father Zossima had broken into the monastery chest and "made tracks from the monastery."

The paragraph in the *Gossip* had the heading, "The Karamazov Case." It was brief, and Madame Hohlakov was not directly mentioned. No names appeared. It merely stated that the criminal, whose approaching trial was making such a sensation— retired army captain, an idle swaggerer, and reactionary bully— was continually involved in amorous intrigues with certain ladies "who were pining in solitude."

One such lady, a pining widow, who tried to seem young though she had a grown-up daughter, was so fascinated by him that only two hours before the crime she offered him three thousand rubles on condition he would elope with her to the gold mines. But the criminal, counting on escaping punishment, preferred to murder his father to get the three thousand rather than go off to Siberia with the middle-aged, pining lady.

"After reading it, Alyosha handed it back to her.

"That must be me," she hurried on. "Scarcely more than an hour before I suggested gold mines to him, and here they talk of 'middle-aged charms' as though that were my motive! He writes out of spite! God forgive him! It's— your friend Rakitin."

"Perhaps," said Alyosha, "though I've heard nothing about it."

"No 'perhaps' about it. You know I turned him out of the house, don't you?"

"I know that you asked him not to visit you for the future, but why it was I haven't heard ... from you, at least."

"Ah, then you've heard it from him! He abuses me?"

"Yes, he does; but then he abuses everyone. But why you've given him up I haven't heard. I seldom meet him now. We're not friends."

"Well, then, I'll tell you about it, for there is one point in which I was perhaps to blame. Only a little point, so perhaps it doesn't count. You see, my dear boy"—Madame Hohlakov suddenly looked arch, a charming smile playing about her lips— "you see, I suspect ... You must forgive me, Alyosha. I am like a mother to you.... No, I speak to you now as though you were my father— it's as though I were confessing to Father Zossima.

"Well, that poor young man, your friend Rakitin, seems to have taken it into his head to fall in love with me. At first—a month ago—he began to come oftener to see me, almost every day; though, of course, we were acquainted before. Suddenly it dawned on me, and I began to notice things with surprise. Two months ago, that charming young man, Pyotr Ilyitch Perhotin, who's in the service here, began to be a regular visitor. You met him here many times. He is an excellent young man, isn't he?

"Altogether, I love young people, Alyosha, talented, modest, like you, and he has almost the mind of a statesman, he talks so charmingly, and I shall certainly try and get a promotion for him. He is a future diplomat. On that awful day he almost saved me from death by coming in the night. And your friend Rakitin comes in such boots, and always stretches them out on the carpet. He began hinting at his feelings, and one day, as he was going, he squeezed my hand terribly hard. My foot began to swell after he pressed my hand. He met Pyotr Ilyitch here before, and would you believe it, he is always growling at him. I looked at the way they went on together and laughed inwardly.

"So I was sitting here alone—I was laid up then. Well, I was lying here alone and Rakitin comes in, and only fancy! He brought me some verses of his own composition—a short poem on my bad foot. Wait a minute—how did it go? A charming little foot. It began.... I can never remember poetry. I've got it here. It's pleasing; and it's not only about the foot, it had a good moral, too, only I've forgotten it; in fact, it was just the thing for an album. So, of course, I thanked him, and he was flattered.

"I'd hardly had time to thank him when in comes Pyotr Ilyitch. Rakitin suddenly looks as black as night. I could see that Pyotr Ilyitch was in the way, for Rakitin wanted to say something after giving me the verses. I had a sense of it. I showed Pyotr Ilyitch the verses and didn't say who the author was. I think he guessed, though he won't own it. Pyotr Ilyitch laughed.

"'Wretched doggerel,' he said, 'some divinity student must have written them,' and with such passion! Instead of laughing, your friend flew into a rage. 'Goodness!' I thought, 'they'll fly at each other.' 'It was I who wrote them,' said he. 'I wrote them as a joke, for I think it degrading to write verses.... But they are good poetry. They'll put up a monument to your Pushkin for writing about women's feet, while I wrote with a moral purpose, and you,' said he, 'are an advocate of serfdom. You've no modern feelings, you are a mere official,' he said, 'and you take bribes.'

"I began screaming and imploring them. And, you know, Pyotr Ilyitch is anything but a coward. He at once took up the most gentlemanly tone, looked at him sarcastically, listened, and apologized. 'I'd no idea,' said he. 'I shouldn't have said it, if I had known. I should have praised it. Poets are all so irritable,' he said. In short, he laughed at him.

"He explained to me afterwards that it was all sarcastic. I thought he was in earnest. As I lay there I thought, 'Would it, or would it not, be the proper thing for me to turn Rakitin out for shouting so rudely at a visitor in my house?' One voice seemed to be telling me, 'Speak,' and the other 'No, don't speak.' And no sooner had the second voice said that than I fainted. Of course, there was a fuss. I got up and said to Rakitin, 'It's painful for me to say it, but I don't wish to see you in my house again'.

"Ah! Alexey Fyodorovitch, I know myself I did wrong. I was putting it on. I wasn't angry with him at all; but I suddenly fancied—that was what did it—that it would be such a fine scene.... And yet, believe me, it was quite natural, for I shed tears and cried for several days afterwards, and then suddenly, one afternoon, I forgot all about it. It's two weeks since he's been here, and I kept wondering whether he would come again. I wondered even yesterday, then last night came this *Gossip*. I read it and gasped. He must have written it, and they put it in. It was two weeks ago, you see. But, Alyosha, it's awful how I keep talking and don't say what I want to say. The words come of themselves!"

"It's very important for me to see my brother today," Alyosha said.

"To be sure! You bring it all back to me. Listen, what is an aberration?"

"What aberration?" asked Alyosha?

"In the legal sense. An aberration in which everything is pardonable. Whatever you do, you will be acquitted at once."

"What do you mean?"

"I'll tell you. This Katya ... she is a charming creature, only I never can make out who she is in love with. She was with me some time ago and I couldn't get anything out of her. Especially as she won't talk to me except on the surface. She is always talking about my health and nothing else, and she takes such a tone with me, too. I simply said to myself, 'Well, so be it. I don't care'...

"Oh, yes. I was talking of oddness. You know a doctor has come? The one who discovers men who are mad. It was Katya's doing. Well, you see, a man may be perfectly sane and suddenly become odd. He may be conscious and know what he is doing and yet be odd. There's no doubt that Dmitri Fyodorovitch was in such a state. The doctor was here and questioned me about that evening, and the gold mines. 'How did he seem then?' he asked me. I told him Dmitri must have been in a state of oddness. He came in shouting, 'Money, money! Give me three thousand!' and then went away and did the murder. 'I don't want to murder him,' he said, and he went and murdered him. That's why they'll acquit him, because he struggled against it and yet he murdered him."

"But he didn't murder him," Alyosha interrupted sharply.

"Yes, I know. It was that old man Grigory murdered him."

"Grigory?" cried Alyosha.

"Yes, it was Grigory. He lay as Dmitri Fyodorovitch struck him down, then got up, saw the door open, and went in and killed Fyodor Pavlovitch."

"But why, why?"

"He was suffering from oddness. When he recovered from the blow Dmitri Fyodorovitch gave him on the head, he was suffering from it; he went and did the murder. As for his saying he didn't, he very likely doesn't remember. Only, you know, it'll be ever so much better, if Dmitri Fyodorovitch murdered him. And that's how it must have been, though I say it was Grigory.

"Oh, not better that a son should have killed his father, I don't defend that. Children ought to honor their parents, and yet it would be better if it were he, as you'd have nothing to cry over then, for he did it when he was unconscious or rather when he was conscious, but did not know what he was doing.

"Let them free him—that's so humane, and would show what a blessing reformed law courts are. And if he is freed, make him come straight from the law courts to dinner with me, and I'll have a party of friends, and we'll drink to the reformed law courts. I don't believe he'd be dangerous; besides, I'll invite a great many friends so he could always be led out if he did anything. And then he might be made a justice of the peace or something, for those who have been in trouble themselves make the best judges.

"And, besides, who isn't suffering from oddness nowadays?— you, I, all of us are a bit odd, so there you are. The doctors are always confirming it. Why, my Lise is in a state of oddness. She made me cry again yesterday, and the day before, too, and today I suddenly realized that it's all due to her oddness. She grieves me so! I believe she's quite mad. Did she send for you?"

"Yes, she sent for me, and I am just going to her."

Alyosha got up, determined.

"My dear Alexey Fyodorovitch, perhaps that's what's most important," Madame Hohlakov cried, bursting into tears. "God knows I trust Lise to you with all my heart, and it's no matter her sending for you on the sly, without telling her mother. But I can't trust my daughter to your brother Ivan Fyodorovitch, though I still consider him the best of young men. But he's been to see Lise and I knew nothing about it!"

"How? What? When?" Alyosha asked, greatly surprised.

"I will tell you; that's perhaps why I asked you to come, for I don't know now why I asked you to come. Well, Ivan Fyodorovitch has been to see me twice since he came back from Moscow. First time he came as a friend to call on me, and the second time because he heard Katya was here. I didn't expect him to come, knowing what a lot he has to do. But I heard he'd been here again, not to see me but to see Lise. That's six days ago. He stayed five minutes, and went away. And I didn't hear of it till three days afterwards, so it was a great shock to me. I sent for Lise directly. She laughed. 'He thought you were asleep,' she said, 'and came in to me to ask after your health.'

"Of course, that's how it happened. But Lise, mercy on us, how she distresses me! Would you believe it, one night, four days ago, just after you saw her last time, she had a fit, screaming and shrieking! Why is it I never have hysterics? Next day another fit, and the same thing on the third, and yesterday too, and then yesterday that aberration.

"She screamed out, 'I hate Ivan Fyodorovitch. I insist you never let him come again.' I was struck dumb, and answered, 'On what grounds could I refuse to see such an excellent young man, a young man of such learning too, and so unfortunate?'—for all this business is a misfortune, isn't it? She suddenly burst out laughing at my words, and so rudely. Well, I was pleased; I thought I had amused her and the fits would pass off, especially as I wanted to refuse to see Ivan Fyodorovitch anyway on account of his visits without my knowledge. But early this morning Lise woke up and flew into a passion with Yulia and, would you believe it, slapped her in the face. That's monstrous; I am always polite to my servants. An hour later she was hugging Yulia's feet and kissing them. She sent a message that she wasn't coming to me at all, and would never come and see me again, and when I dragged myself down to her, she rushed to kiss me, crying, and pushed me out of the room without a word, so I couldn't find out what was the matter.

"Now, dear Alexey Fyodorovitch, I rest all my hopes on you, and my whole life is in your hands. I simply beg you to go to Lise and find out everything from her, as you alone can, and come back and tell me—for it will be the death of me if this goes on, or else I shall run away. Or I may lose patience, and then ... something awful will happen.

"Ah, at last, Pyotr Ilyitch!" cried Madame Hohlakov, beaming all over as she saw Perhotin enter the room. "You are late, you are late! Well, sit down, speak, put us out of suspense. What does the lawyer say? Where are you off to, Alexey Fyodorovitch?"

"To Lise."

"You won't forget what I asked? It's a life and death matter!"

"I won't forget, if I can ... but I am so late," said Alyosha.

"No, be sure to come; don't say 'If you can.' I shall die if you don't," Madame Hohlakov called after him.

But Alyosha had already left the room.

Chapter III

A Little Devil

Alyosha found Lise half reclining in the invalid-chair in which she had been wheeled when unable to walk. She did not move to meet him, but her sharp eyes were fixed on him. There was a feverish look in her eyes, and her face was pale and yellow. He was amazed at the change that had taken place in her in three days. She was much thinner. He touched the thin, long fingers that lay motionless on her dress, then sat down facing her.

"I know you are in a hurry to get to the prison," Lise said, "and mama's kept you there for hours; she's just been telling you about me and Yulia."

"How do you know?" asked Alyosha.

"I've been listening. Why do you stare at me? There's no harm in that."

"You are upset about something?"

"On the contrary, I am very happy. I've only just been reflecting on what a good thing it is I refused you and shall not be your wife. You are not fit to be a husband. If I were to marry you and give you a note to take to the man I loved, you'd take it and be sure to give it to him and bring an answer back. If you were forty, you would still do it."

She suddenly laughed.

"There is something spiteful and yet open-hearted about you," Alyosha said.

"The open-heartedness consists in my not feeling shamed with you. What's more, I don't want to feel shame with you. Alyosha, why is it I don't respect you? I'm very fond of you, but I don't respect you. If I respected you, would I talk to you without shame?"

"No."

"But do you believe I don't feel shame with you?"

"No, I don't believe it."

Lise laughed again.

"I sent your brother, Dmitri Fyodorovitch, some sweets in prison. Alyosha, you are quite pretty! I shall love you awfully for having so quickly allowed me not to love you."

"Why did you send for me today, Lise?"

"I want to tell you of a longing I have. I should like someone to torture me, marry me and torture me, deceive me and go away. I don't want to be happy."

"You are in love with disorder?"

"Yes, I want disorder. I want to set fire to the house. And I shall say nothing. How bored I am!"

She waved her hand with a look of repulsion.

"It's your luxurious life," said Alyosha softly.

"Is it better, then, to be poor?"

"Yes, it is better."

"That's what your monk taught you. That's not true. Let me be rich and all the rest poor, I'll eat sweets and drink cream and not give any to anyone else. Don't say anything," she said, though Alyosha had not opened his mouth. "You've said all that before. If I'm ever poor, I shall murder somebody, and even if I am rich I may murder someone! But do you know, I should like to reap, cut the rye? I'll marry you, and you shall become a peasant; we'll keep a colt, shall we? Do you know Kalganov?"

"Yes."

"He is always wandering about, dreaming. He says, 'Why live in real life? It's better to dream. One can dream the most delightful things, but real life is a bore.' But he'll be married soon for all that; he's been making love to me already. Can you spin tops?"

"Yes."

"He's just like a top: he wants to be wound up and set spinning and then to be lashed with a whip. If I marry him I'll keep him spinning. You're not shamed to be with me?"

"No."

"You are awfully cross because I don't talk about holy things. I don't want to be holy. What will they do to one in the next world for the greatest sin? You must know."

"God will censure you."

"That's just what I should like. I would go up and they would censure me, and I would burst out laughing in their faces. I still want to set fire to the house."

"There are children of twelve who have a longing to set fire to something and they do set things on fire, too. It's a sort of disease."

"That's not true; there may be children, but that's not what I mean."

"You take evil for good; it's a passing crisis, it's the result of your illness."

"You despise me, though! It's simply that I don't want to do good, I want to do evil, and it has nothing to do with illness."

"Why do evil?"

"So that everything might be destroyed. How nice it would be if everything were destroyed! You know, Alyosha, I sometimes think of doing a fearful lot of harm and everything bad, and I should do it for a long while on the sly, and suddenly everyone would find it out. Everyone will stand round and point their fingers at me and I would look at them all. That would be awfully nice. Why would it be so nice, Alyosha?"

"I don't know. It's a craving to destroy something good. It happens sometimes."

"I not only say it, I shall do it."

"I believe you."

"How I love you for saying you believe me. And you are not lying, perhaps thinking I am saying this on purpose to annoy you?"

"I don't think that...though there is a desire to do that, too."

"There is a little. I never can tell lies to you," she declared.

What struck Alyosha above everything was how serious she was. There was not a trace of humor or jesting in her face, though, in old days, fun and gayety never deserted her.

"There are moments when people love crime," said Alyosha.

"Yes! You have uttered my thought; they love crime, everyone loves crime, they love it always, not at some 'moments.' It's as though people have made an agreement to lie about it and have lied ever since. They all declare they hate evil, but they all love it."

"Are you still reading nasty books?"

"Yes. Mamma reads them and hides them under her pillow, and I steal them."

"Don't you feel shame destroying yourself that way?"

"I want to destroy myself. Listen, your brother is being tried for murdering his father; and everyone loves his having killed his father."

"Loves his having killed his father?"

"Yes, loves it; everyone loves it! Everybody says it's so awful, but they love it."

"There is some truth in what you say," said Alyosha softly.

"What ideas you have!" Lise shrieked in delight. "And you a monk, too! You wouldn't believe how I respect you, Alyosha, for never telling lies. Oh, I must tell you a funny dream of mine. It's night; I am in my room with a candle and suddenly there are devils all over the place, in all the corners, and they want to seize me.

"They are just about to seize me, but I cross myself and they all draw back. Though they don't go away, they stand at the doors, and in the corners, waiting. And then I have a longing to curse God, and so I begin, and then they come crowding back, delighted, and seize me again and I cross myself again and they all draw back. It's fun. It takes one's breath away."

"I've had the same dream, too," said Alyosha.

"Really?" cried Lise. "I say, Alyosha, could two people have the same dream?"

"It seems they can."

"Alyosha, I tell you," Lise went on. "It's not the dream, but your having the same dream. You never lie to me; is it true?"

"It's true."

Lise seemed quite impressed and for half a minute was silent.

"Alyosha, come and see me more often," she said.

"I'll always come to see you, all my life," answered Alyosha firmly.

"You're the only person I can talk to. No one but you. And to you more easily than to myself. I feel not a bit of shame with you. Alyosha, why do I not feel shame with you? Alyosha, is it true that at Easter the Jews steal a child and kill it?"

"I don't know."

"I read in a book about the trial of a Jew who took a child four years old, cut off its fingers, then crucified him on the wall, hammered nails into him and crucified him. He said the child moaned and he stood admiring it. That's nice!"

"Nice?"

"I sometimes imagine that it was I who crucified him. He'd hang there moaning, and I would sit eating fruit. I'm awfully fond of fruit. Do you like it?"

Alyosha looked at her in silence.

Her pale, sallow face was bent out of shape, her eyes burned.

"When I read about that Jew I shook with sobs all night. In the morning I wrote a letter to someone begging him to come see me."

"Simply to ask about that child?"

"No, not about that. But when he came, I asked him about that. He answered and went away."

"That person behaved honorably," Alyosha said.

"And did he look down at me? Did he laugh at me?"

"No, for perhaps he believes in the fruit himself, Lise."

"Yes, he does believe in it," said Lise.

"He doesn't look down on anyone," Alyosha went on. "Only he does not believe anyone. If he doesn't believe in people, of course, he does look down on them."

"Then he looks down on me?"

"You, too."

"Good," Lise said. "When he went out laughing, I felt it was nice to be looked down on. To be looked down on is nice...."

She laughed in Alyosha's face, a hateful laugh.

"Do you know, Alyosha—save me!"

She suddenly jumped from the couch, rushed to him and seized him. "Save me!" she groaned. "Is there anyone in the world I could tell what I've told you? I've told you the truth. I shall kill myself, because I hate everything! I don't want to live!

Alyosha, why don't you love me in the least?" she finished in a panic.

"But I do love you!" answered Alyosha.

"And will you weep over me?"

"Yes."

"Not because I won't be your wife, but simply weep for me?"

"Yes."

"Thank you! It's only your tears I want. Everyone else may punish me and trample me under foot, for I don't love anyone. Do you hear, not anyone! On the contrary, I hate him! Go, Alyosha; it's time you went to your brother," she cried.

"How can I leave you like this?" said Alyosha in alarm.

"Go to your brother, the prison will be shut. Give my love to Mitya, go, go!"

She almost pushed Alyosha out the door. He looked at her with pained surprise, when he was suddenly aware of a letter in his hand, a tiny letter folded up tight and sealed. He glanced at it and read the address, "To Ivan Fyodorovitch Karamazov."

He looked quickly at Lise. Her face had become almost hateful.

"Give it to him, you must give it to him!" she ordered, shaking Today, at once, or I'll poison myself! That's why I sent for you."

She slammed the door. The bolt clicked. Alyosha put the note in his pocket and went downstairs without seeing Madame Hohlakov.

As soon as Alyosha had gone, Lise unbolted the door, opened it, put her finger in the crack, and slammed the door.

Chapter IV

A Hymn and a Secret

It was late when Alyosha rang at the prison gate, but he knew he'd be admitted. At first people could only obtain interviews with Mitya by going through the formalities. Later, exceptions were made for some of Mitya's visitors, Grushenka, Alyosha and Rakitin.

When Mitya was summoned from his cell, he went downstairs to the place set aside for interviews. As Alyosha entered the room he came upon Rakitin just leaving. They were both talking loudly. Mitya was laughing as he saw him out, while Rakitin seemed grumbling. Rakitin did not like meeting Alyosha of late. Seeing Alyosha enter, he looked away, as though absorbed in buttoning his coat. Then he began looking for his umbrella.

"I must not forget my belongings," he said.

"Mind you don't forget other people's belongings," said Mitya as a joke.

Rakitin fired up instantly.

"You'd better give that advice to your own family and not to Rakitin," he cried.

"What's the matter? I was joking," cried Mitya. "Damn it all! They are all like that," he said, turning to Alyosha and nodding towards Rakitin's retreating figure. "He was sitting here, laughing and cheerful, and all at once he boils up like that. He didn't even nod to you. Have you broken with him completely? Why are you so late?"

"Why does he come so often? Surely you are not such great friends?" said Alyosha.

"Great friends? No. Is it likely—a pig like that? He considers I am ... a blackguard. They can't understand a joke either, that's the worst of such people. But he is a clever fellow. Well, Alexey, it's all over with me now."

He sat on the bench and made Alyosha sit beside him.

"Yes, the trial's tomorrow. Are you so hopeless, brother?" Alyosha asked.

"What are you talking about?" said Mitya. "Oh, you mean the trial! Damn it all! Till now we've been talking of things that don't matter, but I haven't said a word to you about the chief thing. The trial is tomorrow; but it wasn't the trial I meant."

"What do you mean, Mitya?"

"Ideas! Ethics! What is ethics?"

"Ethics?" asked Alyosha.

"Yes; is it a science?"

"There is such a science...but I confess I can't explain what sort of science it is."

"Rakitin knows, damn him! He's not going to be a monk. He means to go in for criticism. Who knows, he may make his career, too. They are first-rate, these people, at making a career! Damn ethics, I am done for, Alexey!"

"But what is the matter?" Alyosha asked.

"Rakitin wants to write an article about me and my case, and so begin his literary career. That's why he comes, he said. He wants to prove some theory. He wants to say 'he couldn't help murdering his father, he was corrupted by society,' and so on.

"He explained it all to me. He can't bear Ivan, hates him. He's not fond of you, either. But I don't turn him out; he is a clever fellow. But conceited. I said to him, 'The Karamazovs are not blackguards, but philosophers; and though you've studied, you are not—you are a low fellow.' He just laughed."

"Why is it over with you? Alyosha interrupted.

"Why is it all over with me? The fact is ... if you take it as a whole, I am sorry to lose God—that's why it is."

"What do you mean by 'sorry to lose God'?"

"Imagine: inside, in the nerves in the head—in the brain... little tails, the tails of those nerves.... I look at something with my eyes and they begin shaking, and an image appears...or I take an action. That's why I see and think, because of those tails, not because I've got a soul. All that is nonsense! Rakitin explained it to me, brother, and it simply bowled me over. It's magnificent, Alyosha! A new man's rising—that I understand.... And yet I'm sorry to lose God!"

"Well, that's a good thing, anyway," said Alyosha.

"That I am sorry to lose God? It's chemistry, brother! There's no help for it. Rakitin hates God. 'Will you preach this in your reviews?' I asked him. 'If I do it openly, they won't print it,' he said. 'But what will become of men then?' I asked him, 'without God and immortal life? All things are lawful then, they can do anything they like?' 'Didn't you know?' he said, laughing, 'a clever man can do what he likes. A clever man knows his way about, but you've put your foot in it, committing a murder, and now you are rotting in prison.' He says that to my face! A regular pig! I used to kick such people out, but now I listen to them. He talks a lot of sense, too. Writes well. He read me an article of his last week. I copied out three lines. Here it is."

Mitya pulled a piece of paper from his pocket and read: "'In order to determine this question, it is above all essential to put one's personality in contradiction to reality.' Do you understand that?"

"No, I don't," said Alyosha.

"I don't either. It's dark and obscure, but intellectual. 'Everyone writes like that now.' He says, 'It's the effect of society.' They are afraid of society. He writes poetry, too. He's written a poem in honor of Madame Hohlakov's foot!"

"I've heard about it," said Alyosha.

"Have you? And have you heard the poem?"

"No."

"I've got it. Here it is. I'll read it to you. He's a rascal! Three weeks ago he began to tease me. 'You've got yourself into a mess, like a fool, for the sake of three thousand, but I'm going to collar a hundred and fifty thousand. I'm going to marry a widow,' he said, 'and buy a house in Petersburg.' He said he was courting Madame Hohlakov. She hadn't much brains in her youth, and now at forty she has lost what she had. 'But she's awfully sentimental,' he says; 'That's how I'll get hold of her. When I marry her, I shall take her to Petersburg and there I shall start a newspaper.'

"His mouth was simply watering, not for the widow, but for the hundred and fifty thousand. 'She is coming round,' he said. He was beaming with delight. And then, all of a sudden, he was turned out of the house. Perhotin's carrying everything before him! And he had written this doggerel. 'It's to win her heart,' he says, 'so it's in a good cause. When I get hold of the silly woman's fortune, I can be of great social use. But wasn't he stuck up about his doggerel! The vanity! 'On the convalescence of the swollen foot of the object of my affections'—he thought of that for a title.

A captivating little foot,
Though swollen and red and tender!
The doctors come and plasters put,
But still they cannot mend her.

Yet, 'tis not for her foot I dread—
A theme for Pushkin's muse more fit—
It's not her foot, it is her head:
I tremble for her loss of wit!
For as her foot swells, strange to say,
Her intellect is on the wane—
Oh, for some remedy I pray
That may restore both foot and brain!

"He is a regular pig, but he's very arch! Wasn't he angry when she kicked him out!"

"He's taken his revenge already," said Alyosha. "He's written a paragraph on her."

Alyosha told him briefly about the paragraph in *Gossip*.

"That's his doing!" Mitya assented. "That's him! These paragraphs. I know...the insulting things that have been written about Grushenka. And about Katya, too!"

"Brother, I can't stay long," Alyosha said. "Tomorrow will be an awful day for you, the judgment of God. I'm surprised at you, talking of ..."

"Don't be surprised," Mitya broke in. "Am I to talk of that stinking dog? Of the murderer? We've talked enough of him. I don't want to say more of the stinking son of Stinking Lizaveta! God will kill him, you will see!"

He went up to Alyosha and kissed him. His eyes glowed.

"Rakitin wouldn't understand it," he began; "but you'll understand. That's why I was thirsting for you. There's so much I've wanted to tell you, but I haven't said a word about what matters most. Now I can wait no longer. I must pour out my heart to you. Brother, these last two months I've found in myself a new man. He would never have surfaced if it hadn't been for this blow from heaven. What do I care if I spend twenty years in the mines?

"I am not afraid of that—it's something else I'm afraid of now; it's that that new man may leave me. I go because someone must go. I didn't kill father, but I'll accept it. It's all come to me here. There are numbers of them there, under-ground, in chains, but in our great sorrow we shall rise again to joy, for God gives joy.

"Man should be lost in prayer! What should I be underground without God? Rakitin's laughing! If they drive God from the earth, we shall shelter Him under-ground. One cannot exist in prison without God; it's even more impossible than out of prison. We men underground will sing from the bowels of the earth a glorious hymn to God!"

Mitya was almost gasping for breath as he said this.

"Yes, there is life under-ground," he began again. "You wouldn't believe, Alexey, how I want to live now. And what is suffering? I am not afraid of it. Perhaps I won't answer at the trial at all.... I seem to have such strength in me now; I think I could stand anything, any suffering, only to be able to say and to repeat to myself, 'I exist.' Alyosha, my angel, all these philosophies are the death of me. Brother Ivan—"

"What of brother Ivan?" interrupted Alyosha, but Mitya did not hear.

"I never had any of these doubts before, but it was all hidden away in me. It was perhaps because ideas I did not understand were surging up in me that I used to drink and fight and rage. It was to stifle them. But it's God that's worrying me. What if He doesn't exist? If He doesn't exist, man is the chief of the earth, of the universe. Only how is he going to be good without God? That's the question I always come back to. For whom is man going to love then? To whom will he be thankful? To whom will he sing the hymn? Rakitin says one can love humanity without God. Well, life's easy for Rakitin.

"You'd better think about the extension of civic rights, or even of keeping down the price of meat,' he says. 'You will show your love for humanity more directly by that than by philosophy.' I answered him, 'Well, but you, without a God, are more likely to raise the price of meat, if it suits you, and make a ruble on every penny.' He lost his temper. But after all, what is goodness? Answer me, Alexey. You won't laugh if I tell you it's kept me awake two nights. I wonder now how people can live and think nothing about it. Ivan has no God. He has an idea. It's beyond me. But he is silent. I wanted to drink from the springs of his soul—he was silent. But he did drop a word."

"What did he say?" Alyosha took it up quickly.

"I said to him, 'Then everything is lawful if it is so?' 'Fyodor Pavlovitch, our papa,' he said, 'was a pig, but his ideas were right enough.' That was all he said. But that was going one better than Rakitin."

"Yes," Alyosha agreed. "When was he with you?"

"Of that later; now I must speak of something else. I have said nothing about Ivan to you before. When my business here is over and the verdict has been given, then I'll tell you everything. We've something tremendous on hand.... You shall be my judge. But don't begin now. You talk of tomorrow, of the trial; but I know nothing about it."

"Have you talked to the counsel?"

"What's the use? I told him all about it. He's a rogue! He doesn't believe me—not a bit. 'In that case,' I asked him, 'why are you defending me?' They've got a doctor, too, to prove I'm mad. And Katerina Ivanovna wants to do her 'duty' to the end!"

Mitya smiled bitterly.

"Hard-hearted creature! She knows I said of her at Mokroe that she was a woman of 'great anger.' The facts against me have grown. Grigory sticks to his point. Grigory's honest, but a fool.

Many people are honest because they are fools: that's Rakitin's idea. Grigory's my enemy. And some people are better as foes than as friends. I mean Katerina Ivanovna. I am afraid she will tell how she bowed to the ground after that four thousand. She'll pay it back to the last penny. I don't want her sacrifice. Go to her, Alyosha; ask her not to speak of that in court. But damn, it doesn't matter! I shall get through somehow. I don't pity her. It's her own doing. She deserves what she gets. I shall have my own story to tell. Only... Grusha! Good Lord! Why should she have to suffer?" he cried. "Grusha's killing me; the thought of her is killing me. She was with me just now...."

"She told me she was very much grieved by you today."

"Confound my temper! It was jealousy. I was sorry. I didn't ask her forgiveness."

"Why didn't you?" said Alyosha.

Mitya laughed almost mirthfully.

"God preserve you, my dear boy, from ever asking forgiveness from a woman. From one you love especially! Try admitting you are in fault. Say, 'I'm sorry, forgive me,' and a shower of reproaches will follow! Nothing will make her forgive you simply. She'll humble you to the dust, bring forward things that never happened, recall every-thing, forget nothing, add something of her own, and only then forgive you. Even the best of them do it. They are ready to flay you alive, all these angels without whom we cannot live! I tell you, dear boy, every decent man ought to be under some woman's thumb. That's my belief. A man ought to be forgiving. But don't ever beg her pardon for any-thing. Remember that rule given you by your brother Mitya, who came to ruin through women. No, I'd better make it up to Grusha somehow, without begging pardon. I worship her, Alexey. Only she doesn't see it. She still thinks I don't love her enough. She tortures me with her love. The past was nothing! Now I've taken all her soul into me, and through her I've become a man myself. Will they marry us? If they don't, I shall die of jealousy. What did she tell you?"

Alyosha repeated all Grushenka had said to him that day.

Mitya listened, made him repeat things, and seemed pleased.

"Then she is not angry at my being jealous?" he said. "She is a regular woman! 'I've a fierce heart myself!' I love fierce hearts, though I can't bear anyone's being jealous of me. We shall fight. But I shall love her infinitely. Will they marry us? Without her I can't exist...."

Mitya suddenly seemed terribly worried.

"So there's a secret, she says? We have got up a plot against her, and Katya is mixed up in it, she thinks. No, my good Grushenka, that's not it. You are very wide of the mark. Alyosha, darling, well, here goes! I'll tell you our secret!"

He looked round, went close to Alyosha, and whispered to him, though no one could hear them: the old warder was dozing, and not a word could reach the guards.

"I meant to tell you later," Mitya whispered, "for how could I decide on anything without you? You are everything to me. Though I say that Ivan is superior to us, you are my angel. It's your decision will decide. Perhaps it's you that is superior and not Ivan. The secret is so important I can't settle it myself, and I've put it off till I could speak to you.

"Anyway, it's too early to decide now, for we must wait to see what the jury decides. As soon as that is given, you shall decide my fate. I'll tell you, but don't decide now. I won't tell you everything, only the idea, and you keep quiet. You agree?

"Alyosha, listen! Ivan suggests my *escaping*. It can all be arranged. I should go to America with Grusha. You know I can't live without her! What if they won't let her follow me to

391

Siberia? Without Grusha what should I do under-ground with a hammer? I should only smash my skull!

"I should have run away from suffering. A sign has come, I refuse to follow the sign. I have a way of saving myself, and I turn my back on it. Ivan says that in America, 'with good-will,' I can be of more use than under-ground. But what becomes of our hymn from under-ground?

"Alexey, you are the only person who can understand this. It's madness to others, all I've told you of the hymn. They'll say I'm out of my mind or a fool. I am not out of my mind and I am not a fool. Ivan understands about the hymn, too. He understands, only he doesn't believe in it. Don't speak. I see how you look! You've already decided. Spare me! I can't live without Grusha. Wait till after the trial!"

Mitya ended beside himself. He held Alyosha with both hands.

"They don't let convicts marry, do they?" he asked in a begging voice.

Alyosha listened with great surprise, and was deeply moved.

"Tell me one thing," he said. "Is Ivan in on it, and whose idea was it?"

"His. He is very much in on it. He didn't come to see me at first, then he came a week ago and began about it. He doesn't ask me, but orders me to escape. He doesn't doubt of my obeying him, though I showed him all my heart as I have to you, and told him about the hymn, too. He told me he'd arrange it; he's found out about everything. It's all a matter of money: he'll pay ten thousand for escape and give me twenty thousand for America."

"And he told you on no account to tell me?" Alyosha asked.

"To tell no one, and especially not you. He is afraid, no doubt, that you'll stand before me as my conscience. Don't tell him I told you."

"You are right," Alyosha said. "It's impossible to decide anything before the trial is over. After the trial you'll decide yourself. That new man in you will decide."

"A new man or the old one," said Mitya with a bitter grin.

"But, brother, have you no hope of being acquitted?"

Mitya shrugged his shoulders and shook his head.

"Alyosha, darling, it's time you were going," he said. "There's the superintendent shouting in the yard. He'll be here directly. We are late; it's irregular. Embrace me. Kiss me! Sign me with the cross, darling, for the cross I have to bear tomorrow."

They embraced and kissed.

"Ivan," said Mitya, "suggests my escaping; but, of course, he believes I did it."

A sad smile came to his lips.

"Have you asked him whether he believes it?" asked Alyosha.

"No, I haven't. I hadn't the courage. But I saw it from his eyes. Well, good-by!"

Once more they kissed, and Alyosha, just going out, was called back by Mitya.

"Stand facing me! That's right!" And again he seized Alyosha, putting both hands on his shoulders. His face became quite pale, his lips twitched.

"Alyosha, tell me the whole truth, as you would before God. Do you believe I did it? Do you yourself, believe it? The whole truth, don't lie!" he cried.

Everything seemed heaving before Alyosha, and he felt a stab at his heart.

"Hush! What do you mean?" he faltered helplessly.

"The whole truth, don't lie!" repeated Mitya.

"I've never for one instant believed you were the murderer!" broke in a shaking voice from Alyosha, and he raised his right hand in the air, as though calling God to witness his words. Mitya's whole face lit up with bliss.

"Thank you!" he said. "You have given me new life. Would you believe it, till this moment I've been afraid to ask you. Well, go! You've given me strength for tomorrow. God bless you! Come, go! Love Ivan!" was his last word.

Alyosha went out in tears. Such distrust in Mitya, such lack of confidence even to him—all this opened before Alyosha a depth of hopeless grief and despair in the soul of his unhappy brother. Intense compassion overwhelmed him.

"Love Ivan!"—he recalled Mitya's words.

And he was going to Ivan, he was as much worried about Ivan as about Mitya.

Chapter V

Not You, Not You!

On the way to Ivan Alyosha had to pass the house where Katerina Ivanovna was living. There was light in the windows. He resolved to go in. He had not seen her for more than a week. But now it struck him that Ivan might be with her, especially on the eve of the terrible day. Ringing, and mounting the staircase, he met his brother coming down.

"Ah, it's only you," said Ivan dryly. "Well, good-by! You are going to her?"

"Yes."

"I don't advise you to; she's upset and you'll upset her more."

A door was instantly flung open above, and a voice cried:

"No, no! Alexey Fyodorovitch, have you come from him?"

"Yes, I've been with him."

"Has he sent me any message? Come up, Alyosha, and you, Ivan Fyodorovitch, you must come back. Do you hear?"

There was such a note in Katya's voice that Ivan, after a moment's hesitation, went back up the stairs with Alyosha.

"She was listening," he said angrily to himself, but Alyosha heard it.

"Excuse my keeping my coat on," said Ivan in the drawing-room. "I won't sit down. I won't stay more than a minute."

"Sit down, Alexey Fyodorovitch," said Katerina Ivanovna. There was a gleam in her dark eyes. "What did he ask you to tell me?" she asked.

"Only one thing," said Alyosha, "that you would spare yourself and say nothing at the trial of what... passed between you ... at the time of your first acquaintance ...."

"That I bowed to the ground for that money!" She broke into a bitter laugh. "Why, is he afraid for me or for himself? He asks me to spare—whom?"

Alyosha watched her, trying to understand her.

"Both yourself and him," he answered softly.

"I am glad to hear it," she snapped maliciously.

"You don't know me yet, Alexey Fyodorovitch," she said. "I don't know myself yet. Perhaps you'll want to trample me under foot after I testify at the trial tomorrow."

"You will give your evidence honorably," said Alyosha; "that's all that's wanted."

"Women are often dishonorable," she said. "Only an hour ago I was thinking I felt afraid to touch that monster ... but he is still a human being! But is he the murderer?" she cried, hysterical, and turning to Ivan.

Alyosha saw at once that she had asked Ivan that question before, perhaps only a moment before he came in, and not for the first time, and that they ended by quarreling.

"I've been to see Smerdyakov. It was you who persuaded me he murdered his father. It's only you I believed!" she continued, still addressing Ivan.

He gave her a strained smile.

Alyosha started at her tone. He had not suspected such familiar intimacy.

"Well, that's enough, anyway," Ivan said. "I'm going. I'll come tomorrow."

He walked out of the room and went downstairs.

Katerina Ivanovna seized Alyosha by both hands.

"Follow him! Don't leave him alone for a minute!" she said. "He's mad! Don't you know he's mad? He is in a fever. The doctor told me so. Run after him."

Alyosha ran after Ivan, who was not fifty paces ahead.

He turned quickly on Alyosha and said, "What do you want? She told you to catch me up because I'm mad. I know it."

"She is right that you are ill," said Alyosha.

Ivan walked on without stopping. Alyosha followed him.

"Do you know, Alexey Fyodorovitch, how people go out of their mind?" Ivan asked in a voice suddenly quiet.

"No, I don't. I suppose there are all kinds of madness."

"And can one observe that one's going mad oneself?"

"I imagine one can' see oneself clearly at such times," Alyosha answered.

Ivan paused.

"If you want to talk to me, please change the subject," he said.

"While I think of it, I have a letter for you," said Alyosha. He took Lise's note from his pocket and held it out. They were under a lamp-post. Ivan knew the handwriting.

"From that little demon!" he laughed.

Without opening the envelope, he tore it to bits and threw it in the air.

"She's not sixteen yet, I believe, and already offering herself," he said.

"How do you mean, offering herself?" said Alyosha.

"As wanton women offer themselves."

"How can you, Ivan?" Alyosha cried. "She is a child! She is ill, too… on the verge of insanity, perhaps…. I had hoped to hear something from you … that would save her."

"You'll hear nothing from me. If she is a child I am not her nurse. Be quiet, Alexey. Don't go on about her. I am not even thinking about it."

They were silent for a moment.

"She will be praying all night now to the Mother of God to show her how to act at the trial tomorrow," he said, angry again.

"You ... you mean Katerina Ivanovna?"

"Yes. Whether she's to save Mitya or ruin him. She'll pray for light. She can't make up her mind. She takes me for her nurse, too, and wants me to sing lullabies to her."

"Katerina Ivanovna loves you, brother," said Alyosha sadly.

"Perhaps; but I am not very keen on her."

"She is suffering. Why do you ... say things that give her hope?" Alyosha went on. "I know you've given her hope. Forgive me for speaking to you like this."

"I can't behave to her as I ought—break off altogether and tell her straight out," said Ivan irritably. "I must wait till sentence is passed on the murderer. If I break off with her now, she will avenge herself on me by ruining that scoundrel tomorrow at the trial, for she hates him! As long as I don't break off with her, she goes on hoping, and she won't ruin that monster, knowing how I want to get him out of trouble."

The words "murderer" and "monster" echoed painfully in Alyosha's heart.

"How can she ruin Mitya?" he asked. "What evidence can she give?"

"She has a document, in Mitya's writing, that proves he murdered our father."

"That's impossible!" cried Alyosha.

"Why is it impossible? I've read it myself."

"There can't be such a document!" Alyosha repeated. "There can't be, because he's not the murderer. It's not he who murdered father!"

Ivan suddenly stopped.

"Who is the murderer then, according to you?" he asked coldly.

"You know who," Alyosha said in a low voice.

"Who? You mean that crazy idiot, Smerdyakov?"

Alyosha felt himself trembling all over.

"You know who," broke helplessly from him. He could scarcely breathe.

"Who? Who?" Ivan cried almost fiercely.

"I only know one thing," Alyosha went on. "*It wasn't you* killed father."

"'Not you'! What do you mean by 'not you'?" Ivan was thunderstruck.

"It was not you killed father!" Alyosha repeated firmly.

The silence lasted for half a minute.

"I know I didn't. Are you raving?" said Ivan, with a pale, distorted smile.

"No, Ivan. You've told yourself several times that you are the murderer."

"When did I say so? I was in Moscow.... When have I said so?"

"You've said so to yourself many times during these two dreadful months," Alyosha went on softly. "You have accused yourself of being the murderer and no one else. But you didn't do it: you are not the murderer. Do you hear? It was not you!."

They were both silent, gazing into each other's eyes.

Suddenly Ivan began trembling all over, and clutched Alyosha's shoulder.

"You've been in my room!" he whispered. "You've been there at night, when he came.... Confess ... have you seen him?"

"Whom do you mean—Mitya?" Alyosha asked, bewildered.

"Not him, damn the monster!" Ivan shouted. "Do you know he visits me? How did you find out? Speak!"

"Who is *he*! I don't know whom you are talking about."

"Yes, you do know ... or how could you—? It's impossible you don't know."

Suddenly he checked himself. A strange grin contorted his lips.

"Brother," Alyosha began again in a shaking voice, "I have said this to you because you'll believe my word. I tell you once and for all, it's not you. You hear! God has put it into my heart to say this to you, even though it may make you hate me."

By now Ivan had regained his self-control.

"Alexey Fyodorovitch," he said with a cold smile, "I can't endure prophets—messengers from God especially. I break off all relations with you from this moment. I beg you to leave me at this turning. It's the way to your lodgings, too. You'd better be careful not to come to me today! Do you hear?"

He turned and walked on with a firm step, not looking back.

"Brother," Alyosha called after him, "if anything happens to you today, turn to me before any one!"

Ivan made no reply. Alyosha stood under the lamp-post at the cross roads till Ivan had vanished, then walked slowly homewards. He had a furnished room in the house of some working people, while Ivan lived some distance away, in a roomy, comfortable lodge attached to a fine house that belonged to a well-to-do lady.

Ivan reached the gate of the house and had his hand on the bell, when he stopped. He was trembling with anger. Suddenly he let go of the bell, turned back with a curse, and walked with rapid steps in the opposite direction, a mile and a half, to a tiny, wooden house where Marya Kondratyevna, the neighbor who used to come to Fyodor Pavlovitch's kitchen for soup and to whom Smerdyakov had once sung his songs, was now lodging. She had sold their little house, and was now living here with her mother. Smerdyakov, who was ill—almost dying—had been with them ever since Fyodor Pavlovitch's death. It was to him Ivan was going, drawn by an urge he couldn't resist.

Chapter VI

The First Interview with Smerdyakov

This was the third time Ivan had been to see Smerdyakov since his return. The first was on the day of his arrival, then again a fortnight later. It was now a month since he had seen him. Ivan only returned five days after his father's death. The first to meet him was Alyosha, and Ivan was surprised to find that, in opposition to general opinion, he refused to entertain a suspicion against Mitya, and spoke of Smerdyakov as the murderer.

Ivan disliked his brother Dmitri. At most he felt compassion for him, and even that was mixed with contempt. Mitya's whole personality was unattractive to him. Yet he went to see Mitya on the first day of his arrival, and far from shaking his belief in his guilt, it strengthened it. He found his brother talkative, but not entirely coherent. He accused Smerdyakov, and talked mainly about the three thousand rubles he said had been "stolen" from him by his father. "The money was mine," Mitya declared. "Even if I had stolen it, I had the right."

He hardly contested the evidence against him, and if he tried to turn a fact to his advantage, it was in an absurd way. He hardly seemed to wish to defend himself. Quite the contrary, he was angry and scornful of the charges against him. He laughed at Grigory's evidence about the open door, and declared it was "the devil that opened it." But he could not explain it. He even insulted Ivan during their first interview, telling him sharply that it was not for people who declared that "everything was lawful" to question him. Although he was anything but friendly, Ivan went to see Smerdyakov.

In the train on his way from Moscow, he kept thinking of Smerdyakov and of his last conversation with him the evening before he went away. Many things puzzled him and seemed suspicious. But when he gave his evidence to the lawyer, Ivan said nothing of that conversation. He put it off till he had seen Smerdyakov, who was in the hospital.

Herzenstube and Varvinsky, the doctors Ivan met in the hospital, said in reply to his questions that Smerdyakov's attack was genuine, and were surprised at Ivan asking whether he might not have been shamming. They gave him to understand that the attack was an exceptional one, the fits persisting and recurring several times, so that the patient's life was in danger, and it was only now that they could say with confidence the patient would survive. His reason, they said, would be impaired for a considerable period."

On Ivan's asking whether that meant he was mad, they told him that this was not yet the case in the full sense of the word, but that certain abnormalities were evident. Ivan decided to find out what they were. He was allowed to see the patient, whom he found lying on a bed in a separate ward. Smerdyakov grinned uncertainly on seeing Ivan, and in the beginning seemed nervous. But for the rest of the time Ivan was struck by his ease.

From the first glance Ivan had no doubt that he was very ill. He was weak; he spoke slowly, seeming to move his tongue with difficulty, and throughout the interview, which lasted twenty minutes, he kept complaining of headache and of pain in all his limbs. His thin face seemed to have become tiny, his hair was ruffled, and his curls in front stood up. But in the left eye, which was screwed up and seemed to be suggesting something, Smerdyakov showed himself unchanged.

"It's always worth while speaking to a clever man," Ivan remembered him saying.

He sat down on the stool at his feet. Smerdyakov, with painful effort, shifted his position in bed, but he was not the first to speak.

"Can you talk to me?" asked Ivan. "I won't tire you much."

"Certainly I can," said Smerdyakov in a faint voice. "Has your honor been back long?" he added, as though encouraging a nervous visitor.

"I only arrived today.... To see the mess you are in here."

Smerdyakov sighed.

"Why do you sigh? You knew it all along," Ivan blurted out.

Smerdyakov was silent for a while.

"How could I help knowing? But how could I tell it would turn out like that?"

"What would turn out? Don't lie! You foretold you'd have a fit on the way down to the cellar. You mentioned the very spot."

"Have you said so to the lawyers yet?" Smerdyakov asked.

Ivan felt suddenly angry.

"I haven't yet, but I certainly shall. You must explain a great deal to me, my man; and let me tell you, I am not going to let you play with me!"

"Why should I play with you, when I put my whole trust in you?" said Smerdyakov.

"In the first place," began Ivan, "I know that epileptic fits can't be told beforehand. I've inquired; don't try and take me in. You can't foretell the day and the hour. How was it you told me the day and the hour beforehand, and about the cellar, too? How could you tell that you would fall down the cellar stairs in a fit, if you didn't sham a fit on purpose?"

404

"I had to go to the cellar several times a day," Smerdyakov drawled. "I fell from the garret just in the same way a year ago. It's quite true you can't tell the day and hour of a fit beforehand, but you can always have a sense of it."

"But you did foretell the day and the hour!"

"In regard to my epilepsy, sir, you had much better inquire of the doctors here. You can ask them whether it was a real fit or a sham; it's no use my saying anymore about it."

"And the cellar? How could you know beforehand of the cellar?"

"You don't seem able to get over that cellar! What frightened me most was losing you and being left without defense. So I went down into the cellar thinking, 'Here it'll come on directly, it'll strike me down, shall I fall?' And it was through this fear that I felt the spasm that always comes ... and so I went flying. All that, and my conversation with you at the gate the evening before, when I told you how frightened I was and spoke of the cellar, I told all that to Doctor Herzenstube and Nikolay Parfenovitch, the investigating lawyer, and it's all been written down. And the doctor here, Mr. Varvinsky, maintained it was the thought of it brought it on, the fear I might fall. They've written it down, that it's just how it must have happened, simply from my fear."

"Then you have said all that in your evidence?" said Ivan, somewhat taken aback. He had meant to frighten him with the threat of repeating their conversation, and it appeared Smerdyakov had already reported it all himself.

"What have I to be afraid of? Let them write the whole truth," Smerdyakov said. "And have you told them every word of our conversation at the gate?"

"No, not every word."

"And did you tell them that you can sham fits, as you boasted then?"

"No, I didn't tell them that either."

"Tell me now, why did you send me to Tchermashnya?"

"I was afraid you'd go away to Moscow; Tchermashnya is nearer."

"You're lying; you suggested my going away to get out of the way of trouble."

"That was simply out of my devotion to you, foreseeing trouble in the house. I told you to get out of harm's way, that you might understand there would be trouble in the house, and would remain at home to protect your father."

"You might have said it more directly, you blockhead!" Ivan fired.

"How could I have said it more directly? It was my fear that made me speak, and you might have been angry. I might well have been afraid that Dmitri Fyodorovitch would make a scene and carry away that money, for he considered it as good as his own; but who could tell it would end in murder? I thought he would only carry off the three thousand from under the master's mattress, but he murdered him. Who could guess it?"

"But if you say yourself that it couldn't be guessed, how could I have guessed and stayed at home? You contradict yourself!" said Ivan.

"You might have guessed from my sending you to Tchermashnya."

"How could I guess it from that?"

Smerdyakov seemed exhausted, and again was silent for a minute.

"You might have guessed from my asking you not to go to Moscow that I wanted to have you nearer, for Dmitri Fyodorovitch, knowing you are not far off, would not be so bold. And if anything happened, you might have come to protect me, too, for I warned you of Grigory Vassilyevitch's illness, and that I was afraid of having a fit. And when I explained those knocks to you, by means of which one could go in to the deceased, and that Dmitri Fyodorovitch knew them, I thought you would guess he would be sure to do something, and so you wouldn't go to Tchermashnya, even, but would stay nearer at hand."

"He talks very sanely," thought Ivan, "what's the craziness of his thinking that Herzenstube talked of?"

"You are being arch with me, damn you!" he exclaimed.

"I thought at the time you guessed," Smerdyakov replied.

"If I'd guessed, I should have stayed," cried Ivan.

"Why, I thought that it was because you guessed, that you went away in such a hurry, to get out of trouble and save yourself."

"You think that everyone is as great a coward as you?"

"Forgive me, I thought you were like me."

"Of course, I ought to have guessed," Ivan said; "and I did guess you were up to something... only you are lying again," he cried. "Do you remember how you went up to the carriage and said to me, 'It's always worth while speaking to a clever man'? So you were glad I went away, since you praised me?"

Smerdyakov sighed again. A trace of color came into his face.

"If I was pleased," he said, "it was simply because you agreed not to go to Moscow, but to Tchermashnya. For it was nearer should anything happen. When I said these words to you, it was not by way of praise, but of blame. You didn't understand."

"What blame?"

"Why, that seeing such a calamity coming you deserted your father, and would not protect us, for I might have been taken up for stealing that three thousand."

"Damn you!" Ivan swore again. "Did you tell the prosecutor and the investigating lawyer about those knocks?"

"I told them everything just as it was."

"If I thought of anything then," Ivan began again, "it was of some wickedness on your part. Dmitri might kill him, but that he would steal—I did not believe that. But I was ready for any wickedness from you. You told me yourself you could fake a fit."

"It was just through simplicity I said that; I've never faked a fit in my life. I only said so then to boast to you. It was just foolishness. I was open-hearted with you."

"My brother directly accuses you of the murder and theft."

"What else is left for him to do?" said Smerdyakov. "And who will believe him with all the proofs against him? Grigory Vassilyevitch saw the door open. What can he say after that? But never mind him! He is trying to save himself."

He ceased speaking; then, as though on reflection, added: "He wants to throw it on me and make out that it is the work of my hands—I've heard that already. But as to my being clever at shamming a fit: should I have told you beforehand that I could sham one, if I really had had such a design against your father? If I had been planning such a murder could I have been such a fool as to give evidence against myself beforehand? And to his son, too! Is that likely? No one hears this talk of ours now, and if you were to tell of it to the prosecutor and Nikolay Parfenovitch you might defend me completely by doing so, for who would likely be such a criminal if he is so open?"

Ivan got up to cut short their talk, struck by Smerdyakov's argument.

"I don't suspect you at all, and I think it's absurd to suspect you. But I'm grateful to you for setting my mind at rest. Now I am going, but I'll come again. Is there anything you want?"

"I am very thankful for everything. Marfa Ignatyevna does not forget me, and provides me anything I want. Good people visit me every day."

"Good-by. But I shan't say anything of your being able to sham a fit, and I don't advise you to, either," something made Ivan say.

"I quite understand. And if you don't speak of it, I shall say nothing of that conversation of ours at the gate."

Ivan went out, but had only gone a dozen steps when he felt there was something   insulting in Smerdyakov's last words. He was on the point of turning back, but it was only a passing impulse, and he left the hospital. His chief feeling was relief that it was not Smerdyakov, but Mitya, who had committed the murder.

In the following days he became more convinced of Mitya's guilt as he got to know all the evidence against him. There was evidence from people of no importance, like Fenya and her mother, but the effect of it was overpowering. And the evidence of Perhotin, the people at the tavern, and at Plotnikov's shop and Mokroe, seemed conclusive. It was the details that were so damning. The secret of the knocks impressed the lawyers almost as much as Grigory's evidence as to the open door. Grigory's wife, Marfa, declared that Smerdyakov had been lying all night the other side of the partition

"He was not three paces from our bed," and that although she was a sound sleeper she woke several times and heard him moaning, "He was moaning the whole time."

Ivan ended by dismissing all doubts. One thing was strange, however. Alyosha insisted Dmitri was not the murderer, and that "in all probability" Smerdyakov was. Ivan always felt that Alyosha's opinion meant a great deal, and so he was astonished at it now. Another thing that was strange was that Alyosha did not make any attempt to talk about Mitya with him; he never began on the subject and only answered his questions.

On his return from Moscow, Ivan abandoned himself to his passion for Katerina Ivanovna. When, on leaving her with

Alyosha, he told him, "I am not keen on her," it was a lie: he loved her madly, though at times he hated her, too. Many causes brought about this feeling. Shattered by what had happened with Mitya, she rushed on Ivan's return to meet him as her one salvation. She was hurt and humiliated. And here the man had come back to her who had loved her so ardently before, and whose heart and intellect she believed superior to her own. But the virtuous girl did not abandon herself altogether to the man she loved. She was tormented at the same time by remorse for having deserted Mitya, and in moments of discord she told Ivan so. This was what he had called to Alyosha "lies upon lies." There was much that was false in it, which angered Ivan.

He for a time forgot Smerdyakov's existence, and yet, a fortnight after his first visit to him, he began to be haunted by the same strange thoughts as before. Why, he asked himself, on that last night in Fyodor Pavlovitch's house had he, Ivan, crept on to the stairs like a thief and listened to his father below? Why, the next morning, had he been so depressed on the journey? Why had he said to himself, "I am a scoundrel"?

It was just after fancying this, that he met Alyosha in the street. He stopped him at once, and put a question to him: "Do you remember when Dmitri burst in after dinner and beat father, and afterwards I told you in the yard I reserved 'the right to desire'? Tell me, did you think then that I desired father's death or not?"

"I did think so," answered Alyosha softly.

"It was so, too; it was not a matter of guessing. But didn't you fancy that what I wished was just that 'one reptile should devour another'; that Dmitri should kill father as soon as possible ... and that I was even prepared to help to bring that about?"

Alyosha turned pale, looking silently into his brother's face.

"Speak!" cried Ivan, "I want to know what you thought then. I want the truth!"

He drew a deep breath, looking angrily at Alyosha.

"Forgive me, I did think that, too, at the time," whispered Alyosha.

"Thanks," snapped Ivan, and, leaving Alyosha, he went quickly on his way.

From that time Alyosha noticed that Ivan began to avoid him and seemed even to dislike to him, so much so that Alyosha gave up going to see him.

After that meeting with him, Ivan had not gone home, but went to Smerdyakov.

Chapter VII

The Second Visit to Smerdyakov

Smerdyakov had been discharged from the hospital and was now living in a little, old wooden house divided in two by a passage. On the other side of the passage lived Marya Kondratyevna and her mother, and on the other, Smerdyakov. No one knew on what terms he lived with them. It was supposed he had come to stay with them as Marya Kondratyevna's betrothed, and was living there without paying board or lodging.

Ivan knocked and the door was opened by Marya Kondratyevna. He followed her directions and went to the room on the left in which Smerdyakov lived. There was a tiled stove in the room and the walls were gay with blue paper, a good deal used. The room was furnished with benches against two of the walls and two chairs by the table. On the table stood a tea-maker and a tray with two cups. But Smerdyakov had finished tea and the samovar was out. He was sitting at the table on a bench, looking at an exercise-book and slowly writing with a pen. There was a bottle of ink by him and a candlestick.

Ivan saw from Smerdyakov's face that he had completely recovered. It was fuller. He was sitting in a colored dressing-gown, rather dirty, and wearing glasses Ivan had never seen him wear before. This trifling thing redoubled Ivan's anger:

"A creature like that and wearing glasses!"

Smerdyakov looked at him through his glasses; then slowly took them off and rose from the bench. Ivan took it all in and noted most of all the look in Smerdyakov's eyes—evil, churlish and haughty. "What do you want to intrude for?" it said; "we settled everything; why have you come again?"

Ivan could scarcely control himself.

"It's hot here," he said, loosening the buttons on his coat.

"Take off your coat," Smerdyakov responded.

Ivan took it off and threw it on a bench, then took a chair at the table and sat down. "To begin with, are we alone?" Ivan asked. "Can they hear us in there?"

"No one can hear anything. You've seen there's a passage."

"Listen, my good fellow; what was that you babbled as I was leaving the hospital, that if I said nothing about your faculty of shamming fits, you wouldn't tell the lawyer all our conversation at the gate? What do you mean by *all*? Were you threatening me? Have I entered into some sort of compact with you? Do you suppose I am afraid of you?"

Ivan said this in a perfect fury. Smerdyakov's eyes gleamed, his left eye winked, and he at once gave his answer, with his habitual composure and deliberation.

"This is what I meant and why I said that, that you, knowing beforehand of the murder of your parent, left him to his fate, that people mightn't conclude any evil about you, and perhaps of something else, too—that's what I promised not to tell."

Though Smerdyakov spoke calmly, there was something in his voice that was resentful and defiant.

"How? What? Are you out of your mind?"

"I'm perfectly in possession of all my faculties."

"Do you suppose I *knew* of the murder?" Ivan cried, pounding his fist on the table. "What do you mean by 'something else, too'? Speak, scoundrel!"

Smerdyakov, silent, continued to look at Ivan with the same insolent stare.

"Speak, you stinking rogue, what is that 'something else, too'?"

"The 'something else' I meant was that you probably desired your parent's death."

Ivan jumped up and struck him on the shoulder, so that he fell back against the wall. In an instant his face was bathed in tears. Saying, "It's a shame to strike a sick man," he dried his eyes with a dirty handkerchief and began weeping.

A minute passed.

"That's enough! Leave off," Ivan said. "Don't put me out of all patience."

Smerdyakov took the rag from his eyes. His face showed the insult he had received.

"So you thought then, you scoundrel, that, with Dmitri I meant to kill my father?"

"I didn't know what thoughts were in your mind," said Smerdyakov; "and so I stopped you then at the gate to sound you on that point."

"To sound what?"

"Whether you wanted your father to be murdered or not."

What infuriated Ivan more than anything was Smerdyakov's insolent tone.

"It was you murdered him?" he cried suddenly.

Smerdyakov smiled.

"You know for a fact it wasn't me. I should have thought there was no need for a sensible man to speak of it again."

"But why had you such a suspicion about me at the time?"

"As you know, it was from fear. For I was in such a position, shaking with fear, that I suspected everyone. I resolved to sound you, too, for I thought if you wanted the same as your brother, then the business was as good as settled."

"Look here, you didn't say that two weeks ago."

"I meant the same when I talked to you in the hospital; I thought you'd understand without wasting words, and that, being a sensible man, you wouldn't talk of it openly."

"What next! Answer: what could I have done to put such a degrading suspicion into your mean soul?"

"As for the murder, you couldn't have done that and didn't want to, but as for wanting someone else to do it, that was just what you did want."

"Why should I have wanted it; what grounds had I for wanting it?"

"What grounds had you? What about the inheritance?" said Smerdyakov. "After your parent's death there was at least forty thousand to come to each of you, and very likely more, but if Fyodor Pavlovitch had married that lady, Agrafena Alexandrovna, she would have had all his capital made over to her, so that your parent would not have left you two rubles between the three of you. And were they far from a wedding? A hair's-breadth: that lady had only to lift her little finger and he would have run after her to church with his tongue out."

Ivan restrained himself with painful effort.

"Very good," he said. "You see, I haven't jumped up, I haven't knocked you down, I haven't killed you. Speak on. So, according to you, I had fixed on Dmitri to do it"

"How could you help counting on him? If he killed him he would lose all the rights and property, and would go into exile; so his share of the inheritance would come to you and your brother Alexey Fyodorovitch; you'd each have not forty but sixty thousand each. There's no doubt you counted on Dmitri Fyodorovitch."

"What I put up with from you! Listen, scoundrel, if I had counted on anyone it would have been you, not Dmitri, and I swear I did expect some wickedness from you ... at the time.... I remember my impression!"

"I thought, for a minute, at the time, that you were reckoning on me, too," said Smerdyakov with a grin. "It was just by that, more than anything, you showed me what was in your mind. For if you had a foreboding about me and yet went away, you as good as said to me, 'You can murder my parent, I won't hinder you!'"

"You no-good! So that's how you understood it!"

"It was all that going to Tchermashnya. You were meaning to go to Moscow and refused your father's entreaties to go to Tchermashnya—and simply at a foolish word from me you consented at once! What reason had you to consent to Tchermashnya? Since you did, simply at my word, it shows you must have expected something from me."

"No, I swear I didn't!" shouted Ivan.

"You didn't? Then you ought, as your father's son, to have had me taken to the lock-up at once ... or at least given me a punch in the face, but you were not a bit angry. You acted on my foolish word and went away, which was absurd, for you ought to have stayed to save your parent's life. How could I help drawing my conclusions?"

Ivan sat scowling.

"Yes, I am sorry I didn't punch you in the face," he said with a bitter smile. "I couldn't have taken you to the lock-up just then. Who would have believed me and what charge could I bring against you? But the punch in the face ... I'm sorry I didn't think of it. Though blows are forbidden, I should have pounded your ugly face to a jelly."

Smerdyakov looked at him almost with relish.

"In the ordinary occasions of life," he said in the same complacent tone, "blows on the face are forbidden by law, and people have given them up, but in exceptional cases people still fly to blows, not only among us but all over the world, but you did not dare."

"What are you learning French words for?"

Ivan nodded towards the exercise-book lying on the table.

"Why shouldn't I learn them to improve my education, supposing I may chance to go some day to those happy parts of Europe?"

"Listen, you beast." Ivan's eyes flashed. "I'm not afraid of what you may accuse me of; you can say what you like, and if I don't beat you to death, it's because I suspect you of that crime, and I'll drag you to justice. I'll show you for what you are."

"To my thinking, you'd better keep quiet, for what can you accuse me of in view of my innocence? And who would believe you? If you begin, I shall tell everything, for I must defend myself."

"Do you think I am afraid of you now?"

"If the court doesn't believe me, the public will, and you will be shamed."

"'It's always worth while speaking to a sensible man,' eh?" snarled Ivan.

"You hit the mark, indeed. And you'd better be sensible."

Ivan rose, shaking with anger, put on his coat, and without replying further, walked out of the cottage. The cool evening air made him feel better. There was a bright moon, but a nightmare of ideas filled his soul.

"Shall I give information against Smerdyakov? But what information can I give? He is not guilty; he'll accuse me. And in fact, why did I set off for Tchermashnya? Yes, of course, I was expecting something, and he is right...."

He remembered for the hundredth time how, on the last night in his father's house, he had listened on the stairs. He remembered it with such pain that he stood still on the spot as though stabbed.

"Yes, I expected it, that's true! I wanted the murder! I must kill Smerdyakov! If I don't kill Smerdyakov, life is not worth living!"

Ivan did not go home, but went to Katerina Ivanovna, alarming her by his look. He was like a madman. He repeated his conversation with Smerdyakov. He couldn't be calmed. He kept walking about the room, speaking disconnectedly. At last he sat down, leaned his head on his hands, and said: "If it's not Dmitri, but Smerdyakov who's the murderer, I share his guilt, for I put him up to it. If he is the murderer, then I am, too."

When Katerina Ivanovna heard that, she got up from her seat, went to her writing-table, took out a sheet of paper and laid it before Ivan. This was the letter of which he spoke to Alyosha as "proof" that Dmitri had killed his father. It was written by Mitya to Katerina Ivanovna when he was drunk, the evening he was at the "Metropolis." It was there he asked for pen and paper and wrote the letter. It was a wordy letter, like the talk of a drunken man, written at great length, with great excitement and incoherence.

The letter ran as follows:

"FATAL KATYA: Tomorrow I will get the money and repay your three thousand and farewell, woman of great anger, but farewell, too, my love! Tomorrow I shall try and get it from every one, and if I can't borrow it, I give you my word of honor I shall go to my father and break his skull and take the money from under the pillow, if only Ivan has gone. If I have to go to Siberia for it, I'll give you back your three thousand. I bow down to the ground before you, for I've been a no-good. Forgive me! I love another. You got to know her well today, so how can you forgive?

I will murder the man who's robbed me! I'll leave you all and go to the East so as to see no one again.

"P.S. I shall kill myself, but first of all that dog. I shall tear three thousand from him and fling it to you. Though I've been bad to you, I'm not a thief! You can expect three thousand. The dog keeps it under his mattress. Katya, don't look down on me. Dmitri is not a thief! But a murderer! He has murdered his father and ruined himself rather than face your pride. He doesn't love you.

"P.P.S.—I kiss your feet, farewell!

"P.P.P.S.—Katya, pray to God that someone will give me the money. Then I shall not be steeped in blood, but if no one does—I shall! Kill me!

"Your slave and enemy,

"D. Karamazov.

When Ivan read this "document" he was convinced. So then it was his brother, not Smerdyakov. And if not Smerdyakov, then not he, Ivan. This letter at once assumed the aspect of logical proof. There could be no longer the slightest doubt of Mitya's guilt.

The next morning he only thought of Smerdyakov and his gibes with contempt. A few days later he wondered how he could have been so distressed at his suspicions. He resolved to forget him. So passed a month. He made no further inquiry about Smerdyakov, but twice he heard that he was very ill and out of his mind.

"He'll end in madness," the young doctor Varvinsky said, and Ivan remembered this. During the last week of that month Ivan himself began to feel very ill. He consulted the Moscow doctor who had been sent for by Katerina Ivanovna, though his relations with her became very strained. They were like two enemies in love with one another.

Katerina Ivanovna's "return" to Mitya, that is, her brief feeling in his favor, drove Ivan to a perfect frenzy. Strange to say, until that last scene when Alyosha came from Mitya to Katerina Ivanovna, Ivan had never once, during that month, heard her express a doubt of Mitya's guilt. It is remarkable, too, that while he felt he hated Mitya more every day, he realized that it was not on account of Katya, but *because he was the murderer.*

Nevertheless, he went to see Mitya ten days before the trial and proposed a plan of escape. He was partly impelled to do this by a sore place left in his heart from a phrase of Smerdyakov's, that it was to his, Ivan's, advantage that his brother should be convicted, as that would increase his inheritance and Alyosha's from forty to sixty thousand rubles. He determined to sacrifice thirty thousand on arranging Mitya's escape.

On his return from seeing him, he was sad and dispirited, and began to feel anxious for Mitya's escape, not only to heal that sore place, but for another reason.

"Is it because I am as much a murderer at heart?" he asked himself.

Something deep down burned in his soul. His pride above all suffered cruelly all month. But when, after his conversation with Alyosha, he decided to see Smerdyakov, he obeyed a sudden and peculiar impulse. He remembered how Katerina Ivanovna had cried out to him in Alyosha's presence: "It was you who persuaded me of Mitya's "guilt!"

Ivan was thunderstruck when he recalled it. He had never once tried to persuade her that Mitya was the murderer; on the contrary, he had suspected himself in her presence, that time he came back from Smerdyakov. It was *she* who showed him the letter that proved his brother's guilt. And now she exclaimed: "I've been at Smerdyakov's myself!"

When had she been there? Ivan knew nothing of it. So she was not at all so sure of Mitya's guilt! And what could Smerdyakov have told her? His heart burned with anger.

He let go of the bell and rushed off to Smerdyakov.

"I shall kill him, perhaps, this time," he thought.

Chapter VIII

The Third and Last Interview with Smerdyakov

There were scarcely any lamp-posts in the part of the town where
Smerdyakov lived, and Ivan strode alone in the darkness, picking
his way. His head ached and he had a painful throbbing in his
temples. Not far from Marya Kondratyevna's cottage, he came
upon a drunken peasant, stumbling and swearing to himself.

He began singing in a husky drunken voice:

"Vanka's gone to Petersburg;
I won't wait till he comes back."

But broke off and began swearing again.

Ivan felt intense hatred for him. He felt an impulse to knock
him down. As they met, the peasant, with a violent lurch, fell
against him, and Ivan pushed back furiously. The peasant went
flying backwards and fell like a log on the frozen ground. He
cried, "O—oh!" and then was silent, lying on his back without
movement.

"He will be frozen," thought Ivan as he went on his way to
Smerdyakov's.

In the passage, Marya Kondratyevna ran out with a candle,
and whispered that Smerdyakov was ill, "It's not that he's laid up,
but he seems not himself."

"Why, does he make a row?" asked Ivan.

"No, he's very quiet. Only please don't talk to him too long," she begged him.

Ivan opened the door and went in. The room was over-heated as before, but there were changes. One of the benches had been removed; in its place was an old leather sofa on which a bed had been made up. Smerdyakov was sitting on it, wearing the same dressing-gown, with the table in front of him. On the table lay a thick book, but Smerdyakov was not reading it. He seemed to be sitting doing nothing.

He met Ivan with a silent gaze, and was not at all surprised at his coming. There was a great change in his face; he was thinner and sallower. His eyes were sunken and there were blue marks under them.

"Why, you really are ill?" Ivan stopped short. "I won't keep you long, I won't even take off my coat. Where can one sit down?"

He went to the other end of the table, moved up a chair, and sat on it.

"Why do you look at me without speaking? I've only come with one question, and I won't go without an answer. Has the young lady, Katerina Ivanovna, been with you?"

Smerdyakov, still silent, looked at Ivan as before. Suddenly, with a motion of his hand, he turned his face away.

"What's the matter with you?" cried Ivan.

"Nothing."

"What do you mean by 'nothing'?"

"Yes, she has. It's no matter to you. Let me alone."

"No, I won't let you alone. Tell me, when was she here?"

"I'd quite forgotten about her," said Smerdyakov with an evil smile. He stared at Ivan with a look of hatred. "You seem very ill yourself," he said.

"Never mind my health, tell me what I ask you."

"Why are your eyes so yellow? Are you so worried?"

He smiled, and suddenly laughed out loud.

"I've told you I won't go away without an answer!" Ivan cried. "Why do you keep after me? Why do you go on and on?"

"I've nothing to do with you. Just answer my question."

"I've no answer to give you," said Smerdyakov.

"You may be sure I'll make you answer!"

"Why are you so uneasy?" Smerdyakov stared at him with hatred. "Is it because the trial begins tomorrow? Nothing will happen to you. Go home, go to bed and sleep in peace, don't be afraid of anything."

"What have I to be afraid?" Ivan said, surprised, and suddenly a chill breath of fear passed over him.

Smerdyakov measured him with his eyes.

"You don't understand?" he said. "It's strange that a sensible man should care to play such a role!"

Ivan looked at him speechless. The superior air of this man who had once been his valet was extraordinary.

"I tell you you've nothing to be afraid of. I won't say anything about you. I say, how your hands are trembling! Why are your fingers moving like that? Go home, *you* did not murder him."

Ivan started. He remembered what Alyosha had said.

"I know it was not I," he said.

"Do you?" Smerdyakov caught him up again.

Ivan jumped up and seized him by the shoulder.

"Tell me everything, you viper! Tell me everything!"

Smerdyakov riveted his eyes on Ivan with insane hatred.

"Well, it was you who murdered him, if that's it," he whispered furiously.

Ivan sank back on his chair.

"You mean my going away. What you talked about last time?"

"You stood before me and understood it all, and you understand it now."

"All I understand is that you are mad."

"What's the use of keeping up a farce to each other? Are you still trying to throw it all on me? *You* murdered him; you are the real murderer, I was only your instrument, your faithful servant, and I did it following your words."

"*Did* it? Why, did you murder him?" Ivan turned cold.

Something seemed to give way in his brain, and he shuddered. Then Smerdyakov himself looked at him wonderingly; probably the genuineness of Ivan's horror struck him.

"You don't mean to say you really did not know?" he said mistrustfully.

Ivan still gazed at him, and seemed unable to speak.

"Vanka's gone to Petersburg;
I won't wait till he comes back," echoed in his head.

"I'm afraid you're a dream, a phantom sitting there," he said.

"There's no phantom here, only us and one other. No doubt he is here, between us."

"Who is here? What third person?" Ivan cried, looking about.

"That third is God Himself. Only don't look for Him, you won't find Him."

"It's a lie that you killed him!" Ivan cried. "You are mad, or teasing me!"

Smerdyakov watched him with no sign of fear. He could hardly believe it; he still fancied Ivan knew everything and was trying to "throw it all on him."

"Wait a minute," he said at last in a weak voice, and bringing up his left leg from under the table, he began turning up his trouser leg. He was wearing long white stockings and slippers. Slowly he took off his garter and fumbled to the bottom of his stocking.

Ivan gazed at him, and shuddered in terror.

"He's mad!" he cried.

Jumping up, he drew back so that he knocked his back against the wall and stood there looking with terror at Smerdyakov, who, entirely unaffected, continued fumbling in his stocking. At last he pulled out a piece of paper, or perhaps a roll of papers.

Smerdyakov laid it on the table.

"Here," he said quietly.

"What is it?" asked Ivan, trembling.

"Look at it," Smerdyakov answered.

Ivan took up the roll of paper and began unfolding it, but drew back.

"Your hands keep shaking," said Smerdyakov.

He unfolded the bundle himself and displayed three packets of hundred-ruble notes.

"They are all here, the three thousand rubles; you need not count them. Take them," Smerdyakov said.

Ivan sank back in his chair, his face white.

"You frightened me... with your stocking," he said.

"Can you really not have known?" Smerdyakov asked.

"No, I didn't know. I kept thinking of Dmitri. Brother, brother!" he cried, clutching his head in both hands.

"Did you kill him alone? With my brother's help or without?"

"It was only with your help I killed him. Dmitri Fyodorovitch is innocent."

"All right. Talk about me later. Why do I keep trembling? I can't speak properly."

"You were bold enough then. You said 'everything was lawful,' and how frightened you are now," Smerdyakov said. "Won't you have something to drink? I'll ask for some at once. It's very refreshing. Only I must hide this first," he said, motioning at the notes.

He was just going to get up and call at the door to Marya Kondratyevna to make them something cool to drink, but, looking for something to cover up the notes that she might not see them, he first took out his handkerchief, and. as it was very dirty, put the big yellow book Ivan had noticed lying on the table on the notes, instead.

"I won't have anything to drink," Ivan said. "Talk of me later. Tell me how you did it."

"You'd better take off your coat, or you'll be too hot."

Ivan, as though he'd only just thought of it, took off his coat. "Speak, please, speak."

He seemed calmer. He waited, sure Smerdyakov would tell him *all* about it.

"How it was done?" Smerdyakov went on. "In a most natural way, following your very words."

"Of my words later," Ivan broke in. "Tell me how you did it. Everything, as it happened. Don't forget anything. The details, above everything, I beg you."

"You'd gone away, and then I fell into the cellar."

"In a fit or in a fake one?"

"A fake one, naturally. I went quietly down the steps to the bottom and lay down, and as I did I gave a scream, and struggled, till they carried me out."

"Stay! And were you faking it all along, afterwards, and in the hospital?"

"Not at all. Next day, in the morning, before they took me to the hospital, I had a real attack. For two days I was quite unconscious."

"All right. Go on."

"They laid me on the bed. I knew I'd be the other side of the partition, for whenever I was ill, Marfa Ignatyevna used to put me there, near them. She's always been very kind to me. At night I moaned, but quietly. I kept expecting Dmitri Fyodorovitch to come."

"Expecting him? To come to you?"

"Not to me. I expected him to come into the house, for I'd no doubt that he'd come that night, for being without me and getting no news he'd be sure to come and climb over the fence, as he used to, and do something."

"And if he hadn't come?"

"Then nothing would have happened. I should never have brought myself to it."

"All right ... speak clearly, don't hurry; don't leave anything out!"

"I expected him to kill Fyodor Pavlovitch. I had prepared him for it. He knew about the knocks, that was the chief thing. With the fury which had been growing in him, he was bound to get into the house by means of those taps. So I was expecting him."

"Stay," Ivan interrupted. "If he had killed him he would have taken the money and carried it away; you must have considered that. What would you have got by it?"

"He would never have found the money. I told him the money was under the mattress. But that wasn't true. It had been lying in a box. I said to Fyodor Pavlovitch, as I was the only person he trusted, to hide the envelope with the notes in the corner behind the icons, for no one would have guessed that place. So that's where the envelope lay. It would have been absurd to keep it under the mattress. So if Dmitri Fyodorovitch had committed the murder, finding nothing, he would either have run away, afraid of being found and arrested. So I could have climbed up to the icons and taken the money the next morning or even that night, and it would have all been put down to Dmitri Fyodorovitch."

"But what if he did not kill him, but only knocked him down?"

"If he did not kill him, of course, I would not have ventured to take the money, and nothing would have happened. But I calculated that he would beat him senseless, and I should have time to take it, and then I'd make out to Fyodor Pavlovitch that it was no one but Dmitri Fyodorovitch who had taken the money after beating him."

"I'm getting mixed. It was Dmitri who killed him; you only took the money?"

"No, he didn't kill him. I might have told you he was the murderer. But I don't want to lie to you because ... if you really haven't understood till now, as I see for myself, and are not pretending so as to throw your guilt on me, you are still responsible, since you knew of the murder and charged me to do it, and went away knowing about it. So I want to prove to you that you are the real murderer, and I'm not, though I killed him."

"Am I a murderer? Oh God!" Ivan cried. "You mean Tchermashnya? Why did you want my consent if you took Tchermashnya for consent? How will you explain that?"

"Assured of your consent, I should have known you wouldn't make an outcry over the three thousand being lost, even if I'd been suspected; on the contrary, you would have protected me. And when you got your inheritance you would have rewarded me when you were able, all the rest of your life. For you'd have received your inheritance through me, since, if he had married Agrafena Alexandrovna, you wouldn't have had a penny."

"Then you intended to worry me all my life," snarled Ivan. "And what if I hadn't gone away, but had informed against you?"

"What could you have informed? That I persuaded you to go to Tchermashnya? That's all nonsense. Besides, if you had stayed, nothing would have happened. I should have known that you didn't want it done. As you went away, it meant you wouldn't dare to inform against me at the trial, and that you'd over-look my having the three thousand. Indeed, you couldn't have prosecuted me afterwards, because then I should have told it all in the court; not that I had stolen the money or killed him—I shouldn't have said that—but that you'd put me up to the theft and the murder, though I didn't consent to it. That's why I needed your consent, so that you couldn't have cornered me afterwards, for what proof could you have had? I could always have revealed your eagerness for your father's death; the public would have believed it, and you would have been shamed."

"Was I then so eager?" Ivan snarled again.

"To be sure you were; your silence you okayed my doing it."

"Go on," he said. "Tell me what happened that night."

"What more is there to tell! I lay there and thought I heard the master shout. Before that Grigory Vassilyevitch had got up and gone out. He gave a scream, and then all was silence. I lay there waiting, my heart beating; I couldn't bear it. I got up and went out. I saw the window open on the garden. I heard the master moving about, sighing, so I knew he was alive. I went to the window and shouted, 'It's I.'

He shouted, 'He's been; he's run away.' He meant Dmitri Fyodorovitch. 'He's killed Grigory!' 'Where?' I whispered. 'There, in the corner,' he pointed. 'Wait a bit,' I said. I went to the corner of the garden to look, and there I found Grigory Vassilyevitch lying by the wall, covered with blood and senseless. So it's true that Dmitri Fyodorovitch had been here, I thought, and I determined on the spot to make an end of it, as Grigory, even if he were alive, would see nothing of it, as he was senseless. The only risk was that Marfa Ignatyevna might wake up. But the longing to do it was so strong I could scarcely breathe.

"I went back to the window and said, 'She's here, Agrafena Alexandrovna. She wants to be let in.' 'Where is she?' he gasped, but he couldn't believe it. 'She's standing there,' said I. He looked out of the window, half believing and half distrustful. It was funny. I knocked on the window-frame those taps we'd agreed upon as a signal that Grushenka had come. He didn't believe my word, but as soon as he heard the taps, he ran to open the door. I would have gone in, but he stood in the way. 'Where is she?'

"He looked at me, all of a tremble. 'Well,' thought I, 'if he's so frightened of me as all that, it's a bad look out!' My legs went weak with fright that he wouldn't let me in or would call out, or Marfa Ignatyevna would run up, or something else might happen. I whispered to him, 'Why, she's there, under the window; how is it you don't see her?' He said, 'Bring her then, bring her.' 'She's afraid,' said I; 'she was frightened at the noise, she's hidden in the bushes; go and call to her yourself from the study.'

"He ran to the window and cried, 'Grushenka, are you here?' But he didn't want to lean out the window, he didn't want to move away from me, for he was panic-stricken; he was so frightened he didn't dare to turn his back on me.

"'Why, here she is,' said I. I went to the window and leaned out. 'Here she is; she's in the bush, laughing at you, don't you see her?'

"He suddenly believed it, and leaned out the window. I snatched up that iron paper-weight from his table; and I swung it and hit him on the top of the skull with the corner of it. He didn't even cry out. He only sank down, and I hit him again and a third time. The third time I knew I'd broken his skull. He rolled on his back, face upwards, covered with blood. I looked round. There was no blood on me, not a spot. I wiped the paper-weight, put it back, went up to the icons, took the money out of the envelope and flung the envelope on the floor, the pink ribbon beside it. I went into the garden all of a tremble, straight to the apple-tree with a hollow in it—I'd marked it long before and put a rag and a piece of paper in it. I wrapped the notes in the rag and stuffed it deep in the hole. And there it stayed for more than two weeks, until I came out of the hospital.

"Anyhow, I went back to my bed, lay down and thought, 'If Grigory Vassilyevitch has been killed it may be bad for me, but if he is not killed and recovers, it will be first-rate, for then he'll bear witness that Dmitri Fyodorovitch has been here and must have killed him and taken the money.' Then I began groaning to wake Marfa Ignatyevna. At last she rushed in to me, but when she saw Grigory Vassilyevitch was not there, she ran out. I heard her scream in the garden. And that set it all going."

He stopped. Ivan had listened in silence without stirring. As he told his story Smerdyakov glanced at him from time to time, but mostly he kept from looking at him. When he finished he was agitated and breathing hard.

"Stay," cried Ivan. "What about the door? If he only opened the door to you, how could Grigory have seen it open before? For Grigory saw it before you went."

"As for that door, that was only Grigory Vassilyevitch's fancy. He is not a man, I assure you," Smerdyakov said, "but a mule. He didn't see it, but fancied he had, and there's no shaking him. It's just our luck he took that notion into his head, for they can't fail to convict Dmitri Fyodorovitch after that."

"Listen," said Ivan, puzzled. "There are a lot of questions I want to ask you, but I forget them ... and getting mixed up. Tell me this at least, why did you open the envelope and leave it on the floor? Why didn't you carry it with you? When you were telling me, I thought you spoke about it as though it were the right thing to do ... I can't understand...."

"I did that for a good reason. For if a man had known all about it, if he'd seen those notes before, and perhaps had put them in that envelope himself, if such a man had done the murder, what should have made him tear open the envelope in such a desperate hurry, since he'd know for certain the notes must be in the envelope? No, if the robber had been someone like me, he'd have put the envelope in his pocket and got away as fast as he could. But it'd be quite different with Dmitri Fyodorovitch. He only knew about the envelope by hearsay; and if he'd found it, for instance, under the mattress, he'd have torn it open as quickly as possible to make sure the notes were in it. And he'd have thrown the envelope down without having time to consider it would be evidence against him. Because he was not a thief, and if he did steal it would be simply taking what was his own, for he'd told the whole town he meant to, and had even bragged before every one that he'd go and take his property from Fyodor Pavlovitch. I didn't say that openly to the prosecutor when I was being examined, but brought him to it, as though I didn't see it myself, and as though he'd thought of it himself."

"But can you possibly have thought of all that on the spot?"

"Mercy on us! Could anyone think of it all in such a desperate hurry? It was all thought out beforehand."

"Well...well, it was the devil helped you!" Ivan cried. "No, you are not a fool, you are far cleverer than I thought...."

He got up to walk across the room, but was blocked by the table. Irritated, he cried out almost as furiously as before: "Listen, you miserable creature! Don't you understand that if I haven't killed you, it's because I am keeping you to answer tomorrow at the trial? Perhaps I, too, was guilty; perhaps I really had a secret desire for my father's... death, but I was not as guilty as you think, and perhaps I didn't urge you on at all. No, I didn't urge you on! But no matter, I will give evidence against myself at the trial tomorrow. I shall tell everything. We'll make our appearance together. And whatever you may say against me, I'll face it; I'm not afraid of you. I'll confirm everything! But you must confess, too! That's how it shall be!"

Ivan said this solemnly, and his eyes said it would be so.

"You are quite ill. Your eyes are yellow," Smerdyakov said.

"We'll go together," Ivan said. "And if you won't go, I'll go alone."

Smerdyakov paused as though thinking.

"There'll be nothing of the sort, and you won't go," he said.

"You don't understand me," Ivan exclaimed.

"You'll be too shamed if you confess it. And, what's more, it will be no use, for I shall say that I never said anything of the sort to you, and that you are either ill (and it looks like it, too), or that you're sorry for your brother and are sacrificing yourself to save him and have invented it all against me, for you've always thought no more of me than if I'd been a fly. And who will believe you; what proof have you got?"

"Listen, you showed me those notes just now to convince me."

Smerdyakov took the book from the notes and laid it on one side.

"Take that money away with you," Smerdyakov sighed.

"Of course I shall take it. But why do you give it to me, if you committed the murder for the sake of it?" Ivan asked, surprised.

"I don't want it," Smerdyakov said. "I did have an idea of beginning a new life with that money in Moscow or, better still, abroad. I dreamt of it chiefly because 'all things are lawful.' That was what you taught me: if there's no God, there's no such thing as virtue, and there's no need of it. You were right there. So that's how I looked at it."

"Did you come to that of yourself?" asked Ivan.

"With your guidance."

"And now, I suppose, you believe in God, since you are giving back the money?"

"No, I don't believe," whispered Smerdyakov.

"Then why are you giving it back?"

"Leave off ... that's enough!" Smerdyakov cried. "You said yourself that everything was lawful, so why are you so upset? You even want to give evidence against yourself.... Only there'll be nothing of the sort! You won't give evidence!"

"You'll see," said Ivan.

"It isn't possible. You are very clever. You are fond of money, I know that. You like to be respected, too, for you're very proud; you are far too fond of female charms, too, and you mind most of all about living in undisturbed comfort, without having to depend on any one—that's what you care most about. You won't want to spoil your life forever by taking such a disgrace on yourself. You are like Fyodor Pavlovitch, you are more like him than any of his children; you've the same soul as he had."

"You're not a fool," said Ivan, the blood rushing to his face. "It was your pride made you think I was a fool. Take the money."

Ivan took the rolls of notes and put them in his pocket without wrapping them.

"I shall show them at the court tomorrow," he said.

"Nobody will believe you, as you've plenty of money of your own; you may have taken it out of your cash-box and brought it to the court."

Ivan rose from his seat.

"The only reason I haven't killed you," he said, "is that I need you tomorrow, don't forget it!"

"Well, kill me now," Smerdyakov said, looking strangely at Ivan. "You won't dare do that even!" he added. "You won't dare do anything, you who used to be so bold!"

"Till tomorrow," cried Ivan, and moved to leave.

"Stay a moment.... Show me those notes again."

Ivan took out the notes and showed them to him. Smerdyakov looked at them for ten seconds.

"You can go," he said, but called after him, "Ivan Fyodorovitch!"

"What do you want?" Ivan turned.

"Goodbye!"

"Till tomorrow!" Ivan cried again, and walked out.

The snowstorm was still raging. He walked the first few steps boldly, but suddenly began shaking. "It's something physical," he thought. Joy was springing up in his heart.

He would make an end of the lack of decision that had so pained him of late. His mind was made up, "and now it will not be changed," he thought with relief.

At that moment he stumbled against something and almost fell. He made out at his feet the person he had knocked down, still lying motionless. The snow had almost covered his face.

Ivan seized him and lifted him in his arms. Seeing a light in the little house to the right he went up, knocked at the window, and asked the man to whom the house belonged to help him carry the man he had knocked down to the police-station, promising him three rubles. The man came out.

Bringing the man he had knocked down to the police-station, arranging for a doctor to see him, and providing with a liberal hand for the expenses, took a whole hour, but Ivan was well content.

"If I had not taken my decision so firmly for tomorrow," he thought, "I should not have stayed a whole hour to look after the man I had knocked down, but should have passed by without caring about his being frozen. I am quite capable of being sensible, although they have decided that I am going out of my mind!"

Just as he reached his own house he stopped short, asking himself hadn't he better go at once to the prosecutor and tell him everything. He decided the question by turning back to the house. "Everything tomorrow!" he said, and, strange to say, almost all his gladness and self-satisfaction passed in an instant.

As he entered his own room, he felt something like a touch of ice on his heart, like a recollection or, more exactly, a reminder, of something agonizing and revolting that was in the room at that moment, and had been there before.

He sank on his sofa. The old woman brought him a samovar; he made tea, but did not touch it. He sat on the sofa and felt giddy. He felt ill and helpless. He was beginning to drop asleep, but got up uneasily and walked across the room to shake off his drowsiness. At moments he fancied he was not in his right mind, but it was not illness he thought.

Sitting down again, he looked round as though searching for something. This happened several times. At last his eyes fastened on one point. He smiled, but an angry flush filled his face. He sat a long time in his place, his head propped on his arms, though he looked sideways at the sofa against the opposite wall. There was something there that irritated him.

Chapter IX

The Devil: Ivan's Nightmare

Ivan was on the eve of an attack of fever. Though his health had long been affected, it had offered a stubborn resistance to the fever, which in the end gained complete mastery. He had, by an effort of will, succeeded in delaying the attack for a time, hoping to check it completely. He knew he was unwell, but he loathed the thought of being ill at that time.

He consulted the new doctor brought from Moscow by Katerina Ivanovna, who, after listening to him and examining him, concluded he was suffering from some disorder of the brain, and was not at surprised by an admission which Ivan reluctantly made.

"Hallucinations are quite likely in your condition," the doctor said, "though it's better to verify them ... you must take steps at once, or things will go badly with you."

But Ivan did not follow this advice. And so he was sitting, in his room, staring at someone sitting on the sofa against the opposite wall, though who knows how he had got in. He was a gentleman, no longer young, with rather long, thick, dark hair, and a small pointed beard. He looked like a gentlemen of accommodating temper, who could tell a story or take a hand at cards. Ivan was angrily silent and would not begin the talk. The visitor waited like a poor relation who had come down from his room to keep his host company, and was discreetly silent, seeing that his host was frowning and preoccupied. But he was ready for any affable conversation as soon as his host should begin it.

All at once his face expressed a sudden solicitude.

"I say," he began, "excuse me, I only mention it to remind you that you went to Smerdyakov's to find out about Katerina Ivanovna, but came away without finding out anything about her, you probably forgot—"

"Ah, yes," broke from Ivan, his face gloomy. "Yes, I'd forgotten ... but it doesn't matter now," he said. "I should have remembered it in a minute, for that was just what was on my mind! Why do you interfere, as if I didn't remember it myself?"

"Don't believe it then," said the gentleman, smiling, "what's the good of believing against your will? Besides, proofs are no help to believing, especially material proofs. Look at the spiritualists, for instance.... I am very fond of them ... they imagine they are serving the cause of religion because the devils show them their horns. That, they say, is material proof of the existence of another world. If you come to that, does proving there's a devil prove there's a God?"

"I seem to be not in my right mind," Ivan said, getting up from the table. "So say anything you like, I don't care! You won't drive me to fury as you did last time. I sometimes don't see you and don't even hear you, but I always guess what you are saying, for it's *I myself speaking, not you.* Only I don't know whether I was dreaming last time or really saw you. I'll put a wet a towel on my head and maybe you'll go away."

Ivan went into the corner, took a towel, and did as he said.

"I am so glad you treat me so familiarly," the visitor began.

"Fool," laughed Ivan, "do you suppose I would stand on ceremony with you? I am feeling n good, though I've a pain in the top of my head... only please don't talk philosophy, as you did last time. If you can't disappear, talk of something amusing. Talk gossip. What a nightmare to have! But I am not afraid of you. I'll get the better of you."

"That's charming. For what am I on earth but a poor relation? By the way, listening to you I am surprised to find you are beginning to take me for something real, not simply your fancy, as you declared last time—"

"Never for one minute have I taken you for real," Ivan cried. "You are a lie, you are my illness. Only I don't know how to destroy you, and I see I must suffer for a time. You are my imagining, myself, but only of one side of me...of my thoughts and feelings, but only the nastiest and worst of them—"

"Excuse me, I'll catch you. When you flew at Alyosha under the lamp-post this evening and shouted, 'You learnt it from *him*! How do you know that *he* visits me?' you were thinking of me then. So for one brief moment you did believe I really exist."

"That was a moment of weakness...but I couldn't believe in you. I don't know if I was asleep or awake. Perhaps I was only dreaming then and didn't see you at all—"

"Why were you so surly with Alyosha just now? He is a dear; I've treated him badly over Father Zossima."

"Don't talk of Alyosha! How dare you!" Ivan said.

"You scold me—that's a good sign. But you are ever so much more polite than you were last time, and I know why: that decision of yours—"

"Don't speak of my decision," cried Ivan.

"I understand, you are going to defend your brother and give yourself up."

"Hold your tongue, I'll kick you!"

"I shan't be sorry, for then my object will be attained. If you kick me, you must believe in my reality, for people don't kick ghosts. Joking apart, it doesn't matter, say what you like, though it's better to be a bit more polite, even to me."

"If I go after you, I go after myself," Ivan laughed. "You are myself, with a different face. You just say what I'm thinking...and are not able to saying anything new!"

"If I am like you in my way of thinking, it's all to my credit."

"You choose only my worst thoughts, and the stupid ones. You are stupid and vulgar. No, I can't put up with you! What am I to do, what am I to do?" Ivan cried.

"My dear friend, above all I want to behave like a gentleman and be recognized as such," the visitor began. "I am poor, but ... I won't say very honest, but ... it's an axiom generally accepted that I'm a fallen angel. I can't conceive how I can ever have been an angel. If I ever was, it must have been so long ago that there's no harm in forgetting it.

Now I only prize the reputation of being a gentleman, and live as I can, trying to make myself agreeable. I've been greatly lied about! Here, when I stay with you from time to time, my life gains a kind of reality and that's what I like. I wander about here dreaming. What I dream of is becoming a real person, in the form of some merchant's wife, and believing all she believes. My ideal is to go to church and offer a candle in simple-hearted faith. Then there would be an end to my sufferings. I like being doctored, too; in the spring there was an outbreak of smallpox and I was vaccinated—if only you knew how I enjoyed myself that day.... But you are not listening. You are not at all well this evening? I know you went yesterday to that doctor ... well, what did he say?"

"Fool!" Ivan snapped out.

"But you are clever, anyway. You are scolding again? I didn't ask out of sympathy. You needn't answer. Now rheumatism has come in again—"

"Fool!" repeated Ivan.

"You keep saying the same thing; but I had such an attack of rheumatism last year that I remember it to this day."

"The devil has rheumatism!"

"Why not, if I sometimes put on fleshly form?"

"But you didn't get that from me."

"This time I'll be honest. In dreams, especially nightmares, a man sees such artistic visions sometimes, even a whole world of events, woven into a plot, with details from the most exalted matters to the last button on a cuff, as Leo Tolstoy has never invented. Yet such dreams are sometimes seen not by writers, but by the most ordinary people.... A statesman confessed to me that his best ideas came to him when he was asleep. Well, that's how it is now, I am your hallucination, yet just as in a nightmare, I say original things which had not entered your head before. I don't repeat your ideas, yet I am only your nightmare, nothing more."

"You are lying, your aim is to convince me you exist and are not my nightmare, and now you are asserting you are a dream."

"My dear fellow, I've adopted a special method today. Stay, where did I break off? Oh, yes! I caught cold then, only not here but yonder."

"Where is yonder? Tell me, will you be here long?" Ivan exclaimed.

He pulled the wet towel off and threw it away. It was of no use.

"Your nerves are out of order," said the gentleman, with a polite, air. "You are angry with me for being able to catch cold, though it happened in a most natural way. I was hurrying to a diplomatic *soirée* at the house of a lady of high rank in Petersburg, and had to fly through space to reach your earth.... Of course, it took only an instant, but fancy, in an evening suit and open waistcoat. Spirits don't freeze, but when one's in fleshly form, well ... in brief, I didn't think, and set off, and you know in those spaces there's such a frost ... 150 degrees below zero! You know the game the village girls play—they invite the unwary to lick an ax in thirty degrees of frost, the tongue instantly freezes to it and the dupe tears the skin off, so it bleeds. But that's only in 30 degrees, in 150 degrees I imagine it would be enough to put your finger on the ax and it would be the end of it ... if only there could be an ax there."

"And can there be an ax there?" Ivan interrupted.

He was trying his utmost not to sink into complete insanity.

"An ax?" the guest said in surprise.

"Yes, what would become of an ax there?" Ivan cried.

"In space? If it were to fall to any distance, it would begin, I think, flying round the earth without knowing why, that's all."

"You are awfully stupid," said Ivan. "Lie more cleverly or I won't listen. You want to get the better of me, to convince me you exist, but I won't believe you exist!"

"But I am not lying, it's the truth; the truth is unhappily hardly ever amusing. I see you keep expecting something big of me. That's a great pity; I only give what I can."

"Don't talk philosophy, you fool!"

"Philosophy, indeed, when my right side is numb and I'm groaning. I've tried doctors: they can tell you what's wrong beautifully, but they've no idea how to cure you. 'You may die,' they say, 'but you'll know perfectly what disease you are dying of!' And what a way they have sending people to specialists! 'We only tell you what's wrong,' they say, 'but go to such-and-such a specialist, he'll cure you.' What are you to do? I fell back on popular remedies, a German doctor advised me to rub myself with honey and salt in the bath-house. But it did me no good at all. Only fancy, Hoff's malt extract cured me! I bought it by accident, drank a bottle of it, and it took it away completely.

"Boring memories again?" Ivan said angrily.

"God preserve me, but one can't help complaining sometime. You charge me every moment with being dull. My dear fellow, intelligence isn't the only thing! I have naturally a kind and merry heart. Before time was, I was pre-destined 'to deny' and yet I am genuinely good-hearted and not at all inclined to negation.

"'No, you must go and deny; without denial there's nothing interesting to say, and what would a journal be without a column tearing people and things apart?' It would be nothing but one long hymn of praise.' But praise is not enough for life; the praise must be expressed with doubt, and in the same style. But I don't pay any attention to that; I didn't create it, and I am not answerable for it.

"Well, they've chosen their scapegoat, they've made me write all the bad things, and so life was made possible. Live, I am told, for there'd be nothing without you. If everything in the universe were sensible, nothing would happen. There would be no events without you, and there must be events. So I serve to produce events and do what's irrational.

"For all their intelligence, men take this play acting as something serious, and that is their tragedy. They suffer...but then they live, they live a real life, for suffering is life. Without suffering what would be the pleasure of it? It would otherwise be an endless church service; it would be holy, but tedious.

"But what about me? I suffer, but don't live. I am x in an equation. I am a sort of phantom who has lost all beginning and end, and who has even forgotten his own name. You are laughing—no, you are angry again. You are forever angry, all you care about is intelligence, but I repeat, I would give away all this, all the honors, simply to be transformed into the soul of a merchant's wife."

"Then even you don't believe in God?" said Ivan.

"What can I say?—that is, if you are in earnest—"

"Is there a God or not?" Ivan cried.

"You're in earnest! My dear fellow, I don't know. There! I've said it!"

"You don't know but you see God? You are not someone apart, you are myself!"

"Well, if you like, I have the same philosophy. *I think, therefore I am*; all the rest, all these worlds, God and even Satan—all that is not proved, to my mind. Does all exist, or is it only from myself, a logical development of my ego. But I make haste to stop, for next you will be wanting to beat me."

"You'd better tell me some story!" said Ivan.

"There is a story, or rather a legend. You say I have no belief, yet you don't believe. My dear fellow, we are all mixed up now, and all through your science. Once there used to be atoms, five senses, four elements, and everything hung together. Now there's a regular mix-up, superstition, awful scenes; there's as much mix-up among us as among you. Well, this legend belongs to our middle ages—and no one believes it, even among us, except the old ladies. This legend is about Paradise.

"There was, they say, here on earth a thinker who rejected everything, 'laws, conscience, faith,' and, above all, the future life. He died; he expected to go straight to darkness and death and he found a future life before him. He was angry. 'This is against my principles!' he said. And he was punished for that...I am just repeating what I heard. He was sentenced to walk a quadrillion miles in the dark, and when he finished that quadrillion, the gates of heaven would open to him—"

"What tortures have you in the other world besides a quadrillion miles?"

"What tortures? In old days we had all sorts, but now they have taken chiefly to moral punishments—'the stings of conscience' and all that nonsense. We got that, too, from you. And who's the better for it? Only those who have no conscience. But decent people with a conscience and a sense of honor suffer. Reforms, when the ground has not been prepared for them, do nothing but mischief! The ancient fire was better. Well, this man who was condemned to the quadrillion miles stood still, and lay down on the road. 'I won't go, I refuse on principle!'"

"What did he lie on there?"

"Well, I suppose there was something to lie on. Are you laughing?"

"Bravo!" cried Ivan. "Well, is he lying there?"

"That's the point, he isn't. He lay a thousand years and then got up and went on."

"What a fool!" cried Ivan, laughing. "Does it make any difference whether he lies there forever or walks the quadrillion miles? It would take a billion years to walk it?"

"More than that. But he got there long ago, and that's where the story begins."

"He got there? But how did he get the billion years to do it?"

"Why, you keep thinking of our present earth! But earth may have been repeated a billion times. Why, it's become extinct, frozen; cracked, broken into its elements, then again a comet, again a sun, again from the sun it becomes earth—repeated endlessly."

"Well, what happened when he arrived?"

"The moment the gates of Paradise opened, he walked in. Before he had been there two seconds, he cried out that those two seconds were worth walking not a quadrillion but a quadrillion of quadrillions, raised to the quadrillionth power! But he overdid it, so that some persons there of lofty ideas wouldn't shake hands with him at first—he'd become too reactionary, they said."

"I've caught you!" Ivan cried. "That story about the quadrillion years I made up myself! I was seventeen, in high school. I made up that story and told it to a friend called Korovkin.... The story is so like me that I couldn't have taken it from anyone. I thought I'd forgotten it...but you've recalled it—to myself! Thousands of things are remembered without our knowing they are... it has come back to me in a dream. You are that dream!"

"From the heat with which you deny my existence," the gentleman laughed, "I am convinced that you believe in me."

"Not the slightest! I haven't a hundredth part of a grain of faith in you!"

"But you have the thousandth of a grain. Confess that you have faith even to the ten-thousandth of a grain."

"Not for one minute," cried Ivan furiously. "But I should like to believe in you."

"There's an admission! I'll help you. It was I caught you, not you me. I told you a story you'd forgotten to destroy your faith in me."

"You are lying. Your object is to convince me of your existence!"

"Just so. But hesitation, suspense, conflict between belief and disbelief—is such torture to a man such as you, that it's better to hang oneself at once. Knowing you are inclined to believe in me, I gave you some disbelief by telling you that story. I lead you to belief and disbelief by turns. It's the new method. As soon as you disbelieve in me, you'll begin telling me I am not a dream but a reality. Then I shall have gained my object. I shall sow in you only a tiny grain of faith and you will long to enter the ranks of 'the hermits in the wilderness' to save your soul!"

"So it's to save my soul you are working, is it, devil?"

"One must do a good work sometimes. How ill-humored you are!"

"Did you ever tempt those holy men who ate locusts and prayed seventeen years in the wilderness till they were overgrown with moss?"

"My dear fellow, I've done nothing else. One forgets the whole world and all the worlds, and sticks to such a saint, because he is a precious diamond. One such soul, you know, is worth a whole constellation. We have our system of reckoning, you know. The conquest is priceless! They can contemplate such depths of belief and disbelief at the same time that it seems they are within a hair's-breadth of being 'turned upside down.'"

"How stupid!" cried Ivan.

"My dear friend, I only wanted to amuse you.

"Leave me alone, you are beating on my brain," Ivan said, helpless before his imagining. "I'm bored with you. I would give anything to be able to shake you off!"

"Don't expect so much, don't demand of me 'everything great and noble,' and we shall get on," said the gentleman. "You are really angry with me for not having appeared to you in thunder and lightning.

"You keep on saying I am not bright, but I make no claim to be equal to you in intelligence. Mephistopheles declared to Faust that he desired evil, but did only good. It's quite the opposite with me. I am the one man in all creation who loves the truth and desires good. But what would happen if I only did good? Everything on earth would cease to exist, and no events could occur. So, solely from a sense of duty I avoid the good and to stick to my nasty task. Somebody takes all the credit of what's good for Himself, and nothing but what is not good is left for me.

"I don't envy the honor of a life of idle imposture, for I have no desire to be looked up to. But why am I, of all creatures, doomed to be cursed by all decent people? I know there's a secret in it, but they won't tell me the secret, for then perhaps, seeing the meaning of it, I might cry out praises, and the minus we can't do without would disappear. Good sense would reign supreme throughout the whole world.

"And that, of course, would mean the end of everything. I know that at the end of all things I shall be brought into the fold, too. But till that happens I fulfill my destiny, to ruin thousands for the sake of saving one. Till the secret is revealed, there are two sorts of truths for me—their truth yonder, which I know nothing about, and..... Are you asleep?"

"I might well be," Ivan said. "All my stupid ideas—hashed out long ago and thrown aside like a dead carcass—give me as something new!"

"There's no pleasing you! I thought I should fascinate you by my literary style."

"How could my soul create a fool like you? Hold your tongue, or I'll kill you!"

"You'll kill me? No, excuse me, I will speak. I came to treat myself to that pleasure. 'There are new men,' you decided last spring, 'they propose to destroy everything and begin with cannibalism. Stupid fellows! They didn't ask my advice! Nothing need be destroyed, only the idea of God. It's that we must begin with. As soon as men have denied God, the old idea of the universe will fall of itself and, what's more, the old morality, and everything will begin anew. Men will unite to take from life all it can give. Man will be lifted up with a spirit of divine pride and the man-god will appear.

"Extending his conquest of nature by his will and his science, man will feel such lofty joy in doing it that it will make up for all his old dreams of the joys of heaven. Everyone will know that he is mortal and will accept death serenely, like a god. His pride will teach him that it's useless for him to repine at life's being a moment, and he will love his brother without need of reward. Love will be sufficient for a moment of life, but the consciousness of it will intensify its fire, which now is dissipated in dreams of eternal love beyond the grave'... and so on in the same style. Charming!"

Ivan stared at the floor, his hands to his ears, but the voice kept on..

"The question now is, my young thinker, will such a period ever come? If it does, everything is determined and humanity is settled forever. But as, owing to man's inability to think, this cannot come about for at least a thousand years, everyone who sees the truth now may order his life as he pleases. In that sense, 'all things are lawful' for him. What's more, even if this period never comes to pass, since there is no God and no life after death, the new man may well become the man-god, even if he is the only one in the world; he may over-step all the rules of the old morality. There is no law for God. Where God stands, the place is holy. Where I stand will be the foremost place...'all things are lawful' and that's the end of it!"

"That's all very charming; but why do you want a moral sanction for doing it? That's our modern man all over. He can't bring himself to do bad things without a moral sanction—"

The visitor talked on, carried away by the sound of his own voice, speaking louder and louder and staring at his host. But he did not succeed in finishing; Ivan snatched a glass from the table and threw it at him.

"There's that beast again," cried the latter, jumping up from the sofa and shaking the drops of tea off himself. "He remembers Luther's ink-stand! He takes me for a dream and throws glasses at a dream! I suspect you were only making believe to stop up your ears."

A loud knocking was heard at the window.

Ivan jumped up from the sofa.

"You'd better open," cried the visitor. "It's your brother Alyosha with the most surprising news, I'll be bound!"

"Be silent, I knew it was Alyosha, I felt he was coming, and he brings 'news.'"

"Open to him. There's a snowstorm and he is your brother."

The knocking continued.

Ivan wanted to rush to the window, but something seemed to chain his arms and legs. The knocking grew louder. At last the chains were broken and Ivan leapt from the sofa. He looked round him wildly. Both candles had almost burnt out, the glass he had just thrown at his visitor stood before him on the table, and there was no one on the sofa. The knocking went on, but it was by no means so loud as it had seemed.

"It was not a dream! No, I swear it was not a dream, it all happened just now!" cried Ivan.

He rushed to the window and opened the movable pane.

"Alyosha, I told you not to come," he cried to his brother. "What do you want?"

"An hour ago Smerdyakov hanged himself," Alyosha answered.

"Come round to the steps, I'll open at once," said Ivan.

Chapter X

"It Was He Who Said That"

Alyosha told Ivan that a little over an hour ago Marya Kondratyevna ran to tell him Smerdyakov had taken his life. "I went in to clear away the samovar and he was hanging on a nail in the wall." On Alyosha's inquiring whether she told the police, she said she had told no one, "but flew straight to you, I've run all the way."

She seemed perfectly crazy, Alyosha reported, and was shaking like a leaf.

When Alyosha ran with her to the cottage, he found Smerdyakov still hanging. On the table lay a note: "I destroy my life of my own will and desire, and throw no blame on anyone." Alyosha left the note on the table and went straight to the police captain.

"I've come straight to you," said Alyosha. "Brother," he added, "you must be terribly ill. You don't seem to understand."

"It's good you came," said Ivan. "I knew he had hanged himself."

"From whom?"

"I don't know. I knew. He told me. He told me just now."

Ivan stood in the middle of the room.

"Who is *he*?" asked Alyosha, looking round.

"He's slipped away."

Ivan raised his head and smiled.

"He was afraid of a dove like you."

"Brother, sit down," said Alyosha. "For goodness' sake, sit down! You are delirious; put your head on the pillow, that's right. Would you like a wet towel on your head?"

"Give me the towel. It's on the chair. I just threw it there."

"It's not here. Don't worry yourself," said Alyosha, finding a clean towel by Ivan's dressing-table. Ivan looked at the towel: recollection seemed to come back to him.

"Stay"—he got up—"an hour ago I took that towel from there and wet it. I wrapped it round my head and threw it down here ... How is it it's dry?"

"You put that towel on your head?" asked Alyosha.

"Yes, and walked about the room ... What time is it?"

"Nearly twelve."

"No!" Ivan cried. "It was not a dream. He was here, sitting on that sofa. When you knocked at the window, I threw that glass at him. I have dreams now, Alyosha. I walk, talk, and see ... though I am asleep. He was sitting there.... He is frightfully stupid."

Ivan laughed and began pacing about the room.

"Who is stupid? Of whom are you talking?" Alyosha asked.

"The devil! He's taken to visiting me. He's been here twice. He taunted me with being angry at his being a simple devil. But he is an impostor. He is a trivial devil. But if you undressed him, you'd be sure to find he had a tail.... Alyosha, you are cold. You've been in the snow. Would you like some tea?"

Alyosha ran to the wash-stand, wet the towel, got Ivan to sit down again, and put the towel round his head, then sat beside him.

"What were you telling me just now about Lise? I like her ... I am afraid for Katya tomorrow. I'm more afraid of her than of anything. She will cast me off tomorrow. She thinks I am ruining

Mitya from jealousy! But it's not so. Tomorrow the cross, but not the gallows. I shan't hang myself. I can never commit suicide, Alyosha. How did I know   Smerdyakov had hanged himself? Yes, it was *he* told me so."

"And you are convinced that there has been someone here?" asked Alyosha.

"Yes, on that sofa. He disappeared when you arrived. *He* is myself, Alyosha. All   that's base in me, that's mean and shaming. He is so without wit that it's to his advantage. He has animal cunning. He kept accusing me of believing in him."

"He has worn you out," said Alyosha.

"He's been getting to me. He does it so cleverly. Why am I pained by it? From the habit of mankind. So let us give it up, and 'we shall be gods.' He said that!"

"And not you?" Alyosha could not help saying. "Never mind him. Let him take with him all that you curse, and never return!"

"But he is mean. He laughed at me, Alyosha. He was unfair to me about lots of things. He told lies. 'Oh, you are going to perform an act of heroic virtue: to confess you murdered your father, that Smerdyakov murdered him at your order.'"

"Brother," Alyosha said, "it was not you who murdered him. It's not true!"

"That's what he says. 'You are going to perform an act of heroic virtue, and you don't believe in virtue; that's what pains you and makes you angry.'"

"It's you that say that, not he," said Alyosha, "because you are ill and out of your mind."

"No, he knows what he says. 'You are going from pride,' he says. 'You'll stand up and say you killed him. You are longing for their praise—'he is a criminal, a murderer, but what a generous soul; he wanted to save his brother and he confessed.' That's a lie,

Alyosha!" Ivan cried. "I don't want people to praise me! That's why I threw the glass at him and it broke against his ugly face."

"Brother, calm yourself!" Alyosha begged.

"He knows how to anger me," Ivan went on. "I knew why he came. 'You go through pride, still you had a hope Smerdyakov might be convicted and Mitya acquitted, then you would only be punished with moral blame—and some people will praise you. But now Smerdyakov's dead, and who'll believe you?' That's awful, Alyosha. I can't endure such questions. Who dare ask me such questions?"

"Brother," said Alyosha—still hoping to bring Ivan to reason—"how could he have told you of Smerdyakov's death before I came, when no one knew of it?"

"He told me," said Ivan. "It was all he talked about. 'It would be all right if you believed in virtue,' he said. 'You are going for the sake of principle. But you are a pig like Fyodor Pavlovitch, and what do you want with virtue? Why do you want to go sticking your nose in if it is of no use? You'll think about it all night, whether to go or not. But the decision does not depend on you. "You'll go because you won't dare not to!' He called me a coward, Alyosha! And Smerdyakov said the same. He must be killed! Katya despises me. Even Lise will despise me! And you despise me too, Alyosha. Now I am going to hate you again! And I hate the monster, too! I don't want to save him. Let him rot in Siberia! Tomorrow I'll go and spit in their faces!"

He jumped up and paced the room. Alyosha recalled what he just said. "I seem to be sleeping awake.... I walk, I speak, I see, but I am asleep." It seemed to be just like that now. Alyosha wanted to run for the doctor, but was afraid to leave Ivan alone.

By degrees Ivan lost consciousness, though he went on talking incoherently. He staggered; but Alyosha was in time to support him. He put Ivan to bed and sat watching him for another two hours. The sick man slept soundly. Alyosha lay on the sofa. As he fell asleep he prayed for Mitya and Ivan. He began to understand Ivan's illness. It was, "The anguish of a proud soul." God, in Whom he did not believe, was gaining mastery over his heart, which still refused to submit.

"Yes," the thought floated through Alyosha's head, "if Smerdyakov is dead, no one will believe Ivan's evidence; but he will go and give it. God will conquer! He will either rise up in the light of truth, or ... he'll perish in hate, revenging on himself and everyone for having served the cause he does not believe in." And again he prayed.

Book X • A Judicial Error

Chapter I

The Fatal Day

At ten o'clock in the morning of the day following, the trial of Dmitri Karamazov began. Visitors had arrived not only from the chief town of the province, but from several other Russian towns, as well as from Moscow and Petersburg. Every ticket of admission had been snatched up. Many of the ladies were in favor of Mitya's acquittal. This was owing, perhaps, to his reputation as a conqueror of female hearts.

It was known that two women rivals were to appear in the case. One of them—Katerina Ivanovna—was an object of general interest. People said she intended to petition the Government for leave to accompany the criminal to Siberia and to be married to him somewhere in the mines.

The appearance of Grushenka in court was awaited with no less impatience. The public was looking forward to the meeting of the two rivals—the proud aristocratic girl and "the hetaera." But Grushenka, "the woman who had ruined Fyodor Pavlovitch and his unhappy son," was a more familiar figure to the ladies.

Everybody was excited at the presence of the celebrated lawyer, Fetyukovitch. His talent was well known, and this was not the first time he had defended famous criminal cases. And if he defended them, such cases became even more celebrated, and long remembered.

There were stories, too, about the prosecutor, Ippolit Kirillovitch. It was said he was trembling at meeting Fetyukovitch, and that they had been enemies from the beginning of their careers in Petersburg. Ippolit Kirillovitch was a humane and cultured man, with a practical knowledge of his work and progressive views. His attitude to the personal aspect of the case, its tragic importance, and the persons involved, was more a theory.

The court was packed and over-flowing long before the judges made their entrance. On the right of the judges, who were on a raised platform, a table and two rows of chairs had been put for the jury. On the left was the place for the prisoner and the counsel for the defense. In the middle of the court, near the judges, was a table with the "material proofs."

On it lay Fyodor Pavlovitch's white silk dressing-gown stained with blood; the metal tool with which the supposed murder had been committed; Mitya's shirt, with a blood-stained sleeve; his coat, stained with blood in patches over the pocket in which he had put his handkerchief; the handkerchief itself, stiff with blood; the gun loaded by Mitya at Perhotin's with a view to suicide, and taken from him at Mokroe by Trifon Borissovitch; the envelope which had held the three thousand rubles ready for Grushenka, the narrow pink ribbon with which it had been tied; and many other articles. At ten o'clock the three judges arrived—the President, a justice of the peace, and one other. The prosecutor entered immediately after. The President began with asking the court whether all the jury were present. Of the twelve jurymen, four were not very important officials of the town, two were merchants, and six were ordinary people and artisans.

The four officials were men of low rank who spent their leisure over cards and had never read a single book. The two merchants looked respectable, but were strangely silent. There is no need to speak of the artisans and peasants. One might well wonder, "what men like that could possibly make of such a case?" Yet they were imposing with their stern faces.

The President opened the case. The usher was told to bring in the prisoner, and Mitya appeared. Mitya made a most unfavorable impression. He looked a dandy in a brand-new frock-coat he had ordered in Moscow. He wore black kid gloves and exquisite linen, and walked with long strides, looking straight in front of him, and sat down in his place with a most unperturbed air.

At the same moment the counsel for the defense, the celebrated Fetyukovitch, entered, and a subdued hum passed through the court. He was a tall man, with long thin legs and long, thin fingers, a clean-shaven face, rather short hair, and thin lips that were at times curved into something between a sneer and a smile. He was about forty. His face would have been pleasant if it had not been for his small, inexpressive eyes, which were set remarkably close together, with only the thin, long nose as a dividing line.

The President's first questions to Mitya were about his name, his calling, and so on, Mitya answered sharply, his voice so loud it made the President start and look at the prisoner with surprise. Then followed a list of persons who were to take part in the trial. Three of the witnesses were not present—Madame Hohlakov and Maximov, who were absent through illness; and Smerdyakov, through his sudden death. The news of his death produced a stir in the court, for many had not heard of the suicide.

What struck people most was Mitya's outburst when the statement of Smerdyakov's death was made. He cried out: "He was a dog and died like a dog!"

His counsel rushed to him, and the President threatened to take stern measures if such an irregularity were repeated. Mitya nodded and in a subdued voice repeated several times to his counsel, with no show of regret: "I won't do it again. It escaped me."

This brief episode did him no good with the jury. His character was displayed, and it spoke for itself. The opening statement was read. It was rather short, but circumstantial. It stated the chief reasons why he had been arrested, why he must be tried, and so on. It made a great impression. The whole tragedy was unfolded before them in bold relief. After this, the President asked Mitya in a loud voice: "Prisoner, do you plead guilty?"

Mitya rose from his seat.

"I plead guilty to drunkenness and dissipation," he exclaimed, "to idleness and debauchery. I meant to become an honest man for good, just at the moment when I was struck down by fate. But I am not guilty of the death of that old man, my enemy and my father. And I am not guilty of robbing him! I could not be. I'm not a good person, but I'm not a thief."

He sat down again, trembling.

The President briefly, but impressively, told him to answer only what was asked. Then he ordered the case to proceed. The witnesses were led up to take the oath. After a word from the priest and the President, the witnesses were led away and made to sit as far as possible apart from one another. Then they began calling them up one by one.

Chapter II

Dangerous Witnesses

The witnesses for the defense and the prosecution were separated into groups, and called in a certain order. The witnesses for the prosecution were called first.

From the beginning, one characteristic of the case was the overwhelming strength of the prosecution as compared with the arguments the defense had to rely upon. Everyone, perhaps, felt from the first that the case was beyond dispute, that there could be really no discussion, and that the defense was only a matter of form, and the prisoner was guilty.

Even the ladies, who were impatiently longing for the prisoner to be declared not guilty, were, at the same time, without exception, convinced of his guilt. What's more, they would have felt shame if his guilt had not been so firmly established, as that would have lessened the effect of the closing scene of the criminal's being freed. That he would be freed, all the ladies were certain to the very end.

"He is guilty, but he will be freed, from motives of humanity."

That was why they had crowded into the court so impatiently. The men were more interested in the contest between the prosecutor and Fetyukovitch. All were wondering what could even a talent like Fetyukovitch make of such a losing case; and so they followed his defense with close attention.

But Fetyukovitch remained a puzzle to the very end. Persons of experience suspected he had some design he was working towards, but it was almost impossible to guess what it was. His confidence was clear. Everyone noticed with pleasure, moreover, that he, after so short a stay among us, had so wonderfully succeeded in mastering the case and "had studied it to a nicety." People described with relish, afterwards, how cleverly he had "taken down" all the witnesses for the prosecution, had, as far as possible, confused them and, what's more, had lowered their reputation and so the value of their evidence. But it was supposed that he could do no real good by such doings, and probably was more aware of this than anyone, having some concealed weapon of defense, which he would suddenly reveal when the time came.

When Grigory, Fyodor Pavlovitch's old servant, who had given the damning piece of evidence about the open door, was examined, the lawyer for the defense jumped on him. But Grigory, who had entered the hall with a composed, almost stately air, not the least put out by the majesty of the court or the vast audience, gave evidence with as much confidence as though he had been talking with his Marfa, only more respectfully.

It was impossible to make him contradict himself. The prosecutor questioned him in detail about the family life of the Karamazovs. The witness was open and straight-forward. In spite of his deep reverence for the memory of his deceased master, he bore witness that he had been unjust to Mitya and "hadn't brought up his children as he should. It wasn't fair, either, of the father to wrong his son over his mother's property, which was by right his."

In reply to the prosecutor's question on what grounds he had for saying that Fyodor Pavlovitch had wronged his son in their money relations, Grigory, to the surprise of every one, had no proof at all, but still insisted the father was "unfair," and ought "to have paid him several thousand rubles more."

Grigory's description of the scene at the dinner-table, when Dmitri burst in and beat his father, and threatened to come back to kill him, made a strong impression on the court. He said he was not angry with Mitya for having knocked him down; he had forgiven him long ago. Of the deceased Smerdyakov he said, crossing himself, that he was a lad of ability, but stupid and afflicted. But he defended Smerdyakov's honesty, and told how he had once found the master's money in the yard and, instead of keeping it, had taken it to his master, who rewarded him with a "gold piece," and trusted him completely from that time forward.

He also insisted the door into the garden had been open.

At last the lawyer for the defense began to cross-examine him. The first question he asked was about the envelope in which Fyodor Pavlovitch was supposed to have put three thousand rubles for "a certain person." "Have you ever seen it, you, who were for so many years in close attendance on your master?"

Grigory answered that he had not seen it and had never heard of the money from anyone "till everybody was talking about it."

This question Fetyukovitch put to everyone who could conceivably have known of it, and got the same answer from all, that no one had seen it, though many had heard of it.

Everyone noticed Fetyukovitch's persistence on this subject.

"With your permission, I'll ask you a question," Fetyukovitch said. "Of what was that drink made which, as we learn from the preliminary inquiry, you used on that evening to rub on your limbs in the hope of curing it?"

Grigory, after a brief pause, said, "There was saffron."

"Nothing but saffron? Do you remember anything else?"

"There was milfoil in it, too."

"And pepper perhaps?" Fetyukovitch asked.

"Yes, there was pepper, too."

"And all dissolved in vodka?"

"In spirit."

There was a faint sound of laughter in the court.

"After rubbing your back, you drank what was left in the bottle?"

"I did."

"Did you drink much? A wine-glass or two?"

"It might have been a glass-full."

"A glass-full, even perhaps a glass and a half?"

Grigory did not answer. He seemed to see what was meant.

"A glass and a half of neat spirit is not at all bad, don't you think? You might see the gates of heaven open, not only the door to the garden?"

Grigory remained silent. There was a laugh in the court.

"Do you know for a fact," Fetyukovitch persisted, "whether you were awake or not when you saw the open door?"

"I was on my legs."

"That's not proof you were awake." (There was again laughter.) "Could you have answered at that moment, if anyone had asked you a question—say, what year it is?"

"I don't know."

"And what year is it, Anno Domini, do you know?"

Grigory stood with a puzzled look on his face, looking at his questioner. It appeared he really did not know what year it was.

"Can you tell me how many fingers you have on your hands?"

"I am a servant," Grigory said in a loud voice. "If my betters think fit to make game of me, it is my duty to suffer it."

Fetyukovitch was a little taken aback, and the President cut in, reminding him that he must ask more relevant questions.

Fetyukovitch bowed and said he had no more questions to ask the witness. The public and the jury, of course, were left with a grain of doubt in their minds as to the evidence of a man who might, while taking a "cure," have seen "the gates of heaven open," and who did not even know what year it was.

The President, turning to the prisoner, asked him whether he had any comment to make on the evidence of the last witness. "Except about the door, everything he said is true," cried Mitya. "For combing the lice off me, for forgiving my blows, I thank him. The old man has been honest all his life and faithful to my father as a hundred poodles."

"Prisoner, be careful in your language," the President said.

"I am not a poodle," Grigory said.

"All right, it's I am a poodle myself," cried Mitya. "If it's an insult, I take it to myself and beg his pardon. I was a beast and cruel to him."

The President again warned Mitya to be more careful in his language. "You are injuring yourself in the eyes of your judges."

The lawyer for the defense was also clever in dealing with the evidence of Rakitin, who was one of the leading witnesses for the prosecution. He appeared to know everything; to have been everywhere, seen everything, talked to everybody, to know every detail of the life of Fyodor Pavlovitch and all the Karamazovs. Of the envelope, it is true, he had only heard from Mitya himself. But he described minutely Mitya's doings in the "Metropolis," and all his sayings. But he could say nothing about Mitya's inheritance.

"Who could tell which of them was to blame, and which was in debt to the other, with their crazy Karamazov way of muddling things?" He attributed the tragic crime to the habits that had become ingrained by ages of serfdom and the distressed condition of Russia. He was, in fact, allowed some latitude of speech. This was the first occasion on which Rakitin showed what he could do, and attracted notice. The prosecutor knew the witness was preparing a magazine article on the case, and quoted some ideas from it.

The picture drawn by the witness was a gloomy one, and greatly strengthened the case for the prosecution. Rakitin's discourse fascinated the public by its independence and the nobility of its ideas. There were even two or three outbreaks of applause when he spoke of serfdom and the condition of Russia. But Rakitin, in his youthful ardor, made a slight blunder, of which the counsel for the defense at once took advantage.

Answering questions about Grushenka, and carried away by the loftiness of his own sentiments and his success, he went so far as to speak contemptuously of Agrafena Alexandrovna as "the kept mistress of Samsonov." He would have given a good deal to take back his words afterwards, for Fetyukovitch caught him out over it at once. And it was all because Rakitin had not reckoned on the lawyer having been able to become so intimately acquainted with every detail in so short a time.

"Allow me to ask," began the counsel for the defense, with the most affable and respectful smile, "you are, of course, the same Mr. Rakitin whose pamphlet, *The Life of the Deceased Elder, Father Zossima*, published by the diocesan authorities, full of profound and religious reflections and preceded by an excellent and devout dedication to the bishop, I have just read with such pleasure?"

"I did not write it for publication ... it was published afterwards," said Rakitin.

"Oh, that's excellent! A thinker like you can, and indeed ought, to take the widest view of every social question. Your most instructive pamphlet has been widely circulated through the patronage of the bishop, and has been of appreciable service.... But this is the chief thing I should like to learn from you. You stated just now that you were intimately acquainted with Madame Svyetlov." (Grushenka's surname.)

"I cannot answer for all my acquaintances.... I am a young man... and who can be responsible for everyone he meets?" cried Rakitin.

"I quite understand," cried Fetyukovitch, as though he, too, were embarrassed. "You, like any other, might well be interested in knowing a young and beautiful woman who would readily entertain the *élite* of the youth of the neighborhood, but ... it has come to my knowledge that Madame Svyetlov was anxious a couple of months ago to make the acquaintance of the younger Karamazov, Alexey Fyodorovitch, and promised you money if you would bring him to her in his monastic dress. That took place on the evening of the day on which the terrible crime, which is the subject of this investigation, was committed. You brought Alexey Karamazov to Madame Svyetlov. Did you receive twenty-five rubles from Madame Svyetlov as a reward, that's what I want to hear from you?"

"I don't see what interest that can be to you.... I took it for a joke ... meaning to give it back later...."

"Then you did take—. But you have not given it back yet ... or have you?"

"That's of no consequence," said Rakitin. "Of course I shall give it back."

The President cut in, but Fetyukovitch declared he had no more questions. Mr. Rakitin left the witness-box not without a stain upon his character. The effect left by the lofty idealism of his speech was somewhat marred, and Fetyukovitch's expression as he watched him walk away seemed to suggest to the public "this is a specimen of the lofty-minded persons who accuse him."

When, after Rakitin's cross-examination, the President asked the prisoner if he had anything to say, Mitya cried: "Since I've been arrested, he has borrowed money from me! He has no shame; he takes advantage of every opportunity. He doesn't believe in God; he took the bishop in!"

Mitya, of course, was pulled up again for his language, but Rakitin was done for.

Fetyukovitch went on making the most of every opportunity, amazing people by his minute knowledge of the case. For example, Trifon Borissovitch made an impression very prejudicial to Mitya. He calculated that on his first visit to Mokroe, Mitya must have spent three thousand rubles, "or very little less. Just think what he squandered on those gypsy girls alone! And as for our lousy peasants, it wasn't a case of flinging half a ruble; he made them presents of twenty-five rubles each, at least. And what a lot of money was simply stolen from him! And if anyone did steal, he did not leave a receipt. How could one catch the thief when he was flinging his money away all the time?" He recalled, in fact, every item of expense and added it all up. So the theory that only fifteen hundred had been spent and the rest had been put aside in a little bag seemed inconceivable.

"I saw three thousand as clear as a penny in his hands, I saw it with my own eyes; I should think I ought to know how to reckon money," cried Trifon Borissovitch.

When Fetyukovitch cross-examined him, he scarcely tried to refute his evidence, but began asking about an incident at the first carousal at Mokroe, a month before, when Timofey and another peasant called Akim picked up on the floor in the passage a hundred rubles dropped by Mitya when he was drunk, and gave them to Trifon Borissovitch and received a ruble from him for doing so.

"Well, did you give the hundred rubles back to Mr. Karamazov?" he was asked.

Trifon Borissovitch shuffled in vain.... He had, after the peasants were examined, to admit the finding of the hundred rubles, only adding that he had religiously returned it to Dmitri Fyodorovitch "in perfect honesty, and it's only because his honor was in liquor at the time he wouldn't remember it." But, as he had denied the incident of the hundred rubles till the peasants had been called to prove it, his evidence of returning the money to Mitya was regarded with great suspicion. So one of the most dangerous witnesses of the prosecution was again discredited.

The same thing happened with the Poles. Taking an attitude of independence and pride; they said loudly they had both been in the service of the Crown, and that "Pan Mitya" had offered them three thousand "to buy their honor," and that they had seen a large sum of money in his hands. Pan Mussyalovitch introduced a number of Polish words into his sentences, and seeing this only increased his consequence in the eyes of the President and the prosecutor, he grew more and more pompous, and ended by talking in Polish altogether. But Fetyukovitch caught them in his snares. Trifon Borissovitch, recalled, was forced to admit that Pan Vrublevsky had used his own pack of cards of the new pack he had provided, and that Pan Mussyalovitch had cheated during the game. Kalganov confirmed this, and both the Poles left with damaged reputations.

The same thing happened with all the most dangerous witnesses. Fetyukovitch succeeded in casting a slur on all of them, dismissing them with damaged characters. The lawyers and experts were lost in admiration, and were only at a loss to understand what good purpose could be served by it, for all felt the case for the prosecution could not be refuted, but was growing more and more overwhelming. But the confidence of the "great magician" was serene, and they waited, feeling that "such a man" had not come from Petersburg for nothing, and that he was not a man to return unsuccessful.

Chapter III

The Medical Experts and a Pound of Nuts

The evidence of the medical experts was of little use to the prisoner. Fetyukovitch had not counted much on it, and had only taken it up through the insistence of Katerina Ivanovna. Doctor Herzenstube, a bald old man of seventy, much esteemed in the town, was called first. He was a conscientious doctor and a pious man. He had lived in the town for many years and behaved with wonderful dignity. He was kind-hearted and humane. He treated the sick poor and peasants for nothing, visited them in their slums, and left money for medicine, but he was obstinate. Once he got an idea, there was no shaking it.

The famous doctor from Moscow had, within the first days of coming to town, made some extremely offensive allusions about Doctor Herzenstube. Though the Moscow doctor asked twenty-five rubles a visit, several people in the town, who had been patients of Herzenstube, were glad to take advantage of his arrival. The celebrated doctor criticized his treatment with extreme harshness. He had asked the patients as soon as he saw them, "Well, who has been shoving these medications down your throat? Herzenstube?"

Doctor Herzenstube declared that the oddness of the prisoner's mental condition was self-evident, not only in many of the prisoner's actions in the past, but was evidencing itself even now. When asked to explain how it was evidencing itself now, the old doctor pointed out that the prisoner on entering the court had "an odd air under the circumstances", that he "marched in like a soldier, looking straight before him, though it would have been more natural for him to look where the ladies were sitting."

The Moscow doctor, questioned in his turn, also said he considered the prisoner's mental condition odd in the highest degree. He talked at length, with much learning, of "aberration" and "mania," and argued that, from the facts collected, the prisoner had, without doubt, been mentally up-set for several days before his arrest, and, if the crime had been committed by him, it must have been almost without his willing it.

But in the opinion of Doctor Varvinsky, the prisoner was now, and had been all along, in a perfectly normal state, and although he must have been in a nervous and very excited state before his arrest, this might have been due to several obvious causes— jealousy, anger, drunkenness, and so on. But this would not have meant he was crazy.

"Bravo, doctor!" cried Mitya, from his seat, "just so!"

Mitya, of course, was checked, but the young doctor's opinion had an influence on the judges and the public, and, as appeared afterwards, everyone agreed with him. But Doctor Herzenstube, when called as a witness, was unexpectedly of use to Mitya.

As an old resident in the town who had known the Karamazov family for years, he presented facts of great value for the prosecution. As though recalling something, he added: "But the poor young man might have had a very different life, for he had a good heart." A note of feeling and tenderness came into his voice.

"When I was a young man of forty-five," the old man went on, "and had only just come here, I was so sorry for the boy I asked myself why shouldn't I buy him a pound of ... a pound of what? I've forgotten what it's called. A pound of ... what is it?" The doctor waved his hands. "It grows on a tree and is gathered and given to everyone...."

"Apples?"

"No, no. You have a dozen apples, not a pound.... No, there are a lot of them, all little. You put them in the mouth and crack."

"Nuts?"

"Quite so, nuts. I bought him a pound of nuts, for no one had ever bought the boy a pound of nuts before. And I lifted my finger and said to him, 'Boy, *Gott der Vater.*' He laughed and said, '*Gott der Vater.*'... '*Gott der Sohn.*' Then he laughed and said as best he could, '*Gott der heilige Geist.*' I went away, and two days after I happened to be passing, and he shouted to me, '*Uncle, Gott der Vater, Gott der Sohn,*' and he had only forgotten '*Gott der heilige Geist.*' But he was taken away, and I did not see him again.

"Twenty-three years passed. I am sitting in my study, when there walks into the room a young man I should never have recognized, but he held up his finger and said, laughing, '*Gott der Vater, Gott der Sohn,* and *Gott der heilige Geist.* I have just arrived and have come to thank you for that pound of nuts, for no one else ever bought me a pound of nuts.'

"Then I remembered the poor child in the yard, without boots on his feet, and my heart was touched, and I said, 'You are a grateful young man, for you have remembered all your life the pound of nuts I bought you.' I embraced him and blessed him. And I shed tears. He laughed, but he shed tears, too."

"I am weeping now, German, I am weeping, too, you saintly man," Mitya cried.

The story made a favorable impression. But the chief sensation in Mitya's favor was created by the evidence of Katerina Ivanovna. When she was called by the defense and began giving evidence, fortune seemed all at once more favorable to Mitya, and, what was striking, this was a surprise even to the counsel for the defense. But before Katerina Ivanovna was called, Alyosha was examined, and he recalled a fact which seemed to furnish evidence against one important point made by the prosecution.

Chapter IV

Fortune Smiles on Mitya

Alyosha was not required to take the oath, and both sides addressed him very gently. It was evident his reputation for goodness had preceded him. He gave his evidence with restraint, but his warm sympathy for his brother was unmistakable. He sketched his brother's character as that of a bad-tempered man perhaps carried away by his passions, but at the same time honorable. He admitted that, through his passion for Grushenka and his rivalry with his father, his brother had been of late intolerable. But he repelled the idea that his brother might have committed a murder for the sake of gain, though he knew the three thousand rubles had become an obsession with Mitya; that he saw them as part of the inheritance he had been cheated of by his father, and that, indifferent as he was to money as a rule, he could not speak of that three thousand without fury.

"Did your brother tell you that he intended to kill your father?" he was asked. "You can refuse to answer if you think necessary," the prosecutor added.

"He did not tell me so directly," answered Alyosha.

"How so? Did he indirectly?"

"He spoke to me once of his hatred for our father and his fear that at an extreme moment ... at a moment of fury, he might perhaps murder him."

"And you believed him?"

"I am afraid to say that I did. But I never doubted that some higher feeling would save him, as it has, for it was not he killed my father," Alyosha said in a loud voice.

The prosecutor started like a war-horse at the sound of a trumpet.

"Let me assure you that I fully believe in the sincerity of your conviction and do not explain it by your affection for your unhappy brother. Your view of the tragic episode is known to us already from the preliminary investigation. I won't attempt to conceal from you that it is highly individual and contradicts the evidence collected by the prosecution. And so I think it essential to press you to tell me what facts have led you to this belief in your brother's innocence, and of the guilt of another person against whom you gave evidence at the preliminary inquiry?"

"I only answered the questions asked me," replied Alyosha. "I made no accusation against Smerdyakov of myself."

"Yet you gave evidence against him?"

"I was led to do so by my brother Dmitri's words. I was told what took place at his arrest and how he pointed to Smerdyakov before I was examined. I believe my brother is innocent, and if he didn't commit the murder, then—"

"Then Smerdyakov? Why Smerdyakov? And why are you so sure of your brother's innocence?"

"I cannot help believing my brother. I know he wouldn't lie to me. I saw from his face he wasn't lying."

"Only from his face? Is that all the proof you have?"

"I have no other proof."

"And of Smerdyakov's guilt you have no proof but your brother's word and the expression of his face?"

"No, I have no other proof."

The prosecutor dropped the examination at this point. The impression left by Alyosha's evidence on the public was disappointing. Smerdyakov had been talked about before the trial; someone had heard something, someone had pointed out something, it was said Alyosha had gathered proofs of his brother's innocence and Smerdyakov's guilt, and after all there was nothing, no evidence.

Fetyukovitch began his cross-examination. He asked Alyosha when it was the prisoner told him of his hatred for his father and that he might kill him, and whether he had heard it, for instance, at their last meeting before the murder. Alyosha started, as though just remembering something.

"I remember one circumstance which I'd forgotten. It wasn't clear to me at the time, but now—" And he told how, at his last interview with Mitya, Mitya had struck himself on the breast, and said several times that he had a means of getting his honor back, that that means was here, on his breast. I thought, when he struck himself on the breast, he meant heart," Alyosha continued, "that he might find in his heart the strength to save himself from some awful disgrace he did not dare confess.

"I did think at the time that he was speaking of our father, and that the disgrace he was shuddering at was the thought of doing some violence to him. Yet it was just then he pointed to his breast. It struck me at the time that the heart is not on that part of the breast, but below, and that he struck himself much too high, and kept pointing there. It seemed silly at the time, but he was perhaps pointing to that little bag in which were fifteen hundred rubles!"

"Just so," Mitya cried. "That's right, it was the little bag."

Fetyukovitch begged him to keep quiet.

At the same instant he pounced on Alyosha who, carried away by his recollection, expressed his theory that this disgrace was the fifteen hundred rubles, which he might return to Katerina Ivanovna, but which he had not yet determined to do, still wanting to use it to flee with Grushenka.

"It must be so," said Alyosha. "My brother cried several times that half of the disgrace he could free himself from at once, but that he was so unhappy in his weakness that he wouldn't do it... that he knew beforehand he was not able to do it!"

"You clearly remember he hit himself on this part of the breast?"

"Clearly, for I thought at the time, 'Why does he strike himself there when the heart is lower?' But the thought seemed stupid at the time. That's what brought it back just now. It was that little bag he meant when he said he had the means, but wouldn't give back that fifteen hundred. And when he was arrested at Mokroe he cried out—I was told —he thought it the most disgraceful act of his life, when he had the means of paying Katerina Ivanovna half of what he owed her, yet could not bring himself to do it, but would rather be a thief in her eyes!"

The prosecutor, of course, cut in. He asked Alyosha to describe once more how it had all happened, and several times insisted on the question, "Had the prisoner seemed to point to anything? Perhaps he had simply struck himself with his fist on the breast?"

"But it was not with his fist," cried Alyosha; "he pointed with his finger here, high up.... How could I have forgotten it till this moment?"

The President asked Mitya what he had to say to the witness's evidence. Mitya confirmed it, saying he had pointed to the fifteen hundred rubles which were on his breast, just below the neck, and that that was, of course, the disgrace, "The most shameful act of my whole life," cried Mitya. "I might have repaid it and didn't. I preferred to be a thief in her eyes rather than give it back. And the most shameful part of it was I knew I shouldn't give it back! You are right, Alyosha!"

What was important about Alyosha's testimony was that one fact at least had been found, and even though this was only one tiny bit of evidence, it did go a little way towards proving that the bag existed and had contained fifteen hundred rubles, and that the prisoner had not been lying when he said that at Mokroe that money was "his own."

Katerina Ivanovna was next called. As she entered something happened in the court. The ladies clutched their lorgnettes and opera-glasses. There was a stir among the men: some stood up to get a better view. And everybody said afterwards that Mitya had turned "white as a sheet" on her entrance.

All in black, she advanced almost timidly. It was impossible to tell from her face that she was agitated; but there was a resolute gleam in her eyes, and people said she looked very handsome. She spoke softly but clearly, so that she was heard all over the court. She expressed herself with composure, or at least appeared composed.

The President began in a round-about way, but in answer to one of the first questions, Katerina Ivanovna said she had been formerly engaged to the prisoner. When they asked her about the three thousand she had entrusted to Mitya to post for her, she said, "I didn't give him the money simply to send it. I felt at the time he was in great need of money.... I gave him the three thousand on the understanding that he should post it within the month. There was no need for him to worry himself about that debt.

"I was convinced he would send it off as soon as he got money from his father," she went on. "I have never doubted his honesty in money matters. He felt quite certain he would receive the money from his father. I knew he had a fight with his father and

I believed he had been unfairly treated. I don't remember any threat uttered by him against his father. If he had come to me, I should have relieved his anxiety about the three thousand rubles, but he had given up coming to see me...and I was put in such a position ... that I could not invite him.... And I had no right to be exacting as to that money," she added. "I was once indebted to him for assistance in money for more than three thousand, and I took it, although I could not see how I should ever be in a position to repay it."

Then Fetyukovitch began his cross-examination.

"Did that take place at the start of your knowing each other?" he asked, sensing something favorable. It was clear he knew nothing about the four thousand rubles given her by Mitya, and of her "bowing to the ground to him." She had concealed this from him, but she told everything that Mitya had told Alyosha.

The court was quiet, trying to catch each word. From such a proud girl, such a frank avowal seemed incredible. And for what? To save the man who had deceived and hurt her, and to help, in however small a way, in saving him, by creating an impression in his favor. The judges and lawyers listened in silence. The prosecutor did not venture upon even one question on the subject.

Fetyukovitch made a low bow to her.

Much ground had been gained. For a man to give his last four thousand on a generous impulse and then for the same man to murder his father for the sake of three thousand—the idea seemed too out of keeping. Fetyukovitch felt that the charge of theft, at least, was as good as done away with. There was a wave of sympathy for Mitya who, when she finished, cried in a sobbing voice: "Katya, why have you ruined me?" and his sobs were heard all over the court. "Now I am condemned!"

He sat rigid, his teeth clenched. Katerina Ivanovna sat in her place, for a long time shaking.

Grushenka was called.

She, too, was dressed in black, her magnificent black shawl on her shoulders. She walked to the witness-box with her smooth, noiseless tread, slightly swaying, as is common in women of full figure. She looked very handsome, and not at all pale, as the ladies alleged afterwards. They declared, too, that she had a mean expression. But she was simply irritated and painfully aware of the contemptuous and inquisitive eyes of the scandal-loving public.

Sometimes she spoke as though she felt, "I don't care what happens, I'll say it...." In regard to her being familiar with Fyodor Pavlovitch, she said, "That's not true, was it my fault he was always after me?" But a minute later she added, "It was all my fault. I was laughing at them both—at the old man and him, too—and I brought them to this. It was on account of me it happened."

Samsonov's name came up somehow.

"That's nobody's business," she snapped. "He was my benefactor; he took me in when I hadn't a shoe to my foot, when my family had turned me out."

The President reminded her, though very politely, that she must answer the questions without going off into irrelevant details.

Grushenka turned red and her eyes flashed. The envelope with the notes in it she had not seen, but had only heard from "that wicked man" that Fyodor Pavlovitch had an envelope with notes for three thousand in it. "That was foolish. I would never have gone to him."

"To whom are you referring as 'that wicked man'?" inquired the prosecutor.

"Smerdyakov, who murdered his master and hanged himself last night."

She was asked what grounds she had for accusing him; but it appeared that she, too, had no grounds for it.

"Dmitri Fyodorovitch told me so," she said. "The woman who came between us has ruined him; she is the cause of it all," Grushenka added.

She was again asked to whom she was referring.

"The young lady there, Katerina Ivanovna. She sent for me, offered me chocolate, tried to make me like her. There's not much shame about her, I can tell you that...."

At this point the President checked her, asking her to moderate her language. But the jealous woman's heart was burning, and she did not care what she did.

"When the prisoner was arrested at Mokroe," the prosecutor asked, "everyone saw and heard you run from the next room and cry: 'It's all my fault. We'll go to Siberia together!' So you already believed him to have murdered his father?"

"I don't remember what I felt at the time," answered Grushenka. "Everyone was crying out that he had killed his father, and I felt that it was my fault. But when he said he wasn't guilty, I believed him at once, and I believe him now and always shall believe him. He is not the man to tell a lie."

Fetyukovitch began his cross-examination. He asked about Rakitin and the twenty-five rubles "you paid him for bringing Alexey Fyodorovitch Karamazov to see you."

"There was nothing strange about his taking the money," said Grushenka. "He was always coming to me for money: he used to get thirty rubles a month at least out of me, chiefly for luxuries: he had enough to keep him without my help."

"What led you to be so liberal to him?" Fetyukovitch asked.

"He is my cousin. His mother was my mother's sister. But he always asked me not to tell anyone, he is so ashamed of me."

This fact was a surprise to everyone; no one, not even Mitya, knew of it. Rakitin turned purple with shame. Grushenka had somehow heard before she came into the court that he had given evidence against Mitya, and so she was angry. The effect on the public of Rakitin's speech, his noble sentiments, his attacks upon serfdom and the disorder of Russia, was ruined. Fetyukovitch was satisfied: it was another god-send.

Grushenka's cross-examination did not last long and there was nothing new in her evidence. She left a disagreeable impression on the public; hundreds of eyes were fixed on her as she finished giving her evidence and sat down again. Mitya was silent throughout her evidence. He sat as though turned to stone, with his eyes fixed on the ground. Ivan was next called to give evidence.

Chapter V

A Sudden Up-Set

Ivan's entrance was almost unnoticed. He walked slowly, head bowed. His face made a painful impression. His eyes were dull as he looked round the court. The President began by informing him that he was a witness not under oath, and that he might answer or refuse to answer, but that, of course, he must bear witness according to his conscience.

Ivan looked at him blankly, but his face relaxed into a smile and he laughed. "Well, and what else?" he asked in a loud voice.

There was a hush in the court, a feeling of something strange.

"You...are perhaps not well?" the President began.

"Don't trouble yourself, your honor, I am well enough and can tell you something interesting," Ivan answered calmly.

"You have something special to say?" the President asked.

Ivan answered: "No...I have nothing in particular."

He answered each question briefly. To many of the questions he said he didn't know. He knew nothing of his father's money relations with Dmitri. Threats to murder his father he had heard from the prisoner. The money in the envelope he had heard of from Smerdyakov.

"It's the same thing over and over again," he interrupted.

"I see you are not well and I understand your feelings," the President began.

He turned to the prosecutor and counsel for the defense to invite them to examine the witness, when Ivan said in an exhausted voice: "Let me go, your honor, I feel ill."

Without waiting for permission, he started to walk out of the court. But after four steps he stood still, smiled, and went back.

"I want to give you the money that was in the envelope," said Ivan.

"How did you happen to have those notes?" the President asked.

"I got them from Smerdyakov, the murderer.... I was with him just before he hanged himself. It was he, not my brother, who killed our father. He murdered him and I incited him to do it ...Who doesn't desire his father's death?"

"Are you in your right mind?" broke from the President.

"I should think I am ... in the same nasty mind as all of you...." He turned to the audience. "My father has been murdered and they pretend to be horrified," he said. "They keep up the sham with one another. They all desire the death of their fathers. If there hadn't been a murder, they'd have been angry and gone home. It's a spectacle they want! Have you any water? Give me a drink!"

He suddenly clutched his head.

The usher approached. Alyosha jumped up and cried, "He is ill. Don't believe him: he has brain fever." Katerina Ivanovna rose from her seat and gazed at Ivan with horror. Mitya stood up and looked at his brother with a wild, strange smile.

"Don't disturb yourselves. I am not mad, I am only a murderer," Ivan began. "You can't expect fine words from a murderer," he added, laughing.

The prosecutor bent over to the President, obviously up-set. The two other judges whispered with each other. Fetyukovitch pricked up his ears as he listened: the hall was quiet in expectation. The President at last recollected himself.

"Witness, your words cannot be understood. Calm yourself, if you can, and tell your story. How can you confirm your statement ... if indeed you are not out of your head?"

"That's just it. I have no proof. That dog Smerdyakov won't send you proofs from the other world...in an envelope. You think of nothing but envelopes—one is enough. I've no witnesses ... except one, perhaps," he smiled thoughtfully.

"Who is your witness?"

"He has a tail, your Excellency! He is here somewhere, no doubt—perhaps under that table with the evidence on it. Where should he sit if not there? I told him I don't want to keep quiet! Come, release the monster ... he's been singing a hymn. That's because his heart is light! It's like a drunken man in the street crying how 'Vanka went to Petersburg.' Oh, how stupid all this business is! Come, take me instead of him!"

He began slowly looking about. The court was in an up-roar.

Alyosha rushed towards him, but the usher had already seized Ivan by the arm.

"What are you about?" the usher cried, staring into Ivan's face.

Seizing him by the shoulders, Ivan flung him to the floor.

The police were on the spot and he was seized. All the time he was being removed, he yelled and screamed.

The whole court was thrown into an up-roar.

When everything was quiet again, the usher came in for a talking to, though he explained that the witness had been quite well, that the doctor had seen him an hour ago, and that until he came into the court he had talked reasonably, so that nothing could have been foreseen—he had, in fact, insisted on giving evidence.

Before everyone had completely recovered, this scene was followed by another. Katerina Ivanovna had an emotional attack. She sobbed, shrieking loudly, but refused to leave the court.

"There is more evidence I must give!" she cried. "Here is a letter...read it! It's a letter from that monster...that man there!" She pointed to Mitya. "It is he killed his father. He wrote to me how he would do it! The other one is ill, out of his mind!"

The usher took the document to the President, while she, Katerina Ivanovna, dropped into her chair, and hiding her face in her hands, began noiselessly sobbing. The document was the letter Mitya had written at the tavern. Its proof was recognized, and had it not been for that letter, Mitya might have escaped his doom.

The President passed the document to the judges, the jury, and the lawyers. After they had studied it, the examination of Katerina Ivanovna began.

On being asked by the President whether she had recovered sufficiently, Katerina Ivanovna exclaimed, "I am quite equal to answering you." She was asked to explain in detail what this letter was and under what circumstances she received it.

"I received it the day before the crime was committed, but he wrote it the day before, at the tavern—two days before he committed the crime. Look, it is written on some sort of bill!" she cried. "He hated me at that time because he had behaved so badly to me and was running after that creature...and because he owed me that three thousand.... He was shamed by that three thousand on account of his own meanness!

"This is how it happened. Three weeks before he murdered his father, he came to me one morning. I knew he was in want of money, and what he wanted it for. Yes—to win that creature and carry her off. I knew then he had been false to me and meant to abandon me, and it was I who gave him that money, using the excuse of his sending it to my sister in Moscow.

"As I gave it him, I looked him in the face and said that he could send it when he liked, 'in a month's time would do.' How could he have not known that I was telling him to his face, 'You want money to be false to me with your creature, so here's the money. Take it, if you have so little honor!' I wanted to prove what he was, and what happened?

"He took it, and threw it away with that creature in one night.... He understood, too, that I gave him that money to test him, to see whether he was so lost to all honor as to take it from me. I looked into his eyes and he looked into mine, and he knew!"

"That's true, Katya," Mitya roared, "I looked into your eyes and I knew you were shaming me, and yet I took your money. Look upon me as a no good, all of you!"

"Prisoner," cried the President, "another word and I will order you to be removed."

"That money was a torment to him," Katya went on. "He wanted to repay it. That's true; but he needed money for that creature, too. So he murdered his father, but he didn't repay me, and went off with her to that village where he was arrested. There, again, he threw away the money he had stolen after the murder of his father. And a day before the murder he wrote me this letter. He wrote it from spite, certain I would never show it to anyone, even if he did kill him, or else he wouldn't have written it. He knew I shouldn't want to revenge myself and ruin him! Read it, please, and you will see that he described it all in his letter, how he would kill his father and where his money was kept. He thought it all out beforehand," Katerina Ivanovna pointed out with hateful triumph. "If he hadn't been drunk, he wouldn't have written to me; but everything is written there just as he committed the murder!" she exclaimed.

She was reckless now of all consequences, though, no doubt, she had foreseen them even a month ago, for even then, shaking with anger, she had thought whether to show it at the trial or not. Now she had taken the plunge. The letter was read aloud by the clerk. It made an overwhelming impression. They asked Mitya if he had written the letter.

"It's mine!" cried Mitya. "I shouldn't have written it, if I hadn't been drunk! We've hated each other for many things, Katya, but I swear, I loved you even while I hated you, and you didn't love me!" He sank back on his seat, wringing his hands in despair.

The prosecutor and counsel for the defense began cross-examining her, chiefly to determine what had made her conceal such a document and to give her evidence.

"Yes, I was telling lies just now. But I wanted to save him, for he has hated and despised me!" Katya cried. "He has despised me from the moment I bowed to him for that money. How often I have read it in his eyes, 'You came of yourself.' He had no idea why I ran to him. He suspected nothing but baseness. He thought everyone was like himself! He was convinced I should be trembling with shame all my life because I went to him, and he had a right to despise me, and feel superior to me—that's why he wanted to marry me! I tried to conquer him by love—a love that knew no bounds. I even tried to forgive his faithlessness; but he understood nothing! He is a monster! I received that letter the next evening: and only that morning I wanted to forgive him everything!"

The President and the prosecutor tried to calm her. They felt shame taking advantage of her hysteria and of listening to such avowals. "We understand how hard it is for you," they said. "We feel for you." And yet they dragged the evidence out of the raving woman. She described how Ivan had been nearly driven out of his mind during the last two months trying to save "the monster and murderer," his brother.

"He tortured himself," she exclaimed. "He was always trying to ease his brother's guilt, confessing to me that he, too, had never loved his father, and perhaps desired his death. He tormented himself! He came every day and talked to me as his only friend. One day he came and said, 'If it was not my brother, but Smerdyakov who committed the murder, then I too am guilty, for Smerdyakov knew I didn't like my father and desired his death.' Then I brought out that letter and showed it him.

"He was convinced his brother had done it, and was overwhelmed. He couldn't endure the thought that his own brother was a parricide! Only a week ago I saw it was making him ill. During the last few days I saw his mind giving way. He walked about raving. The doctor from Moscow examined him and told me he was on the eve of brain fever—all on account of this monster! And last night he learnt that Smerdyakov was dead! It was such a shock it drove him out of his mind...!"

Such an outpouring is only possible once in a lifetime! But it was in Katya's character, and it was such a moment in her life. It was the same Katya who had thrown herself on the mercy of a young profligate to save her father; the same Katya who had just sacrificed herself before all these people, telling of Mitya's generous conduct in the hope of softening his fate. And now, again, she sacrificed herself; but this time it was for another, and perhaps only now she felt and knew how dear that other was to her! Sensing he had ruined himself by his confession that he had committed the murder, not his brother, she sacrificed herself to save him!

And yet one terrible doubt occurred—was she lying about her former relations with Mitya? No, she had not intentionally slandered him when she cried that Mitya despised her for her bowing down to him! She had loved him, but only from wounded pride, which was more like revenge. Perhaps Katya longed for nothing more than that, but Mitya's faithlessness had wounded her to the bottom of her heart, and her heart could not forgive him. The moment of revenge had come suddenly, and all that had been accumulating so long and so painfully burst out. She betrayed Mitya, but herself, too. And no sooner had she given full expression to her feelings than the tension was over and she was over-whelmed with shame. She fell on the floor, sobbing and screaming, and was carried out.

At that moment Grushenka, with a wail, rushed towards Mitya before they had time to prevent her. "Mitya," she cried, "your serpent has destroyed you! She has shown you what she is!" At a signal from the President they seized her and tried to remove her from the court, but she wouldn't allow it. She fought and struggled to get back to Mitya.

Mitya cried out and struggled to get to her. He was overpowered.

Then the Moscow doctor appeared, for the President had sent the court usher to arrange for medical aid for Ivan. The doctor announced to the court that the sick man was suffering from a dangerous attack of brain fever, and that he must be at once removed. In answer to questions from the prosecutor and counsel for the defense, he said the patient had come to him of his own accord the day before yesterday and that he had warned him that he had such an attack coming on, but he had not consented to be looked after.

"He was certainly not in a normal state of mind: he told me himself that he saw visions, that he met several persons in the street who were dead, and that Satan visited him every evening," said the doctor.

After giving his evidence, the celebrated doctor withdrew. The letter produced by Katerina Ivanovna was added to the material proofs. After some deliberation, the judges decided to proceed with the trial and to enter both pieces of evidence given by Ivan and Katerina Ivanovna.

The other witnesses only repeated what had been said. Everyone was excited by what had happened, and were waiting for the speeches of the prosecution and the defense. Fetyukovitch was obviously shaken by Katerina Ivanovna's evidence. But the prosecutor was triumphant. When all the evidence had been taken, the court was adjourned for an hour. It was just eight o'clock when the President returned to his seat and the prosecutor, Ippolit Kirillovitch, began his speech.

Chapter VI

The Prosecutor's Speech

Ippolit Kirillovitch began, trembling with nervousness. He put everything he had into that speech. Where it really excelled was in its sincerity. He really believed in the prisoner's guilt; he accused him not as an official duty only, and in calling for vengeance quivered with passion "for the security of society." He began in a breaking voice, but it soon gained strength and filled the court to the end of his speech.

"Gentlemen of the jury," he began, "this case has made a stir throughout Russia. But what is there so horrifying in it? We are so accustomed to such crimes! That's what's so horrible, that such dark deeds have ceased to horrify us. We read almost daily of things beside which the present case grows pale. Our national crimes of violence bear witness to a widespread evil, so general among us, that it is difficult to contend against it.

"Perhaps people will cry out against me that that it is a slander. Let them say so—I should be the first to rejoice if it were so! Don't believe me, but remember my words; if only a twentieth of what I say is true—it's awful! Look how our young people commit suicide. Look at our vice, at our profligates. Fyodor Pavlovitch, the victim in the present case, was an innocent babe compared with many of them. Yet 'he lived among us!'

"One day perhaps the leading intellects of Russia will study the psychology of crime, for the subject is worth it. But now we are either horrified, or pretend to be, though we really gloat over the spectacle, and love strong sensations. Or, like children, we brush the dreadful ghosts away and hide our heads so as to return to our sports and pleasure as soon as they have vanished. But we must one day begin in earnest to look at ourselves."

Ippolit Kirillovitch's speech was interrupted by applause. The significance of what he said was appreciated. The applause was brief; the President did not think it necessary to caution the public, and only looked severely at the offenders. But Ippolit Kirillovitch was encouraged; he had never been applauded before! He had been all his life unable to get a hearing, and now he suddenly had an opportunity of securing the ear of all Russia.

"What, after all, is this Karamazov family which has gained such notoriety in all Russia?" he continued. "It seems to me that certain fundamental features of the educated class of today are reflected in this family. Think of that unhappy old man who has met with such a sad end! Beginning life of noble birth, but in a poor, dependent position, through an unexpected marriage he came into a small fortune. A petty knave, a toady and buffoon, he was a money-lender who grew bolder with growing prosperity. His abject and servile characteristics disappeared; his malicious and sarcastic cynicism was all that remained. On the spiritual side he was undeveloped, while his vitality was excessive. He saw nothing in life but sensual pleasure, and brought his children up to be the same. He had no feelings for his duties as a father. He left his children to the servants. He was an example of everything that is opposed to civic duty, the most complete individualism.

"'The world may burn so long as I am all right' was his belief. He was content and eager to go on living in the same way for another twenty or thirty years. He swindled his own son and spent his money on trying to get his mistress from him. No, I don't intend to leave the prisoner's defense altogether to my talented colleague. I can understand the resentment heaped up in his son's heart against him. But enough of that unhappy old man; he has paid the penalty. But let us remember that he was a father, and a typical father, who only differ in not openly professing such cynicism, but their philosophy is the same.

"Now for the children of this father. One of them is the prisoner, and the rest of my speech will deal with him. Of the other two I will speak only briefly. The elder is one of those modern young men of brilliant education and intellect who has lost faith in everything. We have all heard him. He never hid his opinions, which justifies me in speaking openly of him now, not as an individual, but as a Karamazov.

"Another person closely connected with the case died here by his own hand last night. I mean an afflicted idiot, formerly the servant, and possibly the illegitimate son, of Fyodor Pavlovitch, Smerdyakov. At the preliminary inquiry, he told me with tears how the young Ivan Karamazov horrified him by his spiritual audacity. 'Everything in the world is lawful according to him, and nothing must be forbidden in the future—that is what he taught me.' I believe he was driven out of his mind by this theory, though the epileptic attacks from which he suffered, and this terrible murder, helped to unhinge his faculties. But he made one very interesting observation: 'If there is one of the sons that is like Fyodor Pavlovitch, it is Ivan Fyodorovitch.' With that remark I conclude my sketch of his character, feeling it indelicate to continue further. We've seen today in this court that there are still good impulses in his young heart, that family feeling has not been destroyed by lack of faith and cynicism.

"The third son is a devout and modest youth who does not share his elder brother's destructive theory of life. He clings to the 'ideas of the people,' or to what goes by that name in some circles. He was within an ace of becoming a monk. He seems to me to have betrayed that timid despair which leads so many in our unhappy society who dread cynicism and its corrupting influences, and mistakenly attribute it to European enlightenment. Like frightened children, they yearn to fall asleep on the withered bosom of their decrepit mother to escape the horrors that terrify them. For my part I wish the excellent young man every success; I trust his youthful idealism and impulse towards the ideas of the people may never degenerate, as often happens, into gloomy mysticism, and blind chauvinism—two elements which are even a greater menace to Russia than the decay, due to the adoption of European ideas from which his elder brother suffers."

Two or three people clapped at the mention of chauvinism and mysticism. Ippolit Kirillovitch had been, indeed, carried away by his own eloquence. All this had little to do with the case in hand, but the sickly and consumptive man was overcome by the desire to express himself once in his life. People said afterwards that he was actuated by unworthy motives in his criticism of Ivan, because the latter had on one or two occasions got the better of him in argument, and Ippolit Kirillovitch tried now to take his revenge.

"But to return to the eldest son," Ippolit Kirillovitch went on. "He is the prisoner before us. We have his life and his actions, too, before us. While his brothers seem to stand for 'Europeanism' and 'the principles of the people,' he seems to represent Russia as she is. Not all Russia! God preserve us! Yet, here we have the very scent and sound of her. Oh, he is spontaneous, a mingling of good and evil, he is a lover of culture, yet he brawls in taverns. But he, too, can be good and noble, but only when all goes well with him. He dislikes paying for anything, but is very fond of receiving. Give him every possible good in life, put no obstacle in his way, and he will show that he, too, can be noble. He is not greedy, but he must have a great deal of money, and you will see how generously he flings it all away in reckless dissipation. But if he has not money, he will show what he is ready to do to get it. But let us take events in their chronological order.

"First, we have before us a poor abandoned child, running about the yard 'without boots on his feet,' as our worthy and esteemed fellow citizen, of foreign origin, expressed it just now. I repeat, I yield to no one the defense of the criminal. I am here to accuse him, but to defend him also. Yes, I, too, am human; I, too, can weigh the influence of home and childhood on the character. But the boy grows up and becomes an officer; for a duel and other reckless acts he is exiled to one of the remote frontier towns of Russia. There he led a wild life as an officer. And, of course, he needed money, and more money, and so after prolonged disputes he came to a settlement with his father over his inheritance, and the last six thousand was sent him. A letter is in existence in which he gives up his claim to the rest on the payment of this six thousand.

"Then came his meeting with a young girl of lofty character and brilliant education. I do not venture to repeat the details; you have only just heard them. Honor, self-sacrifice   were shown there. The young officer, frivolous and profligate, doing homage to true nobility and a lofty ideal, was shown in a very sympathetic light. But the other side of the medal was unexpectedly turned to us immediately after. Again I will not conjecture why it happened so, but there were causes. The same lady, bathed in tears of long-concealed indignation, alleged that he, of all men, had despised her for her action, which, though incautious, reckless perhaps, was still dictated by lofty and generous motives.

497

"He, the girl's betrothed, looked at her with that smile of mockery which was more insufferable from him than from anyone. Knowing he had already deceived her, she offered him three thousand rubles, and clearly let him understand she was offering him the money to deceive her. 'Well, will you take it or not, are you so lost to shame?' was the question in her eyes. He looked at her, saw clearly what was in her mind, took that three thousand, and squandered it in two days with the new object of his affections.

"What are we to believe? The legend of the young officer sacrificing his last penny in a noble impulse of generosity and doing reverence to virtue, or this other revolting picture? As a rule, between two extremes one has to find the mean, but in the present case this is not true. The probability is that in the first case he was truly noble, and in the second as truly base. Because he was of the Karamazov character—that's just what I am leading up to—capable of combining contradictions, and capable of the greatest heights and greatest depths. Remember the brilliant remark made by a young observer who has seen the Karamazov family at close quarters—Mr. Rakitin: 'The sense of their own degradation is as essential to those reckless, unbridled natures as the sense of their lofty generosity.' And that's true, they need this unnatural mixture. Two extremes at the same moment, or they are miserable and dissatisfied and their existence is incomplete.

"By the way, gentlemen of the jury, we've just touched upon that three thousand rubles. Can you conceive that a man like that, on receiving that sum and in such a way, at the price of such shame, such disgrace, could have been capable that very day of setting apart half that sum and sewing it up in a little bag, and would have the firmness of character to carry it about with him for a whole month, in spite of every temptation and his extreme need of it! Neither in drunken debauchery in taverns, nor when he was flying into the country, trying to get from God knows whom, the money so essential to him to remove the object of his affections from being tempted by his father, did he bring himself to touch that little bag! If only to avoid abandoning his mistress to the rival of whom he was so jealous, he would have been certain to have opened that bag and to have stayed at home to keep watch over her, and to wait for the moment she would say to him at last 'I am yours,' and to fly with her far from their fatal surroundings.

"But no, he did not touch that money, and what is the reason he gives for it? The chief reason, as I have just said, was that when she would say, 'I am yours, take me where you will,' he might have the wherewithal to take her. But that first reason, in the prisoner's own words, was of little weight beside the second. While I have that money on me, he said, I am a scoundrel, not a thief, for I can always go to my insulted betrothed and, laying down half the sum I have appropriated, say to her, 'You see, I've squandered half your money, and shown I am a weak and immoral man, but though I am a scoundrel, I am not a thief, for if I had been a thief, I shouldn't have brought you back this half of the money!' A marvelous explanation! This weak man, who could not resist the temptation of accepting the three thousand rubles at the price of such disgrace, suddenly develops the most stoical firmness, and carries about a thousand rubles without touching it. Does that fit in with the character we have analyzed? No, and I venture to tell you how the real Dmitri Karamazov would have behaved if he really had put away the money.

"At the first temptation—for instance, to entertain the woman with whom he had already squandered half the money—he would have unpicked his little bag and have taken out some hundred rubles, for why should he have taken back precisely half the money, that is, fifteen hundred rubles? Why not fourteen hundred? He could just as well have said then that he was not a thief, because he brought back fourteen hundred rubles. Then another time he would unpick it again and taken out another hundred, and then a third, and then a fourth, and before the end of the month he would have taken the last note but one, feeling that if he took back only a hundred it would answer the purpose, for a thief would have stolen it all. And then he would have looked at this last note and have said to himself, 'It's really not worth-while giving back one hundred; let's spend that, too!' That's how the real Dmitri Karamazov, as we know him, would have behaved. One cannot imagine anything less believable than this legend of the little bag. Nothing could be more inconceivable. But we shall return to that later."

After touching upon what had come out in the proceedings about the money relations of father and son, arguing that it was impossible, from the facts known, to determine who was in the wrong, Ippolit Kirillovitch passed to the evidence of the medical experts about Mitya's fixed idea of the three thousand owed him.

Chapter VII

An Historical Survey

"The medical experts have tried to convince us that the prisoner is out of his mind and, in fact, a maniac. I maintain that he is in his right mind, and that if he had not been he would have behaved more cleverly. I agree with the doctor who maintained that the prisoner's mental faculties have always been normal. The prisoner's continual and violent anger was not the money itself; there was a special motive—jealousy!"

Here Ippolit Kirillovitch described the prisoner's passion for Grushenka. He began from the moment when the prisoner went to her lodgings "to beat her"—I use his own expression," but instead of beating her, he remained there at her feet. That was the beginning of the passion. At the same time the prisoner's father was captivated by the same person—a strange coincidence, for they both lost their hearts to her at the same time. And she inspired both of them with the most violent passion.

"We have her confession: 'I was laughing at both of them.' Yes, the desire to make a jest of them came over her, and she conquered both of them at once. The old man, who worshiped money, set aside three thousand rubles as a reward for one visit from her, but soon after that he would have been happy to lay his property and his name at her feet, if only she would become his wife. As for the prisoner, the enchantress gave the unhappy

501

young man no hope until the last moment, when he knelt before her, stretching out hands already stained with the blood of his father. It was at that point he was arrested. 'Send me to Siberia with him, I am to blame,' the woman cried at the moment of his arrest.

"The talented young man, to whom I have referred, Mr. Rakitin, characterized this heroine in brief terms: 'She was disillusioned early in life, deceived and ruined by a man who seduced and abandoned her. She was left in poverty, cursed by her family, and taken under the protection of a wealthy old man, whom she still considers as her benefactor. There was perhaps much good in her young heart, but it was hardened too early. She became prudent and saved money. She grew sarcastic and resentful against society. After this it easy to understand how she might laugh at them both simply from malice.

"After a month of hopeless love and moral degradation, during which he betrayed his betrothed and used money entrusted to him, the prisoner was driven to madness by jealousy—and of his father! And the worst of it was the crazy old man was using the three thousand rubles the son looked upon as part of his inheritance to steal the object of his affection. I admit it was hard to bear! It might well drive a man to madness. It was not the money, but the fact that this money was being used to ruin his happiness!"

The prosecutor went on to describe how the idea of murdering his father had entered the prisoner's head. "At first he only talked about it in taverns. But those who heard the prisoner began to think at last that such anger might turn into action."

Here the prosecutor described the scene of violence when the prisoner rushed into his father's house after dinner. "I cannot positively assert," he said, "that the prisoner fully intended to murder his father before that incident. Yet the idea had several times presented itself to him, and he had deliberated on it—for that we have witnesses, and his own words. I confess, gentlemen of the jury," he said, "that till today I was uncertain whether to charge the prisoner with conscious premeditation. I was convinced he had pictured the fatal moment beforehand, but only pictured it as a possibility. He had not definitely considered when and how he might commit the crime.

"But I was only uncertain till today, till that fatal document was presented to the court just now. You yourselves heard the young lady's exclamation, 'It is the plan, the program of the murder!' That is how she defined that letter of the unhappy prisoner. And from that letter we see that the murder was premeditated. It was written two days before, and so we know for a fact the prisoner swore that, if he could not get money next day, he would murder his father and take the envelope with the notes from under his pillow. So he had thought everything out, weighing every circumstance, and he carried it out just as he had written it. The proof of premeditation is conclusive; the crime was done for the sake of the money, that is clear. The prisoner does not deny his signature.

"I shall be told he was drunk when he wrote it. But that does not diminish the value of the letter. Quite the contrary; he wrote when drunk what he had planned when sober. Had he not planned it when sober, he would not have written it when drunk. I shall be asked: Then why did he talk about it in taverns? A man who premeditates such a crime will keep it to himself. Yes, but he talked about it before he had formed a plan, when he had only the desire. Afterwards he talked less about it.

"On the evening he wrote that letter he was, in fact, silent, though he had been drinking. He did not play billiards; he sat in a corner, talked to no one. He did indeed turn a shop man out of his seat, but that was done almost unconsciously, because he could never enter a tavern without making a disturbance. It is true that after he made the decision, he must have realized that he had talked too much about it beforehand, and that this might lead to his arrest and prosecution afterwards. But his luck had served him before, it would serve him again. I must confess, too, that he did a great deal to avoid the fatal crime. 'Tomorrow I shall try to borrow the money from every one,' he writes, 'and if they won't give it to me, there will be bloodshed.'"

Ippolit Kirillovitch passed to a detailed description of Mitya's efforts to borrow the money. He described his visit to Samsonov, his journey to Lyagavy. "Harassed, jeered at, hungry, after selling his watch to pay for the journey (though he tells us he had fifteen hundred rubles on him—a likely story), tortured by jealousy, suspecting that the object of his love would go to Fyodor Pavlovitch in his absence, he returned at last to the town, to find, to his joy, that she had not been near his father.

"He accompanied her himself to her protector. Then he hastens back to his ambush in the garden, and there learns that Smerdyakov is in a fit, that the other servant is ill—the coast is clear and he knows the 'signals'—what a temptation! Still he resists it; he goes off to a lady living in the town, Madame Hohlakov. That lady, who had watched his career with compassion, gave him the most judicious advice, to give up his dissipated life, his love-affair, the waste of his youth in debauchery, and to set off to Siberia to the gold mines: 'that would be an outlet for your energies, your thirst for adventure.'"

After describing the result of this conversation and the moment when the prisoner learnt that Grushenka had not remained at Samsonov's, the luckless man, worn out with jealousy, thought she had deceived him and was now with his father, it was the last straw. Ippolit Kirillovitch concluded by dwelling upon the fatal influence of chance. "Had the maid told him her mistress was at Mokroe with her former lover, nothing would have happened. But she lost her head, she could only protest her ignorance, and if the prisoner did not kill her on the spot, it was only because he flew in pursuit of his false mistress.

"But note, frantic as he was, he took with him a brass pestle. Why that? Since he had been contemplating his plan and preparing himself for it for a whole month, he would snatch up anything like a weapon that caught his eye. He had realized for a month past that any object of the kind would serve as a weapon, so he, without hesitation, recognized that it would serve his purpose. And then we find him in his father's garden—the coast is clear, there are no witnesses. The suspicion that she was with his father, and perhaps laughing at him—took his breath away. And it was not mere suspicion, the deception was obvious. She must be there in that lighted room; and the unhappy man would have us believe he stole up to the window, peeped in, and withdrew for fear something terrible should happen. He tries to persuade us of that, we who understand his character, who know his state of mind and that he knew the signals by which he could enter the house."

At this point Ippolit Kirillovitch discussed the suspected connection of Smerdyakov with the murder. He did this very circumstantially, and every one realized that, although he professed to despise that suspicion, he thought the subject of great importance.

Chapter VIII

A Treatise on Smerdyakov

"To begin with, what was the source of this suspicion?" Ippolit Kirillovitch began. "The first person who cried out that Smerdyakov had committed the murder was the prisoner himself at the moment of his arrest, yet from that time to this he has not brought forward a single fact to confirm the charge. The charge is confirmed by three persons only—the two brothers of the prisoner and Madame Svyetlov.

"The elder of these brothers expressed his suspicions only today, when he was out of his mind. But we know that for the last two months he has shared our conviction of his brother's guilt. The younger brother has admitted he has not the slightest fact to support his notion of Smerdyakov's guilt, and has only been led to that conclusion from the prisoner's own words. What Madame Svyetlov said was even more astounding. 'What the prisoner tells you you must believe; he is not a man to tell a lie.' That is all the evidence against Smerdyakov produced. Yet the theory of Smerdyakov's guilt is still maintained."

Ippolit Kirillovitch described the character of Smerdyakov, "who had cut short his life in a fit of insanity." He depicted him as a man of weak intellect, with little education, who had been thrown off his balance by philosophical ideas above his level and modern theories of duty, which he learnt from his master, who was also perhaps his father—Fyodor Pavlovitch; and from philosophical talks with the elder son, Ivan Fyodorovitch, who probably indulged in this diversion to amuse himself at the valet's expense.

"He spoke to me himself of his spiritual condition during the last few days at his father's house," Ippolit Kirillovitch said; "but others too have borne witness to it—the prisoner himself, his brother, and the servant Grigory—all knew him well. Moreover, Smerdyakov, whose health was shaken by attacks of epilepsy, had not the courage of a chicken. 'He fell at my feet and kissed them,' the prisoner told us. And yet the prisoner chose him for his confidant, and frightened him into acting as a spy for him.

"In that capacity he deceived his master, telling the prisoner of the envelope with the notes in it and the signals by means of which he could get into the house. How could he help telling him? 'He would have killed me,' he said at the inquiry, trembling before us, though his tormentor had been arrested and could do him no harm. 'He suspected me at every instant. In fear I hurried to tell him every secret that he might see I had not deceived him, and let me live.' Those are his own words.

"He was naturally honest and enjoyed the complete confidence of his master, ever since he had returned him some money he had lost. So it may be supposed that the poor fellow suffered pangs of remorse at having deceived his master, whom he loved as his benefactor. Persons severely afflicted with epilepsy are, so the doctors tell us, prone to self-reproach. They worry over their 'wickedness,' they are tormented by conscience, often without cause; they exaggerate and often invent all sorts of faults. And here we have a man of that type who had been driven to wrong-doing by intimidation.

"He had a sense that something terrible would be the outcome of the situation. When Ivan Fyodorovitch was leaving

507

for Moscow just before the murder, Smerdyakov begged him to remain, though he was too timid to tell him what he feared. He confined himself to hints, but his hints were not understood. It must be understood he looked on Ivan Fyodorovitch as a protector, whose presence in the house was a guarantee no harm would come. Remember the phrase in Dmitri Karamazov's letter, 'I shall kill the old man, if only Ivan goes away.' So Ivan Fyodorovitch's presence seemed a guarantee of peace.

"But he went away, and within an hour of his departure Smerdyakov was taken with an epileptic fit. Here I must mention that Smerdyakov, oppressed by terror and despair, had felt during those last few days that one of the fits might be coming on. The day and hour of such an attack cannot, of course, be known. But every epileptic can feel before it happens that he is likely to have one. So, as soon as Ivan Fyodorovitch had driven out of the yard, Smerdyakov, depressed by his lonely and unprotected position, went to the cellar, wondering as he went down the steps if he would have a fit, and that very fear brought on the spasm that always precedes such attacks, and he fell unconscious into the cellar. In this perfectly natural occurrence people try to detect a suspicion that he was shamming an attack *on purpose*. But, if it were on purpose, the question arises at once, what was his motive? What motive had he for such falsity? Could he, plotting the murder, have desired to attract the attention of the household by having a fit?

"Gentlemen of the jury, on the night of the murder, there were five persons at Fyodor Pavlovitch's—Fyodor Pavlovitch himself; his servant Grigory, who was almost killed, Grigory's wife, Marfa Ignatyevna, but it would be shameful to imagine her murdering her master. Two persons are left—the prisoner and Smerdyakov. If we are to believe the prisoner's statement that he is not the murderer, then Smerdyakov must have been, for no one else can be found. That is what accounts for the astounding accusation against the unhappy idiot who committed suicide yesterday. Had a shadow of suspicion rested on anyone else, had there been a sixth person, even the prisoner would have been ashamed to accuse Smerdyakov, for that is perfectly absurd.

"Gentlemen, let us lay aside psychology, let us lay aside medicine, let us even lay aside logic, let us turn only to the facts and see what the facts tell us. If Smerdyakov killed him, how did he do it? Alone, or with the assistance of the prisoner? Consider the first alternative—that he did it alone. If he had killed him, it must have been for some advantage to himself. But not having a motive, Smerdyakov could only have murdered him for the sake of gain, for the three thousand rubles he had seen his master put in the envelope. And yet he tells another person—the prisoner— everything about the money and the signals, where the envelope lay, what was written on it, what it was tied up with, and, above all, told him the signals by which he could enter the house. Did he do this to betray himself, or to invite to the same enterprise one who would be anxious to get that envelope for himself? 'Yes,' I shall be told, 'but he betrayed it from fear.' How do you explain this? A man who could think of such a savage act and carry it out tells facts known to no one else, and which, if he held his tongue, no one would ever have guessed!

"No, however cowardly he might be, if he had plotted such a crime, nothing would have induced him to tell anyone about the envelope and the signals, for that was as good as betraying himself. He would have invented something, he would have told some lie if he had been forced to give information, but he would have been silent about that. For if he had said nothing about the money, but had been the murderer and stolen the money, no one in the world could have charged him with murder for the sake of robbery, since no one but he had seen the money, no one but he knew of its existence in the house.

"Even if he had been accused of the murder, he committed it from some other motive. But since no one had seen any such motive in him, and everyone saw, on the contrary, that his master was fond of him and honored him with his confidence, he would, of course, have been the last to be suspected. People would have suspected first the man who had a motive, a man who had himself declared he had such motives, who had made no secret of it; they would, in fact, have suspected the son of the murdered man, Dmitri Fyodorovitch. Had Smerdyakov killed and robbed him, and the son been accused of it, that would, of course, have suited Smerdyakov. Yet are we to believe that, plotting the murder, he told that son about the money, the envelope, and the signals? Is that logical?

"When the day of the murder planned by Smerdyakov came, we have him falling downstairs in a *feigned* fit—with what object? In the first place that Grigory, who had been intending to take his medicine, might put it off and remain on guard, seeing there was no one to look after the house, and, in the second place, I suppose, that his master seeing that there was no one to guard him, and in terror of a visit from his son, might redouble his vigilance. And, most of all, I suppose that he, Smerdyakov, disabled by the fit, might be carried from the kitchen, where he always slept, apart from all the rest, and where he could go in and out as he liked, to Grigory's room at the other end of the lodge, where he was always put, shut off by a screen three paces from their own bed. This was the custom established by his master and the kind-hearted Marfa Ignatyevna, whenever he had a fit. There, lying behind the screen, he would most likely, to keep up the sham, have begun groaning, keeping them awake all night. And all this, we are to believe, that he might more conveniently get up and murder his master!

"But I shall be told that he shammed illness that he might not be suspected and that he told the prisoner of the money and the signals to tempt him to murder his father, and when he had murdered him and had gone away with the money, making a noise most likely, and waking people, Smerdyakov got up, am I to believe, and went in—what for? To murder his master a second time and carry off the money that was already stolen?

Gentlemen, are you laughing? It shames me to put forward such suggestions, but, incredible as it seems, that's just what the prisoner alleges. When he had left the house, had knocked Grigory down and raised an alarm, he tells us Smerdyakov got up, went in and murdered his master and stole the money! I won't press the point that Smerdyakov could hardly have reckoned on this beforehand, and have foreseen that the son would simply peep in, though he knew the signals, and left, leaving Smerdyakov his booty. Gentlemen of the jury, I ask you, when could Smerdyakov have committed his crime? Tell me that, or you can't accuse him.

"But, perhaps, the fit was real, the sick man recovered, heard a shout, and went out. What then? He looked about him and said, 'Why not kill the master?' And how did he know what had happened, since he had been lying unconscious till that moment? 'Quite so,' some astute people will tell me, 'but what if they were in agreement? What if they murdered him together and shared the money?' A serious question, truly! And the facts to confirm it are astounding. One murders the father and takes all the trouble. while his accomplice lies on one side shamming a fit, apparently to arouse suspicion in everyone, and alarm his master and Grigory. It would be interesting to know what motives could have induced the two to form such an insane plan.

"But perhaps it was not a case of being active on Smerdyakov's part, but only of being still; perhaps Smerdyakov, out of fear, agreed not to prevent the murder, and foreseeing that he would be blamed for letting his master be murdered without screaming for help or resisting, he may have obtained permission from Dmitri Karamazov to get out of the way by shamming a fit— 'you may murder him as you like; it's nothing to me.' But as this attack of Smerdyakov's was bound to throw the household into confusion, Dmitri Karamazov could never have agreed to such a plan. But supposing he did agree, it still follows that Dmitri Karamazov is the murderer and Smerdyakov only agreed to be quiet about it, against his will through terror.

"But what do we see? As soon as he is arrested the prisoner throws all the blame on Smerdyakov, not accusing him of being his accomplice, but of being the murderer. 'He did it alone,' he says. 'He murdered and robbed him.' Strange sort of accomplices who begin to accuse one another at once! And think of the risk for Karamazov. Murdering his father while his accomplice lay in bed, he throws the blame on the sick man, who, in self-preservation might have confessed the truth. For he might have seen that the court would at once judge how far he was responsible, and so he might well have reckoned that if he were punished, it would be far less severely than the real murderer. In that case he would have been certain to make a confession, yet he has not done so.

"Smerdyakov never hinted at their complicity, and the actual murderer insisted he committed the crime alone. What's more, Smerdyakov at the inquiry volunteered the statement that it was *he* who had told the prisoner of the envelope and the signals, and that, but for him, he would have known nothing about them. If he had really been an accomplice, would he so readily have made this statement? No one but an innocent man could have acted as he did. And in a fit of melancholy arising from his disease and this catastrophe, he hanged himself yesterday. He left a note: 'I destroy myself of my own will and inclination so as to throw no blame on any one.' What would it have cost him to add: 'I am the murderer, not Karamazov'? But he did not. Did his conscience lead him to suicide and not to avowing his guilt?

"And what followed? Notes for three thousand rubles were brought into the court, and we were told that they were the same that lay in the envelope now on the table before us, and that the witness had received them from Smerdyakov the day before. I need not recall the painful scene, though I will make a few comments.

"First, Smerdyakov must have given back the money and hanged himself yesterday from guilt; he confessed his guilt to Ivan Karamazov, as the latter informs us. If it were not so, why should Ivan Fyodorovitch have kept silence till now? And if Smerdyakov confessed, why, I ask again, did he not avow the truth in the letter he left behind, knowing the innocent prisoner had to face this terrible ordeal?

"The money alone is no proof. A week ago it came to our knowledge that Ivan Fyodorovitch sent two five per cent coupons of five thousand each to the chief town of the province to be changed. I only mention this to point out that anyone may have money, and that it can't be proved that these notes are the same as were in the envelope.

"Also, Ivan Karamazov, after receiving yesterday a communication of such importance from the real murderer, did not stir. Why didn't he report it at once? Why did he put it off till morning? I think I can guess why. His health had been giving way for a week: he told a doctor and his closest friends that he was seeing things, and was on the eve of the attack of brain fever by which he was stricken today.

"In this condition he heard of Smerdyakov's death, and at once reflected, 'The man is dead, I can throw the blame on him and save my brother. I have money. I will take a roll of notes and say Smerdyakov gave them to me before his death.' You will say it's not honorable to say bad things of the dead, even to save a brother. But what if, unhinged by the news of the valet's death, he believed it really was so? You have seen the witness's condition.

"Then followed the prisoner's letter, written two days before the crime, with a   complete plan of how the murder was to be done. Why are we looking for any other plan? The crime was committed according to this plan, and by no other than the writer of it. Yes, gentlemen of the jury, it went off without a hitch!

"He did not run respectfully and timidly away from his father's window, though he was firmly convinced that the object of his affections was with him. That is crazy! He went in and murdered him. Most likely he killed him in anger, burning with resentment as soon as he looked on his hated rival. But having killed him, probably with one blow of the metal tool, and having convinced himself after a careful search that she was not there, he did not forget to put his hand under the pillow and take out the envelope that lies now on the table.

"I mention this that you may note one circumstance. Had he been an experienced murderer and committed the murder for the sake of gain only, would he have left the torn envelope on the floor beside the corpse? Had it been Smerdyakov, for instance, who murdered his master to rob him, he would have simply carried the envelope with him, without opening it, for he would have known the notes were in the envelope—they had been put in and sealed in his presence—and had he taken the envelope, no one would ever have known of the robbery. Would Smerdyakov have left it?

"No, this was the action of a frantic murderer, a murderer who was not a thief and had never stolen before, who snatched the notes from under the pillow, not like a thief, but as though seizing his own property. For that was the idea which Dmitri Karamazov had been unable to get out of his mind. Pouncing on the envelope, which he had never seen before, he tore it open to make sure the money was in it, and he ran away with the money in his pocket, forgetting to consider he had left a key piece of evidence against himself in that torn envelope on the floor.

"Because it was Karamazov, not Smerdyakov, he didn't think. He ran away; the old man caught him and was felled to the ground by the metal tool, the pestle. The prisoner, moved by pity, leapt down to look at him. Would you believe it, he tells us he leapt down out of compassion, to see whether he could do anything for him. No; he jumped down simply to make certain the only witness of his crime was dead. Any other motive would not be natural.

"Note the trouble he took over Grigory, wiped his head with his handkerchief and, convincing himself he was dead, ran to the house of his mistress, dazed and covered with blood. He wanted to find out at once where she was, so he ran to her lodging and learnt an unexpected piece of news—she had gone to Mokroe to meet her first lover."

Chapter IX

The End of the Prosecutor's Speech.

At this moment in his speech, Ippolit Kirillovitch went off into a dissertation on Grushenka's "first lover," and brought forward several interesting ideas.

"Karamazov, who had been frantically jealous of everyone, effaced himself before this first lover. What makes it all the more strange is that he seems to have hardly thought of this rival. Possibly he regarded him as a fiction. But his wounded heart grasped that the woman had been concealing this new rival and deceiving him, because he was the one hope of her life. Grasping this instantly, Dmitri Karamazov resigned himself.

"Gentlemen of the jury, I can't help dwelling on this trait in the prisoner. He shows suddenly an irresistible desire for justice, a respect for woman's right to love whom she pleases. At the moment when he had stained his hands with his father's blood for her sake! He was forced to ask himself what he was and what he could be now to her, in comparison with the former lover who had returned with new love, to the woman he once betrayed, promising a new and happy life. What could he offer her now?

"Karamazov knew that all ways were barred to him by his crime and that he was a criminal under sentence, and not a man with life before him! This thought crushed him. And so he instantly flew to a mad plan, which, to a man of Karamazov's character, must have appeared the one way out of his terrible position. That way was suicide. He ran for the pistols he had left with his friend Perhotin, pulling out of his pocket the money for the sake of which he had stained his hands with blood.

"Now he needed money more than ever. Karamazov would shoot himself and it should be remembered! To be sure, he was a poet and had burnt the candle at both ends all his life. 'To her I will give a feast such as never was before, that will be remembered and talked of long after! In the midst of shouts of wild merriment, reckless gypsy songs and dances, I shall raise the glass and drink to the woman I adore and her new-found happiness! And then, on the spot, at her feet, I shall dash out my brains! She will remember Mitya Karamazov, she will see how I loved her, she will feel for me!'

"Here we see in excess love a romantic despair and the wild recklessness of the Karamazovs. Yes, but there is something else, gentlemen of the jury, something that cries out in the soul, throbs in the mind and poisons the heart —that *something* is conscience! The pistol will settle everything, it is the only way out!" Here Ippolit Kirillovitch drew a picture of Mitya's preparations. He quoted words and actions, confirmed by witnesses. The guilt of this desperate man stood out clear and convincing.

"What need had he of precaution? Two or three times he almost confessed. He even cried out to the peasant who drove him, 'Do you know, you are driving a murderer!' But it was impossible for him to speak out, he had to get to Mokroe and finish his romance. But almost from the first minute at Mokroe he saw that his invincible rival was perhaps by no means so invincible, that the toast to their new-found happiness was not desired. But you know the facts, gentlemen of the jury. Karamazov's triumph over his rival was complete and his soul passed into a new phase, the most terrible phase.

"One may say with certainty," the prosecutor went on, "that the criminal heart brings its own vengeance, more complete than any earthly justice. What's more, justice and punishment on earth are essential to the soul of the criminal at such moments as the only escape from despair. I cannot imagine the horror and moral suffering of Karamazov when he learnt that she loved him, that for his sake she had rejected her first lover, that she was bidding him, Mitya, to a new life. She was promising him happiness—when everything was over for him and nothing was possible!

"I will note in passing a point of importance for the light it throws on the prisoner's position at the moment. This woman, the love of his, had been till the last moment out of his reach, though passionately desired by him. Yet why did he not shoot himself then, why did he give up his plan, and even forget where his pistol was? It was just that passionate desire for love and the hope of satisfying it that held him back.

"Throughout their revels he kept close to his adored mistress, now more charming and fascinating than ever. His passion might well stifle not only the fear of arrest, but even the torments of conscience. I can picture the state of mind of the criminal—first, drink, the noise and excitement, the thud of the dance and the scream of the song, and her, flushed with wine, singing, dancing, and laughing!

"Secondly, the hope that the end might still be far off, till next morning, at least, before they would come and take him. So he had a few hours, and in a few hours one can think of many things. This must be how it was with Karamazov. 'I may still find some way out,' he must have thought, 'there's still time to make some plan of defense!'

"His soul was full of confusion and dread, but he managed to put aside half his money and hide it somewhere. He had been in Mokroe before, he had caroused there, he knew the old big house with its passages and outbuildings. I imagine that part of the money was hidden in that house. With what object? Why, he hadn't yet considered how to meet his fate, he hadn't the time, his head was throbbing and his heart was with *her*, but money was needed in any case! With money a man is always a man.

"Perhaps such foresight at such a moment may strike you as unnatural? But he assures us himself that a month before, at a critical moment, he had halved his money and sewn it up in a little bag. And though that was not true, it shows the idea was familiar to him. When he declared at the inquiry that he had put fifteen hundred rubles in a bag, because he had two hours before divided his money and hidden half of it at Mokroe till morning, in case of emergency, simply not to have it on himself.

"We have looked in the house, but we haven't found the money. It may still be there or it may have disappeared next day and be in the prisoner's hands now. In any case he was at her side, on his knees before her, she was lying on the bed, he had his hands out to her, and had so forgotten everything that he did not even hear the men come to arrest him. He hadn't time to prepare any line of defense. He was caught unawares.

"Gentlemen of the jury, there are moments in the execution of our duties when it is terrible for us to face a man! Seeing that animal fear when the criminal knows all is lost but still struggles, the moment when every instinct of self-preservation rises up in him. He looks at you, studying your face, uncertain on which side you will strike, and his mind frames thousands of plans in an instant, but he is still afraid to speak, of giving himself away! This thirst for self-preservation, this humiliating moment, is awful, and sometimes arouses horror and compassion for the criminal. This is what we witnessed.

"At first he was thunderstruck, and in his terror said some very compromising things. 'Blood! I've deserved it!' But he quickly restrained himself. He had not prepared what to say, what answer to make, he had nothing but a bare denial ready. 'I am not guilty of my father's death.' That was his fence for the moment, behind which he hoped to throw up a barricade of some sort. His first compromising exclamations he hastened to explain by declaring that he was responsible for the death only of Grigory.

"'Of that bloodshed I am guilty, but who has killed my father, gentlemen, who has killed him? Who can have killed him, *if not I?*' Do you hear, he asked us that, we who had come to ask him that question! Do you hear that phrase—'if not I'—the cunning, the Karamazov impatience of it? 'I didn't kill him and you mustn't think I did! I wanted to kill him, gentlemen,' he admitted, 'but I am not guilty, it is not I murdered him.' He concedes he wanted to murder him, as though to say, you can see for yourselves how truthful I am, so you'll believe that I didn't murder him.

"At that point one of the lawyers asked him, as if incidentally, the most simple question: 'Wasn't it Smerdyakov killed him?' As we expected, he was angry at our having anticipated him and caught him unawares, before he had time to choose the moment when it would be most natural to bring in Smerdyakov's name. He rushed to the other extreme and began to assure us that Smerdyakov could not have killed him, was not capable of it. But that was only his cunning; he didn't really give up the idea of Smerdyakov; on the contrary, he meant to bring him forward perhaps next day, or even a few days later, choosing an opportunity to cry out to us: 'You know I was more skeptical about Smerdyakov than you, but now I am convinced he killed him!' But for the present he falls back upon an irritable denial. Impatience and anger prompted him to the most incredible explanation of how he looked into his father's window and withdrew. The worst of it was that he was unaware of the evidence given by Grigory.

"We proceeded to search him. The search angered, but encouraged, him, the whole three thousand had not been found on him, only half of it. And no doubt only at that moment did the fiction of the little bag first occur to him. No doubt he was conscious himself of the improbability of the story and strove painfully to make it sound likely, to weave it into a romance that would sound plausible. In such cases the chief task of the investigating lawyers is to prevent the criminal being prepared, to pounce upon him unexpectedly so that he may blurt out his cherished ideas in all their improbability.

"The criminal can only be made to speak by the apparently incidental mention of some new fact of great importance in the case, which he could not have foreseen. We had such a fact in readiness—that was Grigory's evidence about the open door through which the prisoner had run out. He had completely forgotten about that door and had not even suspected that Grigory could have seen it. The effect was amazing. He leapt up and shouted, 'Then Smerdyakov murdered him!' and so betrayed the basis of the defense he was keeping back, betrayed it in its most improbable shape, for Smerdyakov could only have committed the murder after he had knocked Grigory down and run away.

"When we told him that Grigory saw the door was open before he fell, and heard Smerdyakov behind the screen as he came out of his bedroom—Karamazov was crushed. And to improve matters, the prisoner hastened to tell us about the much-talked-of bag!

"Gentlemen of the jury, I have told you already why I consider this tall tale the most unlikely invention that could have been brought forward. If one tried to invent the most unbelievable story, one could hardly find anything more unbelievable than this. The worst of such stories is that they can always be crushed by the very details in which real life is so rich and which these unhappy story-tellers neglect as trifles. Oh, they have no thought to spare for such details, their minds are concentrated on their grand invention as a whole, and fancy anyone daring to pull them up for a trifle! But that's how they are caught.

"The prisoner was asked: 'Where did you get the stuff for your little bag and who made it for you?' 'I made it myself.' 'And where did you get the linen?' He was offended; he thought it insulting to ask such a trivial question. 'I tore it off my shirt.' 'Then we shall find that shirt among your linen tomorrow, with a piece torn off.' And only fancy, gentlemen of the jury, if we really had found that torn shirt that would have been a material fact in support of his statement! But he was not capable of that reflection. 'I don't remember, it may not have been off my shirt, I sewed it up in one of my landlady's caps.' 'What sort of a cap?' 'It was an old cotton rag lying about.' 'And do you remember that clearly?' 'No, I don't.' He was very angry!

"Gentlemen of the jury, why do I tell you all these details, trifles?" cried Ippolit Kirillovitch. "Because the prisoner persists in these absurdities to this moment. He has not explained anything since that fatal night two months ago; he has not added one actual fact to his former fantastic statements. 'You must believe it on my honor.' Oh, we are glad to believe it, we are eager to believe it, even if only on his word of honor! Are we jackals thirsting for human blood?

"Show us a single fact in his favor and we shall rejoice; but let it be a substantial, real fact, and not a conclusion drawn from the prisoner's expression by his own brother, or that when he beat himself on the breast he must have meant to point to the little bag. We shall rejoice at the new fact, and be the first to drop our charge. But now justice cries out and we persist."

Ippolit Kirillovitch passed to his final speech. He spoke of the blood that cried to be paid for, the blood of the father murdered by his son, with the base motive of robbery! He pointed to the tragic and glaring consistency of the facts.

"And whatever you may hear from the talented and celebrated counsel for the defense," Ippolit Kirillovitch could not resist adding, "whatever touching appeals may be made, remember that you are in a temple of justice. Remember that you are the champions of our justice and our holy Russia!"

Though Ippolit Kirillovitch was genuinely moved, he wound up his speech with this appeal—and the effect was extraordinary. When he finished, he went out and almost fainted in the next room. There was no applause in the court, but serious persons were pleased. The ladies were not so satisfied, though even they were pleased with his speech, especially as they had no doubts as to the out-come of the trial.

"He will speak at last and of course carry all before him."

Everyone looked at Mitya; he sat silent through the prosecutor's speech, his head bowed. From time to time he raised his head and listened, especially when Grushenka was spoken of.

When the prosecutor mentioned Rakitin's opinion of her, a smile of contempt and anger passed over his face.

When Ippolit Kirillovitch described how he had questioned him at Mokroe, Mitya raised his head and listened with intense curiosity. At one point he seemed about to jump up and cry out, but controlled himself.

The court was adjourned for a short interval. There was a hum of conversation in the court. But the bell rang, all rushed to their places. Fetyukovitch mounted the tribune.

Chapter X

The Speech for the Defense

All was hushed as the first words of the famous orator rang out. He began simply and directly, with an air of conviction, but not the slightest trace of conceit. He made no attempt at eloquence, pathos, or emotional phrases. He was like a man speaking in a circle of intimate friends. His voice was sympathetic, and there was something genuine and simple in the sound of it. But everyone realized at once that the speaker might rise suddenly to pathos and "pierce the heart with untold power."

At the beginning he dealt with facts separately, though, at the end, they formed a whole. His speech might be divided into two parts, the first consisting of refutation of the charge, sometimes malicious and sarcastic. But in the second half he changed his tone, and at once rose to pathos by saying that although he practiced in Petersburg, he had more than once visited towns like this one to defend prisoners of whose innocence he had a conviction.

"That is what has happened to me in the present case," he said. "From the very first accounts in the newspapers I was struck by something which made me believe strongly in the prisoner's favor. What interested me most was a fact which often occurs in legal practice, but rarely in such an extreme and peculiar form as in the present case. I ought to note that peculiarity at the end

of my speech, but I will do so at the very beginning, for it is my
weakness to go to work directly, not keeping effects in reserve.
That may not be wise on my part, but at least it's sincere. What
I have in my mind is this: there is an overwhelming chain of
evidence against the prisoner, and at the same time not one fact
that will stand criticism if it is examined separately. As I followed
the case more closely, my idea was more and more confirmed,
when I suddenly received from the prisoner's relatives a request
to undertake his defense. Here I became completely convinced.
It was to break down this terrible chain of facts, and to show
that each piece of evidence taken separately was unproved, that
I undertook the case."

So Fetyukovitch began.

"Gentlemen of the jury," he said, "I am new to this district.
I have no preconceived ideas. The prisoner, a man of unbridled
temper, has not insulted me. But he has insulted perhaps
hundreds of persons in this town, and so prejudiced many people
against him. Of course I recognize that the moral sentiment
of local society is justly excited against him. The prisoner is
of violent temper. Yet he was received in society here, even
welcomed in the family of the prosecutor. Nevertheless, in spite
of his independent mind and character, my opponent may have
formed a prejudice against my unfortunate client. That is natural;
outraged morality, and outraged taste, is often relentless. We
heard, in the prosecutor's speech, a stern analysis of the prisoner's
character and conduct, and his severe critical attitude to the case
was evident.

"What's more, he went into psychological subtleties he could
not have entered if he had the least conscious and malicious
prejudice against the prisoner. But there are things which are even
worse. It is worse if we are carried away by the artistic instinct,
by the desire to create a romance, especially if we are endowed

with psychological insight. Before I started here, I was warned in Petersburg that I should find here a talented opponent whose insight and subtlety had gained him renown in legal circles.

"But profound as psychology is, it's a knife that cuts both ways. I will take as an example any point in the prosecutor's speech. The prisoner, running away in the garden in the dark, climbed over the fence, was seized by the servant, and knocked him down with a brass pestle. Then he jumped back into the garden and spent five minutes over the man, trying to discover whether he had killed him or not. The prosecutor refuses to believe the prisoner's statement that he ran to old Grigory out of pity. 'No,' he says, 'he ran to find out whether the witness of his crime was dead or alive, and so showed he had committed the murder, since he would not have run back for any other reason.'

"Here you have psychology; but let us take the same method and apply it to the case the other way round, and our result will be no less probable. The murderer, we are told, leapt down to find out, as a precaution, whether the witness was alive or not, yet he had left in his murdered father's study, as the prosecutor himself argues, an amazing piece of evidence in the shape of a torn envelope, with an inscription that there had been three thousand rubles in it. 'If he had carried that envelope away with him, no one in the world would have known of that envelope and of the notes in it, and that the money had been stolen by the prisoner.' Those are the prosecutor's own words.

"So on one side you see a complete absence of precaution, a man who has lost his head and run away in a fright, leaving that clue on the floor, and two minutes later, when he has killed another man, we are entitled to assume the most heartless and calculating foresight in him. But even admitting this, it is more complex than that. It supposes that, under certain circumstances, I become bloodthirsty, while at the next I am as timid and blind as a mole.

"But if I am so bloodthirsty and calculating that when I kill a man I only run back to find out whether he is alive to witness against me, why should I spend five minutes looking after my victim at the risk of encountering other witnesses? Why soak my handkerchief, wiping the blood off his head so that it may be evidence against me later? If he were so cold-hearted, why not hit the servant on the head again with the pestle to kill him outright and relieve himself of all anxiety?

"Again, though he ran to see whether the witness was alive, he left another witness on the path, that metal tool he had taken from the two women, which they could always recognize afterwards as theirs and prove he had taken it from them. And it is not as if he had forgotten it on the path, dropped it through carelessness or haste; no, he had flung away his weapon, for it was found fifteen paces from where Grigory lay.

"Why did he do so? Because he was grieved at having killed an old servant; and he flung away the pestle with a curse, as a murderous weapon. What other reason could he have had for throwing it so far? And if he was capable of feeling grief and pity at having killed a man, it shows that he was innocent of his father's murder.

"Had he murdered him, he would never have run to another victim out of pity; he would have felt differently; his thoughts would have been centered on self-preservation. He would have had none to spare for pity. On the contrary, he would have broken his skull instead of spending five minutes looking after him. There was room for pity and good-feeling because his conscience had been clear till then.

"Here we have psychology also. I have purposely used this method, gentlemen of the jury, to show that you can prove anything by it. It all depends on who makes use of it. Psychology lures even most serious people into making up fanciful theories. I am speaking of the abuse of psychology."

Sounds of approval and laughter were audible in the court.

Chapter XI

There Was No Money. There Was No Robbery

There was one point that struck everyone in Fetyukovitch's speech. He flatly denied the   existence of the three thousand rubles, and consequently their having been stolen.

"Gentlemen of the jury," he began. "Every unprejudiced observer must be struck by a peculiarity in the present case, namely, the charge of robbery, and the impossibility of proving that there was anything to be stolen. We are told three thousand rubles were stolen, but whether those rubles ever existed nobody knows. Who has seen the notes? The only person who saw them, and stated that they had been put in the envelope, was Smerdyakov. He spoke of it to the prisoner and his brother, Ivan Fyodorovitch. Madame Svyetlov, too, had been told of it. But no one actually saw the notes but Smerdyakov.

"Here the question arises, if they did exist and Smerdyakov had seen them, when did he see them for the last time? What if his master had taken the notes from under his bed and put them back in his cash-box without telling him? According to Smerdyakov, the notes were kept under the mattress; the prisoner must have pulled them out, and yet the bed was absolutely not messed. How could the prisoner have found the notes without disturbing the bed? How could he have helped soiling with his blood-stained hands the spotless linen with which the bed had been made?

"But I shall be asked: What about the envelope on the floor? Yes, it's worth saying a word or two about that envelope. I was surprised to hear the talented prosecutor declare that but for that envelope left on the floor, no one would have known of its existence and the notes in it, and therefore of the prisoner's having stolen it. And so that torn scrap of paper is, by the prosecutor's own admission, the sole proof on which the charge of robbery rests. But is the mere fact that that piece of paper was laying on the floor a proof that there was money in it, and that that money had been stolen?

"It will be objected, Smerdyakov had seen the money in the envelope. But when had he seen it? I talked to Smerdyakov, and he told me that he had seen the notes two days before the murder. Then why not imagine that old Fyodor Pavlovitch may have broke open the envelope and taken out the notes. 'What's the use of the envelope?' he may have asked himself. 'She won't believe the notes are there, but when I show her the thirty rainbow-colored notes in one roll, it will make her mouth water.' And so he tears open the envelope, takes out the money, and flings the envelope on the floor.

"Gentlemen, could anything be more likely than this theory? Why is it out of the question? But if anything of the sort could have taken place, the charge of robbery falls to the ground; if there was no money, there was no theft. If the envelope on the floor may be taken as evidence that there had been money in it, why may I not maintain the opposite, that the envelope was on the floor because the money had been taken from it by its owner? But, I shall be asked, what became of the money if Fyodor Pavlovitch took it, since it was not found when the police searched the house?

"First, part of the money was found in the cash-box, and secondly, he might have taken it out that morning or the evening before to make some other use of it, to give or send it away; he may have changed his plan of action completely, without thinking it necessary to announce the fact to Smerdyakov. And if there is the barest possibility of such an explanation, how can the prisoner be positively accused of having committed murder for the sake of robbery, and of having actually carried out that robbery? This is a romance. If it is maintained that something has been stolen, the thing must be produced, or at least its existence must be proved. Yet no one had seen these notes.

"Yes, I shall be told, but he was carousing that night, squandering money; he was shown to have had fifteen hundred rubles—where did he get the money? But the very fact that only fifteen hundred could be found, and the other half of the sum could not be discovered, shows that that money was not the same, and had never been in any envelope. It was proved at the preliminary inquiry that the prisoner ran straight from those women servants to Perhotin's without going home. So he had been all the time in company and therefore could not have divided the three thousand in half and hidden half in the town.

"This led the prosecutor to assume that the money is hidden in some crevice at Mokroe. Why not in the dungeons of the castle of Udolpho, gentlemen? Isn't this idea really too fantastic? And if that supposition breaks down, the whole charge of robbery is scattered to the winds, for in that case what could have become of the other fifteen hundred rubles? By what miracle could they have disappeared, since it's proved the prisoner went nowhere else? And we are ready to ruin a man's life with such tales!

"I shall be told that he could not explain where he got the fifteen hundred, and everyone knew he was without money before that night. Who knew it, pray? The prisoner has made a clear statement of the source of that money, and if you will have it so, gentlemen of the jury, nothing can be more probable than that statement is more consistent with the temper and spirit of the prisoner. The prosecutor is charmed with his own romance. A man of weak will, who had brought himself to take the three thousand so insultingly offered by his betrothed, could not, we are told, have set aside half and sewn it up, but would, even if he had done so, have unpicked it every two days and taken out a hundred, and so would have spent it all in a month. All this was put forward by the prosecutor in a tone that brooked no contradiction. But what if it happened quite differently? What if he's been weaving a romance about a different kind of man? Maybe that's it!

"I shall be told there are witnesses who say he spent on one day all three thousand given him by his betrothed a month before the murder, so he could not have divided the sum in half. But who are these witnesses? The value of their evidence has been shown in court already. Besides, no one of them counted the money; they all judged simply at sight. And the witness Maximov testified that the prisoner had twenty thousand in his hand. You see, gentlemen of the jury, psychology is a two-edged weapon. Let me turn the other edge now and see what comes of it.

"A month before the murder the prisoner was entrusted by Katerina Ivanovna with three thousand rubles to send off by post. But is it true they were entrusted to him in such an insulting and degrading way as was proclaimed just now? The first statement made by the young lady on the subject was different. In the second we heard only resentment and revenge. And the very fact that the witness gave her first evidence incorrectly, gives us a right to conclude that her second piece of evidence may have been incorrect also. If a lofty and high-principled person such as that young lady allows herself in court to contradict her first statement with the obvious motive of ruining the prisoner, it is clear this evidence has been given not impartially. Have not we the right to assume that a revengeful woman might have exaggerated? In particular, the insult and humiliation of her offering him the money? No, it was offered in such a way that it was possible for him to take it, especially as he expected to receive shortly from his father the three thousand rubles that was owed him. It was unreflecting of him, but it was his want of reflection that made him so confident his father would give him the money, and so could always dispatch the money entrusted to him and repay the debt.

"But the prosecutor refuses to allow that he could the same day have set aside half the money and sewn it up in a little bag. That's not his character, he tells us. He talked of the Karamazov nature; he cried out about the two extremes a Karamazov can contemplate at once. Karamazov is just such a two-sided nature, fluctuating between two extremes, that even when moved by strong craving for riotous gayety, he can pull himself up, if something strikes him on the other side. And on the other side is love—that new love which had flamed up in his heart, and for that love he needed money; far more than for carousing with his mistress. If she were to say to him, 'I am yours, I won't have Fyodor Pavlovitch,' then he must have money to take her away. That was more important than carousing. Could a Karamazov fail to understand it? That anxiety was just what he was suffering from—what is there not probable in his laying aside that money?

"But time passed, and Fyodor Pavlovitch did not give him the three thousand; on the contrary, the latter heard that he meant to use this sum to seduce the woman he, the prisoner, loved. 'If Fyodor Pavlovitch doesn't give me the money,' he said to himself, 'I shall be put in the position of a thief before

Katerina Ivanovna.' And then the idea came that he would go to
Katerina Ivanovna, lay before her the fifteen hundred rubles he
still carried round his neck, and say, 'I am a scoundrel, but not a
thief.' So here we have a two-fold reason why he should guard
that sum of money, why he shouldn't unpick the little bag and
spend it a hundred at a time. Why should you deny the prisoner
a sense of honor? Granted it's misplaced, yet it exists.

"But now the affair becomes even more complex; his jealous
torments reach a climax, and those same two questions torture
him more and more: 'If I repay Katerina Ivanovna, where can I
find the means to go off with Grushenka?' If he behaved wildly,
drank, and made disturbances in the taverns in the course of that
month, it was perhaps because he was wretched and strained
beyond his endurance. These questions became so acute that they
drove him at last to despair. He sent his younger brother to beg
for the three thousand rubles, but without waiting for a reply
burst in and ended by beating the old man in the presence of
witnesses. After that he had no prospect of getting it.

"The same evening he struck himself on the breast where the
little bag was, and swore to his brother he had the means of not
being a scoundrel, but that still he would remain a scoundrel, for
he foresaw he would not use that means, that he wouldn't have
the will-power. Why does the prosecutor refuse to believe the
evidence of Alexey Karamazov, given so genuinely and sincerely?
And why, on the contrary, does he force me to believe in money
hidden in a crevice in the castle of Udolpho?

"The same evening, after his talk with his brother, the
prisoner wrote that fatal letter, and that letter is the chief proof
of the prisoner having committed robbery! 'I shall beg from
everyone, and if I don't get it I shall murder my father and
take the envelope from under his mattress as soon as Ivan has

gone.' A full program of the murder, we are told, so it must have been he. 'It has all been done as he wrote,' cries the prosecutor.

"But in the first place, it's the letter of a drunken man, written in great irritation; secondly, he writes of the envelope he has only heard of from Smerdyakov, for he has not seen the envelope himself; and thirdly, though he wrote it, how can you prove he did it? Did the prisoner take the envelope from under the pillow, did that money even exist? And was it to get money the prisoner ran off? He ran off not to steal, but to find out where she was, the woman who had crushed him. He was not running to carry out what he wrote, but in a jealous fury. Yes! I shall be told, but when he got there and murdered him he seized the money, too. But did he murder him? The charge of robbery I repudiate. A man cannot be accused of robbery if it's impossible to prove what was stolen. But did he murder him without robbery? Isn't that, too, a romance?"

Chapter XII

And There Was No Murder Either

"Allow me, gentlemen of the jury, to remind you that a man's life is at stake and that you must be careful. We have heard the prosecutor admit that until today he hesitated to accuse the prisoner of planning the crime advance; he hesitated till he saw that fatal, drunken letter which was produced in court today, 'All was done as written.'

"But the prisoner was running to her solely to find out where she was. Had she been at home, he would have stayed at her side, and so would not have done what he promised in the letter. He ran unexpectedly, and by that time it was very likely he did not even remember his drunken letter.

"'He picked up the pestle,' they say, and a whole psychology was built on that pestle. A very commonplace idea occurs to me at this point: What if that pestle had not been in sight? It would not have caught the prisoner's eye, and he would have run away with empty hands, and would not have killed anyone. How then can the pestle prove the murder was planned?

"Yes, he talked in the tavern of murdering his father, and two days before, on the evening when he wrote his drunken letter, he was quiet! But my answer to that is, if he was planning such a murder in accordance with his letter, he probably would not have gone into the tavern at all, because a person plotting such a crime seeks to avoid being seen and heard.

"Gentlemen of the jury, the psychological method is a two-edged sword, and we, too, can use it. As for all this shouting in taverns, don't we often hear children, or drunkards coming out of taverns, shout, 'I'll kill you'? But they don't murder anyone. And that fatal letter—isn't that simply the shout of the brawler outside the tavern, 'I'll kill you!' Why could it not be that? What reason have we to call that letter 'fatal' rather than absurd?

"Because his father was found murdered, because a witness saw the prisoner run out of the garden with a weapon in his hand, and was knocked down by him: therefore, we are told, everything was done as planned, and the letter was not 'absurd,' but 'fatal.'

"Now we've come to the real point: 'Since he was in the garden, he must have murdered him.' In those few words: 'since he *was*, then he *must*' lies the prosecutor's whole case. He was there, so he must have. And what if there is no *must* about it? I admit the chain of evidence—the coincidences—are really suggestive. But examine the facts separately. Why, for instance, does the prosecution refuse to admit the truth of the prisoner's statement that he ran away from his father's window?

"Remember the sarcasms in which the prosecutor indulged at the expense of the respectful and 'pious' sentiments which suddenly came over the murderer. What if there *was* a feeling of religious awe, if not of filial respect? 'My mother must have been praying for me at that moment,' were the prisoner's words at the preliminary inquiry, and so he ran away as soon as he found out that Madame Svyetlov was not at his father's.

"'But he could not convince himself by looking through the window,' say the prosecutors. But why couldn't he? The window opened at the signals given by the prisoner. Some word might have been uttered by Fyodor Pavlovitch, some exclamation which showed the prisoner she was not there. Why should we assume everything as we make up our minds to imagine it?

"'Yes, but Grigory saw the door open, and so the prisoner was in the house and therefore killed him.' Now about that door, gentlemen of the jury. Observe that we have only the statement of one witness as to that door, and he was at the time in such a state that— But supposing the door was open; supposing the prisoner has lied in denying it; supposing he did go into the house—well, what then? How does it follow that because he was there he committed the murder? He might have dashed in, pushed his father away; might have struck him; but as soon as he made sure Madame Svyetlov was not there, he may have run away rejoicing that she was not there and that he had not killed his father. And it was perhaps because he had escaped from the temptation to kill his father, because he had a clear conscience, that he was capable of feeling pity, and leapt to the assistance of Grigory after he had, in his excitement, knocked him down.

"With terrible eloquence the prosecutor has described to us the dreadful state of the prisoner's mind at Mokroe, when love again lay before him calling him to a new life, while love was impossible because he had his father's bloodstained corpse behind him, and beyond that corpse—retribution. And yet the prosecutor allowed him love, which he explained, according to his method, talking about his drunken condition, and so on.

But again I ask, Mr. Prosecutor, have you not invented a new personality? Is the prisoner so coarse and heartless as to be able to think at that moment of love and of dodges to escape punishment if his hands were really stained with his father's blood?

"As soon as it was made plain she loved him, promising him a new happiness, he must have felt the impulse to suicide doubled, and must have killed himself if he had his father's murder on his conscience. The savage, stony heartlessness ascribed to him by the prosecutor is inconsistent with his character. He would have killed himself, that's certain. But he did not, because 'his mother's prayers saved him,' and he was innocent of his father's blood. He was grieving that night at Mokroe only about old Grigory, praying to God that the old man would recover. Why not accept such an interpretation of the facts? What proof have we that the prisoner is lying?

"But we shall be told, 'There is his father's corpse! If he ran away without killing   him, who did murder him?' Here, I repeat, you have the whole logic of the prosecution. Who murdered him, if not he? There's no one to put in his place. Gentlemen of the jury, is that really so? Is it actually true that there is no one else? We've heard the prosecutor count on his fingers all the persons who were in that house that night. They were five in number; three of them, I agree, could not have been responsible—the murdered man, old Grigory, and his wife.

"There are left then the prisoner and Smerdyakov, and the prosecutor exclaims that the prisoner pointed to Smerdyakov because he had no one else to fix on, that had there been even a phantom of a sixth person, he would have abandoned the charge against Smerdyakov and accused that other. But, gentlemen of the jury, why may I not draw the very opposite conclusion? There are two persons—the prisoner and Smerdyakov. Why can I not say that you accuse my client simply because you have no one else to accuse? And you have no one else only because you have determined to exclude Smerdyakov.

"It's true, Smerdyakov is accused only by the prisoner, his two brothers, and Madame Svyetlov. But there are others who accuse him: there are vague rumors of suspicion. But we have the evidence of a combination of facts that are very suggestive, though, I admit, not actual proof. In the first place we have precisely on the day of the murder that fit, for the genuineness of which the prosecutor has felt obliged to make a careful defense.

"Then we have Smerdyakov's suicide on the eve of the trial. And the equally startling evidence given in court today by the elder of the prisoner's brothers, who had believed in his guilt, but has today produced a bundle of notes, proclaiming Smerdyakov as the murderer. I fully share the conviction of the court and the prosecutor that Ivan Karamazov is suffering from brain fever, that his statement may really be a desperate effort to save his brother by throwing the guilt on the dead man. But when Smerdyakov's name is mentioned, there is a suggestion of mystery. There is something incomplete.

"The court has resolved to go on with the trial, but, meantime, I might make a few remarks about the character of Smerdyakov, drawn with subtlety by the prosecutor. But while I admire his talent, I cannot agree with him. I have visited Smerdyakov, I have seen him and talked to him, and he made a very different impression on me. He was weak in health, but in character, in spirit, he was by no means the weak man the prosecutor has made him out to be. I found in him no trace of the timidity on which the prosecutor so insisted. There was no simplicity about him, either. I found in him, on the contrary, an extreme mistrustfulness concealed under a mask of *naïveté*, and an intelligence of considerable range. The prosecutor was too simple in taking him for weak-minded.

"He made a very definite impression on me: I left him with the conviction that he was a spiteful creature, ambitious, and intensely envious. I made some inquiries: he resented his parentage, was ashamed of it, and would clench his teeth when reminded that he was the son of 'stinking Lizaveta.' He was disrespectful to the servant Grigory and his wife, who had cared

540

for him in his childhood. He jeered at Russia. He dreamed of going to France and becoming a Frenchman. He used often to say that he hadn't the means to do so. I fancy he loved no one but himself and had a high opinion of himself. His idea of culture was limited to good clothes, clean shirts, and polished boots.

"Believing himself to be the illegitimate son of Fyodor Pavlovitch, he might well have resented his position, compared with that of his master's legitimate sons. They had everything, he nothing. They had all the rights, and the inheritance, while he was only the cook. He told me he had helped Fyodor Pavlovitch put the notes in the envelope. The destination of that sum—a sum which would have made his career—must have been hateful to him. Beware of showing an ambitious and envious man a large sum of money! It was the first time he had seen so much money. The sight may have made a morbid impression on his imagination.

"The talented prosecutor, with great skill, sketched all the arguments for and against the theory of Smerdyakov's guilt, and asked us in particular what motive he had in feigning a fit. But he may not have been feigning, the fit may have happened quite naturally, but it may have passed off quite naturally, and the sick man may have recovered, as happens with epileptics.

"The prosecutor asks at what moment Smerdyakov could have committed the murder. But it is very easy to point out that moment. He might have waked from deep sleep at that moment when old Grigory shouted at the top of his voice, 'Parricide!' That shout in the dark may have waked Smerdyakov. Getting out of bed, he goes with no definite motive towards the sound to see what's wrong.

"His head is still clouded with sleep; but, once in the garden he walks to the lighted windows and he hears terrible news from his master, who would be, of course, glad to see him. He hears all the details, and gradually there shapes an idea in his brain—terrible, but seductive. To kill the old man, take the three thousand rubles, and throw all the blame on his young master.

"A terrible lust of money might have seized upon him as he realized his security from being caught. These sudden impulses come often when there is a favorable opportunity, and especially with murderers who have had no idea of committing a murder in advance. Smerdyakov may have gone in and carried out his plan.

"With what weapon? With any stone picked up in the garden. With what object? Why, the three thousand, which means a career for him. Oh, I am not contradicting myself—the money may have existed. And perhaps Smerdyakov alone knew where to find it.

"And the covering of the money—the torn envelope on the floor? Just now, when the prosecutor was explaining his theory that only an inexperienced thief like Karamazov would have left the envelope on the floor, and not one like Smerdyakov, who would have avoided leaving a piece of evidence against himself, I thought as I listened that I was hearing something very familiar, and, would you believe it, I heard that very theory, of how Karamazov would have behaved, precisely two days before, from Smerdyakov himself. What's more, it struck me at the time that there was a false simplicity about him; that he was in a hurry to suggest this idea to me that I might fancy it was my own. Did he not, at the inquiry, suggest it to the prosecutor?

"I shall be asked, 'What about Grigory's wife? She heard the sick man moaning all night.' Yes, she heard it, but that evidence is unreliable. I knew a lady who complained that she had been kept awake all night by a dog in the yard. Yet the poor dog, it appeared, had only yelped once or twice in the night. And that's natural.

"If anyone is asleep and hears a groan he wakes up, annoyed at being waked, but instantly falls asleep again. Two hours later, again a groan, he wakes up and falls asleep again; and the same thing again two hours later—three times altogether in the night. Next morning the sleeper complains that someone was groaning all night and keeping him awake. It is bound to seem so to him: the hours of sleep he does not remember, only the waking moments.

"But why, asks the prosecutor, did not Smerdyakov confess in his last letter? Why did his conscience prompt him to one step and not to both? But, excuse me, conscience implies penitence, and the suicide may not have felt penitence, but only despair. Despair and penitence are two very different things. Despair may be vindictive, and the suicide, laying his hands on himself, may well have felt redoubled hatred for those he had envied all his life. Gentlemen of the jury, beware of a miscarriage of justice!

"What is there unlikely in all I have put before you? Find the error in my reasoning; find the impossibility. If there is but a shade of possibility in my propositions, do not condemn him. And I swear I fully believe in the explanation of the murder I have put forward. What troubles me and makes me indignant is that of all the mass of facts heaped up by the prosecution against the prisoner, not a one is irrefutable. And yet the unhappy man is to be ruined by the accumulation of these facts.

"Yes, the accumulated effect is awful: the blood dripping from his fingers, the blood-stained shirt, the dark night resounding with the shout 'Parricide!' and the old man falling with a broken head. And then the mass of phrases, statements, gestures, shouts! This has so much influence it can bias the mind; but, gentlemen of the jury, can it bias *your* minds? Remember, you have been given absolute power to bind and to loose, but the greater the power, the more terrible its responsibility.

"I do not draw back one word from what I have said, but suppose for one moment I agreed with the prosecution that my luckless client had stained his hands with his father's blood. This is only hypothesis, I repeat; I never for one instant doubted his innocence. But, so be it, I assume my client is guilty of parricide. Even so, hear what I have to say. I have it in my heart to say something more to you, for I feel there must be a great conflict in your hearts and minds.... Forgive, but I want to be truthful and sincere to the end!"

At this point the speech was interrupted by applause. The last words, indeed, were pronounced with a note of such sincerity that everyone felt he really might have some-thing to say, and that what he was about to say would be of the greatest consequence. But the President, hearing the applause, threatened to clear the court if such an incident were repeated. Every sound was hushed, and Fetyukovitch began in a voice full of feeling.

Chapter XIII

A Corrupter of Thought

"It's not only the accumulation of facts that threatens my client with ruin, gentlemen of the jury," he began. "What is really damning for my client is one fact—the dead body of his father. Had it been an ordinary case of murder you would have rejected the charge in view of the triviality and fantastic character of the evidence if you examine each part separately; or, at least, you would have hesitated to ruin a man's life simply from the prejudice against him, however well deserved. But it's not an ordinary case of murder, it's a case of parricide. That impresses men's minds, to such a degree that the very triviality and incompleteness of the evidence becomes less trivial and less incomplete even to an open mind. How can such a prisoner be acquitted? What if he committed the murder and gets off unpunished? That is what everyone feels at heart.

"Yes, it's a fearful thing to shed a father's blood—the father who has begotten me, loved me, grieved over my illnesses from childhood up, troubled all his life for my happiness, and has lived in my joys and successes. To murder such a father—that's inconceivable. But, gentlemen of the jury, what is a real father? We have just indicated in part what a true father is and what he ought to be. In the present case, the father, Fyodor Pavlovitch

Karamazov, did not correspond to that conception. That's the misfortune.

"In the course of his heated speech, my opponent exclaimed several times, 'I will not yield the defense of the prisoner to the lawyer who has come from Petersburg. I accuse, but I defend also!' He said that several times, but forgot to mention that if this terrible prisoner was for twenty-three years so grateful for a mere pound of nuts given him by the only man who had been kind to him as a child, might not such a man well have remembered for twenty-three years how he ran in his father's back-yard, 'without boots on his feet and with his trousers hanging by one button'— to use the expression of the kind-hearted doctor, Herzenstube?

"Gentlemen of the jury, why need we look more closely at this misfortune? What did my client meet with when he arrived here at his father's house, and why depict my client as a heartless egoist and monster? He is uncontrolled, he is wild and unruly— we are trying him now for that—but who is responsible for his life? Who is responsible for his having received such an unseemly bringing up, in spite of his excellent disposition and his grateful and sensitive heart? Perhaps he may, recalling his childhood, have driven away the loathsome phantoms that haunted his childish dreams and with all his heart he may have longed to embrace and to forgive his father! And what awaited him? Cynical taunts, suspicions, and wrangling about money. He heard nothing but revolting and vicious talk uttered daily over the brandy, and at last he saw his father seducing his mistress from him with his own money. Gentlemen of the jury, that was cruel and revolting! And that old man was always complaining of the disrespect and cruelty of his son. He slandered him, injured him, lied to him, and bought up his unpaid debts to get him thrown into prison.

"Gentlemen of the jury, people like my client, who are fierce and uncontrolled on the surface, are frequently exceedingly tender-hearted, only they don't express it. Don't laugh! The talented prosecutor laughed mercilessly just now at my client for loving Schiller—for loving the sublime and beautiful! I should not have laughed in his place. For such natures often thirst for tenderness, goodness, and justice. Passionate and fierce on the surface, they are painfully capable of loving a woman, for instance, with a spiritual and elevated love. But they cannot hide their passions; that is noticed, but the inner man is unseen. Their passions are quickly exhausted; but, by the side of a noble and lofty woman that rough man seeks a new life, seeks to correct himself, to become a man of honor, 'sublime and beautiful,' however much the expression has been ridiculed.

"I said just now that I would not venture to touch upon my client's engagement. But I may say half a word. What we heard just now was not evidence, but only the scream of a frenzied and revengeful woman, and it was not for her to reproach him with treachery, for she has betrayed him! If she had had but a little time for reflection she would not have given such evidence. Do not believe her! My client is not a monster, as she called him!

"I asked just now what does 'father' mean, and said it was a great word, a precious name. But one must use words honestly, gentlemen, and I venture to call things by their right names: such a father as old Karamazov cannot be called a father and does not deserve to be. Filial love for an unworthy father is an absurdity, impossibility. Love cannot be created from nothing: only God can create something from nothing.

"'Fathers, provoke not your children to wrath,' the apostle writes. It's not for the sake of my client I quote these sacred words; I mention them for all fathers. Let us first fulfill Christ's injunction ourselves and only then venture to expect it of our children. Otherwise we are not fathers, but enemies of our children, and we have made them our enemies. 'What measure ye mete shall be measured unto you'—it's not I who say that, it's the Gospel. How can we blame children if they measure us by our own measure? The father is not he who begets the child, but he who does his duty by it.

"Of course, there is the other interpretation of the word 'father,' which insists that any father, even though he be a monster, still remains my father simply because he begot me. But this is the mystical meaning which I can only accept *on faith*. But in that case let it be kept outside the sphere of actual life. In that sphere, if we want to be humane, we must act only upon convictions justified by reason and experience; in a word, we must act rationally, and not ruin a man. Then it will be not only mystic, but rational and loving."

There was violent applause at this passage, but Fetyukovitch waved his hands as though imploring them to let him finish without interruption.

"Do you suppose that our children as they grow up and begin to reason can avoid such questions? No, they cannot, and we will not impose on them such a restriction. The sight of an unworthy father suggests tormenting questions to a young creature, especially when he compares him with the fathers of his companions. The conventional answer to this question is: 'He begot you, you are his flesh and blood, and therefore you are bound to love him.' The youth reflects: 'But did he love me when he begot me? Was it for my sake he begot me? He did not know me at that moment of passion, and has only given to me a propensity to drunkenness—that's all he's done for me. Why am I bound to love him for begetting me when he has cared nothing for me all my life?'

"Those questions may strike you as coarse and cruel, but do not expect something impossible from a young mind. 'Drive nature out of the door and it will fly in at the window.' Above all, let us not be afraid of words, but decide the question according to the dictates of reason and humanity, not of mystic ideas. Let the son say to his father, 'Father, tell me, why must I love you? If that father is able to answer and show him good reason, we have a real parent, not one resting on mystical prejudice, but on a rational, responsible and humane basis. But if he does not, he is not a father to him.

"Gentlemen of the jury, you remember that awful night of which so much has been said today, when the son got over the fence and stood face to face with the enemy and persecutor who had begotten him. It was not for money he ran to his father's house: the charge of robbery is an absurdity. And it was not to murder him he broke into the house! If he had had that design he would have taken the precaution of arming himself, and not with a pestle which he caught up instinctively without knowing why.

"Granted that he deceived his father by tapping at the window, granted that he made his way in—I've said already I do not for a moment believe that legend, but let's suppose it for a moment. Gentlemen, I swear to you by all that's holy, if it had not been his father, but an ordinary enemy, he would, after running through the rooms and satisfying himself that the woman was not there, have made off without doing any harm to his rival.

"He would have struck him, pushed him away perhaps, nothing more, for he had no thought and no time to spare for that. What he wanted to know was where she was. But his father! The mere sight of the father who had hated him from his childhood, had been his persecutor, and now his unnatural rival, was enough! A feeling of hatred came over him, clouding his reason. It all surged up in one moment! It was an impulse of madness and insanity, but also an impulse of nature, avenging the violation of its eternal laws.

"But the prisoner even then did not murder him—he only brandished the pestle in a burst of angry disgust, not meaning to kill him, not knowing that he would kill him. Had he not had this pestle in his hand, he would have only knocked him down perhaps, but would not have killed him. As he ran away, he did not know whether he had killed the old man. Such a murder is not a murder. Such a murder is not a parricide. No, such a murder can only be reckoned parricide by prejudice.

"But I appeal to you again; did this murder actually take place? Gentlemen of the jury, if we convict and punish him, he will say: 'These people have done nothing for my bringing up, for my education, nothing to improve my lot, nothing to make me better, nothing to make me a man. These people have not given me to eat and to drink, have not visited me in prison, and here they have sent me to penal servitude.

"I owe them nothing. They are wicked and I will be wicked. They are cruel and I will be cruel.' That is what he will say, gentlemen of the jury. By finding him guilty you will only make it easier for him: you will ease his conscience, he will curse the blood he has shed and will not regret it. At the same time you will destroy the possibility of his becoming a new man, for he will remain in his wickedness all his life.

"Do you want to punish him with the most awful punishment and at the same time save him and regenerate his soul? If so, overwhelm him with your mercy! That wild but grateful heart, gentlemen of the jury, will bow before your mercy; it thirsts for a great and loving action. Subdue such a soul with mercy, show it love, and it will curse its past. It will expand and see that God is merciful and that men are good and just. He will be crushed by remorse, and will say, 'I am guilty in the sight of all men and more unworthy than all.' With tears of penitence, he will cry out: 'Others are better than I, they wanted to save me, not to ruin me!' This act of mercy is so easy for you, for in the absence of anything like real evidence it will be too awful for you to say: 'Yes, he is guilty.'

"Better acquit ten guilty men than punish one innocent man! The Russian court does not exist for punishment only, but for the salvation of the criminal! Let other nations think of retribution and the letter of the law, we will cling to the spirit and meaning—the salvation and reformation of the lost. If Russia and her justice are such, she may go forward with good cheer! In your hands is the fate of my client, in your hands the fate of Russian justice. You will defend it, save it, and prove there are men to watch over it!"

Chapter XIV

The Common Folk Stand Firm

This was how Fetyukovitch concluded his speech, and the enthusiasm of the audience burst like a storm. It was out of the question to stop it: the women wept, many of the men, too. The President postponed ringing his bell. The suppression of such an enthusiasm would be the suppression of something sacred.

The orator himself was touched. And when Ippolit Kirillovitch got up to make certain objections, people looked at him with hatred. "What's the meaning of it? He dares to make objections," the ladies cried. But if the whole world of ladies, including his wife, had protested, he could not have been stopped. He was pale, shaking with emotion. But he soon recovered and began.

"I am reproached with having woven a story. But what is this defense if not one story on top of another? Fyodor Pavlovitch, while waiting for his mistress, tears open the envelope and throws it on the floor. We are even told what he said while doing this strange act. Is not this a flight of fancy?

"And the weak-minded idiot, Smerdyakov, was changed into a Byronic hero, avenging society for his illegitimate birth? And the son who breaks into his father's house and murders him without murdering him is not even a story—this is a riddle he cannot solve himself. If he murdered him, what's the meaning of murdering him without having murdered him?

"Then we are told that our trial is a trial of true and sound ideas, and from this 'trial' is heard a declaration that to call the murder of a father 'parricide' is nothing but a prejudice! But if parricide is a prejudice, and if every child is to ask his father why he is to love him, what will become of us? Parricide, it appears, is the most precious, the most sacred guarantee, for the destiny and future of Russian justice are presented to us in a tricky way, simply to justify what cannot be justified.

"'Crush him by mercy,' cries the lawyer for the defense; that's all the criminal wants. And is not the lawyer for the defense too modest in asking only that the defendant be freed? Why not found a charity in the honor to commemorate his exploit? 'What measure you mete so it shall be meted unto you,' cried the lawyer for the defense! But what Christ commands is something very different: He bids us beware of doing this, because the wicked world does this, but we ought to forgive and to turn the other cheek. This is what God taught, not that to forbid children to murder their fathers is prejudice."

At this the President intervened and checked the speaker, begging him not to exaggerate. The audience, too, was uneasy. There were exclamations of indignation. Fetyukovitch did not so much as reply; he mounted the tribune to lay his hand on his heart and, in an offended voice, utter a few words full of dignity. He touched lightly on "romancing" and "psychology," and quoted, "Jupiter, you are angry, therefore you are wrong," which provoked a burst of approving laughter, for Ippolit Kirillovitch was by no means like Jupiter.

Regarding the accusation that he was teaching the young generation to murder their fathers, Fetyukovitch observed with dignity that he would not even answer. As for the prosecutor's charge of uttering opinions that were no acceptable, Fetyukovitch said it was a personal insinuation and that he had expected in this court to be secure from such charges that were "damaging to my reputation as a citizen and loyal subject." But at these words the President pulled him up, and Fetyukovitch concluded his speech with a bow.

Then the prisoner was allowed to speak. Mitya stood up, but said little. He was exhausted, physically and mentally. The look of strength and independence with which he had entered in the morning had almost disappeared. He seemed as though he had passed through an experience that day which had taught him, for the rest of his life, something important he had not understood till then. His voice was weak, he did not shout as before. In his words there was a new note of humility and submission.

"What am I to say, gentlemen of the jury? The hour of judgment has come! The end has come to a man who has done wrong! But, before God, I repeat, I am innocent of my father's blood! For the last time I repeat, it wasn't I killed him! I did not always behave properly, but I loved what is good. Every instant I strove to reform, but I lived like a wild beast. I thank the prosecutor, he told me many things about myself I did not know; but it's not true that I killed my father.

"I thank my counsel, too. But don't believe the doctors. I am perfectly sane, only my heart is heavy. If you spare me, if you let me go, I will pray for you. I will be a better man. I give you my word before God! And if you condemn me, I'll break my sword over my head and kiss the pieces. But spare me, do not rob me of my God!"

He fell back in his place: his voice broke: he could hardly speak the last phrase. The judges proceeded to put questions and to ask both sides to come up with conclusions. At last the jury rose to retire for consultation. The President was tired, and his last charge to the jury was rather feeble. "Be impartial, don't be influenced by the eloquence of the defense, but weigh the arguments," and so on.

The jury withdrew and the court adjourned. People could move about, exchange impressions, refresh themselves. It was almost one o'clock, but no one could think of sleep. All waited with sinking hearts; though the ladies thought acquittal was inevitable. They all prepared themselves for a dramatic moment of general enthusiasm. Many among the men, too, were convinced that acquittal was inevitable. Some were pleased, while some were simply dejected. Fetyukovitch himself was confident of his success. He was surrounded by people congratulating him and fawning upon him.

"There are," he said to one group, "invisible threads binding the counsel for the defense with the jury. One feels during one's speech if they are being formed. I was aware of them. They exist. Our cause is won. Set your mind at rest."

"What will our peasants say now?" said one stout, cross-looking gentleman.

"But they are not all peasants. There are four government clerks among them."

"You don't suppose they won't acquit him?" one of the young officials exclaimed.

"They'll acquit him for certain," said a resolute voice.

"It would be shameful not to acquit him!" cried the official. "Suppose he did murder him—there are fathers and fathers! And, besides, he was in such a fury. He may have done nothing but swing the pestle in the air, and so knocked the old man down. It was a pity they dragged the valet in. That was absurd! If I'd been in Fetyukovitch place, I should have said straight out: 'He murdered him; but he is not guilty!'"

"What did you think of what he said about children? Splendid, wasn't it?"

"And about mysticism, too!"

"Oh, drop mysticism, do!" cried someone else. "Think of Ippolit and his fate from this day forth. His wife will scratch his eyes out tomorrow for Mitya's sake."

"I dare say they will acquit Mitenka, after all."

"Well, gentlemen, I admit it was eloquent. But still it's not the thing to break your father's head with a pestle! Or what are we coming to?"

"What cunning chaps there are these days! Is there any justice to be had in Russia?"

The bell rang. The jury had deliberated for exactly an hour.

A deep silence reigned in the court as soon as the public had taken their seats.

"Did the prisoner commit the murder for the sake of robbery," asked the President.

There was a complete hush. The foreman of the jury, the youngest clerk, said in a clear, loud voice, amidst the deathlike stillness of the court: "Yes, guilty!"

The same answer was repeated to every question, without the slightest extenuating comment. This no one had expected. The deathlike silence in the court was not broken—all seemed petrified. But that was only for an instant; it was followed by a hubbub. Many of the men in the audience were pleased. Those who disagreed with the verdict seemed crushed. The ladies, at first, could scarcely believe their ears. Then suddenly the whole court rang with cries: "What's the meaning of it?"

They leapt up from their places, fancying the verdict might be at once reconsidered. And at that instant Mitya stood up and cried in a heartrending voice, stretching his hands out before him: "I swear by God and the dreadful Day of Judgment I am not guilty of my father's blood! Katya, I forgive you! Brothers, friends, have pity on the other woman!"

He could not go on, and broke into a terrible sobbing that was heard all over the court. From the farthest corner at the back of the gallery came a piercing shriek—it was Grushenka. She had succeeded in begging admittance to the court again. Mitya was taken away. The passing of the sentence was deferred till next day. The court was in a hubbub.

"He'll have a twenty years' trip to the mines!"

"Not less."

"Well, our peasants have stood firm."

"And have done for our Mitya."

JOSEPH COWLEY, born October 9, 1923, graduated from Columbia University in 1947, interrupting his academic career to serve two and a half years with the Army Air Force during World War II. The last few months were spent as a bombardier with the Eighth Air Force, for which he was awarded a Bronze Star.

He earned his M.A. from Columbia in 1948 and taught English at Cornell University before entering sales. Most of his career was spent writing on sales and management for The Research Institute of America. He retired in 1982 to devote himself to his own writing.

His published work includes the novels: The Chrysanthemum Garden, Home by Seven, Landscape With Figures, Dust Be My Destiny, and The House on Huntington Hill; the plays: The Stargazers, Twin Bill, and A Jury of His Peers; shorter fiction: The Night Billy Was Born and Other Love Stories, and Do You Like It and Other Stories; non-fiction: *John Adams: Architect of Freedom (1735-1826)*, and (with Robert Weisselberg) *The Executive Strategist, An Armchair Guide to Scientific Decision-Making*.

His favorite writings can be found in *The Best of Joseph Cowley*.

For the past few years he has been adapting the classics for ESL students under the over-all title of *Classics Condensed by Cowley*. They include *Crime and Punishment* by Fyodor Dostoevsky, *The Scarlet Letter* by Nathaniel Hawthorne, *The Kreutzer Sonata* by

LeoTolstoy, *Alice's Adventures in Wonderland* by Lewis Carroll, *The Golden Bowl* by Henry James, *The Brothers Karamazov* by Fyodor Dostoevsky, and *The Aspern Papers* by Henry James. He is also writing a book on old age to which he has given the working title: *Journey to the End of Time, Reflections on life and Aging.*

Joseph Cowley has been listed in Who's Who, International Who's Who of Writers and Authors, Who's Who in the World, the Cambridge Blue Book, 2000 Outstanding Intellectuals of the 21st Century, and many other reference volumes. The organizations to which he has belonged include Mensa, Great Books, the Authors Guild of America, and a twelve-step program.

OTHER BOOKS BY JOSEPH COWLEY

NOVELS

The Chrysanthemum Garden
Home by Seven
The House on Huntington Hill
Dust Be My Destiny
Landscape with Figures

STORIES

The Night Billy Was Born and Other Love Stories
Do You Like It and Other Stories

PLAYS

The Stargazers
A Jury of His Peers
Twin Bill (Women I Have Known and I Love You, I Love You)

NON-FICTION

John Adams (1737-1826): Architect of Freedom
The Executive Strategist: An Armchair Guide to Scientific
Decision-Making (with Robert Weisselberg)

ANTHOLOGY

The Best of Joseph Cowley

CLASSICS CONDENSED BY COWLEY

Crime and Punishment by Dostoevsky
The Aspern Papers by Henry James
The Golden Bowl by Henry James
The Kreutzer Sonata by Tolstoy
Alice's Adventures in Wonderland by Carroll

Review Requested:

If you loved this book, would you please provide
a review at Amazon.com?